MW00534114

DISTURBING THE PEACE

DISTURBING
—THE—
PEACE

Black Culture and the Police Power
after Slavery

BRYAN WAGNER

HARVARD UNIVERSITY PRESS
Cambridge, Massachusetts, and London, England
2009

Library of Congress Cataloging-in-Publication Data

Wagner, Bryan.
Disturbing the peace : Black culture and the police power after slavery / Bryan Wagner.
p. cm.
Includes bibliographical references and index.
ISBN 978-0-674-03508-9 (alk. paper)
1. African Americans—Social life and customs.   2. African Americans—Music—History and criticism.   3. Legends—History and criticism.   4. Ballads—History and criticism.   5. Police power—Southern States—History.   6. Police-community relations—Southern States—History.   7. African Americans—History—1863–1877.   8. African Americans—History—1877–1964.
I. Title.
E185.86.W334   2009
305.896'073—dc22   2009001685

CONTENTS

ILLUSTRATIONS

DISTURBING THE PEACE

INTRODUCTION

Perhaps the most important thing we have to remember about the black tradition is that Africa and its diaspora are older than blackness. Blackness does not come from Africa. Rather, Africa and its diaspora become black during a particular stage in their history. It sounds a little strange to put it this way, but the truth of this description is widely acknowledged. Blackness is an adjunct to racial slavery. Certainly we will continue to discuss and disagree about the determinants that made blackness conceivable as well as about the pacing of their influence. That process is very complex, mixing legal doctrine from ancient slave systems with social customs from the long history of enslavement between Christians and Muslims to produce a new amalgam that would become foundational to the modern world. Blackness is an indelibly modern condition that cannot be conceptualized apart from the epochal changes in travel, trade, labor, consumption, industry, technology, taxation, warfare, finance, insurance, government, bureaucracy, communication, science, religion, and philosophy that were together made possible by the European systems of colonial slavery. Due to this complexity, we will likely never be able to say with confidence whether blackness begins before or during the sugar revolution, or consequently whether slavery follows from racism or racism follows from slavery. We do know, however, what blackness indicates: existence without standing in the modern world system. To be black is to exist in exchange without being a party to exchange. Being black is belonging to a state organized according to its ignorance of your perspective—a state that does not, that cannot, know your mind. To borrow a formulation from the eve of decolonization, we might say that blackness suggests a situation in which you are anonymous to yourself. It is a kind of invisibility.[1]

Taken seriously, these facts about blackness are enough to make problems for anyone who wants to talk about blackness as founding a tradition.

Conceptualized not as a shared culture but as a condition of statelessness, blackness would appear to negate the perspective that would be necessary to found a tradition. To speak as black, to assert blackness as a perspective in the world, or to argue the existence of the black world is to deny the single feature by which blackness is known. Because blackness is supernumerary, it is impossible to speak as black without putting yourself into tension with the condition that you would claim. Speaking as black can mitigate your condition, or make you into an exception or a credit to your condition, but it cannot allow you to represent your condition, as speaking is enough to make you unrepresentative. You can be clean and articulate and also black, but to be all these things at once is to admit to an existence defined by its division (or its doubleness). From *Somerset*, there comes a line of thought that would deny these facts on the grounds that individuals are audible to one another in nature before there is a law to intercede between them. The politics in this line is communicated as a chiasmus about persons made into slaves and slaves made into persons, a trope whose limitation lies in the fact that it takes for granted a term ("person") that is unevenly intelligible in the natural rights tradition that determines what blackness means. Returning to that lineage, and especially to the scene where the enemy combatant is made into the slave, we can think again about the position of the ex-slave without recourse to the consolation of transcendence.[2]

Taking up this challenge, this book tries to think again about the predicament of the black tradition after slavery. It does so by returning to some of the foundational myths that have been indispensable to the documentation of black vernacular expression ever since it first became possible to represent blackness as a culture. By thinking again about W. C. Handy hearing the blues at a train station in Mississippi, Buddy Bolden experiencing the drumming at Congo Square, or John Lomax porting his wax cylinder recorder into the southern penitentiary, my aim is not to propose a canon or to suggest that these cases are representative in the sense that many have presumed. On the contrary, I am hoping for something like the opposite. I am hoping to find a way to name the blackness in the black tradition without recourse to those myths that have made it possible up to this time to represent the tradition as cultural property. By tracking the emergence of the black tradition from the condition of statelessness, I believe we can learn a lot about the songs and stories that were recorded by cultural collectors like Handy and the Lomaxes: why, for instance, certain recognizable speaking positions are assumed (criminal, beggar, outcast) when the tradition stoops to dramatize its own perspective, or why the topos of warfare appears across the tradition in the service of a critique of law, or why the grain of the black voice is often suggested, even inside its own tradition, to approximate noise. Contrary to the notion that the perspective in the black tradition is foreclosed by the ethnographic norms that condition our knowledge of its history, I am arguing that it remains possible to describe its contours by tracking the tradition's engagement with the law. The law does not provide evidence for uninterrupted contact, or scenes where we can see the torch being passed, but it does offer cues that can lead us backward through the accumulated layers of anthropological description to specific points in these songs, stories, and sayings where it is possible to perceive the black tradition invoking the historical language of natural rights as an index to its own formal development.[3]

Given that there was no blackness before there was racial slavery, it would seem that a reasonable place to begin such an inquiry is with the earliest slave codes. Written week by week and line by line as the idea of blackness was being constructed to justify slavery as an indefinite and heritable condition, these codes are coincident not only with racial slavery but also with blackness as such. The English colonies present a special challenge, as their slave codes exhibit a resistance to abstraction that makes it hard to see how they could facilitate a theory about slavery, much less a theory about blackness. Unlike Portugal, Spain, and France, which wrote comprehensive legal codes derived from Roman example to administer the slave systems in their colonies, England gave its empire no coherent guidance on slavery. There was no English equivalent to the *Code noir* or *Codigo negro*. Instead of converting inherited doctrine into a code that could be imposed by fiat, as was done by other imperial powers, English lawmakers were extremely reticent about slavery, leaving colonists to their own devices when it came to managing chattel. The few cases prior to *Somerset* that speak to slavery in the colonies are obscure in their content and vague in their language, offering no foundation for the many statutes that were being drafted on the empire's margin. With no doctrine to guide them, the colonists improvised. The Barbados Act of 1661 became the model for the slave codes drafted elsewhere in the West Indies and on the North American continent, but its example was neither systematic nor exhaustive. It made no general propositions about slavery, nor did it tackle the problems associated with the private law of slavery, especially those having to do with manumission and inheritance. Following Barbados, legislators in Jamaica, Antigua, Georgia, and South Carolina produced slave codes without any pretense to unity, as did Virginia and Maryland. Slavery appeared within these legal systems merely as an arbitrary inventory of forbidden actions, situations, and associations.[4]

These codes employ neither principle nor example to organize their long lists of heterogeneous threats to the public peace. Statutes governing clothing, trade, domicile, outlawry, miscegenation, baptism, permits to travel, custody of firearms, hiring out, false petitions to indenture, flight, literacy, inveigling, insurrection, lurking, keeping livestock, and religious observance are enumerated, without subordination or any indication as to how their entries are supposed to be combined or connected to one another. Neither do the codes profess anything like comprehensive coverage. The entries are presented merely as consecutive illustrations. They say nothing about the limit to the law's breadth. It is always possible to attach new entries to the list, and it is always conceivable that some threat may arise that is wholly unanticipated in the existing law, to which the law's authority nonetheless immediately applies.[5]

According to the analytical norms that characteristically apply in the civil and the common law, these slave codes are unfinished and insufficient. But from the standpoint of the police power, a principle that was not codified in Anglo-American jurisprudence until the middle of the eighteenth century, these codes have nothing to apologize for. Their resistance to theoretical justification is not only predictable but indispensable to their basic purpose. What looks like conceptual disorganization becomes, from the policing perspective, rigorous adherence to principle. Read through the police power, these statutes seem focused and coherent. The police power, furthermore, is not limited to a single legal system, as it derives from a legal process that predates the great divergence between civil and common law. The police power is broadly relevant and entirely appropriate, if differently instantiated, within the law of racial slavery throughout the Americas, and when it is referenced with precision, the concept easily answers the objections that are sometimes raised about the law's probative value for the comparative study of modern slavery.[6]

Reading these slave codes, it is vital to know that most police regulations, not only those directed at slaves, are represented as lists. This layout is determined by the nature of the police power. The term "police" designates the state's right and duty to dispose threats to public welfare. Due to the potential seriousness of the threats, it was often acknowledged that the state's discretion in police cases was absolute. The police power could tolerate no delays, no formal or substantive limitations, that might interfere with its ability to protect the public from harm. In situations where the public's survival could be at risk, it made sense to allow the state to act by whatever means necessary. Put simply, the police power is about self-defense, and this is why so many of the laws implemented under its authority employ enumeration, rather than deduction, to define their range. No matter its particular focus—a slave, a vagrant, liquor, a rabid dog, a fire-prone building—the police power remains opposed to generalization on the grounds that petitions to principle place inappropriate limits on its autonomy. Like the statutes themselves, early writings on the police power, from William Blackstone's *Commentaries on the Laws of England* (1765–1769) to Patrick Colquhoun's *Treatise on the Police of the Metropolis* (1806), resort to inconclusive catalogues, rather than theoretical exposition, in order to keep the law open-ended and ready for unpredictable threats. After a rambling list that includes vagabonds, passengers on public conveyances, poisonous drugs, and navigable waterways as legitimate objects for police action, Fortunatus Dwarris finishes the discussion in his *General Treatise on Statutes* (1873) with a disclaimer. "This enumeration may suffice," he states, "though it is but a portion of the instances in which this police power may be and has been exerted." "Nor can it be deemed necessary," he adds, "to cite authority to sustain the principle upon this enumeration of powers." It is not enough to leave the catalogue open ended; Dwarris stresses the implied ellipsis at its end. It is not enough to leave the concept of police unspecified; Dwarris insists that the police power requires no theoretical justification to sustain its sway over an indefinite series of cases, only some of which are numbered in his preceding sentences.[7]

What was true for Dwarris was also true for the legislators writing slave codes in the English colonies, even if they failed to understand the nature of the prerogative they were bringing into play. Classifying their slave laws as police measures, for this reason, is much more than accurate description. It is the prerequisite for discovering what is systematic in their legal approach to the enslaved. Unlike Roman slave law, and unlike the *Code noir*, which attempt to define the slave in every dimension, the police measures adapted from Barbados to Virginia were concerned with the slave, first and foremost, as a potential threat. Whereas slavery was certainly conceived in these colonies in relation to the master, it was also defined (distinctively so) as a relation, or more precisely a non-relation, to society at large. When the South Carolina legislature in 1696 described the slave as "wholly unqualified to be governed by the laws, customs, and practices of the province," it was stating explicitly something that was implied elsewhere by its police regulations. The ungovernable slave, the slave as outsider to the state, the slave as fugitive—this is a trope that looks backward to classical thinking about enslaving infidels or captives taken in a just war even as it also looks forward, in the history of the United States, to the beginnings of a systematic jurisprudence on slave status during the decade prior to independence; to the widening of police initiatives against free negroes in the antebellum years; to *Prigg v. Pennsylvania* and *Dred Scott v. Sandford* on the fugitive slave's unlawful standing; to the Thirteenth Amendment's exception clause; to *Roberts v. City of Boston* and *Plessy v. Ferguson* on segregation and public welfare; to the new police departments, magistrate's courts, and convict lease operations that were introduced after emancipation.[8]

This book, however, does not attempt to write a positive genealogy in law. Nor does it tarry with the early statutes that have thus far claimed its attention. Its interest in the police power is more hermeneutic than scholastic. It invokes the police power, in other words, as a framework for interpretation. I make this decision partly because I take the judges and jurists who defined the police power at their word when they say that the police power cannot be defined. Writing for the majority in the *Slaughterhouse Cases* (1873), Justice Samuel Miller explains this premise: "The power is, and must be from its very nature, incapable of any very exact definition or limitation." For Miller, society owes its security, and the citizen his or her life, to the police power, whose importance is evidenced by its resistance to representation. Police is not disposed to definition, because it relates to threats whose character cannot be known in advance. From Cesare Beccaria to Jeremy Bentham, William Blackstone to James Kent, Lemuel Shaw to Samuel Miller, John Marshall to Roger Taney, this much is apparent. In this book, I invert this premise. In the cases I examine, it is not the unpredictability of the threat that keeps the police power from being known. It is, rather, the discretionary license in the police power that excludes everything that might be known about its object besides its threat potential. Seen from the standpoint of the police power, blackness is imperceptible except for the presumed danger it poses to public welfare. The book presses this idea as far as it can—stressing, in particular, its implications for the theory of the black vernacular tradition. Returning to examples (trickster tales, outlaw legends, blues lyrics) that have been indispensable to previous studies of black vernacular expression, this book develops an analytical framework from the historical language of the law to read these sources in new ways. In doing so, it does not shy away from the larger questions. It asks again about the connection between these songs and sayings and the history that gives blackness its meaning. It asks again about what makes the black tradition black.[9]

Before we can get to this core issue, we need to measure the historical range of the police power. This means, in the first place, separating the word "police" from its current association with the specific department charged with stopping or detecting crime. Restricting the word "police" to its idiomatic association would be wrong for this book, because it would mean assuming something that did not exist under slavery. In this idiomatic sense, "police" implies a situation where there is at least some pretense to a state monopoly on violence. Such a monopoly was unthinkable under a slave system in which most crimes were punished extralegally, usually at a master's discretion, and in which the power to police was considered not as a state prerogative but as a racial privilege of all whites over all blacks, slave or free. Nor does it make sense to discuss a formal monopoly on violence after slavery in the United States. Marked by the breakneck expansion of state institutions for criminal justice, these decades were defined at the same time by the founding of the Ku Klux Klan, the lynching epidemic, and mob activities (often enough styled "race riots") that overturned legitimate elections and removed black politicians from public office. During these decades, the ex-slave was portrayed, in the press and on the stump, as a threat to society. This threat was invoked to win support for new police and prison systems, but it was also turned against the state by advocates who felt that vigilante violence was the only way to proceed in extreme situations, where the well-being of individuals, or the peace of the society, was potentially at stake. Holding onto a narrow conception of police is obviously inadequate to these contexts. Only by turning to a more capacious definition of police, as the discretion to dispose threats to public welfare by any means necessary, can we begin to conceptualize what the law means, and what it does, for the black tradition.[10]

Police, for the purposes of this book, is not a specific institution, nor is it a category of practice. Although it is easy to imagine the relationship between policing and blackness through on-the-street practices like racial profiling, this is not the level at which their fundamental association becomes available to analysis. Police relates to blackness not as practice but simply as a power. It has always been possible to debate the practices to which the power applies, but the power's existence has never been open to discussion. This foreclosure is significant. Though the controlling cases on the police power from the antebellum decades concern not slaves but wharves and paupers and liquor, these cases are directly relevant to blackness because they declare the self-evidence of the police power, and police comes closest to blackness at the point where it passes into self-evidence. At times the topic of vigorous debate in congress, legislatures, and the courts, the power's existence has nevertheless always been taken for granted.[11]

When judges and jurists debate the police power, they talk about which statutes should be counted as police measures, not about the rightness of police. They ask questions about classification, in other words, always with the knowledge that classification as police is sufficient to insulate a measure from constitutional scrutiny on the grounds that it is needed to protect society from harm. Judges and jurists have disagreed over where to draw the line between federal and state government's seemingly concurrent powers over commerce and welfare. They have disagreed over the distinction between the police power and eminent domain, with the latter dictating compensation for those adversely affected by government action and the former conceding no such responsibility. They have argued over Mill's harm principle, or the proposition that the state has no business regulating individuals when their conduct poses risk only to themselves. Especially after the passage of the Fourteenth Amendment, which restricted the state's power to make laws infringing on due process, they argued over what constituted a true risk to society, questioning whether statutes were public necessities (and therefore authentic police measures) or arbitrary policies infringing on property rights (by constraining those willing to purchase an article in spite of its known health effects) or the right to free contract (by establishing minimum wage rates or maximum hours in a work week). Finally, they have addressed procedural restrictions on the power to search or informally detain suspected criminals, creating a set of standards distinct from the constitutional norms for probable cause, booking, and arraignment that distinguish an arrest. Judges and jurists have often looked to these limit cases to determine what does and does not constitute a legitimate application of the police power, but never have they doubted the function of police as a bedrock assumption in their thinking.[12]

The argument that the power to police was self-evident was already commonplace in the 1770s and 1780s, when pamphleteers and constitutional committees were actively railing against anyone who dared to doubt the need for "internal police," a public need whose "necessity" was "so strikingly obvious," according to Thomas Paine, that "no sufficient objection can be made against it." After all, Paine says in his third number of *The Crisis* (1777), it was pointless to question the justice of an idea when "the safety of all societies depends upon it." From another direction, Alexander Hamilton argues the case for overruling necessity in the thirty-first installment of *The Federalist* (1788). Hamilton writes that police discretion must be considered as axiomatic; he associates its existence with the rules of mathematics and with "other maxims in ethics and politics," like the one that says "there cannot be an effect without a cause." Of this variety, according to Hamilton, is the rule that says "every power ought to be commensurate with its object." Because degrees of threat cannot be known in advance, police should have no ascribed limitations. Or as Hamilton puts it: "there ought to be no limitation of a power destined to effect a purpose which is itself incapable of limitation." Given that "securing the public peace against foreign or domestic violence" involves "dangers to which no possible limits can be assigned," it is obvious that police "ought to know no other bounds than the exigencies of the nation and the resources of the community." Lawmakers and jurists in the ensuing decades would supplement this homegrown thinking by looking to English opinion on "public police and economy," in particular to the fourth volume of William Blackstone's *Commentaries* (1769), as they crafted the laws and opinions that would establish, once and for all, the self-evidently natural connection between police sovereignty and overruling necessity.[13]

The phrase "the police power," as opposed to early variants like "police" and "internal police," is coined in an opinion by Chief Justice John Marshall in *Brown v. Maryland* (1827), a case concerning a state's right to restrict the selling of imported goods. Marshall's tenure was the last gasp for the court's federalism, and with his retirement and Roger Taney's ascendancy to Chief Justice, the balance of the court shifted, and there arose a new philosophy in its decisions on the police power. Marshall and Taney had agreed about the existence of the police power, but under Taney's direction, the power was given new latitude. Newspapers became interested in this sudden shift in the court, and with the battle over slavery brewing, they injected the term "the police power" to common parlance. In *State of New York v. Miln* (1837), the court made its first full attempt to delineate the police power. The case concerned an immigration statute requiring ship captains to post bond for the passengers they disembarked at New York City. The statute's stated purpose was to curtail the influx of paupers and criminals into the city, and it was challenged on the grounds that it represented an unconstitutional regulation of foreign commerce. As is generally true in these leading cases on the police power, the problem is remembered as a conflict between federal and state jurisdiction. The case, however, does not try to redivide sovereignty. Rather, it asserts the indivisibility of sovereignty in situations where the public is potentially at risk. Upholding the statute, Justice Barbour, writing for the court majority, argues for the "indefinite supremacy" of the police power. For Barbour, police discretion is "complete, unqualified and exclusive." By its nature, the police power possesses an "undeniable and unlimited jurisdiction over all persons and things."[14]

Taney would put his own stamp on a definition in the *License Cases* (1847), a decision concerning a statute requiring a permit to retail liquor imported from out of state. Taney's definition would prove no more limiting than Barbour's attempt in *Miln*—in fact, it might be considered even more expansive insofar as it makes the police power indistinguishable from sovereignty as such. Taney defines the police power as "nothing more or less than the powers of government inherent in every sovereignty to the extent of its dominion." It does not matter whether the statute in question is a "quarantine law" or "a law to punish offenders." In both cases, government "exercises the same power; that is to say, the power of sovereignty, the power to govern men and things within the limits of its dominion." The definition that counted most often for subsequent jurisprudence, however, came not from the Taney Court but from the Supreme Court in Massachusetts, where Justice Lemuel Shaw would stipulate in *Commonwealth v. Alger* (1851) the implications following from Taney's equation between sovereignty and police, making police decisive not only to government but to society itself. By most assessments, it was *Alger* that furnished the "starting point for citations directly relating to the police power in most of the constitutional discussions that embrace the subject." Upholding a statute governing the size and shape of wharves in Boston Harbor, Shaw describes the police power in familiar terms as the prerogative to protect the "welfare of the commonwealth," but he goes on to insist that police must be treated not as a court opinion but as a warrant underlying all aspects of reasonable jurisprudence. It was a "settled principle, growing out of the nature of well ordered civil society." Without the police power, there would be no society to protect in the first place. Shaw's stroke of genius is to connect police's lack of definition to its efficacy as a precondition for social existence. This primacy explains why it is so "much easier to perceive and realize the existence and sources of this power, than to mark its boundaries, or prescribe limits to its exercise." This is why Shaw sees no need to venture further in his definition. Having asserted its inevitability, Shaw goes on to enumerate, in no particular order, with no claim to comprehensiveness, "cases in which such a power is exercised by all well ordered governments, and where its fitness is so obvious, that all well regulated minds will regard it as reasonable."[15]

Thinking about the police power changed after the Civil War. Prompted by the procedural limitations upon state sovereignty introduced through the Fourteenth Amendment, the courts in these years began to focus increasing attention on the criteria employed in cases like *Miln* and *Alger* to determine the constitutionality of police measures. Their purpose, however, was never to overturn these antebellum precedents but to think harder and better about what fell inside and what fell outside the domain of the police power. Many treatises on the police power were published in these years, with bulky volumes like Thomas Cooley's *Treatise on Constitutional Limitations* (1868, 720 pages), Christopher G. Tiedeman's *Treatise on the Limitations of Police Power in the United States* (1886, 662 pages), and Ernst Freund's *The Police Power* (1904, 819 pages) exercising the greatest influence. The tenor and undoubtedly the amount of writing on the police power changed in these decades, but everyone involved in this expanded enterprise retained the central assumption inherited from Taney that any government without police "would scarcely be worth preserving." They retained as well the assumption that police could not be defined, albeit with a heightened sense of the paradoxes that were produced when its indefinite power was fitted inside a constitutional framework. "The term police power," Freund says, "while in constant use, and indispensable in the vocabulary of American constitutional law, has remained without authoritative or generally accepted definition." Resignation on this point was conjoined to familiar standards of necessity and reasonableness. These standards remained intact across an increasingly skeptical line of decisions, from the *Slaughterhouse Cases* (1873) to *Lochner v. New York* (1905), only to emerge once again in subsequent decades as the self-evident baseline for all practices that aspired to the name of good government.[16]

The controlling cases on the police power from the antebellum decades routinely appeal to imagined threat scenarios to communicate these high stakes. The favorite example was the storage of gunpowder. Acknowledging a dissenting point made by Taney in *Brown v. Maryland*, Marshall was forced to admit in his opinion that "removal of gunpowder" was "unquestionably" a "branch of the police power." Governments had the unconditional authority to confiscate or destroy a cache of gunpowder if it was improperly stored or kept in a populous area. Marshall realized that he was asserting an "express exception" to laws (in this instance property laws) that would otherwise govern the situation he was addressing, but he deduced that the potential danger in this situation was reason enough to suspend the owner's property right by removing the powder. This specific scenario was reiterated in the ensuing decades by other judges as a substitute for strict definition. The gunpowder scenario resurfaced at crucial junctures in majority opinions in *Miln*, the *License Cases*, and *Alger*, where the powder trope is supplemented by other accidents-waiting-to-happen (medicines poorly manufactured, fire-prone buildings) and threats-in-the-making (would-be incendiaries, rabid dogs) whose existence was thought to warrant preventative action. These thought experiments used narratives of imminent peril, or situations where something must be done before it is too late, to argue that it was occasionally necessary to relax restrictions on police authority. The classic instance of this thinking is Jeremy Bentham's limited defense of torture, which says the torture of one individual is just if it can prevent the torture of one hundred others. "For the purpose of rescuing from torture these hundred innocents," Bentham says, "should any scruple be made of applying equal or superior torture, to extract the requisite information from the mouth of one criminal, who having it in his power to make known the place where at this time the enormity was being practiced, should refuse to do so?" This fragment on torture was written in 1776, the same year the time bomb was invented by a Yale student named David Bushnell. Unrelated at the time of their discovery, the ticking time bomb would eventually summarize, in one figure, every step in Bentham's utilitarian calculus. With a suspect in custody who knows the location of a bomb soon to explode, how could you not resort to torture? In the 1830s, the time bomb was not yet the favorite trope that it would become, but the message stayed the same. These were situations where the state required a free hand.[17]

What the police power cases share with Bentham's torture scenario is an orientation—to prevention rather than punishment—and it is this preventative orientation that makes them into police cases rather than criminal cases where the normal procedural restrictions on state action would remain in force. Exigency, whether represented as the ticking time bomb or gunpowder waiting to detonate, is the only occasion for police activity in the strict sense of the term. Claiming that this prerogative is "brought into active exercise for the protection of the citizen by the sovereign power in all needful emergencies," Fortunatus Dwarris names police as "a natural right, arising from inevitable, and pressing necessity." "The moment the police power is destroyed or curbed by fixed and rigid rules," William Packer Prentice concurs, "a danger is introduced into our system." For this reason, police must remain "the exception to all human ordinances and constitutions." Its exercise follows from the axiom that says that "the safety of society is the paramount law." It is this natural law that is represented in the compulsive imagination of the threat scenario, where the right to self-preservation is evoked time and again to trump the protections customarily afforded by positive law. Whether the protections involve your property (the gunpowder you paid good money for) or your person (the bundle of rights eventually known as due process), the result is the same. All such positive considerations must yield to the law of necessity. Borrowing liberally from the language of the police power cases, William Stevens would write in his temperance novel, *The Unjust Judge* (1854), about the need to impart "primary importance" to the police statutes for "the preservation of the public peace." As these statutes involve the "protection of life and liberty," it is right that they "compel all laws on subjects of secondary importance . . . to recede when they come into contact or collision." The "free operation" of the police power, which allows the state or its proxies to behave "according to the exigency which requires their interference," supplies a discretionary authority that is necessary for "the correction of the great evils" confronting society. After all, Stevens writes, "the framers of the constitution never contemplated taking away from the citizen, the natural right of self preservation." For Stevens, nothing more need be said.[18]

Although the police cases only occasionally look back much further than Blackstone, their reasoning has a history that is much longer. Self-preservation is paramount in both the reason-of-state tradition and the natural rights tradition. An emphasis in the former tradition was to define the prince's absolute privilege to preserve his state (and himself) by extraordinary measures, without any concern for independent moral considerations, whether the threat in question was economic, political, or military. For natural rights philosophers like Hugo Grotius or Thomas Hobbes, self-preservation was the universal principle from which other moral considerations derived. It was argued that there never existed, nor could there exist, a society that denied its members the right to self-defense, and that all other rules and conventions should therefore be treated as dependent upon its precedence. There could be no moral obligation to look after another's welfare unless your own was already secure. It was said on these grounds that exceptions to the law should always be made in cases of necessity. A starving man who takes the food he needs from another's larder commits no crime, because the law that pertains to his case is not the positive law of property but the natural law of self-preservation. For the same reason, the property owner has no right to demand restitution from the starving man once he is no longer starving. There was real difference of opinion over whether the property owner (or anyone else) could discriminate between true and false necessity, and several attempts were initiated to distinguish the particular degrees of necessity (dire or relative) that legitimated reversion to the rule of primitive right. This debate, however, never came to the tipping point where the priority of self-preservation was itself open to question.[19]

The police cases draw selectively from this philosophical tradition on overruling necessity. They take their emphasis on prevention from this tradition, looking not only to Grotius and Hobbes but to much earlier philosophers who sought to justify preemptive strikes in warfare. When Barbour and Shaw make the leap from preventing a direct threat to eliminating something that is not threatening at present but could become threatening in the future, they are following this established line on preemption. At the same time, however, the police power cases tend to downplay the skepticism that remains pronounced across the natural rights tradition. Hobbes and his followers emphasize that the appeal to necessity is always open to question by an injured party or impartial observer, and they make much of the fact that there is no objective criterion for resolving the resulting disagreements. Often enough, it was admitted, there was no way to say for sure what was really dangerous or what was necessary for self-preservation. Bentham attempts to allay this skepticism by imagining a situation where all the variables are known, but the leading cases on the police power would take no such precaution. Knowledge was not a problem for these cases, and it was not until after the Civil War that skepticism (eventually leading to *Lochner*) would return to police thinking.[20]

Moreover, the police cases receive their most important warrant from the natural rights tradition. Time and again, they sketch the analogy between the state and the individual in nature. In the *License Cases*, Justice McLean takes the familiar tack, naming police as "essential to self-preservation," only to suggest that this essential right was nothing more than the extension of an entitlement "possessed by man in his individual capacity." "It is not singular that an analogy to the law of self-defense should have been thus early suggested," William Prentice reflects, "but the distinction is obvious when we consider the plea of self-defense is founded upon a right, belonging to the individual by the law of nature, to repel violence against his person." Nature, in this analogy, is operating in a double sense. In the police cases, it is used as a heuristic method naming the logical presuppositions of the state. This is the way it is used in *Alger* when Shaw describes the police power as a prerequisite to political society. Shaw employs nature not only to validate police measures based on their presumed priority to the social contract; he maintains that the social contract would be impossible without recourse to these police measures in the event of a potential emergency. But it is important to recognize that this is not the only way in which nature, as a political category, matters for these cases. For Grotius, who takes the hardest line on the analogy between the state and the natural person, and for the majority of thinkers who follow in his direct wake, natural law is not merely conjectural, nor is it in any respect prehistorical. Natural law derives from actually existing circumstances, which continue to exist after the social contract is created. It is a law that refers to people, places, and associations outside the state's domain. It refers to the relations between states, whether or not they are at war, just as it also references the usage of wastelands, negotiations between vessels on the open sea, and the management of outlaws whose legal recognition by the polity has been withdrawn.[21]

It is in this empirical sense that natural law is relevant to the world history of colonization and enslavement. European states routinely justified their imperial adventures on the moral grounds that they were fitting punishments for infidels who had sinned against natural law. The expropriation of land (depicted as uncultivated) was rationalized on this basis, as was the enslavement of captives taken in just warfare. It was considered a plain right of warfare that an enemy could be killed or spared at the conqueror's discretion to survive as a slave. This tradition begins to disappear from public life even as it continues to enlarge philosophically, as it descends to Hegel to Alexandre Kojève. But its original relevance is for premodern slavery, conceptualized as a substitute for death. There were long-standing disagreements inside this tradition over the natural justice of slavery, over whether the requirements for a just war should be met before captives could be made into slaves, or whether the opportunity to enslave infidels (who were natural slaves by definition) was enough on its own to rationalize warfare. Recall John Locke in his *Second Treatise of Civil Government* (1690) advocating the abandonment of slaves to the "absolute dominion and arbitrary power of their masters." Like many before him, Locke uses the premise that says people who violate laws of nature are fit for enslavement. Having "forfeited his own life" through his transgression, the criminal "declares himself to quit the principles of human nature, and to be a noxious creature." Like the enemy in a just war, the criminal has no rights that others are bound to respect, and so it is acceptable that he is enslaved, as reparation for wrongdoing or as preventative self-protection. Having "[quitted] reason," he can "be destroyed" by the "injured person" or the "rest of mankind," as if he were a "wild beast . . . with whom mankind can have neither society nor security." It is this abandonment that stands in Locke's philosophy as the premonition to slavery.[22]

If Aristotle formulated his theory of natural slavery in part to separate slavery from sovereignty by showing how society's power over its slaves differs from the state's power over its citizens, Locke restores this ambiguity by attributing to slavery and society the same cause. The state is necessary for the same reason slavery is necessary: for self-protection against those who violate natural law. This ambiguity is preserved by later philosophers who develop their concept of police from the natural rights tradition. "What is the Police?" Johann Fichte inquires in his *Science of Rights* (1796). "The state," Fichte begins, "entered into a common compact with its citizens by which each party assumes certain duties." When someone violates the law, the state originally has but one recourse. It terminates "the civil agreement between it and the criminal, thereby making the criminal an outlaw." Given that "the state exists for the individual as state only through the compact," it follows that the "highest punishment which the state can inflict" is declaring "this compact annulled." Past this threshold, the state and the individual no longer "exist for each other," as "the legal relation between them, and indeed all relation between them, has been utterly canceled." This may lead to death, but death would come then not "as a punishment, but as a means of security; and hence it is not at all an act of the *judicial*, but simply of the *police* power." Executing the criminal, the state acts, not as a state, but as a superior force of nature, which is to say that its action is guided not by the text of positive law but by the nature of police.[23]

"Placed beyond the pale of the judiciary," Fichte says, the outlaw "belongs to the police." When the outlaw is killed, it is "not done by virtue of a positive right, but from sheer necessity." Fichte notes that being outlawed does not limit how the criminal can relate to other individuals; it says only that the criminal's relation to other individuals is no longer mediated by the state. There is no law to prevent others from brutalizing the criminal if they wish. The withholding of legal protection, however, does not ensure that others will choose to abuse the criminal. "Supposing some citizens should thus treat the outlaw, what would follow?" Fichte inquires. "No proceeding against them on the part of the state, for the outlaw has no rights; but certainly the contempt of all men." Fichte says that anybody "who tortures an animal for mere pleasure, without having any positive advantage in view, is justly held in abhorrence as an inhuman barbarian." The limit on gratuitous cruelty is social not legal. Individuals refrain from gratuitous abuse, because they are governed by "self-respect" and the desire for "the esteem of other men." Here are both the positive (sympathizing) and negative (not brutalizing) relations, formed by outlawry, when coupled with the citizen's desire for the regard of others. This is what makes criminals (or slaves) into appropriate objects for sentimentality.[24]

The distinction between law and necessity would become decisive for police cases in the United States; it was first made, however, not by Fichte but by earlier philosophers who dissented from Grotius's argument that the state's power to punish criminals came from natural right. Most notable among these thinkers is Samuel Pufendorf. Although Pufendorf retained the analogy between the state and the individual in nature, he held that this analogy did not account for the state's power to punish criminals, as it ignored punishment's main purpose, which was deterring crime. For punishments to discourage would-be criminals, they had to be "threatened before, and . . . inflicted after the Crime is known," and this was only possible when punishments were written in law and administered by a state. Punishment was therefore different from self-defense or retribution in nature. Like Pufendorf and others before him, Fichte drew this same line between police and criminal law to differentiate two kinds of legal violence—one based on natural right and another on positive jurisprudence. For Fichte, the implication is that criminal regulation allowed for expiation and rehabilitation where abandonment to police was irrevocable. In the United States, judges asserted this distinction for a different purpose. They used it to shield police discretion from procedural limitations such as *actus reus* (necessitating proof of a crime committed) and *mens rea* (necessitating proof of criminal intent) that were traditional to criminal law. Pointing out the difference between natural and positive law became a powerful way for judges to distinguish the exceptionally dangerous instances to which the police power self-evidently applied.[25]

It may seem odd to suggest that these cases, on the vanguard of legal thinking, were compatible with the arguments that were being made by slavemasters, and later by lynch mobs, in defense of their own sovereignty. Although the lynch mob, in particular, operated outside the law, arrogating to itself a purpose reserved for the state, it is still worth noting that lynching advocates tended to speak in terms that were consistent with police cases like *Miln* and *Alger*. In truth, lynching advocates were probably more thoroughgoing, and closer to the spirit of the police power, in their refusal to acknowledge the difference between legal and extralegal means of prevention. If *Miln* and *Alger* were content to characterize police as a state capacity, lynching advocates pressed further, all the way to the point where attacks against ex-slaves, pursued by the state or by the mob, for prevention or punishment, were formally indistinguishable. These acts register only as "natural force," in Fichte's terms. When these defenses of lynching are taken seriously, it becomes impossible to brook the historical distinction that is often drawn between extralegal violence (barbarism) and legal violence (the prerequisite for modernization). The formal composition of the threat scenario, the identity between prevention and punishment, the suspension of due process, the blurring of the distinction between human and nonhuman, the petition to self-defense as natural right—these rhetorical features are commonly shared between the discourse on lynching and the discourse on police.[26]

Due to this surprising cohesion, it is revealing to compare seemingly barbarous statements from negrophobic newspapers like the *Wilmington*

Messenger to the leading police cases. Consider the following editorial, which was reprinted in the *Messenger* in 1898:

> Should a rattlesnake, or a mad dog, be tried before killing? Should a murderer, incendiary, or highwayman, caught in the act, be allowed to complete it and to appeal to all the delays and chances of law? If you, or your people, or your property, be feloniously attacked, will you await the laws, or will you act at once in self-defense? If a mad man be on the streets, marauding and slaying all he meets, must we take out a warrant for him, arrest and try him, before we disable him and stop his wild career? The negro who has just been lynched at Charlottesville was far worse than any rattlesnake or mad dog, far worse than any mad man or criminal and by his nature and course had outlawed himself utterly. To recognize in him any right to the protections and processes of law would be to mitigate his offence, aggravate the outrage upon the lady, and to add to the shame and horror already inflicted upon her. No decent white man endowed with reason and the proper respect of manhood, should or could restrain himself in the presence of so foul a crime. It would disgrace justice and defile the courts to treat him as an innocent man.

As far as this reasoning is concerned, the time is always right for action whether the offense is happening in the past, present, or future. Delay in every case is fatal. The stakes remain the same whether the offender completes his action (as purportedly is the case with the negro in Charlottesville), is caught red-handed (the case with the incendiary or highwayman), or merely implies the threat by his nature (like the rattlesnake or mad dog). As with the police power, it does not matter here whether a crime has been committed. There is only one course of action to be pursued, and that course does not change depending on whether or when the offense is registered. The key details in the passage, for this reason, are implied: they are the swish of the rattle, and the specks of foam on the dog's lips. These details mark the self-evidence of the threat, and in the process, they define their bearers, which is to say that all other details are void once the threat is perceived, from the finest points like the texture of the fur or the design on the skin, to the largest, in this case, qualification as human or animal. By these lights, it is foolish to put a snake on trial, not because he will have nothing to say in the witness box, but rather because he will bite you before you get him there. In fact—and this is the strangest thing about the passage—knowing that the snake will have nothing to say in the witness box has nothing to do with the fact that snakes cannot speak. The rattlesnake is barred from testimony not because he is an animal but because the possibility of his speaking is continually preempted by the threat he poses. The passage's racism is not the idea that the negro is like an animal. It does not matter whether the negro is human or animal; that is the racism. The only thing you need to know is that the negro is a threat, and threats are meant to be exterminated. In no sense is the crescendo, which arrives with the concluding appeal to white manhood, extrinsic to this principal line of argument. It only expands the passage's reasoning. Like the terrorist or the ticking time bomb, the negro will kill you if you waste time deliberating over his rights. Indeed, it appears that the only other choice is suicide.[27]

The editorial's allusion to the ancient precedent of outlawry reminds us how seriously we need to take the legal history of this threat scenario before we venture arguments about the power it is thought to warrant. It reminds us as well that we should not mistake the widespread claim about police's resistance to definition to mean that police authority was unrepresentable in an absolute sense, as if it could outstrip the need for legitimation or exist apart from the storylines where it is named. Far from being anti-mimetic in orientation, the police power has to stage continuously its inevitability before the public. Police may be opposed to the limitation that comes with definition, but it is also necessary to note that its stakes are recounted compulsively across its history. In James Kent's phrase, police pertains only to "cases of urgent necessity." Those cases, whether enumerated or narrated in all their lurid particularity, derive from threats that put society at risk. In these scenes, where the stakes could not be higher, where one thing always leads to another, the only hope is acting on the early warning signs. Police thrives on this rhetorical intensification. It has to put everything at stake, at least hypothetically, before its indefinite supremacy makes sense in modern society.[28]

By paying attention to the details of this history, we can begin to grasp the resistance that conditions black expression. Importantly, we can also come to appreciate that the unavoidable fact of this resistance does not mean that black expression is impossible, unknowable, or unrecoverable.

Primo Levi's proviso that the drowned, or those lost to history, are the only complete witnesses may be incontrovertible in the abstract, but it cannot comprehend the movement that has kept the black tradition going since its inception. The witnessing from the black tradition is admittedly incomplete and often corrupted by the very procedures that have facilitated its historical preservation. Nevertheless, I find it bitterly ironic that so many of the most thoroughgoing efforts to respect the integrity (or even the singularity) of the witness have begun to seem less like the antidote to anthropology than like its apogee. Most approaches to the so-called state of exception tend to oversimplify a history where the difference between those who survived and those who drowned can be difficult to determine. Black speaking should not be taken for granted but neither should it be discounted as impossible. As Du Bois says, it is a problem. Specifically it is a problem about predication, or more specifically about the burden of self-predication, a problem that becomes meaningful, in this respect, as a specific instance of the general problem of political subjectivity.[29]

Contrary to the claim that the black tradition is somehow unrepresentable, I am arguing that it is possible to detect the tradition's contours against the background conditions of its legal history. It is the history of law that gives us what we need to discern the tradition's ongoing self-predication. This is a critical approach that will allow us to expand on the argument, recently formulated by Hortense Spillers, that black culture is "compounded of a disposition that carries both its *statement* and *counter-statement*" in its expression, meaning that the tradition is forced continually to mimic the conditions of its alienation before it can inject into this inherited framework a "repertoire of predicates that were not there before so far as we can see." It is the insertion of these predicates into a scene in which they were previously invisible, where by all rights they should still be invisible, that initiates the process by which the tradition is able to "constitute its own standpoint." Spillers supplies a solution to a long-standing problem in interpretation: the tendency to abstract black expression from the history that is referenced in its performance, a tendency that has led many critics to mischaracterize the voice's insistence for a positive property such as soulfulness. In this book, my aim is to specify the historical statement against which the black tradition has dramatized its own emergence. Whether it is abstracted in codes or embedded in cases, the law leaves a paper trail that can be used to reconstruct the historical coordinates that are invoked in the tradition's representative structures of self-address.[30]

This approach compels us to take seriously statements that we would otherwise be inclined to dismiss, such as the often-quoted metaphor coined by John W. Burgess in 1891 to describe the police power. "The police power," Burgess pronounces, "is the 'dark continent' of our jurisprudence." This remark was meant to be critical. Concerned that police seemed to serve as a "repository of everything for which our juristic classifications can find no other place," Burgess decided the best way to convey his concern was by summoning the "barbaric anarchy" of the world's least civilized continent. For Burgess, Africa signifies a repository for legally unclassifiable persons and things. I realize that it may seem perverse to take this thinking seriously. Taking Burgess seriously does not mean, however, accepting the substitution proposed in his statement. It means, rather, staying between the terms of the metaphor and working carefully to keep its tenor ("police") from dissolving into its vehicle ("Africa"). This approach places us at the historical occasion, described so powerfully by Colin Dayan, where the captive's crime against nature becomes transmissible to descendants as the corruption of blood. It places us, in other words, where it is possible to recognize the black tradition intensely, even distinctively, engaged at the second order with its own conditions.[31]

Clearly, the cases that this book inherits from impresarios such as W. C. Handy and John Lomax come with strings attached. The book's compass is constrained by its criteria of selection. It chooses cases from the late nineteenth and early twentieth centuries according to the influence that they exercised over the framing of the black tradition during the decades when it first became possible to represent blackness as a culture. Given that I am trying to say something, however preliminary, about blackness in general, this archive is most remarkable for its limitations. The evidence appears unacceptably narrow and disproportionate in its distribution of attention, whether its scope is measured by nation (most examples view the African diaspora from the United States), gender (men are overrepresented), religion (examples are overwhelmingly secular), or medium (there is an aversion to mass culture and especially to the legacy of blackface in mass culture). I mean it when I say that my examples should not be thought to represent the black tradition in its extant diversity. I am writing about characters like Bras-Coupé and Uncle Remus, not because they are representative, but instead because they are the characters around which the black vernacular tradition was framed, for the first time, as a cultural inheritance, and I think that many of the assumptions about black expression formed at that time, around these cases, are still with us. The intent of this book is not to reproduce the mistakes that made blackness seem consubstantial with masculinity or opposed to technology. On the contrary, my aim is to write a history of these mistakes.[32]

At issue here, finally, is the applicability of the culture concept to black vernacular expression. Even as the disciplinary methods of description in literature and anthropology have changed, sometimes radically, in recent decades, most practitioners have retained the central assumption that blackness is a culture, an ensemble of symbolic practices, that can be bounded and thickly described. Not so long after Sidney Mintz and Richard Price published *An Anthropological Approach to the Afro-American Past* (1976), it became customary to assert that slaves were active in selecting, adapting, and mixing their cultural legacies. By and large, the standard emphasis on cultural survival was replaced by a new emphasis on creative recombination. Since the 1990s, critics have continued to explore, with increasing theoretical sophistication, the idea that blackness is a practice and not a stable identity. The diaspora is now often conceived less as a hereditary circumstance and more as a connection that is forged through alliances and claims. In this book, I engage with this powerfully practical orientation to blackness by asking what I see as a related question about the standpoint from which blackness is put to use. Is this standpoint already black? If so, what makes it black? How does this blackness condition or predicate the choice that occurs when blackness becomes a practice? In this respect, my argument is addressed to the presuppositions that we bring to the study of black culture. I want to know what we mean when we talk about the blackness in black politics or expression. My intent is not to downplay the diversity of the social practices identified as black. Rather, it is to ask what it is about these practices that makes them count as black in the first place.[33]

Once blackness is defined not as a common culture but instead as a species of statelessness, we can no longer take for granted the perspective in the black tradition. We have no choice but to account for its predication. Addressing this challenge, this book distills a few ideas from recent thought about experimental black aesthetics, particularly from Fred Moten, applying these ideas to a representative set of case studies from the vernacular archive. The tradition revealed by this approach certainly seems less like folk expression and more like an avant-garde. The notion that the black tradition is an avant-garde from its start is classically stated by Amiri Baraka, who associates the tradition's penchant for experimentation and its resistance to commodification with the continuing retention of socially functional music from the African continent. This is a strong notion that begs questions about how art relates to commerce, how leaders relate to masses, how form relates to innovation, and how authenticity relates to inauthenticity. Much of its strength, in fact, derives from its refusal to provide any easy answers to these questions. It is an idea that has also been redirected, to quote Fred Moten quoting Cedric Robinson, to name a tradition that "cannot be understood within the particular context of its genesis." Observing that the black tradition is always escaping an original situation to which it remains attached is one way to get to the bottom of what it means to say that the tradition is an avant-garde from its start. It is also a way to understand in the abstract what I have been trying to show about the black tradition's relation to the law. By specifying the tension between the tradition and the context that can be recovered through the law, this book catches a few glimpses of an alternative to the tradition's established line of descent. For now, they remain glimpses, although I have attempted to specify them as fully as possible in the ensuing chapters.[34]

1

THE BLACK TRADITION FROM
IDA B. WELLS TO ROBERT CHARLES

Although the actual origin of the blues is unknown, and maybe at this point unknowable, we do know exactly when and how this little-known regional vernacular became an international phenomenon. More than anyone else, it was W. C. Handy who communicated the music to a mass audience, standardizing the format for twelve-bar blues in the process. Although Handy was not the first to notate the blues, it was the publication of compositions like "Memphis Blues" (1912) and "St. Louis Blues" (1914) that facilitated the music's wider circulation. Drawing on the vernacular materials that he gathered around the Delta, Handy became a prolific songwriter and a cultural entrepreneur, writing tune after tune, many of which became popular standards. Handy's knack for self-promotion was key for his success given the racism that he encountered in the publishing industry. Before long, he was introducing himself as the "Father of the Blues," a tagline that eventually became the title for his autobiography. This is an assertion that has long been questioned and contested, most famously by Jelly Roll Morton in an angry letter to *Down Beat*, which attacked Handy's credibility and frankly doubted whether Handy had ever created anything. The letter's heading summarizes Morton's argument: "I Created Jazz in 1902, Not W. C. Handy." As if there could be any doubt as to his point, under his signature Morton added the sobriquet, "Originator of Jazz and Stomps."[1]

The intention of this chapter is not to take sides in this well-known dispute between Handy and Morton. It is, instead, to contemplate the structure of these paternity claims in light of their lasting impression upon the recording and transcription of the modern black tradition in jazz and blues. This is an inquiry that will involve several detours as well as the consideration of a song that Morton refuses to sing on tape, a tragic song about an outlaw named Robert Charles, whose characterization closely matches the profile of a ragged songster that Handy meets a few years later in a train station in Mississippi. I am not so mystical as to say that Robert Charles was reincarnated as Handy's songster. I do believe, however, that for all intents and purposes Charles and the ragged songster might as well have been the same person. The best way to understand their similarity, I will propose, is through a pamphlet that Ida B. Wells-Barnett wrote about Charles, in which she offers her most complete account of the relationship between blackness and the law. With guidance from Wells-Barnett, I intend to trace some of the deeper lines of determination that remain legible within Handy and Morton's long-standing dispute.

The first thing we need to observe about Handy and Morton's disagreement is that Handy never says that he made the blues by himself. By his own admission, the blues form was "used by Negro roustabouts, honky-tonk piano players, wanderers and others of their underprivileged but undaunted class from Missouri to the Gulf" long before he introduced it to the "general public." Accordingly, the most celebrated scene in *Father of the Blues* (1941) concerns discovery and not invention. Having fallen asleep on a station platform in Tutwiler, Mississippi, while waiting for an overdue train, Handy awoke to find someone next to him playing a guitar. This was the first time that Handy heard the blues:

> A lean, loose-jointed Negro had commenced plunking a guitar beside me while I slept. His clothes were rags; his feet peeped out of his shoes. His face had on it some of the sadness of the ages. As he played, he pressed a knife on the strings of the guitar in a manner popularized by Hawaiian guitarists who used steel bars. The effect was unforgettable. His song, too, struck me instantly. Goin' where the Southern cross the Dog. The singer repeated the line three times, accompanying himself on the guitar with the weirdest music I had ever heard. The tune stayed in my mind. When the singer paused, I leaned over and asked him what the words meant. He rolled his eyes, showing a trace of mild amusement. Perhaps I should have known, but he didn't mind explaining. At Moorhead the eastbound and the westbound met and crossed the north and southbound trains four times a day. This fellow was going where the Southern cross the Dog, and he didn't care who knew it. He was simply singing about Moorhead as he waited. That was not unusual.

Southern Negroes sang about everything. Trains, steamboats, steam whistles, sledge hammers, fast women, mean bosses, stubborn mules—all become subjects for their songs. They accompany themselves on anything from which they can extract a musical sound or rhythmical effect, anything from a harmonica to a washboard. In this way, and from these materials, they set the mood for what we now call the blues.

Handy says that this experience altered his life, putting him on the path to success as a big-time composer. He would tell this story for many years before it was eventually printed in his autobiography, with an earlier version appearing in Abbe Niles's preface to Handy's *Blues: An Anthology* (1926). Subsequent to its publication, the tale became a legend. It has been told again and again in interviews, liner notes, and influential books such as Robert Palmer's *Deep Blues* (1981) and David Evans's *Big Road Blues* (1982). Some writers are quick to label the encounter as the starting point to the "remarkable odyssey of the blues." Others take the time to dwell on whatever additional details they can infer: the closed-up shop windows in the middle of the night, the rustle of the cypress and willow trees, the exhaustion that comes from shifting your weight for hours while trying to get comfortable on a hard bench. The critical theory of the black vernacular that emerged in the 1980s pressed this ambition even further, using this archetypal scene to frame the tradition as a whole. Works including Houston Baker's *Blues, Ideology and Afro-American Literature* (1984) turn not to Handy but to his native informant—the ragged songster—to show the continuity in the tradition. For Baker, it is the songster, and the desperate class to which he belongs, that "constitute the vernacular."[2]

In the reception of this scene, it is the native informant that matters most. Through his origin story, Handy helped to sanctify the train-hopping threadbare drifter as a central character in the iconography of the black tradition. It is easy to see the terms of this canonization at work in the encounter. As Handy constructs the scene, the spotlight never leaves the informant. His own position vis-à-vis the informant is carefully circumscribed. Everything in the scene is stage-managed to limit his ability to shape its circumstances. The loose-jointed vagrant catches Handy off guard. He emerges as if from a dream, a phrase that never leaves the vagrant's reality in doubt even as it strips the background that would bring him into focus. As the meeting is accidental, it involves no criteria for selection, no preconceptions, and no intercession of categories. In the present moment, the songster is unaccountable, like his music. The scene is supposed to stand as an example of pure induction—at least that is how it is performed in retrospect. Nothing is planned ahead of time or processed according to expectation. The most important thing to notice here is how Handy manages to idealize the conditions for ethnographic exchange by giving away all his power in the scene. It is only by staging his own disempowerment that Handy is able to take for granted the cultural authenticity of the gift that he receives. He is able to intuit the true nature of the gift, only because he has denied himself the capability to corrupt or interfere with its performance. The irony is that Handy's power is enhanced under these constraints. He gets what every collector desires—immediate access to the taproot of the vernacular tradition—by structurally limiting his own potential power over his native informant.[3]

The telling moment comes when the songster rolls his eyes after Handy asks about the meaning of the song. What the informant knows at this moment that Handy does not know is that the song's meaning is available to direct observation. The irony of Handy's ignorance, in other words, is the failure to notice something that he could hear with his own ears and see with his own eyes. The ragged songster is someone waiting for a train singing about waiting for a train. He is singing what he is doing, and he is doing what he is singing. He is the subject of the song. In this scene, music is a primary mode of self-consciousness. For Handy, this is "not unusual." People like this singer transform experiences into songs, accompanying themselves on homemade instruments built from objects near at hand, and it is this closed circuit between environment and expression that qualifies their music as real folk music. The fact that the singer looks down-and-out is decisive to the authenticity of his expression, but it is not the whole story. What makes for vernacular authenticity, in this instance, is the songster's capacity to embody what he sings. He is someone who hops freights who sings about hopping freights. When he sings, he sings about himself. Others may sing about the Southern crossing the Dog, but their music would not be folk music unless they too were hopping freights by night. This idea—that the singer is the subject of the song—further aggrandizes the collector's power by providing access not only to the song but to the mind of the singer. It establishes an approach that can solve ambiguity in any structure of address ("What Dog?")

through the presumption that the standpoint in the song is always the singer's own.[4]

Among would-be collectors around the turn of the twentieth century, there were many fortunate accidents like the encounter between Handy and his songster. In addition to Handy's legend, there are retrospective stories by inadvertent anthropologists like John Jacob Niles, and contemporary writings by researchers like Charles Peabody, an archaeologist from Harvard who published some of the music sung by the black workers he hired to excavate American Indian burial mounds in the Mississippi Delta. Decades earlier, Joel Chandler Harris prefaced his Uncle Remus tales by describing a similarly accidental encounter at a train station at Norcross, Georgia, with a cluster of railroad workers, perched upon a stack of cross-ties, whose storytelling was in Harris's estimation more than equal to Uncle Remus. Like Handy, these collectors look backward, sometimes quite explicitly, to T. D. Rice, the blackface player who—one legend has it—learned to Jump Jim Crow by imitating a black stablehand whom he met by chance in Cincinnati. In contrast to these accidental collectors, who are going about their daily business when they are surprised by a song, story, or dance that they never could have imagined, their successors tend to know ahead of time what they are trying to find. And what they want is somebody who looks exactly like the loose-jointed songster on Handy's train platform at Tutwiler. If Handy discovers gold without foreknowledge of its value, his successors already realize that vagabonds, outcasts, and drifters are the black singers whose songs are most true to themselves. Poised for action, they know a good source when they see one, the indicators being the rags and broken shoes needed for a singer to personify the perspective in the black tradition.[5]

Judging from Handy's tale, it would seem the best folklorist is the accidental folklorist. But increasingly, negrophile collectors in the opening decades of the twentieth century were treating fieldwork as a science requiring a hypothesis about where the best sources were located. If Handy imagined his informant's rags retrospectively to authenticate his own blues compositions, folklorists like Howard Odum and Will Thomas were prepared to predict ahead of time that the music made by threadbare drifters was bound to be culturally valuable. They formed a definite hypothesis about the black tradition and kept a specific profile in mind when they were in the field. "Wherever Negroes work, or loaf, or await judgment," Odum guarantees, "there may be heard the weary and lonesome blues so strange and varied as to reveal a sort of superhuman evidence of the folk soul." Employing this criterion in selecting his informants, Odum looked for black men who were wandering, or who looked like they had been wandering, and accepted the music he took from them as autobiographical expression. For Odum, the proper informants were those ramblers passing from "section to section, loafing in general, and working only when compelled to do so." In "Some Current Folk-Songs of the Negro" (1912), Will Thomas agrees that the ideal informant is someone who tries to "live in this world without working." "So far as my observation goes," Thomas writes, "the property-holding negro never sings." Because "property lends a respectability" and "respectability is too great a burden" for any tradition to bear, the only "negro" who "sings" is the one who is losing, or has never found, his "economic foothold." A good worker makes a bad informant because he is too respectable to waste time singing, and a bad worker makes for the best kind of informant because the dearth in industry and respectability is richly compensated by musical genius. Collecting authentic black expression became a matter of knowing where to look. Canvassing "wayside roads and camps" was a good start, according to the strategy Odum recommended, and even better was "the chain gang."[6]

Among the collectors following in this line were E. C. Perrow, Anna Kranz Odum, Newbell Niles Puckett, Natalie Curtis-Burlin, John Lomax, Abbe Niles, Josh Dunson, Dorothy Scarborough, Robert Winslow Gordon, Newman White, Nettie McAdams, Guy B. Johnson, Alan Lomax, Zora Neale Hurston, Sterling Brown, Lawrence Gellert, Arna Bontemps, Langston Hughes, Robert Bass, Edward C. L. Adams, Mary Wheeler, Thomas W. Talley, John W. Work, and Harold Courlander. By the 1920s, the interest widened from professional journals into the book trade, as university presses at Harvard and North Carolina started printing compilations—including Howard Odum and Guy Johnson's *The Negro and His Songs* (1925) as well as its sequel *Negro Workaday Songs* (1926), Dorothy Scarborough's *On the Trail of Negro Folk-Songs* (1925), and Newman White's *American Negro Folk-Songs* (1928). Other books, advertised as all-purpose affairs, began to feature black songs as essential to the national folk tradition. Most important in this regard were the best-selling collections by John and Alan Lomax like *American Ballads and Folk Songs* (1934) and *Our Singing Country* (1941). Some collectors tried their hands at fiction, yielding works like Howard Odum's *Rainbow Round My Shoulder* (1928), *Wings on My Feet* (1929), and *Cold Blue Moon* (1931)—a trilogy based on the life of Odum's informant, Left Wing Gordon. This ethnographic romance would also inform the works by artists associated with the Harlem Renaissance and the Popular Front. In the Harlem number of *Survey Graphic* magazine and the movement-defining anthology *The New Negro* (1925) that came in its wake, Alain Locke would announce that the "answer" to modernization lay "in the migrating peasant." Many literary experiments at the time were catalyzed by a desire to harness the energy of "the man farthest down" (Locke's words) and structured by the presumed mutual dependence between the avant-garde and the itinerant black masses. Writers including Langston Hughes, Zora Neale Hurston, and Sterling Brown combined folklore collection with literary vocation in works that featured "permanent transients with no attachments" as full-fledged characters, such as Big Boy Davis, an itinerant songster whom Brown met in Lynchburg and used as the basis for a number of poems—one of which is dedicated, according to its headnote, to the memory of all the days before Davis was "chased out of town for vagrancy." This enthusiasm was carried into left-wing periodicals like *New Masses*, which published some of the pathbreaking prison fieldwork by Lawrence Gellert, as well as anthologies like Nancy Cunard's *Negro* (1934), Sterling Brown's *Negro Caravan* (1941), and Arna Bontemps and Langston Hughes's *The Book of Negro Folklore* (1958).[7]

By the late 1920s, this thinking was also exerting influence on the commercial recording industry. Looking for the traditional music that was thought to be thickest and least adulterated among no-accounts and loafers became not only an academic pursuit but a principal business enterprise. The sudden vogue for black street performers dates to 1926 when Blind Lemon Jefferson, an itinerant songster who played for spare change, was suggested to Mayo Williams, a scout for Paramount Records, by a record store in Dallas. Taken off guard by Jefferson's wild success in the national market, record companies dispatched field outfits and cultivated local contacts, flooding the market with street corner musicians whose repertoires were in many respects continuous with the singers who thrilled Handy and Odum. After the early records by Blind Lemon Jefferson, Papa Charlie Jackson, and Peg Leg Howell, companies recorded singers like Charley Patton, Skip James, Tommy Johnson, and Son House—who almost certainly would have remained obscure were it not for the new formula that talent

Display advertisement by Paramount Records for Blind Blake, "He's in the Jailhouse Now," from the *Chicago Defender*, 31 December 1927. Reprinted with permission from John Tefteller.

brokers like Ralph Peer, H. C. Speir, and Williams (the one black scout in the group) employed to select and then promote their discoveries in venues like the *Chicago Defender*. The production, recording, and reception of this music, retrospectively termed country blues, was shaped by new migration patterns, innovations in electrical recording equipment, and the brisk exchange between string-driven regional styles and the better-known style of blues performed by female singers accompanied by horns and piano, which had long dominated the tent shows and the phonograph. But country blues never would have been preserved on record were it not for the common sense that told folklorists and commercial scouts who was most likely to have stayed in contact with the tradition.[8]

Much has been made of the important differences among these folklore collectors and cultural impresarios: Alan Lomax (a white man) versus Zora Neale Hurston (a black woman), or John Lomax (a moderate conservative) versus Lawrence Gellert (a Communist Party member), or even Alan Lomax (who was enraged by the cruelty and injustice that he viewed in southern prisons and considered folksong collecting some small gesture toward redress) and John Lomax (who joked that his son wanted to set all the prisoners free). So much has been made of these differences, in fact, that it may be worth recalling how much these collectors had in common. When Hurston produces her pathbreaking ethnography on the juke joint, or collects blues by migrant fruit-pickers during her fieldwork with Alan Lomax, she is guided by principles that are generally shared by folklorists at the time. When Gellert classifies his informants as vagrants who fall as "easily as small change" into the pockets of the police, he means something different from what Will Thomas means when he says the worst employees make the best songsters. Gellert means something different, but he has the same person in mind. Thomas lectures an audience that is presumed to know this informant only from the other side of the labor contract, and names the informant through the struggle to extract value from him. Gellert, on the other hand, sees little distinction between this silent compulsion and the primitive violence of the chain gang. Thomas and Gellert have nothing in common intellectually except for what matters most—their mutual participation in the folklore movement that turned the nameless and ragged drifter into the representative subject of black history. Despite their differences in approach, these collectors are unified by the idea that the folk tradition was encapsulated by the generations of ragged singers that took to the roads after slavery. This common criterion has counted for more in the long run than the diversity in approach among these collectors, who are bound despite their differences by the collective intuition that people who look like Handy's songster are self-expressive in a way that other people are not. When closer attention is given to the assumptions applied by these collectors in their fieldwork and reporting, we may start to see them in a new light, not only as cultural entrepreneurs, or salvage specialists, or romantic racialists, but as thinkers who were to a significant degree responsible for the major declension of the race concept after emancipation.[9]

The key here is recognizing how these negrophile collectors facilitated not the discovery but the artificial instigation of folk expression through their fieldwork. In this respect, it is telling that the impression established in the Handy legend—that the singer is the subject of the song—is explicitly asserted by later collectors. "A negro singing the folk-songs of his race," John Lomax writes, "might be termed a negro thinking aloud." Characterizing music as what the negro says when nobody is listening, Lomax idealizes the ethnographic scene to the point where there is nothing separating the collector from the informant. Lomax declares, in other words, what Handy enacts in his stage-management of the scene at Tutwiler. In both cases, what matters most is not the singer's demographic profile but the alignment between this demographic profile and the particular structure of address in the song. When Odum proposes that black songsters in work camps, penitentiaries, and street corners manifest a "superhuman evidence of the folk soul" in their singing, he is responding not to the music alone but to the perceived alignment between the music and its singers, alignment that is not natural but carefully engineered before the collector enters the field. The reason manual laborers, loafers, and near-criminals are more soulful than other members of the race is not that they have something special inside them. Rather, it is that they are the only ones who can be so easily mistaken for the perspective within their songs and sayings. Odum knew this well enough to say ahead of time where the folk soul could be located, but his prediction only affirms something that many others knew or would soon come to know, which was where to track down the last remaining examples of truly black expression. Some went so far as to justify this intuition by suggesting that the black tradition had developed: although its original source was the suffering slave, its new focus was the black prisoner. Demands to "let my people go" expressed in the "old spirituals" were not only matched but exceeded by the "determined call for freedom" from "the Negro singer behind the bars." Songs by "the wanderer, the migrant, the black man offender" were described by this new generation of collectors as the most "eloquent successors to the old spirituals with their sorrow-feeling."[10]

This perceived relay between the music and the singer's mind was a benchmark for folklore collectors who judged songs by their "trueness" to the "actual workaday experience" of "the negro." The best songs, it was said, were like a "folk-mirror." As soon as this cross-referencing is under way, nothing else has to happen for the black tradition to become a folk tradition. Based on the glow of natural alignment between the tradition and its speakers, ethnographers were free to follow their presumption that black culture came from a traditional world where expression was still indexed directly to its producers. The black tradition was a folk culture where singing and storytelling retained the stamp of its authors, a tradition unlike modern communications that lost their aura as they became standardized, market-based, and mediated by mechanically reproduced image and sound. Unaccountably self-expressive by these modern standards, the black tradition was identified by its collectors as among the last remnants from a disappearing world where artistic expression maintained its individuality. Many people who wrote about black expression into the 1920s tended to think that they were describing a premodern tradition that was gradually withering away in a world where market relationships were predominant and individuals were becoming increasingly dissociated from organic kinship groups as they were compelled by economic necessity into contractual association with strangers. According to this model, it was the economic failure of loose-jointed and lazy singers that insulated them from the deracinating forces of the market. The collector's criterion for selection (ragged clothes, broken shoes) may have been shaped by the pleasure of condescension, but it was also governed by a systematic rationale, which correlated economic failure with cultural authenticity.[11]

Certainly, there were valuable innovations in this fieldwork. Collectors did much to recompose the rigid canon inherited from Francis James Child, which had little use for American folklore, much less African American. The old developmental prejudice, which assumed that folklore was premodern, also gradually gave way to a novel consensus that insisted folklore was contemporary and vibrant, even as it preserved the standard assumption about folklore's resistance to the alienation that came with modern living. Again, it is good to emphasize the continuity in these common assumptions, given the customary critical tendency to stress the divisions between collectors. There is much that is traditional in their methods, including a practical focus on salvaging materials that were soon to disappear, an emphasis that is attributable to Thomas Percy's *Reliques of Ancient English Poetry* (1765), as well as the connected imperative for direct transcription from a live informant, an imperative that extends back to Joseph Ritson's critique of Percy's methods in *A Select Collection of English Songs* (1783). When a collector named Walter Prescott Webb, working in South Texas in 1915, pinpoints an informant, fresh from the local jail, and praises his music for its synopsis of the "desires and aims" of the negro race, he continues the line of romantic nationalism not only by equating race with culture but also by choosing Floyd Canada, a drifter and jailbird, as a representative speaker for this racial tradition. Webb leverages an established presumption that says the finest folklore resides with the people most down-and-out. Although Johann Gottfried von Herder and his followers first looked to the peasantry as the source of folk tradition, already in the early nineteenth century there existed a pronounced tendency to assimilate migrant workers, vagabonds, and criminals to this romantic framework. Handy and his cohort were not the first to associate vagrancy with cultural authenticity, but it was their combined influence that made this association structural to the recording and documentation of the black vernacular tradition.[12]

Given the breadth of this influence, it is important to consider the structural tensions that collectors like Handy failed to resolve in transcription in spite of their best efforts. Regarding Handy's encounter at Tutwiler, for instance, we have already noticed how the scene is stage managed to allow a fantasy of uncontaminated induction: it establishes an opportunity for cultural collection that is supposed to be unmediated by the categories of selection and interpretation that otherwise constitute ethnographic fieldwork. The irony is that, for all the effort to dispel the mediation of social categories, the ragged songster remains available to representation in this encounter only as a social type. There is nothing that we know about him in particular; he is apprehensible only as a representative of the horde or mass to which he belongs. We do not know his name. There is nothing that Handy says about the songster that differentiates him from others like him. Given this lack of individuation, we can ask a deeper question about the scene's composition. Why would Handy arrange the encounter in a way that undercuts the importance of everything that can be known about his native informant? The ragged songster is present in the encounter only as a social type, and yet his social legibility is the one thing about him that is not allowed to affect Handy's experience of his song. Whether the resulting tension between individuality and typicality is registered in time (as ethnographic knowledge deferred until after the scene is over) or in space (as the mismatch between the scene's form and content), we are still forced to confront the strange disparity between the apparent objectivity of Handy's social description of the ragged songster and the singularity of the self-expression that Handy claims to hear in his music.[13]

This formal disparity becomes available to historical analysis when we consider the specific type that the songster is supposed to represent. He is a vagrant. Or, to be precise, the ragged songster is not individuated except as a vagrant, which is to say that he is "unindividuated," to borrow a term from Lawrence Gellert.[14] It follows that one thing we can know for sure about Handy's songster is that he is legally vulnerable. The dilapidation of his garments, his loitering in the train station, the fact that he is unknown to Handy and likely a stranger in Tutwiler, even the guitar he strums— these details combine to imply a demographic profile with predictable legal implications. If Handy were a police officer, he could arrest the songster on the spot. The vagrancy laws that were resuscitated in states like Mississippi after emancipation were expressly designed to target people like the songster. Outlined in the discourse of the state, so-called black vagrants were assigned an array of emblematic habits (loafing and stealing), inclinations (shiftlessness and intemperance), and attributes (dirtiness and disease) that left them vulnerable to legal prosecution. With characteristics that would have been recognizable from blackface entertainments and narrative representations of fugitive slaves and free blacks, the vagrant became the subject of intense scrutiny in public debates about the meaning and impact of slave emancipation in the United States. This background has to be taken into account if we want to understand the social type that Handy's songster is meant to embody, and it is precisely this background that is wished away when Handy has the songster emerge from a dream, as if he had no history relevant to the scene.[15]

On its own, however, this immediate background does not give us everything we need. To appreciate the mystery of Handy's songster we need to consider not only the function but also the form of vagrancy laws, which means reading them specifically as police statutes. Since the eighteenth century, vagrancy has been indispensable to jurisprudence about the police power. Blackstone's *Commentaries* (1765–1769) cite "rogues and vagabonds" most prominently in their list of police offenses, an emphasis carried into controlling decisions, like *Miln*, whose influence was enough to assure that vagrancy would persist in the legal thought of the United States as the paradigm case in most major considerations concerning police. In this jurisprudence, serious questions have been raised about the breadth of the police power—concerning its relation to commerce, for example, or the prescribed limitation known as substantive due process—but its service in vagrancy laws has never been subject to constitutional scrutiny. The application of the police power in vagrancy law has been seen as self-evidently legitimate, so much so that vagrancy has often supplied the benchmark against which other police statutes have been appraised. Controversial police laws were described by their advocates as equivalent to vagrancy laws. Their opponents, by contrast, have made their cases by arguing against the analogy. Vagrancy was even strong enough to function as a benchmark in cases concerning the state's relationship to fugitive slaves, such as *Prigg v. Pennsylvania* (1842), which confirms the power of states to "arrest and restrain runaway slaves" on grounds that these actions are analogous to those taken against "idlers, vagabonds and paupers." The reasoning in *Prigg,* as in kindred cases like *Moore v. Illinois* (1852), is tortured, implying that fugitive slaves are police targets (not property) when the statute provides for their rendition but property (not police targets) when rendition is opposed. Perhaps the one baseline that remains consistent across these decisions is the warrant that says statutes governing fugitives are legitimate whenever they can be analogized to vagrancy statutes and illegitimate when the analogy does not hold. Even before the fugitive slave, the vagrant was imagined in antebellum courtrooms as a self-sufficient cause for police action. The ragged character who served as the prototypical informant for cultural collectors like Handy, it follows, was also the prototypical target for the police power. When collectors talked about the wandering drifter who was the modern carrier for the black tradition, they were picturing a character that appeared first in the law. This is a relationship that needs to be tracked.[16]

Among the most influential writings on the legal example of vagrancy is Christopher Tiedeman's *A Treatise on the Limitations of the Police Power* (1886). Tiedeman follows his predecessors in citing vagrancy as a quintessential example for the police power, making much of the discretion given the police and the courts in processing vagrants. No evidence, or even a cause, is required in these cases. It is left to the police officer to "trace the lines of criminality upon the face." Discretion is exercised not only in the arrest but in its prosecution in a summary proceeding before a magistrate's court where there is no jury, no written record, no consideration of criminal intention, no rules on the use of evidence, no presumption of innocence. Unlike in criminal trials, where the prosecution bears a burden to prove guilt, a vagrant must establish his innocence by giving a good account of himself. In making the determination as to whether the account is sufficient, the magistrate is under no constraints; his decision is formally identical to the decision to arrest. Tiedeman notes that in both cases the decision is "unchecked" and "external" to law. The proceeding is shaped not by procedure but by the power, shared by officer and magistrate, to discern the "indelible stamp of criminal propensity" in the face of the accused.[17]

Tiedeman sees this infringement upon "individual liberty" as a potential problem and argues for this reason that police must be limited to actual emergencies. Nothing but "public necessity," concludes Tiedeman, is sufficient to warrant the wide discretion that is granted by vagrancy statutes. "The vagrant," Tiedeman proposes in definition, "has been very appropriately described as the chrysalis of every species of criminal. A wanderer through the land, without home ties, idle, and without apparent means of support, what but criminality is to be expected from such a person?" As the vagrant is the "chrysalis" of every criminal, policing the vagrant is a way to stop crime before it happens. One polices vagrants not for what they have done, or for who they are, but for who they may become. The criminal apparently counts as a person for Tiedeman, but the vagrant is a legal abstraction, an unpredictable and destructive possibility that cannot register as a person as it has no consistency across time.[18]

Tiedeman pauses over the difficulty in this definition, observing that the properties that would seem to distinguish the vagrant—itinerancy, unemployment, raggedness, absence of visible property, criminal countenance—were never entered into evidence in the courts where vagrants were processed. Pushing the point, he mulls over the reasons why these properties, including the "tattered and otherwise dilapidated condition" of one's clothes do not, and indeed cannot, stand as prima facie evidence for vagrancy. "The man may be a miser," Tiedeman writes, "possessed of abundant means, which he hoards to his own injury." Applying vagrancy law to a ragged miser is a "plain violation" of liberty. Does not the miser have the right to "wear old clothes . . . and may he not, thus clad, indulge in a desire to wander from place to place?" Tiedeman emphasizes that the problem is not merely that rags are unreliable evidence, pointing at once in opposite directions, to rich as well as poor. It is, rather, that rags are not registered as

evidence at all. There is no occasion either in the arrest or at trial when rags
are evidence, because there is no point where evidence is considered. The
magistrate may ask the vagrant about his rags, but there is no requirement
to take the explanation into account. The discretion granted by the police
power allows the magistrate to count or discount the explanation without
regard for its content. There are no rules on how rags are interpreted, so
they cannot be evidence. It does not matter if the vagrant wears rags at all,
as they are not necessary for the arrest or for the determination of guilt.
Counterintuitive as it may seem, rags cannot be one of the properties that
defines a vagrant. What the rags symbolize is that the vagrant can exhibit no
properties that matter from the standpoint of the law.[19]

Rags stamp the vagrant as a vagrant by rendering all other properties irrelevant to consideration. Once you have seen the rags and tatters, you
know all you need to know. Vagrancy has no empirical reference. It is a
term that cannot be defined like a word in the dictionary, as it references
a category whose members have nothing in common besides their identification as vagrants. Commenting on the catalogues in vagrancy statutes,
Tiedeman notes that there are often entries on lewdness, juggling, assembly, and other actions that have nothing to do with vagrancy in any strict
sense of the word. Though these entries would never appear under "Mr.
Webster's definition" for vagrancy, they appear in the law. "The only apparent object of incorporating them into the vagrant act," Tiedeman
resolves, "is to secure convictions of these offenses by the summary proceeding created by the act." Pushing the point again, Tiedeman then asks
whether Webster's definition should be revised accordingly to name "all
acts" policed as vagrancy, a correction that would change not only its substance but its form, stretching the definition to the point where it would
have no positive content whatsoever. Inclusion in Webster's as a vagrant
would not indicate that you have certain properties (rags, for instance) but
merely that you have been named as a vagrant by the law. This definition,
which would say only that vagrants are persons policed as vagrants, cannot tell us anything about what does and does not count as vagrancy, but
it does tell us how vagrancy law was enforced in the time between emancipation and Handy's meeting with his ragged songster.[20]

Tiedeman explains the rags that define Handy's songster, and he also
tells us something more. He follows his analysis of the vagrant's rags with
an account of the style in which these rags as well as kindred markers of social disqualification are named. The catalogue, Tiedeman affirms, is not

only formally important to collectors like Handy who found their informants on highways and in prisons yards but to the laws that told these collectors where to pursue their fieldwork. Whenever Handy starts to list the "Negro roustabouts, honky-tonk piano players, wanderers and others of their underprivileged but undaunted class" who knew the blues, he is adapting a style of description—the catalogue—that Tiedeman identifies as requisite to vagrancy law. Asking about these catalogues, Tiedeman quotes an Ohio statute that lists the "street beggar, common prostitute, habitual disturber of the peace, known pickpockets, gambler, burglar, thief, watch-stuffer, ball-game player, a person who practices any trick, game, or device with the intent to swindle, a person who abuses his family . . . and any suspicious person who cannot give a reasonable account of himself." Although it may be possible to conjecture some unity behind the diversity in this catalogue, a unity that is perhaps perceptible in the rags shared by Handy's songster and the watch-stuffer in Ohio, Tiedeman shows that the catalogue is first and foremost a legal convention that derives negatively from the discretionary license in police power.[21]

Tiedeman forces us to remember that naming your object over and over again is not the same thing as thickly describing your object; there is no sense that you are learning more as you go along or getting closer to the object in the aggregate. There are always more elements to come, whose nature cannot be anticipated based on the elements that precede them. The lumpenproletariat is unlike other classes as its members have no characteristics that can be used to designate them as a class. *Lumpen* (meaning "rags and tatters") names a class whose members have nothing in common with one another besides their membership in the class. Vagrants share nothing with each other, and they share nothing with the individuals who belong to other classes, whose existence does not have to be enumerated, because it can be identified by the qualities (culture, wealth, occupation, status) that organize them as a class. Vagrants, on the other hand, are not vagrants because they satisfy some condition. They are vagrants because they do not satisfy any condition that would qualify them for another class in society. Vagrants cannot be classified, and it is their resistance to classification that makes them invisible. They register, in law or in any other medium, only through the qualities they are presumed to lack.[22]

Looking to these legal precedents, we can understand aspects of ethnographic practice that would otherwise remain obscure, including the tendency to enumerate informants in catalogues. Handy, for instance, emphasizes that his ragged songster is one of many. The songster arrives on his own, but Handy is quick to assert that he is one among the multitude of "footloose bards" who are "forever coming and going" on the rivers and highways. When collectors like Handy named informants in long lists, they were imitating a paratactic method that was already prevalent among lawmakers, novelists, muckrakers, philosophers, and social scientists who wrote about the so-called dangerous classes. When Handy enumerates the "barroom pianists, careless nomadic laborers, watchers of incoming trains and steamboats, street corner guitar players, strumpets and outcasts" who played the blues, he is drawing on a tradition of social representation whose milestones include Karl Marx's *Eighteenth Brumaire of Louis Bonaparte* (1852) and Henry Mayhew's *London Labour and the London Poor* (1861), works that reckon the lumpenproletariat not analytically as a class but theatrically as a proliferation of unassimilated elements. In his anecdote, Handy adapts this inherited framework for representing individuals who are presumed to lack the capacity for self-representation. As Tiedeman explains, this mode of representation ultimately derives from the vagrancy laws that defined the classes that writers like Marx and Mayhew were considering, laws whose regularity is discernible only when they are read as police measures.[23]

These legal precedents also reveal something about the songs transcribed by collectors like Handy, which is the energy that the songs have to expend to occupy the vagrant's position. This is a position that cannot be intuitively inhabited. Vagrancy supplies no natural standpoint to express in a song. To speak as a vagrant is to make your own existence into a problem. In effect, it is to deny the social existence of the perspective that is performed in your singing. Even before this background is sketched, it is easy enough to show that collectors had to resort to trickery to insinuate the identity between the songs they gathered and the people who sang them. Occasionally, collectors will make the effort to demonstrate this connection by matching a song to perceived patterns in black society, but more often the black mind is derived analytically from the music in which it gets communicated, which is merely to say that both terms of the correspondence—singer and song—are found inside the music.[24] In a limited sense, the continuing existence of this trickery is enough to unsettle the claim that there is any necessary or inevitable connection between ragged singers and their songs. It is, however, difficult to show empirically the consequences of this non-identity. The relay between the singer and the song may be established through circular reasoning that is easy enough to debunk, but the hard work commences when we try to specify alternative grounds for black expression. In the remainder of this chapter, I take up this challenge by reconsidering Handy's anecdote in light of his famous dispute with Jelly Roll Morton. In my view, there are structural reasons why Handy and Morton's competing demands for cultural recognition are forced to circle back continuously to the character of the ragged vagrant, a character who assumed a starring role in folklore, literature, and commercial recording during the decades between Handy's legendary encounter with his ragged songster (in 1903) and Morton's celebrated interviews with Alan Lomax at the Library of Congress (in 1938).

Unlike Handy, who was calling himself "Father of the Blues" for much of his career, Morton staked his claim on two specific occasions: first, in the 1938 letter to *Down Beat*, and second, in his interviews with Lomax later that year. It was the interviews that would have the most enduring impact on Morton's reputation. After reading the letter in *Down Beat*, Lomax made arrangements to meet with Morton, who was playing at a ramshackle bar across town in Washington, D.C., having fallen on hard times as he battled for the royalties that he had never been paid. Conducted over the piano in the main auditorium at the Library of Congress, the interviews gave Morton the chance to showcase his music and to recreate the styles of turn-of-the-century contemporaries whose work was not recorded. Morton presented these recitals as "proof" that he was the "Originator of Jazz and Stomps," as he endorsed his letter about Handy. An enthusiast with a particular affection for music he believed was misunderstood, Lomax knew that many listeners in the 1930s, under the spell of swing, were unaware of the stunning innovations in timekeeping and melodic development evidenced in Morton's early style. The intention behind the interviews was to rectify this situation by making the case that Morton deserved consideration as a founding father of the jazz tradition. Nevertheless, the first thing that anyone recalls about these interviews is Morton's wild claim that he invented jazz, a claim that rings false before it is heard. The irony is even more pronounced when the suggestion is repeated in the book that Lomax based on the interviews, *Mister Jelly Roll* (1950), a book that was responsible for establishing the lasting impression of Morton as a cantankerous hustler, past his prime but still skillful when playing in the old style, demanding as ever more than his due.[25]

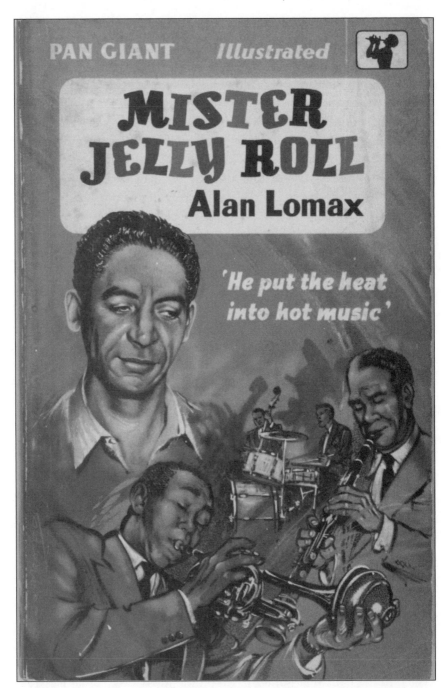

David Stone Martin, cover design from Alan Lomax, *Mister Jelly Roll: The Fortunes of Jelly Roll Morton, New Orleans Creole and "Inventor of Jazz"* (London, 1959; first published 1950). Reprinted with permission from Macmillan Publishers Ltd.

In *Mister Jelly Roll*, Lomax represents Morton's declaration that he invented jazz with a not-so-gentle irony. Morton's paternity claim is not debunked exactly, but it is left hanging as colorful boasting, turning pathetic at times. Certainly it is not presented as a claim to be taken seriously. Nevertheless, it must have exerted a powerful influence upon Handy, who published the definitive version of his fable about the ragged songster in his autobiography in 1941, three years after Morton's challenge was featured on the cover of *Down Beat*. Understanding how the fable about the ragged songster is shaped by Morton's challenge is a complicated enterprise. It is frequently said that Handy made the decision to dramatize his relationship with the songster to bolster his own importance to the blues. But it is worth taking a closer look—for instance, at how Handy's fable shifts the terms of the discussion from invention to discovery, or at how Handy transforms his implied antagonist into another native informant, given that Morton was working as one of the "honky-tonk piano players" enumerated in Handy's catalogue alongside the ragged singer. We should also ask about Handy's relative success and Morton's failure in staking this claim. Critics tend to take Handy seriously, citing his anecdote in their histories, while winking at the tall tales that Morton offers in response.[26]

Morton's response to Handy, I will propose, is made available to structural analysis particularly at the pressure points in the Library of Congress interviews where Morton fails to supply what Lomax demands. One such moment arrives when Lomax asks Morton to perform the Robert Charles Song, and Morton does not comply. To be sure, it is hard to know what to make of this noncompliance. The Robert Charles Song was a special point of interest to Lomax, as the song had never been recorded and its words never written down. It was known to have been sung, almost certainly with piano accompaniment, at after-hours parties in New Orleans in the first decade of the twentieth century, but to this day, that is all we are able to say. We are able to compare Morton's reflections on the song to rough accounts in as-told-to autobiographies by other musicians, including Sidney Bechet and Louis Nelson Delisle. Like Morton, these musicians are willing to admit that they once knew the song, but each maintains that they long ago forgot the music and words. This hearsay is all that is left from the song.[27]

We already know as much as we are ever likely to know about the individual whose life inspired the eponymous song, thanks to the remarkable research of William Ivy Hair. Robert Charles was born free, probably in 1865 or 1866, to parents who were working as sharecroppers. Charles grew up in Copiah County, Mississippi, a hotbed of anti-black violence where masked vigilantes killed black community leaders and made nightly visits to dissuade black families from political participation. Lynching was the common punishment in Copiah for infractions real or imagined and large or small. "Bloody Copiah" more than one person called it. Like many others, Robert Charles fled from this violence, first for Vicksburg and then, around 1894, for New Orleans, looking for better work and the relative safety that came with urban living. Whether by choice or necessity, Charles found himself piecing together short stints at a variety of jobs around New Orleans. The summer when he was murdered, he was stacking lumber for the Pelican Sawmill Company. Before then he worked as a roustabout unloading cargo on the docks at Port Chalmette, as a construction worker for the contractor Wolf and Seeman, as a cutter for sugar planters, as a street cleaner for the city, and as a manual laborer for the St. Charles Hotel, where he laid cables then stayed on for a few months shoveling coal in the boiler room.[28]

By all accounts, Charles was literate and absorbed in the politics of the day. He was active in emigrationist circles, serving both as collector for the International Migration Society and as a door-to-door subscription agent for Bishop Henry M. Turner's *Voice of Missions*. His commitment to the Back-to-Africa movement intensified in 1899 after he learned that Sam Hose (a migrant farmhand who lived outside Atlanta) was lynched, burned, and dismembered after an altercation with his employer. According to his coworkers on the levee, Charles began to advocate self-defense, urging them to "buy a rifle" and "keep it ready." In July 1900, he was given the chance to put his ideas into action when he was accosted by a police patrol while sitting on some steps with a bunkmate a few blocks from their boarding house, waiting for two friends to get off work. After answering a series of questions about where he was employed and how long he had been in the city, Charles rose to his feet. He was grabbed by one officer and then clubbed by another. He broke free, exchanged gunfire, and fled the scene wounded. When the police tracked him to his bunk house, Charles shot and killed one of the officers, and escaped again. Fanned by inflammatory reports in the morning papers, rioting commenced the next day. "Mobs rushed up and down the streets assaulting Negroes wherever they could be found," Benjamin Brawley writes in an early account of the violence, describing the shots fired at random into black houses and the black pedestrians who were killed indiscriminately by the white mob that roamed the city under the pretext of searching for Robert Charles. Four days into the riot, Charles's hideout was found, and a crowd gathered outside, peppering the wood-frame building with bullets. A stand-off followed. Charles, aiming his Winchester rifle through an open window, managed to pick off dozens of his assailants, killing at least seven, before someone finally set fire to the building. Forced to flee, Charles was killed by the mob, and his body dragged through the city.[29]

What makes the Robert Charles Song unusual as a case study is how little we know about the song itself and how much we know about the history evoked in its performance. There is almost nothing about the song's words or music that can be positively described. The song cannot be empirically examined, because it does not exist in the available archive. At the same time, there is a lot that we know about the police encounter that the song purportedly cites as a framework for its own perspective. This kind of imbalance is the reverse of what is usually found in the vernacular archive, and my intention in this chapter is to take advantage of these unusual circumstances to explore what the Robert Charles Song can tell us, if anything, about the general character of the black vernacular tradition.

The best contemporary source on the song's background remains the pamphlet printed by Ida B. Wells-Barnett soon after Charles was murdered in 1900. Wells-Barnett solicited testimony for the pamphlet, but she mainly relied upon her usual mode of immanent critique, reassembling passages from newspapers into a patchwork designed to intensify their internal contradictions. "The press of the country has united in declaring that Robert Charles was a desperado," she acknowledges. Without "evidence to justify the assertion," even the "most conservative of journals" is ready to broadcast the proposition that "the dead man was a criminal" whose "life had been given over to law-breaking." We might think based on the tone of these propositions that the pamphlet takes a positivist approach, undercutting the news accounts by exposing their insufficient basis in the facts, but that interpretation would misrepresent the pamphlet's wider aims. By figuring the structural disconnection between everything that is known about Robert Charles and the criminal identity foisted upon him, the pamphlet registers the irrelevance of his personal history to his legal status as nonperson. It suggests, in other words, that his condition hinges not on his guilt or innocence but on a previous determination that says his acts and intentions have no bearing on his existence. The power of this critical analysis lies in its capacity to connect the original scene of routine harassment to the violence that ensues. Ultimately it shows that the law's overenforcement (during the initial encounter) and the law's underenforcement (during the riot) develop from the same source: the suspension of recognition that is accomplished at the start through the identification of Robert Charles as "desperado."[30]

In her pamphlet, Wells-Barnett goes to great lengths to show that statelessness, and not some other procedural consideration, is what is at stake in Charles's first encounter with the police. Charles is not subject to what subsequent commentators would call racial profiling, if racial profiling is supposed to indicate the disproportionate enforcement of the law. Neither is he subject to what criminologists would call deviance amplification, if that refers to the exaggerated representation and selective punishment of minor offenses disproportionate to their social costs. Neither is he subject to police brutality, if that is supposed to refer to police who are somehow overstepping their authority, breaking instead of enforcing the law. The claim is not that the law is being enforced inappropriately. Rather, the claim is that there is a separate authority functioning in this encounter, a power whose enforcement does not concede the protections that would otherwise obtain in law, a power technically known as "police."[31]

It is important to see how this first encounter is structured by the police power. The officers have the authority to approach in this situation not because Charles and his bunkmate have done anything wrong, but because they could potentially pose a threat. Charles is never put under arrest. An arrest is distinguished not by the police power but by constitutional constraints (probable cause) and procedural safeguards (arraignment and booking) that exist to protect the individual's liberty by restricting state action. Unlike an arrest, a summary street inquiry is not subject to these constraints. Police are able to stop and informally confine individuals as they see fit. The standard in these instances is not the constitutional standard of probable cause but instead the statutory standard of suspicion, a standard that affirms, rather than constrains, the subjective license accorded to the police. It is for this reason that distinctions otherwise indispensable to criminal law, such as the distinction between omission and commission, are irrelevant to Charles, and why restraints upon procedure such as *actus reus* (barring punishment for status) and *mens rea* (barring punishment without consideration of intention) do not apply to him even as they are standard in criminal law.[32]

In this encounter with the police, Charles is like a vagrant. He is not a vagrant in name, as he is not named a vagrant by the police, but he is structurally indistinguishable from a vagrant in relation to the summary inquiry of the police officer. The police power that sanctions the summary inquiry is the same power that makes the arrest for vagrancy different from other kinds of criminal arrests. In police cases, there is never presumption of innocence. Like a vagrant who is compelled to give a good account of himself to the presiding magistrate, Charles is compelled to explain himself to Officer Mora even as Mora is not bound to take Charles's explanation into account when deciding whether further detention is warranted. In this analysis, Wells-Barnett is close to Tiedeman, who makes the same point about the nonregistration of the vagrant's rags in the magistrate's courtroom, and yet she goes further than Tiedeman in generalizing its implications.[33]

"They had not broken the peace in any way whatsoever," Wells-Barnett says. "No warrant was in the policemen's hands justifying their arrest, and no crime had been committed of which they were the suspects." The "only evidence" that Charles could possibly be a criminal "lay in the fact that he had refused to be beaten over the head by Officer Mora for sitting on a step quietly conversing with a friend. Charles resisted an absolutely unlawful attack, and a gun fight followed." This is a key transition in the logic of the pamphlet. Wells-Barnett suggests Charles has a natural right to resist, given that the legal authority governing the encounter was dissolved by the unlawful blow from the police, which initiated a state of war (a "gun fight") between the officer and the person wronged. At the same time, Wells-Barnett perceives that self-preservation is complicated in this instance by the fact that the person wronged, and therefore the self preserved, is unrecognizable within the given structure of the situation. Natural right can take nothing for granted here, as Charles's humanity is irrelevant to the original encounter and illegible in the newspaper reporting that provides the primary evidence for the pamphlet. Because Charles's humanity cannot be assumed, it needs to be written into the encounter. Indeed, the foreclosure of his humanity is the reason that an argument for the possibility of self-defense is required in this case.[34]

The law's ignorance of Charles's perspective, analyzed first in the structure of the police encounter, is shown to carry over into the presentation of the encounter in the news. Wells-Barnett notes that Charles's standpoint does not register in the stories circulated about him, which are organized

"Scene of the Double Murder," from the *New Orleans Times-Democrat*, reprinted in Ida B. Wells-Barnett, *Mob Rule in New Orleans: Robert Charles and His Fight to the Death, the Story of His Life, Burning Humans Alive, Other Lynching Statistics* (Chicago, 1900), 1.

around the foreclosure of his point of view. This foreclosure is figured in the epithets that appear throughout the news coverage of the riot: "monster," "desperado," "desperate darky," "fiend," "beast," "outlaw." For Wells-Barnett, being a monster means having no perspective that others can imagine in relation to themselves, and this is why she insists that Charles must be seen first as a legal abstraction, a person made from newspaper, before it is possible to imagine his humanity. Rather than taking his humanity for granted, she forces the point into a framework committed to its denial, affirming its implications at every opportunity, knowing that they cannot be brooked by the prevailing reason of state. Across the pamphlet, Wells-Barnett advances this claim in the negative. She may not know for certain what happened in the initial police encounter, but she bases her claim on the certainty that Charles's actions cannot be seen as self-defense in a situation structured by the police power, as the police power does not consider intent, and intent must be registered for self-defense to become imaginable. She may not know who he is, but she does know that he is not who they say he is. Charles appears in this way as an echo unrelated to its source, adrift in the epithets that the pamphlet reprints, as a somebody who is imaginable only because he is a nobody.[35]

Wells-Barnett speaks for Charles by speaking through Charles, and the force of her commitment can restore depth and dimension to the rumors and second-order reflections that are otherwise all that remain from his song. There is a special affinity between the accounts offered by Wells-Barnett and Morton. Though Morton never performs the Robert Charles Song for Lomax, there still is much to learn from the reasons that Morton gives for not singing. We can learn, in particular, about the song's resistance to the ethnographic conventions that determine, at each instant, what can and cannot pass between Lomax the collector and Morton his informant. Morton's insistence on the song's obsolescence, his idiosyncratic retelling of the Charles story, the validation he demands for not singing a song he may or may not have known—all of these aspects of the interview deserve close scrutiny.

"What about, uh, Robert, uh," Lomax stammers at one point in the interview, breaking off before the name escapes his mouth. "Robert Charles?" Morton responds. "Well they never, there was a little song about Robert Charles, but I don't remember it. Robert Charles, would you like to hear about that?" "Yeah," Lomax repeats, "I want to hear it." Morton provides a summary of the police assault and the riot, and suggests that these facts comprised the primary contents of the song, but he maintains that he cannot sing the song anymore because he does not recollect the words. Lomax persists: "You can't remember any of it? Not one word or not one line or anything?" In response, Morton is unwilling or unable to fulfill Lomax's requests, except by recounting the conditions that made the song disappear:

> They had a song out on Robert Charles, like many other songs
> and like many other, uh, badmen that always had some kind of
> a song and somebody originated it on 'em. But this song was
> squashed very easily by the [police] department. And not only
> by the department, by any of the surrounding people that ever

heard the song. Due to the fact that it was a trouble breeder and it never did get very far. I used to know the song, but I found it was best for me to forget it. And that I did, in order to go along with the world on the peaceful side.

It is hard to know what to make of this moment. We cannot say why Morton does not sing as requested. Whether he has forgotten the song, or refuses the request for his own reasons, is not readily apparent from the transcript. At this instant, Morton could be incredulous, or uncharacteristically bashful, or even expressing solidarity with Robert Charles. On the other hand, it could be a mistake to look inside Morton for reasons to explain the song's truancy. Maybe he does not know the song. Maybe the song is not just unknown but unknowable, having disappeared by 1938 not only from Morton's memory but from the tradition, a possibility that is given some credence by the similarity between this transcript and the excuses given by other musicians whenever the request is made to perform the song. There is another possibility, which is that the song is neither withheld nor forgotten but intractable. It is possible, in other words, that forgetting stands in this interview as the subjective figure for the procedural limit to ethnographic testimony. Morton may have no recourse other than asserting the song's obsolescence, but he explains its absence in terms that are not only individual but structural, marking what might be conceived as an objective resistance to exchange.[36]

This ambiguity is reinforced when Morton attributes the song's absence not only to a conscious decision to forget the words but also to the police who squash the song before it gets very far. Courting redundancy, Morton suggests the song is not simply unknown (whether forgotten or withdrawn) but unknowable due to the completed action of an external authority. Morton's attempt to forget what he may still know is thereby linked to a prefigurative occasion where the police command those who sing for the black population to forget what they know. Forgetting the words to the song is thereby turned into an imperative for self-preservation, an imperative that Morton must internalize to keep the police from hitting him. It is at this moment, when the police department is internalized as the superego, that the two reasons for the song's absence become one. Already, then, it would seem an oversimplification to describe this one reason for the song's absence as a well-formed intention. Proposing that the song is intentionally withheld, moreover, only doubles what Lomax has already said—both in this interview and in the ethnographic collections he would produce with his collaborators, where the informant's reluctance normally functions, not as an obstacle to collection, but instead as the prelude to authentic expression. The ostensibly naïve or spurious excuses tendered by informants, who proposed they had found religion, or worried that the Lomaxes were spies for the police, or professed never to have known such songs in the first place, postpone narrative progress only long enough to heighten satisfaction when the performance begins. To get to the real folklore, the Lomaxes emphasized, the collector had to "penetrate" the "zone of silence" insulating black folk culture. If the pleasure from this penetration is intensified when the gratification is delayed, the desire dissipates when gratification never arrives at all, which is what occurs with the Robert Charles Song. The tension builds, but there is no release. Morton follows the right script with gestures that could be heard as delaying the song, but when it comes down to it, he is unable to provide the satisfaction that Lomax demands.[37]

From this point in the interview, it is possible to begin to consider how Morton's not singing about Robert Charles prevents Lomax from redressing the jazz establishment's unjust neglect of its founding father. Throughout *Mister Jelly Roll,* Lomax treats the paternity claim ironically not because he fails to sympathize with Morton but instead because Morton fails to make this claim felt during their encounter. Morton says, "Call me father!" But Lomax cannot do it. The moment that Morton and Lomax are both anticipating—the moment when Lomax cries "Daddy!"— never comes, and the tape runs out. This is why the claim sounds so contrived, as if it were not convinced of its own merits. They are faking it. It is the symbolic failure to sing about Robert Charles that robs the climax to the exchange, frustrating the claim behind the interview before it can be substantiated in performance.

We can see why the claim to fatherhood has to be suspended in the interview when we look closer at the reasons Morton gives for not singing. Morton responds to Lomax's demands for the song by restating what happened in the riot. The violence was foregone, Morton maintains, from the moment that Charles shot the first officer, which guaranteed that another and another "officer'd come to take his place." Morton's second summary concludes with a non sequitur: "So, the song was quelled, as I 'fore stated," he starts. "And, of course, I'm a little bit ahead of my time—before the song came out." Doubling the song's foreclosure as something that already has been "stated" in his own discourse, Morton cannot help but notice that foreclosure in this case is sequentially out of joint. Morton names this prolepsis by routing the expected phrase "ahead of its time" into the first person. "I'm a little bit ahead of my time," he falters, referring not to his innovations in jazz composition but to his odd substitution of a second summary for the song that Lomax demands—a song that could not have been sung, much less forgotten, before the riot began. This swerve into the first person marks a pressure point in the encounter, where the perspective inside the Robert Charles Song becomes fused to the perspective of the native informant. This process is under way even before the interview starts. "I guess I am 100 years ahead of my time," Morton estimates in his letter to *Down Beat,* a claim that returns accompanied, not by the "conclusive proof" that Morton promises, but as the song that Lomax fails to register as evidence despite his best efforts. This failure arrests the ethnographic exchange after it is already under way, catching the encounter at the moment when the native informant's perspective is still being articulated to the dispossessed perspective that is claimed inside the music, before those two perspectives have become indistinguishable.[38]

Although the two perspectives remain separated in this case, we can see them starting to join together in the interview. We can see, for instance, how the solidarity that comes from knowing the Robert Charles Song is aligned with the desire for libidinal release against the internalized authority of the police. That alignment would seem to synchronize the performer's desire to sing about Robert Charles with the folklorist's desire to make the native informant speak. It would appear, in other words, to make the music's perspective accessible to the folklorist as a positive property of the black voice. This dashing of expectation arrives as a moment of clarity in the interview. When Morton says that the reason he cannot sing the song is that the police forced him to forget, he leaves himself in a position where, rather than singing, he is forced to reenact the police encounter that made Robert Charles into an outlaw. We witness Morton putting himself in a place where it might be possible to embody what he sings, where the perspective in the song might begin to look like his own perspective, but when the song is a no-show, this promise is unfulfilled. The frustration of ethnographic expectation triggers the return to another scene where the collector and the informant are gone and in their places, standing face to face, are the police and the outlaw. We arrive just in time to witness the direct address from the police ("Don't sing!") that seems intended, at once, for both Morton and Charles. The coincidence is crucial here. We discover that the song can be perceived as a response to the police at the same moment we learn that the response cannot be transacted ethnographically. The resistance registered intermittently across the ethnographic transcript is rendered, in this interview, as a flickering back and forth between two scenes: one where a native informant fails to sing at his collector's request and another where the outlaw speaks back unaccountably to the initiating address from the police. The song is not exactly squashed by the police, as Morton would have it. On the contrary, we can follow the song as it is detached from the scene of the police encounter and gradually assimilated to the only standpoint that is open to assignment: the standpoint from which the song is supposed to originate, the standpoint of the informant, whose incipient genius is nothing more than the trace of the impossible perspective expressed in the song. Though Morton's failure to sing about Charles stalls this transaction, everything else in the interview still follows from this point where the law's exception is claimed as culture's origin.[39]

In the attempt to dethrone Handy as the father of the modern black tradition, Morton unwittingly calls into doubt whether the black tradition has anything like a paternity or a culturally continuous bloodline. His inability to wrest the title from Handy leaves not only his own particular claim, but the very pretense to fatherhood and succession, open to examination. If Handy is able to stake his claim as blues father by telling a story about a songster who embodied the music he sang, it would appear that Lomax's request is a golden opportunity for Morton to advance his competing claim by performing Charles's perspective as if it were his own. In the encounter with Lomax, Morton accepts a special burden when he says he is the "originator" of jazz. To be the music's origin, he needs to show that he embodies the tradition that he claims to have invented. Singing the song would, at the very least, lubricate the exchange with Lomax, making it easier for Lomax to mistake the standpoint inside the song, which is presumably forced in the music in much the same way that it is forced into existence by Wells-Barnett, for the unfathomable originality of its singer. As an ethnographic reproduction, the Robert Charles Song's excess to its occasion would become audible as the difference between a genius and his followers or a founder and his tradition. However, Morton does not sing the song, and this absence indexes, more powerfully than anything Morton sings or says, his inability to stake his claim as father of jazz.[40]

When Morton and Handy's competing claims are read together, we can understand better not only what goes wrong for Morton but also what goes right for Handy. We can describe better what feels laughable at certain moments in Morton's interviews, and we can gauge better the reasons for Handy's success in pitching a tale that has been told over and over by music critics and cultural historians. Handy succeeds because his legend accomplishes what Morton fails to achieve in his interview. He succeeds in making an outlaw into a native informant, a process that establishes the compound character of the ragged songster as the beginning for the modern tradition in blues and jazz. Handy's legend is often repeated, moreover, because this work is never done. It is labor that needs to happen continuously if the blues tradition is to remain comprehensible as self-expression. This ongoing work is evident in mid-century books including Samuel Charters's *Country Blues* (1959) and Frederick Ramsey Jr.'s *Been Here and Gone* (1960) and in the cover designs and liner notes for long-playing records of reissued songs like Robert Johnson's *King of the Delta Blues Singers* (1961). The blues iconography from the original marketing of artists like Blind Lemon Jefferson returns in these contexts, and generally, in the revivalism of the 1950s and 1960s, which continued to showcase the itinerant singer—a "beggar, outcast, near criminal" in Ramsey's words— as the one true ambassador for the black tradition. The folklore process started earlier in the century by Handy, Odum, and their cohort came to fruition in the efforts of these later collectors, whose first principle was that the "personal and immediate experience" expressed in blues had nothing to do with the political domain proper to the state.[41]

Without realizing it, Lomax and Morton appear to have undone the ethnographic transaction that these blues revivalists copied from Handy's tale—a transaction that made the music's standpoint definitively into its source. We can observe this strange alchemy beginning to happen when Morton says he is ahead of his time, and we can also observe it happening again and again in the opening decades of the twentieth century as collectors ascribed a sublime expressive capacity to informants they corralled in labor camps, train stations, passageways, saloons, and state penitentiaries. What these collectors were doing was transacting (albeit awkwardly) the impossible selves that were being invented in the discourse of their informants. What these collectors were hearing was not cultural expression but legal incapacity, or more precisely, the mnemonics that enabled informants to sing themselves from incapacity into hypothetical existence. Black singers were able to invent a perspective from which people without perspective could begin to speak only because their music allowed them to proceed as if such things were possible even when they were not. The music's capacity to convey hypothetical experience — experience that could be imagined but not known and felt but not named — was celebrated by collectors who took its artifice for authentic self-expression. The authenticity that these collectors thought they had found was nothing more than the residue from personification, the trace left by the outlawed speaker whose humanity is continually staked on its invisibility in political society. Writing the history of black authenticity, it follows, means thinking backward through the equation that would make this political invisibility into cultural property. Documented as unconditioned and unconditional, black music had to be split from its original predication against the law before its meaning was made available not only to the renewed project of natural rights, where musical intelligence was evoked to prove the inhumanity of the convict labor routine, but also to the regular daydreams of romantic racialists who held that blacks were not only human but more human, deeper in their souls, than other races. This equation does not put the outlaw in the singer's place; it conjoins outlaw and singer without dissolving one into the other, yielding a common sense that has since oriented collectors to their informants, and record companies to their biggest stars, who are represented as looking, acting, and most importantly sounding like Robert Charles, someone who, to the best of our knowledge, may never have sung a note.

2

THE STRANGE CAREER OF BRAS-COUPÉ

In the history that has been written about the United States, there is a long-standing tendency to differentiate the South from the rest of the nation. Often, the South has been singled out as the exception to the normative pattern of institutional development exemplified in big cities on the northeastern seaboard. A case in point is police history, which from its beginning has tended to construe the difference between North and South in the strictest terms. Take the following passage from "The Mind that Burns in Each Body" (1983), the classic essay by Jacquelyn Dowd Hall. As background for its analysis of lynching and sexual violence, the essay names two systems of criminal justice:

> In the nineteenth century, the industrializing North moved toward a modern criminal justice system in which police, courts, and prisons administered an impersonal, bureaucratic rule of law designed to uphold property rights and discipline unruly workers. The South, in contrast, maintained order through a system of deference and customary authority in which all whites had informal police power over all blacks, slave owners meted out plantation justice undisturbed by any generalized rule of law, and the state encouraged vigilantism as part of its overall reluctance to maintain a strong system of formal authority that would have undermined the planter's prerogatives. . . . And each tradition continued into the period after the Civil War.

This strict opposition has become untenable as critics have started to question not only its accuracy but the role that it has played in constituting national history. It is now openly doubted whether the slow development to impersonal bureaucracy ever could have been measured so confidently without the baseline offered by southern barbarism. The resulting stress is greatest when it comes to lynching—a tradition that could not be more southern, or less American, according to the implied framework that Dowd Hall takes over from a previous generation of police historians.[1]

The traditional story about law enforcement in the United States was established between the 1960s and the 1980s. It says that modern police bureaucracy in the United States was modeled on the London Metropolitan Police, which was organized by Robert Peel in 1829. Cities such as Boston, Philadelphia, and New York followed London's lead in creating the first modern police forces in the United States. In the 1830s and 1840s, these cities implemented consecutive reforms that led to recognizably modern departments with salaried, centrally administered, well-armed, uniformed, around-the-clock patrols. These departments replaced the loose combination of independent officials that had previously managed criminal justice—a combination featuring constables who worked in the daytime as process servers for the courts, the watch that patrolled at night, and sheriffs who looked after prisons, elections, and taxation. Under the old system, officials did not wear uniforms or carry guns. The only option in an emergency was to call up the militia. All of this changed rapidly at midcentury, when cities moved to modernize their police systems.[2]

This traditional story mostly ignores what was happening in southern cities. Thanks to the renewed interest, now decades long, in the police institutions of slavery, we can see not only what has been absent from the traditional story about police reform but also what about the story has to change before it can account for a city like Charleston, South Carolina. Focusing on such apparently anomalous cases, historians have started asking why our standard narratives of modern law enforcement begin in Boston and New York when southern cities used fully equipped police patrols long before they appeared in the northeast, in some cases as early as the 1780s. These police forces (termed "city guards") were paramilitary in organization, with officers enrolling for fixed tours and living together in barracks, but in every other respect, they were modern. Officers wore uniforms. They were paid salaries not fees. They were heavily armed with swords and guns, and permitted to use deadly force in the course of their duties. Southern police outfits began earlier and evolved faster than their northern counterparts. Police arrived in southern cities whose populations had reached about 10,000 residents; they arrived in northern cities ten to twenty times that size. Police organizations in southern cities were much grander in scale, with a police-to-population ratio two to three times greater than in northern cities. Once the guards in places like Richmond and New Orleans are taken seriously as police, it is impossible to preserve the distinction between rule-bound bureaucracy (in the North) and informal racial prerogative (in the South). Indeed, we have to wonder whether the first modern police in the United States were created not for the general maintenance of the public peace, on the London model, but for a more specific purpose: the restraint of urban slave populations.[3]

This is more than a question about timing. It is a question about institutions such as the slave patrols, which become thinkable not merely as vigilante groups, anticipating the Ku Klux Klan, but as auxiliaries whose police powers are continuous with those of the state. On this basis, it has even been suggested that the formal relationships between town councils and slave patrols, in many municipalities, established the blueprint for modern policing for the region. This is also a question about the slaveowners who claimed that their relationship to their chattel was unmediated by the state. Although often repeated by historians, this claim is untenable, especially in urban areas such as Savannah or Mobile where the main point of the police was regulating slavery. There were many laws on the books saying where slaves could be, when they could be there, what they could do with whom while they were there—and the agency responsible for enforcing these laws was the police. There were also laws against cruelty to slaves, which were rarely enforced except in exceptional high-profile cases. Nonetheless, it was possible to imagine the police as a paternalistic institution that could intervene when necessary to protect slaves from their masters. In practice, officers spent much of their time managing the pass systems in their cities, enforcing curfews and stopping slaves they found on the street to see whether they were on an errand or otherwise authorized to be away from their masters. Capturing fugitives was a primary duty, accounting for more than half of slave arrests in many locations. This was complicated business, due to the proportion of slaves that worked and lived away from their masters. It was complicated, as well, by the fact that many masters became annoyed when their slaves were detained by the police. Slaveowners tended to be powerful people with influence in the political parties to which police owed their patronage jobs. Policing slavery meant striking a delicate balance between these individual interests and the public interest in subduing unruly slaves. The police were not a mere extension of the master's will. Still, their existence had everything to do with slavery.[4]

Police departments in the United States are managed locally, rather than nationally as in England or France, which is why historians have tended to confine their research to one city at a time. Among the greatest of these local studies is Dennis C. Rousey's *Policing the Southern City* (1996), which tracks the early fortunes of the New Orleans Police. A port city with a majority-black population, including many free persons of color, and unusual proximity to an enormous tract of unenclosed swampland, New Orleans looks like an anomalous case. It is Rousey's considerable achievement to show precisely what can be extrapolated from the city's history: evidence for how the southern states were not only mainstream in their police thinking, but in many respects, far ahead of the national curve. This chapter turns to a remarkable case from the annals of the New Orleans Police that has yet to be addressed by its historians. It focuses upon a single character from the city's police history: the legendary fugitive slave, Bras-Coupé. The reputed commander of the maroons who subsisted in the cypress swamps outside the city, Bras-Coupé was brought to public attention during the 1830s as the target for a protracted manhunt sponsored by the city government. A kind of cipher for the police power, Bras-Coupé was used by the city to explain its jurisdiction over its citizens as well as its slaves. This is only the beginning, however, as Bras-Coupé flew instantly from the newspapers into oral tradition, and from oral tradition into memoirs, folklore archives, novels, an opera, a feature film, and ultimately into the history of jazz. By following this strange career all the way from the 1830s to the 1970s, this chapter presses hard on the inferences made in recent historical research—expanding them to the limit where we can note not only the connection between slavery and police but also the strong cross currents that connect the history of the police power to the formal development of the black vernacular tradition.[5]

New Orleans organized a slave patrol for the first time in 1764. This was critical to individual slaveowners, who had previously been forced to rely on their own resources to recapture their fugitives, but it was also stimulated by the need to provide for the common defense. The creation of a formal patrol was only one part of a larger history in which the city was cast against the swamps. A decisive event in this history is the maroon revolt in 1729, the first major offensive launched against the city by the communities on its outskirts, which were gradually established as the fugitive slaves who escaped to the swamps intermarried with the Natchez and Choctaw. In 1733, the French colonial government announced a campaign to break

this alliance, kicking off the evolution that eventually led to the institutionalization of a slave patrol thirty years later. This cycle of warfare was
also behind the growth in the militia, which increased its numbers and its
stockpile of weapons as the battles intensified during the late eighteenth
century, with the biggest changes coming in response to planned upris-
ings like the Point Coupée conspiracy in 1795.[6]

These battles were seen by the government as a war between civilization and the wilderness, but from the perspective of the people living in
the swamp, the dividing line was never so clear. Literally it was hard to tell
where the city ended and the wilderness began, as the estates demarcated
on the riverfront stretched backwards indefinitely into unenclosed wetlands. "Slaves and maroons from various plantations met regularly in the
ciprière," Gwendolyn Midlo Hall writes, "Huts were built, with secret
paths leading to them. A network of cabins of runaway slaves arose behind
plantations all along the rivers and bayous." Much of the social life of the
city's slaves became concentrated in the swamps where they could talk,
dance, drink, trade, hunt, fish, and garden without supervision. The set-
tlements were hidden away, but they were also integrated with the life of
the city. Unlike in some places in the United States, these maroon com-
munes had many women and children. There were families, intertwined
with the bloodlines of the city, that reproduced over generations. The maroons cultivated corn and squash and sweet potatoes, but mostly they
were growing rice. The technology for turning wetlands into rice paddies
was African. Brought over the Atlantic by slaves, it became no less indispensable to the city than it did to the swamp. There was also active trade
that brought manufactured goods from the city into the swamp as well as
foodstuffs (roots, vegetables, sassafras, fish, game) and crafts (reed baskets,
tools, wooden bowls) from the swamp into the city. Especially in the very
early years when the indigo crops were failing to turn a profit, the swamp
was a resource for the subsistence of the city's population.[7]

The tension with the maroons became so intense in the 1790s, following the revolution in Saint-Domingue, that the government moved to
prevent the immigration of free blacks as well as the importation of slaves
to the city. It was this lasting tension, among other factors, that led to the
militarization of the police in 1805. The department's early years were
scored by a series of experimental efforts at reorganization, which came as
quickly as they went, as patronage positions were refilled with every transition in government and the bureaucracy was redrawn accordingly. But

there was no mistaking the conspicuous difference between the new police (uniformed, salaried, and armed) and the loose network of patrols
that were in operation before the Louisiana Purchase, just as there was no
mistaking its difference from the decentralized and lightly armed foot patrols in northern cities. This was a distinctive police, one whose features
were carefully annotated by northern travelers such as Joseph Holt Ingraham, who wrote back to his northern public about the "well-filled
armory" and "plain blue uniforms" that distinguished this exotic arrangement. The new city guard was quite similar to the institutions in other
southern cities like Richmond and Charleston, but it remained controversial in New Orleans. The earliest campaigns to restrict the police were
launched soon after the guard was reorganized, but the public demands
to demilitarize the police did not reach their fever pitch until the first police homicide in 1830, which intensified the campaign to take away the
police's heavy weaponry. This campaign triggered policy changes, such as
a regulation that said three warnings must be given before violence could
become an option. In 1836, the reformers got their wish and the city council passed an ordinance that removed all weapons from the police except
their spontoons, a slightly larger version of what were later called night-
sticks. Other reforms were adopted as well that established a civil administration for the police, and in consequence, the guard suddenly started
to look more like the lightly armed patrols in New York, Boston, and
Philadelphia. Although its results were dispersed by an ill-conceived plan
to partition the city into three municipalities, the reform campaign achieved
its central purpose. The police would not win back their legal right to
firearms for decades to come.[8]

The reform campaign is traceable through the records of the mayor's
office, city council transcripts, and the editorial pages from newspapers
like the *Louisiana Advertiser* and *New Orleans Daily Picayune*, which
were eagerly asserting the need for significant "alterations" to the "present
system" of the police. In the realm of local politics, the controversy was
spurred by several factors—by the struggle between the mayor and the
city council for control over patronage appointments, by the friction between incompatible modes of law inherited from England and France,
and by new patterns of immigration that altered the city's demographics.
As the ratio of slaves to citizens decreased with the ongoing influx of
European immigration, many longer-term residents began to worry less
about the possibility of a slave revolt and more about daily conflicts with

the new immigrant class, many of whom were Irish or German, and many of whom took jobs as police officers. A proposal to disband the police was vetoed by Mayor Denis Prieur in 1830, but the reformers continued to press for demilitarization until they had their way six years later. Many issues were raised by the reformers, but above all else they wanted to take the guns from the hands of the police.[9]

The forces shaping the reform campaign were particular to their time and place, but they fed into a rhetoric that was cast in the broadest possible terms. The reformers went so far as to imply their own theory of world history. New Orleans, as they saw it, was suspended between two stages of civilization. It was still to be determined whether the city would progress into the future (where the law rules without violence) or backslide into the past (where there is no law, only violence between individuals). Among the broadsides published on this question, the most frequently reprinted was the following editorial. This version was printed in February 1834 in the *Louisiana Advertiser:*

> Founded on the customs, and continued by the prejudices of ancient despotic governments . . . our police establishment still remains a blot on the face of a free country, an ancient barbarism in a great commercial and REPUBLICAN city, an inefficient and utterly useless incumbrance, a system of petty sinecures as well as a glaring remnant of despotism in a land of LIBERTY. Are we not sufficiently enlightened? Have we not sufficient energy and decision of character in our present city government to cast off this offending remnant of barbarism—annihilate this remaining leaven of ancient despotic custom and inherited prejudice—to dispense with the sword and pistol, the musket and bayonet, in our civil administration of *republican* laws, and adopt or create a system more congenial to our feelings, to the opinions and *interests* of a free and prosperous people, more in accordance with the spirit of the age we live in.

According to this reasoning, armed police prove that the city government had yet to evolve from a patriarchal stage of history where violence remains the sovereign's uninhibited prerogative. The trace of this violence is described as a blot or remnant within republicanism that can be dissolved by rigorous adherence to principle. This was a favorite trope for the reformers, who tended to rationalize the unevenness of their present by describing the police as a "foul stain" that adheres to the letter of the law and obstructs its development. Implicit in this trope is the fact that history has a telos. Progress is measured by how little remains in the present from the barbarism of the past. History reaches its endpoint when the stain is removed, and the law achieves a stable state where violence is no longer necessary.[10]

This argument deviates from many classic theories of modern state formation, which claim that modernity begins when the government claims a monopoly on legitimate violence in its territory. In the line that stretches from Thomas Hobbes to Max Weber to Norbert Elias, the state's presumptive monopoly on violence is a turning point in world history. Political society begins when individuals transfer their claim on personal violence to a sovereign with a near-exclusive right to the initiation of force, except in those exigent circumstances where individuals are acting in defense of themselves or others. In turn, this new security facilitates an increasingly complex economic and cultural interdependence. On this account, it is the police that trigger progress from the archaic to the modern. Altering this history, the reformers decided that history had reached a stage where violence was no longer requisite for the organization of the polity. The law was ready to stand alone as the basis for civilization. Police violence was not a signal of progress but a holdover from an archaic past. Police represented the abrogation, rather than the foundation, of the rule of law.[11]

The rhetoric of the reformers was ambitious, even grandiose, but it was also communicated concretely as a practical problem that could be solved by procedural measures. The reform campaign concentrated much of its imagination on the scene of arrest, especially on the split second when an officer decided whether to use violence. Because this decision required discretion and hence could not be regulated by legal norms, the reformers interpreted its existence as a threat to law. What was there to prevent the police from firing their weapons on "slight occasions"? If you give guns to police officers and put them in situations where discretion is essential, you have to be prepared to accept that the officers will use their guns, at least some of the time, without legitimate cause. To the reformers, this was not acceptable. "Citizens of New Orleans," they demanded, why should the police walk the streets "beating and maiming" persons on the slightest pretense when the law states that "no man, no matter how vile or how worthless" should suffer "without trial"? "In what free country" are there such patrols "parading the streets" in "all the panoply of war" as if they were the "guard of an eastern despot"? Equipped with "sword belt and pistol," with "musket and bayonet," authorized to act all at once as "judge, jury and executioner," the firearms holstered by the police were the proof that the city was under "military rule." "Are we freemen? Have we laws?" the reformers concluded. "Citizens, shall we bear this any longer? Shall we not demand the disbanding of these men? . . . Shall the ordinances creating a military police still remain the opprobria of our city laws, or shall they be expunged forever?"[12]

Others were quick to defend the police. Remarking wryly that it had "become fashionable once more to rail and cry aloud against the police," the department's supporters were quick to dispute the claim that its officers were a "band of miscreants." When the right to arms was disputed by the reformers, the police used a crafty line of defense. The police did not propose, as they might have, that their violence could be regulated and therefore did not pose the risks that were alleged by the reformers. Instead, the department argued that an absolute right to violence was crucial to the defense of the city. Their aim was not to propose their own theory of law but to attack the assumption that law could exist without violence, an assumption that was duplicitous because it denied the need for violence from within a legal system where violence was the only recourse in the event of an emergency. The reformers could not account for these exceptional circumstances, and the police attempted to make this obvious to their constituency. Leaving the police without their guns was impractical. It was a concept that sounded good "in theory" when "hot headed writers" were "speaking of liberty," but it was a proposal that could not be "safely carried into operation" without imperiling the city. This was the argument that was most often made by Mayor Denis Prieur, a strong supporter of the police in its existing configuration. "Let us ameliorate it, improve it, but let us not change it," Prieur declared in 1836, months before the reform was adopted without him. As far as Prieur was concerned, police without guns were not police.[13]

In a city as violent as New Orleans, with a sizable population of transient riverworkers, it would have been easy to refer to many familiar situations where it would be good for the police to have guns, but the supporters of the department decided to evoke a more traditional rationale. When they argued that the police needed weapons to protect the city, the threat they summoned was from slavery. Often, it was from the fugitive slaves in the swamps. Whether they were reminding citizens about the potential for an organized slave revolt, or publicizing the occasional raids on outlying parts of the city, or decrying the damage that the maroons had done to the discipline of their slaves, the police were clear that they could never protect the city against the slave population without their weaponry. Even a single fugitive could prove too much for an unarmed guardsman. The following article, from March 1830, printed in the arch-conservative and bilingual creole newspaper, the *New Orleans Bee,* is a good illustration:

> Yesterday afternoon about 4 o'clock, an application was made to the city guard by the owner of a runaway negro, to have him arrested, having discovered where he was. The officer of the guard enquired whether it was necessary to send two men, and was answered that the negro was very submissive, and that one man would be enough to conduct him; notwithstanding, the officer ordered two of the guards to go with the owner, and they went on the Bayou road where they found the negro in a hut belonging to Mr. Milns. As he was almost naked, his master ordered him to put on his clothes and to follow him. The negro feigned to obey and pretended to look for his coat, when all at once he rushed on one of the guards, wrung his sword out of his hands, and at the same moment applied a severe blow with it on the head of the other guard, which cut his hat, and with another blow severely wounded him in the wrist. The master of that negro irritated at this daring impudence fired two pistols at him and wounded him in the arm; another person who was present fired a third pistol but missed him. The negro then seized an ax, and breaking down some planks, escaped through the garden. A hunter who happened to be there at the moment fired at the request of the master his two loads at the negro, which hit him in the back and the thigh and brought him down: it was only then that he could be mastered. How many such occurrences will it require . . . to corroborate the opinion which we expressed a few days ago, and to convince those who pretend that the city guard ought on no occasion to make use of their arms? We do not wish to influence the opinion of any one, but it seems to us that this last occurrence will be sufficient to

enlighten those who will be called upon to decide on the fate of
the city guard, who is to be brought in a few days before the
criminal court for having killed a sailor.

Any slave no matter how submissive may drop the charade at any moment, this report suggests, picturing the change from household servant
to sword-stealing and ax-wielding supervillain in just a few sentences. The
firepower that it takes to "master" this single slave—a sword, three pistols,
and a rifle—is enough to make the idea of unarmed police seem preposterous. You can never have enough weaponry to deal with this kind of
threat. Following this line, Prieur held that the police's proper model was
not the constable-watch systems on the northern seaboard, in which officers were armed exclusively with small clubs, but the Charleston police,
who were given more weapons and were trained with greater precision
than their counterparts in New Orleans. Charleston was the better model
given the "similarity existing between their social system and ours." The
similarity to which the mayor refers, of course, is slavery. In the final gesture from the *Bee*, we witness the crucial exposition of this claim. Having
predicated the necessity of police upon the existence of slavery, the *Bee*
sees a general rationale for the police power that counts in all cases, including the case of the sailor that led to the first effort at police reform in
1830, which was vetoed by Prieur. The unresolved question here—whether
the slave's precedent applies to the sailor—would shape the debate for the
next six years.[14]

This, then, is the context in which Bras-Coupé was turned into a legend. The public controversy over police violence is the background that
must be taken into account before we can appreciate how his legend came
into being and how it was put to use by the advocates for the city guard.
When the coalition allied with the city council tried to strip the police of
their weapons, the department responded by initiating what appears to
have been a well-publicized operation against Bras-Coupé, a maroon
leader who was meant to epitomize the indistinct threat emanating from
the swamps. Who will defend you from Bras-Coupé, it was suggested, if
not the police? And how will the police defend you if they are stripped of
their ability to act by any means necessary? Invoked to affirm the state's
right to deadly force, Bras-Coupé became a paradigm case in local police
history for reasons that have less to do with the details from his career
than with the exigencies of local politics. Singled out from the swamp

and made larger than life, Bras-Coupé was dramatized by the police as an exemplary threat, the type of problem to which the reformers had no solution.

The records from the police campaign against Bras-Coupé are ambiguous. There are records concerning a slave named "Squire," which was Bras-Coupé's legal name before he became an outlaw, who was arrested "comme marron" in 1834–1835. On more than one occasion, Squire was said to have escaped police custody. The dates of these arrest records correlate with a sheriff's notice to claim a captured maroon called Squire, found by Marcus Christian, but there remain problems of corroboration, especially concerning the master's identity. The arrest records designate Squire's master as Monsieur Gurly, but the legend refers to General William De Buys and occasionally to Joseph Le Carpentier, John Freret, or a "Mr. D." These municipal documents, if verified, would locate the official beginning of the fugitive's career (and the loss of his arm) within months of the publication of the reform campaign's most heated rhetoric. Still, additional evidence is required before the relevance of these municipal documents is confirmed.[15]

The other materials that have survived, however, particularly from the newspapers, are entirely consistent with the general defense of the police department in these years. If timing is an indication, it seems that Bras-Coupé was a centerpiece for the campaign to support the police's right to legitimate violence, as a manhunt was announced just as the reformers were gaining momentum in the early 1830s. The hair-raising tales of Bras-Coupé and his band of fugitives returned the city's imagination to the cypress swamps bordering Lake Pontchartrain, which became the scene for countless gunfights between maroons and the police. These battles were widely reported. Even abolitionist publications like *The Liberator* saw fit to mention the "band of runaway negroes" living in "the Cypress Swamp in the rear of the city." The coverage of Bras-Coupé's death in 1837 was quick to capitalize on the outlaw's notoriety. "It will be remembered by all our citizens," one obituary from the *Daily Picayune* says, that Bras-Coupé "prowled about the marshes" for years, organizing the maroon resistance against the police and leading raids on the outlying areas of the city. According to the newspaper, Bras-Coupé was "a terror to the community." Known to everyone in the area by his fearsome reputation, his "cruelty" and "crime" are said to have been recorded at great length in the "annals of the city." Having murdered "several white men" before he "fled to the swamp," Bras-Coupé eluded "the searching efforts of justice" for years until he was betrayed and killed by someone who was once an accomplice.[16]

Using his slave name (Squire) instead of the name he would assume in legend (Bras-Coupé), the *Picayune* summarizes the outlaw's legendary career as the formidable leader of the maroons with the following statement:

> This demi-devil has for a long time ruled as the "Brigand of the Swamp." A supposition has always found believers that there was an encampment of outlaw negroes near the city, and that Squire was their leader. He was a fiend in human shape and has done much mischief in the way of decoying slaves to his camp, and in committing depredations upon the premises of those who live on the outskirts of the city. His destruction is hailed, by old and young, as a benefit to society. . . . It is hoped that the death of this leader of the outlaw negroes supposed to be in the swamp will lead to the scouring of the swamp round about the city. This nest of desperadoes should be broken up. While they can support a gang and have a camp, we may expect our slaves to run away and harrowing depredations to be committed upon society.

Even in death, it is Bras-Coupé who guides police action. His demise brings not the cessation of the police campaign but its expansion to a diverse population on the periphery of the slave economy, all of whom are deemed enemies of the state by virtue of their supposed affiliation with the rebel leader. An incorrigible terror to the community, whose crimes scorched the city's annals, Bras-Coupé was alleged to warrant, at the very least, the reward of "two thousand dollars" offered for his head by Denis Prieur. This reputed bounty—an extraordinary sum for a single slave—played an important role in the events leading to the fugitive's capture and in the legend that surfaced after his career.[17]

In offering this bounty, Prieur was working with the symbolism of the police, hoping to explain their power through the ancient practice of outlawry. Prieur began the manhunt for Bras-Coupé by declaring him an outlaw. This was a familiar procedure for dealing with fugitive slaves in the seventeenth and eighteenth centuries. A proclamation was posted on public buildings naming the slave and declaring him outlawed if he did not surrender. Once outlawed, a slave could be slain without fault. If the outlaw were killed, the person responsible could never be tried for murder nor compelled to compensate the owner for destruction of property. As far as the law was concerned, the outlaw did not exist. Though outlawry was infrequently used in the nineteenth century, there were some spectacular exceptions such as those annotated in Harriet Beecher Stowe's *Dred* (1856), a novel where a character named Harry Gordon is outlawed after he escapes to the Great Dismal Swamp and joins the maroons there. Closer in space if not in time to Bras-Coupé is Robert Charles, who was outlawed by New Orleans Mayor Paul Capdevielle at the end of the century. In the case of Bras-Coupé, the symbolic impact of the proclamation is immediately discernible in what it does to the relationship between the city and the swamp. Gone is the city's long-standing interdependence with the swamp. What comes in its place, maybe more clearly than ever before, is a city under siege. Correspondingly, the swamp becomes an archetypal wilderness, a wasteland, by virtue of its association with the outlaw. Banished from organized society, the outlaw's traditional habitat is the unenclosed land beyond the boundary of civilization—a land that is pictured as empty, forbidding, perilous—a land that stands, in other words, for the natural state from which society emerged.[18]

By outlawing Bras-Coupé, Prieur was seeking to control the symbolic associations of the police. There is a genealogy implied by this proclamation, which tracks the discretionary authority of the police back to its origin. Prieur was employing a legal procedure that many have acknowledged as the root of criminal jurisprudence. As Frederick Pollock and William Maitland notice in their *History of English Law before the Time of Edward I* (1898), outlawry is the original punishment in the Anglo-Saxon tradition: lesser penalties such as fines or amercements all "have their root in outlawry" as they are "mitigations of that comprehensive penalty." Following the work of Heinrich Brunner, Pollock and Maitland note that the ongoing allowance for "arbitrariness" or "discretion" in criminal process derives from this original and absolute penalty, where the outlaw's fate is left to the discretion of the person he has wronged. It has proven possible to distinguish several stages to this genealogy through the centuries, as outlawry becomes the prototype for the royal prerogative, and the prerogative becomes the prototype for the police power as it was defined by Blackstone and subsequently by legislators in the United States. This history of patriarchal authority—where the householder's right to defend his land becomes the lord's right to defend his fiefdom and then the king's unqualified right to safeguard the peace of his kingdom—is the prehistory to the discretionary authority given the police.[19]

In New Orleans, this history was known by both sides in the debate over the police. For the reformers, there was no absolute difference between the discretionary entitlement granted to traditional proxies for the sovereign and the judgment calls made by the city guardsmen in the normal course of their duties. "It is the opinion of some men," one pundit remonstrates, "that a 'City Guard' should have the same power as that of 'Hangman,' and exclude a man from society, or its laws altogether. . . . We say shame upon those who seek to bring about such things." By making Bras-Coupé into an outlaw, Prieur engages with this history to make the opposite point. By his lights, the police are not an obstacle to modernization. It is, rather, their power that has made modernization possible. Without the police, there is no way for society to fight back against the forces of nature that would lead backwards into chaos. To catch all of these associations, we need to read the proclamation of outlawry as a response to the reform campaign. Prieur agreed with the reformers about what was at stake in this controversy, but he came to the opposite conclusion about the role of the police in world history. The vehicle for expressing his dissenting opinion was Bras-Coupé.[20]

When Bras-Coupé is understood in the context of the municipal debate over police violence, the first thing we notice, perhaps surprisingly, is how modern he is. The legal theory behind the manhunt is neither eccentric nor incompatible with the police thinking occurring in courtrooms in Massachusetts and New York, where the most robust precedents were being established, for what would emerge after the Civil War as a national police doctrine. Unlike their counterparts from the northern states, southern thinkers like John C. Calhoun did not refer to "police power" or to cognates like "residual sovereignty," but they were coming to similar conclusions about police discretion. Placed in this company, Prieur is in no sense outside the national mainstream. In crucial respects, he even appears to anticipate solutions that would not be applied elsewhere until decades later. In New Orleans, police thinking was ahead of its time in at least two ways. First, it extended the police power to its structural limit—the right to informal deadly violence. The New York Police would not acquire their right to revolvers for another two decades, and even then, the introduction of firearms was greeted with resurgent public skepticism about "the danger of placing deadly weapons in the hands of men who may use them with impunity at their own discretion." Second, as we have already seen, this entitlement was justified in New Orleans on racial grounds. The reformers forced Prieur to create a rationale that would dictate when to trade liberty for security, and in response, he launched the legend of Bras-Coupé, which deserves to be read in these terms as a myth of modern government. If Prieur lost the local battle over the right to firearms, he won the war in the sense that the rationale that he tried to dramatize through Bras-Coupé eventually became so pervasive that it no longer had to be explicitly labeled. In the end, there was no longer a need to argue for the police's right to firearms, because the right was no longer open to question, and the reason it was no longer open to question was the collective recognition that there would always be social threats like Bras-Coupé. Based upon this threat assessment, the police power came to seem socially necessary not only in New Orleans but in every other city and town that followed its precedent.[21]

As an archetype, Bras-Coupé is defined by his missing arm. The missing part connects him to other maroon rebels, like Three-Fingered Jack, the so-called "Terror of Jamaica," but it also literally instantiates the legal doctrine that makes him into an enemy of the city, given that forfeiture of a limb, according to Pollock and Maitland, was the typical manner in which outlaws were branded before they were banished into the wastelands. Bras-Coupé embodies this legal abstraction, and it is for this reason that his story provides such an exceptional vantage on modern slavery. This perspective is valuable for how it cuts through legal complexity. The competing precedents that remained alive in the law of slavery; the confusion that scuttled every effort to define "slave" as a positive status in law; the struggle to specify when slaves counted as persons and when they counted as property; the ambiguity that made it impossible to distinguish absolutely between slavery and sovereignty—these problems are resolved when they are viewed from the standpoint afforded by the legend of Bras-Coupé. Obviously we must continue to pay attention to this complexity. The reason, however, that Bras-Coupé is potentially so important is that his story simplifies what is at stake in the law of slavery, allowing us to think clearly, if tentatively, about issues that have otherwise remained muddled in our commentary.[22]

It has often been said, for example, that the slave's concurrent status as person and property was a problem for the law. David Brion Davis famously proposes that this "essential contradiction" formed the laws in "every slave society." Starting with antiquity, slaves were granted no ordinary personal rights to marriage, testimony, inheritance, or ownership, yet there were always moments when slaves had to be treated as legal persons, particularly in criminal trials where volition had to be recorded to hold the slave accountable. Given the history of these exceptional cases, it has even been said that a slave's capacity for self-directed action could only be portrayed in law as criminal liability. Judges tied themselves into knots trying defendants who as property had no capacity to posit a legally valid act, and their sophistry has been thought to illustrate the bad thinking endemic to slavery. The intellectual quandary posed by thinking property (as Aristotle put it) or persons made things (as Harriet Beecher Stowe put it after him) is presumed to demonstrate slavery's irrationality, and slavery's irrationality is presumed to demonstrate, at a second remove, its immorality. We presume that it is illogical to treat persons as property, and we attribute the patterns of casuistry and prevarication evidenced within the historical documentation of slave trials to this fundamental moral mistake.[23]

When this record is viewed from the perspective of Bras-Coupé, the slave's concurrent status as subject and object no longer seems like a problem. It no longer looks like logical inconsistency, disorganization, malfunction, or a mistake the system has to make. It looks instead like a precondition for the system's normal operation. Bras-Coupé explains slavery because he is a vehicle for the police power, and the police power explains slavery because it takes something that has been seen as anomalous but ever-present in all slave societies, and shows why it is indispensable. The police power can aid us in clarifying an aspect of slavery that has often appeared confused, telling us that slavery's indignity is not about being turned from a person into a thing but rather about being in a position where it does not matter if you are a person or a thing. Reflecting on outlawry in his *Science of Rights* (1796), Johann Fichte clarifies this point: "The outlaw is considered simply as a wild beast, which must be shot; or as an overflowing river, which must be stopped; in short, as a force of nature, which the state must render harmless by an opposing force of nature." For Fichte, it is key that the outlaw, like the slave, has a relation to the state: the outlaw is always potentially (and therefore actually) a threat, and it is the perception of this threat, on its own, that cancels everything else that might be known about the outlaw. This assumption is eventually rolled into the leading cases on the police power from the antebellum decades, which insist across the board that "police" applies indistinguishably to "persons and things." As far as the police power is concerned, it does not matter whether the threat is posed by a "rational man" or "senseless material," an "assassin" or "his poison," a "maniac" or "his torch." When judges attempted to describe "slave" as a positive status in the law, this ambiguity was a problem, but when they considered slaves as police objects, as in *Prigg v. Pennsylvania* (1842), it became possible for them to analogize the slave's situation, apparently with little cognitive dissonance, to previous police cases involving persons (vagrants, entertainers) as well as things (liquor bottles, counterfeit coins).[24]

Although Orlando Patterson long ago deposed the fallacy about slaves having no legal standing as persons, we are still trying to specify the terms of their liminal incorporation into society, and the police power is relevant in this regard. As Patterson says, the problem is not that slaves were barred from representation. Slaves could and often did appear as persons in the law. The problem, rather, is that their representation tends to lapse before it can count for anything. The legal device that keeps slaves from counting as persons comes from the police power, and further back, from the natural rights tradition. Although it is true that increasing attempts were made to recognize slaves as persons by placing limits on the violence they should have to endure, one fact remains constant across this history: these reforms typically remained unenforced, if not unenforceable, in law. Whenever positive protections were extended, they could easily be outstripped by the claim to exigency. It was the claim to self-defense, depicted not as a source for slavery but as an exceptional petition, that time and again diminished the slave's legal personality to the point where it was an empty technicality. Winning conviction in cases concerning violence against slaves was very nearly impossible, as prosecutors needed to prove not only the aggressor's guilt but also that the wronged slave was not "in revolt" or otherwise posing some threat. To establish unlawful violence against a slave, it was compulsory to prove the negative that the slave was "unoffending and unresisting" at the time of the attack. Slaves were countable as persons, in other words, only so long they were not construed as agents with their own rights to self-defense.[25]

Through Bras-Coupé, we can see this legal history in the making, as it passed into common sense. But as we have noted with Robert Charles, this history is fully revealed only as it is turned over in vernacular expression. By moving from the police campaign to the sketchy remains of the vernacular record, we can see Bras-Coupé not only as a racial trope of public right but as a character incarnating the historical consciousness of the black tradition. In the first place, the oral tradition appears willing to preserve the polarized language of the police campaign. During battle scenes that might as well have been reprised from the newspapers, the legend defines Bras-Coupé by his "utter contempt for law" and his willingness to "shoot it out" with the city guard. Hyperbolized by the police, Bras-Coupé turns supernatural in black tradition. His gaze can turn an officer into a statue, a toad, or a puff of smoke. Fire shoots from his eyes. The police's guns are rendered useless when bullets ricochet from his "iron-like" torso, or when their muskets float into the air after he utters a mysterious incantation. Given this bevy of superpowers, the battle between Bras-Coupé and the city guard begins to look like an altogether unfair fight. It is no wonder that many of the patrols sent after Bras-Coupé become "lost in the mists of the Louisiana swamps never to be seen again." In contrast to the newspapers, which see these brutal battles as scandalous deviations from everyday civility, the oral tradition accepts them as the pivots for its own counterhistory, converting what was once a topical rhetoric of racial emergency into a general theory of society. It gets a lot of mileage, that is to say, simply from taking the state at its word.[26]

It is important to realize that these battle sequences do not represent the primary axis of the legend. What matters most to its narrators is not the immediate confrontation with police authority. Their intent is not merely to turn the police's words backwards, exchanging villainy for heroism. Their labor, rather, is more subtle: it is to impress Bras-Coupé with the capacity for political speech. This involves not resuscitation, or bringing the outlaw back to life after he has been put to death, but inventing a person where before there was none, discovering speech where before there was only noise. To see how this happens, we need first to acknowledge that Bras-Coupé is never meaningfully individuated from the perspective of the police. He is subtracted from the city, reduced to nonpersonhood ("a fiend in human shape"), and imprisoned by a perspective from which he is imperceptible except as a threat. He is less like a person than like a blot upon the horizon. He has no positive qualities (no age, no occupation, no tastes or preferences, no grain to his voice) that are relevant to his given identity and no perspective that counts as far as the law is concerned. Reading the papers, it is not possible to see the battle from his point of view. This blockage was indispensable to the campaign for the city guard, which was structured to keep its audience from imagining police violence from the standpoint of its potential targets. To feel addressed by the police campaign was to know that their guns were reserved for somebody different from you. It was to feel, in other words, that you were a citizen in a city where others were slaves. Most of the time, it is true, the oral tradition reproduces this blockage in chase-and-escape scenes where Bras-Coupé enters the frame "laughing at his would-be captors" only to vanish without warning. But every once in a while, an attempt is made to predicate a political perspective outside the law. Among these instances of flickering interiority, the best example is when Bras-Coupé loses his arm and thereby gains his name. Formerly known by the slave name of Squire, the fugitive is renamed Bras-Coupé after he loses his arm in a skirmish with a police officer. Confined to a hospital where his arm is amputated, he gets dysentery. As he falls into this "state of feebleness," the city guard suspends its surveillance. Taking advantage of the situation, Bras-Coupé leaps through an open window and flees to the swamp, where he organizes the band of fugitives that subsequently terrorizes the city.[27]

It is through this primary event of police violence that the tradition signals its awareness of the state's role in the making of the legend. Cutting the arm, the police convert the ordinary fugitive ("Squire") into the superheroic outlaw ("Bras-Coupé") whose name would soon be on everyone's lips. This injury recasts the law's power to assign identity, its capacity to name through violence, by connecting the moniker "Bras-Coupé" to its source. As the sign of his inadmissibility to the city, the lost arm gives the fugitive his perspective. It is this loss that gives Bras-Coupé his name and instigates his career. Putting this violence at the start of the story, the oral tradition inverts the propaganda that brought the legend into being. According to that propaganda, it is the violence of the fugitive slave that precedes (and therefore legitimates) the violence of the city guard. Once this violence is shown not only to precede but also to produce the outlaw, a new kind of inquiry is begun that reads blackness as the signature of violence. From that point, the legend can accept the lost arm as the occasion for insinuating the standpoint denied by the state. In this sequence, psychic interiority emerges as a relation to injury. The subjectivity accorded Bras-Coupé grows like a phantom limb that is felt by the legend's narrators even as it is known not to be there. In pursuing this strategy, the legend skips the most economical choices for representing emotion (feeling depressed about losing an arm) and cognition (examining its absence) to adopt a looser strategy involving dreams, premonitions, and prophecies that predict the amputation of the arm before it happens. Before he becomes an outlaw, Squire sees the future. He "practices his marksmanship not only with one hand but with both," as he knows ahead of time that he will "lose an arm" and "become Bras-Coupé." This visionary sequence does not suggest a fantasy of personal wholeness before the acquisition of identity so much as it seizes and insistently enlarges the missing arm as the source for an unnatural subjectivity that can only be depicted as prophecy. Once this prophecy is postulated from the pretext of the injury, the outlaw assumes an external relation to his body that looks like self-consciousness distributed over time. A self emerges where it is not supposed to exist. It emerges, moreover, from inside a story that denies its existence. Here, as elsewhere, we notice the black tradition reenacting its own beginning, and therefore beginning again, by indexing its negative relationship with the law.[28]

In the earliest cycles of the oral tradition, the historical emergence of this political perspective registers first at the level of narration, where Bras-Coupé gets represented both as subject and object in his warfare with the police. This process neither romanticizes the outlaw's guilt nor does it presume his innocence. Instead, it calls a person into being whose nonpersonhood establishes the unstated grounds for police action. Throwing their voices to speak back to the city from the perspective of the swamp, the legend's narrators assume a kinship to Bras-Coupé that repeats his own relation to his missing arm in refusing the equivalence between part and whole as the crux for common identity. In rejecting this consolation, the legend gradually subtracts its orators as well as its auditors from the law's language in order to build an alternative perspective from which the state can be engaged without acceding to its universality. That the legend never sustains this ventriloquism for more than a few moments at a time is evidence of its continual struggle to predicate a political subjectivity upon statelessness. Because its political content is not prescribed by this manner of predication, the vernacular tradition is not committed to any position ahead of time. The pressing question of whether a particular claim has value, whether it leads to a genuine or a false politics, is not prejudged so much as usurped by the prior need to construct a standpoint from which such claims can be made in the first place. More than mere romance, the tradition is not single-mindedly dedicated to the state's elimination, nor is it incompatible with a willingness to punish those who harm. It does not suspend the law; it speaks from the point where the law has been suspended, generating the proleptic potential for a new law from an unstructured point in the existing situation. The legend takes seriously the fact that claims made in the fugitive's name are nondemonstrable from the perspective of the citizenry, given that their expression violates the process by which the city recognizes its members. Such claims cannot be logically derived from the situation at hand, and they intrude as a result with the unexpected forcefulness of an axiom promising to make its own law. The fugitive's standpoint, in short, is both immanent and unimaginable to the city. His legend is therefore not a cultural agency intervening from outside the city but a political perspective that is founded upon and named for the blackening that occurs when the existing law becomes deformalized.[29]

These, then, are the legend's outlines as revealed in its first cycle. A favored slave escapes from his master. He loses an arm after he is shot by the police only to reappear stronger than ever as the leader of the maroons. From this point, the legend stretches into a series of repeatable chase-and-escape sequences and battle scenes, in which the fugitive's violence may seem either valiant or terrifying, depending on the perspective from which the legend is told. These outlines are accessible in multiple forms, including first-hand reminiscences by locals like Henry Castellanos, dedicated sketches by collectors like Lafcadio Hearn, and varorium albums by historians like Marcus Christian. The legend would enter its second cycle after a bookkeeper named George Washington Cable heard the tale from a black porter in the counting room where he worked. Cable decided to "make a story" about Bras-Coupé and struggled first to transcribe then to publish the results. Rejected twice by *Scribner's*, once by *Appleton's*, and once by the *Atlantic*, Cable's version would not see print until it was made into the "foundation" for *The Grandissimes*, a novel published serially in *Scribner's* in 1879–1880. Given its lasting impact on the tradition as well as the commanding extent of its revisions, it is indisputable that *The Grandissimes* is the turning point in the legend's transmission. Its impact has been decisive for the history of the legend. Many renditions, like Frederick Delius's blackface opera *Koanga* (1897), dispense altogether with the oral tradition to base their plots directly on the novel, whereas others, such as the version in Herbert Asbury's *The French Quarter* (1936), combine early components from the oral tradition with innovations introduced by Cable. Looking to Cable's revisions and the later responses to these revisions, my aim is to show how the blackness in black tradition persists under these mixed conditions—through, and not despite, its historicity.[30]

To understand the lasting influence that *The Grandissimes* has exercised on the legend, we need to consider what brought Cable to Bras-Coupé in the first place. In his reflections on the novel's composition, Cable is clear that his revisions to the legend were guided by a legal philosophy that is systematically presented in landmark essays like "The Freedman's Case in Equity" (1885) and "The Convict Lease System in the Southern States" (1884), whose aim was to criticize the failure within the southern states to extend equality to their former slaves. Lamenting the growth of segregation and the escalating rate of penal exploitation, Cable censures the southern states for lagging behind the national mainstream. Proposing a new narrative for southern history that moves forward from a benighted past when public associations are irredeemably determined by racial status to an enlightened future when they are arbitrated by the privileges and immunities of citizenship, Cable represents the failure to assimilate the ex-slave as a failure to be fully modern. The switching point in this story is the emptiness of the present, where slavery hovers as a ghost yet to be dispelled. Acknowledging that many whites in the region would never peaceably concede to the government their "broad powers of police over any and every person of color," Cable still insists that the southern states would remain a backwater until this occurred. All such powers needed to become the state's exclusive prerogative before a modern civilization could take root. According to Cable's vision of the civilizing process, the pursuit of justice is the pursuit of the modern, and the pursuit of the modern is the pursuit of a world where the state trumps all competing modes of social organization. If modernization begins when the individual's natural entitlement to personal violence is surrendered to the state, it matures when the state administers its resulting monopoly without regard for the inherited custom that would divide the population into parts and stipulate rights and duties, part by part, according to racial status.[31]

Cable came to this position gradually over the course of a decade when he was also pondering Bras-Coupé. His revisions to the legend betray this concurrent engagement with the problem of formal equality; indeed they may even suggest that he adopted Bras-Coupé precisely as a narrative vehicle for thinking through the law's limit cases. Cable found Bras-Coupé troubling because his story exposed an impediment built into the social contract that could not be overcome by invoking the prospect of legal development. Faced with this problem, Cable changed the legend in an attempt to detach the police power from its racial moorings, devising a thought experiment that he hoped could make a future for law by laying the fugitive to rest. The best way to fit the legend into his idea of historical progress, Cable realized, was to revise its plot from the perspective of evolutionary anthropology. Remembering his discovery of the legend in the counting room, Cable goes so far as to enclose its transmission with an ethnographic tableau that includes its own "old darkey informant" who reverts to Bras-Coupé no matter what question is asked. By presenting this workplace conversation as ethnographic fieldwork with a native informant, Cable fixes the legend's authenticity as a cultural item. "In those days," he says, "I took great pains to talk with old French-speaking negroes, not trusting to the historical correctness of what they told me, but receiving what they said for its value as tradition, superstition, or folklore." Given his conviction that folklore never rises to the level of history, Cable's framing of the legend begs the question of why he would use "folklore" as a way to talk about the history of law. But that is precisely the point. Folklore is valuable for Cable because the line between "folklore" and "history" is what makes history, in his sense, possible. Bras-Coupé is the perfect kernel for this project, not because his story is a self-evident example of folklore, but because the historical dilemma posed by his existence can be resolved only by turning his story into folklore.[32]

As with the law, Cable was very close to the cutting edge in his conceptualization of culture. The claim that culture is a "complex whole" dates to E. B. Tylor's *Primitive Culture* (1871), which argues that culture, like biology, obeys the natural laws of evolution. Cable, like Tylor, does not believe that there are many cultures in the world. On the contrary, he believes there is one culture in the world that is unevenly distributed among its peoples. Individuals differ from one another not because they come from separate cultures but because they have reached separate stages along the single trajectory of world history. From this perspective, folklore marks the persistence of a previous age's politics into the present day. Folklore encompasses many systems of explanation that were at one time integral to the political organization of society. Rendered obsolete by progress, these systems become increasingly extraneous until they are finally reduced to crude customs, soon to disappear altogether. Collecting the songs and stories from slavery was an urgent project, according to this thinking, which had to happen before the last remnants of slave culture were gone for good. This was an orientation that Cable shared with many contemporary thinkers. If there was something distinctive in Cable's approach, it was his creative reliance on a corollary to this claim. For Cable, the cultural value of these slave-made songs and stories was predicated upon their growing irrelevance to contemporary society.[33]

Cable's research into racial folkways has long been seen as setting the groundwork for the supposition that race is culturally constructed. But his research needs to be seen not only as anticipating this eventual commonplace but also as engaging with the law of its own time. Ethnographic knowledge of black culture should be construed as necessary (and not merely coincident) to his advocacy for color blindness. Collecting black folklore helped Cable to imagine a future where the state could lay claim to universality by providing an orientation that perceived the law's limits as remnants that would one day decompose into culture once history reached greater levels of rationalization. It was the culture concept, albeit in an embryonic condition, that allowed Cable to reconcile the persistence of black identity with the normative self-description of modern law. Through this structural dependency, we can begin to see why folklore became indispensable to progressive narratives of political modernization, and why blackness has been so persistently imagined as a condition that is culturally prolific yet politically and economically hopeless. This method is evidenced in Cable's famous essays of the 1880s, which intuitively divide their attention between culture and politics in a manner that prevents the slightest possibility of their commingling at the level of analysis. It is also evidenced in the changes he made to Bras-Coupé. Cable rewrites the legend in his first novel, *The Grandissimes*, to illustrate the legacies that had to be overcome before his region could catch the advance guard of world history. By the novel's lights, progress is measured by whether the legend continues to provide a reliable map to current politics. Color blindness is achieved when the legend turns atavistic, its strength pale in contrast to the rational organization of modern law, whose bureaucratic protocols supply the all-encompassing coordinates for political deliberation.[34]

The key to interpreting *The Grandissimes* is realizing how Cable's commitments to "politics" and "culture" are unified in the novel by his approach to the historical process, an approach that is applied with equal intensity and methodological consistency to matters that have been pictured ever since as belonging to distinct domains of society. Some of the novel's amendments to the legend (such as the inclusion of a failed romance plot) may be perceived as resulting from its transmission from an oral to a written medium with a greater capacity for thematic subordination, but other changes to the legend are plainly motivated by Cable's aspiration to put the law upon a new foundation by relieving the fugitive of his supporting role in the local development of police power. Framing devices are employed throughout the novel to facilitate the translation of Bras-Coupé into folklore by sealing his story into its own diegetic level. Dead for eight years before the novel starts, Bras-Coupé survives only in the tales told about his tragic career. Three characters—two of them white, one a creole of color—recount the legend over the course of a single day, but it is printed in full only once. This version does "not exactly follow the words of any one" of these narrators. Rather, it mixes their language to form a group rendition whose texture bears the markings of oral transmission. Framed as a story-within-a-story, connected to and divorced from its tellers, the legend is punctuated by cursory digressions from its assorted narrators as well as blanket references to the authority of "tradition." For Cable, it is important that these colloquial channels are untouched by the state. The wanted posters and newspaper headlines that focus the manhunt for Bras-Coupé are cultivated as second-order objects of interest in other versions of the legend, but they are excised from *The Grandissimes*. Filtering from its plot all details that would suggest the state's role in facilitating the legend, the novel also removes from its plot—with one notable exception—all references to the police. Given their centrality to the manhunt and their prevalence in the oral tradition, the police's absence in the novel is striking. The purpose of this exclusion, however, is clear. By removing from Bras-Coupé all traces of the state, Cable removes from the state all traces of Bras-Coupé. The legend becomes the unadulterated expression of cultural tradition, and the police are freed to develop into an authority uncorrupted by the taint of race. Subtracting the mark of each from the other, the novel redraws the line between culture and state in a way that conflates culture with race and thereby cleanses the state of racial contamination, preserving the possibility of a law that can make good on the pledge of equality.[35]

This is an imperative that can elucidate certain revisions to the legend that are otherwise inexplicable, even the oddest of them all: the restoration of the arm. Cable is clear that Bras-Coupé has "two goodly arms intact."

In the novel, the outlaw is not maimed by the state. He names himself, looking not outward to the police but homeward to Africa:

> His name . . . was —— ——, something in the Jaloff tongue, which he by and by condescended to render into Congo: Mioko-Koanga, in French Bras-Coupé, the Arm Cut Off. Truly it would have been easy to admit, had this been his meaning, that his tribe, in losing him, had lost its strong right arm close off at the shoulder; not so easy for his high-paying purchaser to allow, if this other was his intent; that the arm which might no longer shake the spear or swing the wooden sword, was no better than a useless stump never to be lifted for aught else. But whether easy to allow or not, that was his meaning. He made himself a type of all Slavery, turning into flesh and blood the truth that all Slavery is maiming.

In the novel, this ritual of self-naming stirs a series of improvisations on injury, value, and violence that rise and fall only to be shut down by the passage's conclusion, when the phrase is deemed unambiguous: it signals Bras-Coupé's representative status as a "type of all Slavery." By turning a slave maimed by the police into the unmaimed vehicle for the expression of the truth that all slavery is maiming, Cable sublimates violence into metaphysics. Locking the slave into an earlier phase of history, the novel extracts from his legend the brutality that supplies his name.[36]

This is a grave departure from the oral tradition, which furnishes several explanations for the missing limb but never deigns to preserve the arm whole. Cable reports that readers were outraged by this alteration to the legend. "They considered . . . my version . . . was faulty," he confesses, "because I had . . . trifled" with that "precious verity of history." Cable offers no explanation, however, for his intervention. It would be a mistake, I believe, to construe this reticence as a sign that Cable was merely trifling when he decided to restore the missing arm. By every account, the missing arm is the crux of the vernacular tradition. Restoring the arm is the most radical change one could make to the legend without rendering its storyline unrecognizable. It stands to reason that Cable would have a good reason even for contemplating such a desperate measure. As I understand it, Cable's reticence on this point indicates not the absence of a rationale but its structural importance to the novel. Literally everything about the novel's project hinges upon its recasting of the primary scene where the outlaw gets his name from the injury he is given by the police. Not only is this scene unspeakable in the novel, the reason why it is unspeakable cannot be spoken by its author. There is nothing accidental about this resistance. It is a structural condition for the history that the novel attempts to envision. Once we recognize this imperative, other revisions start to make more sense. We can grasp, for instance, why Cable backdates the legend from the 1830s to the 1790s—a change that means, when Bras-Coupé is mutilated in the novel, his punishment derives not from the police powers legitimated in enlightened courts but from the *Code noir*, whose colonial character the novel emphasizes to maximize the measurable distance between its past and its future. Backdating the legend also facilitates the analogy between the world in the novel and the world where the novel was being written and read—such that, famously, the Louisiana Purchase becomes an equivalent to Reconstruction—and clearly there is nothing that this analogy needs more than the distance that also makes development imaginable.[37]

There is more to say about the moment in the novel when Bras-Coupé names himself. We want to consider what the novel is resisting in this scene, but we also want to think about how this scene fits in the novel's framework for the legend. Something we might notice about this scene of self-naming is how the novel manages to displace the cutting of the arm only by looking back to a prior determination for identity, linking the arm not to the outlaw's war with the police but to the relation between the "prince" and his "tribe." This is a second major change to the legend. Although early versions of the legend typically identify Bras-Coupé as a creole and sometimes as a "mulatto," Cable makes him into an African prince who is newly arrived to America. Bras-Coupé keeps his arm, and instead it is the tribe, missing its leader, that is said to have lost its "right arm close off at the shoulder." In the vernacular tradition, Bras-Coupé is an outlaw who confronts the police as an authority that is unrestricted. As prince, he wields the same unfettered sovereignty over his tribe. Bras-Coupé becomes not only an enemy of the state but also a personification of the state, and not just any state but precisely the kind of antiquated military state the New Orleans reformers saw in their police. Under these conditions, society's artificial part is not its head but its arm. What the arm names is the despotic violence that organizes social relations in primitive society. By collapsing the entire circuit of violence into the character of Bras-Coupé, Cable secures its placement in the storyline of modernization.

Bras-Coupé, pictured with "two goodly arms intact." Albert Herter, "Bras-Coupé," from George Washington Cable, *The Grandissimes: A Story of Creole Life* (New York, 1899), 260.

Whereas the violence looks in oral tradition like the self-perpetuating cycle of racial warfare that drives the development of modern sovereignty, *The Grandissimes* is willing to permit its historical representation only under the atavistic sign of the African.[38]

In remaking the legendary fugitive as an enslaved prince, the novel cites a venerable tradition that begins with Aphra Behn's *Oroonoko* (1688). In the spirit of this tradition, Cable solicits sympathy for Bras-Coupé on the basis of his nobility. It is the prince's honor, written into his "fine" features and "royal" stature, that transforms the dishonor of his slavery into a tragedy. These petitions to nobility counteract his standing as a "type of all Slavery" because they present a case that cannot be universalized. Even as Cable removes the scene where the arm is severed, his sublimation of this injury into a meditation on enslaved royalty preserves the legend's resistance to the teleology of equal protection. The novel is able to claim sympathy for Bras-Coupé, but only on restricted grounds that indicate the structural incapacity to transform the legend into a direct appeal for natural rights. This resistance should be read back to its source: the appeal to rights is subverted not because the novel secretly believes in nobility but because the prince's exceptional status is the insoluble (albeit coded) remainder of the police violence that has to disappear from the historical process before black equality can be represented as developing from the law as it actually exists.[39]

Furthermore, by appealing to his African homeland, Bras-Coupé consecrates his blackness as a relation to origin. This appeal makes the state's implication in the fugitive's identity unavailable to representation, indicated by the noninscription of his initial name. The dashes that substitute for the African name ("—— ——") denote an unspeakable origin that only becomes an origin by virtue of the translation that converts "Bras-Coupé" from Jaloff to Congo to French. Although we might read these dashes as the sign for something withheld, their presence on the page also indicates the novel's apprehension of a phenomenon that ethnographers at the time were calling an alternating sound, a unit of language that resisted transcription because of its phonetic variation in the native tongue. The dashes, in this regard, indicate the line beyond which sound refuses to resolve into sense. This line is drawn again in the curse that Bras-Coupé puts upon his master's house. Unlike the muddled translation of his name, and unlike the confused negotiations over the terms of his enslavement, this curse needs "no interpreter" to convey the threat that is audible to everyone within earshot even though it is spoken in his "mother tongue." Most anthropologists at the time were attributing this phonetic intractability to the primitive condition of the languages they were studying, which in their minds had not yet evolved to a stage where pronunciation had become standardized. Cable's thinking is closer to the landmark essay by Franz Boas, "On Alternating Sounds" (1889), which asserted to the contrary that there was no such thing as an alternating sound, that the variance collectors thought they were hearing resulted from their own incapacity to hear the gradations in an informant's speech. Boas redescribes the intractability of primitive culture as the noise endemic to the encounter between cultures, establishing in the process the modern concept of human diversity, but it is less evident what Cable is doing with his dashes and his evocation of an incantation that need not be printed. This uncertainty persists, I would suggest, because Cable's innovations in the theory of culture result from a struggle to resolve a problem that was not a cultural problem at all. For Cable, sound's refusal to resolve into sense evidences not the foreignness of the prince's native tongue, whether the foreignness is measured in space or time, but rather the identity-forming violence that cannot be admitted to the scene of self-naming without splitting the controlling fiction of origin. What cannot be translated is the violence that gives Bras-Coupé his name. This violence resurfaces in this passage only as an absence ("— —"), which rapidly gives way to racial presence secured through a repetition that conceals its source. Denied social recognition, the outlaw discovers the fullness of identity only in relation to an absent homeland. At this point, Cable introduces Africa into his novel to provide an alibi for the police.[40]

After restoring the arm and turning the maroon leader into a captive prince, Cable also changes the legend's climax. More than the others, this third change arguably made the biggest difference for the legend's later cycles. To understand this third intervention, first we need to consider the conventional climax that is not depicted in the novel. Traditionally, the legend concludes with Denis Prieur exhibiting Bras-Coupé's corpse on the Place d'Armes. "That thousands and thousands rushed to that historic square" was "a matter of notoriety," the legend concludes. "Surging crowds" gathered "under that broiling solstitial sun" to catch a glimpse of the fugitive with its "unhealed and gaping wounds, alleged to have been inflicted by the city guard." Many of the slaves in attendance were reputedly not there by choice but were told to go by their masters "for the sake of example." As

Bras-Coupé was "so well known among the negroes," it was considered "salutary" for slaves to "gaze upon" the corpse "bleeding and weltering in his gore." In this final recursive turn, we can perceive the oral tradition concluding by narrating its own beginning in the pageantry that fixed the fugitive's place in local memory. Adopting the perspective of the slaves scattered about the plaza, the legend submits its own existence as evidence that these slaves lived to tell about what they saw.[41]

In the novel, Bras-Coupé is never hung in effigy. The public exhibition that routinely brought the legend to its end is excluded from *The Grandissimes*. Turning away from the Place d'Armes, the novel looks to Congo Square for its public climax. In this scene, Bras-Coupé emerges from the cypress swamp and joins the crowd that gathers in the square to sing, dance, and socialize on Sunday afternoons. Upon arrival, the fugitive takes center stage and executes a series of dazzling moves that catch the crowd's attention. He hurdles with "tinkling heels" over the head of his "bewildered partner," and everyone there "[howls] with rapture." The "blackest of black men" in this performance, Bras-Coupé epitomizes the "whole company of black lookers-on." The novel waits for Bras-Coupé to push the scene to its saturation point: it is his entrance that sparks the experience of "unison." If Place d'Armes acts as an allegory by orchestrating the meeting of Denis Prieur and Bras-Coupé as a confrontation between sovereignty and its enemy, Congo Square betrays a similar degree of ambition, imagining blackness as an organic and therefore primitive identification between a sovereign and his followers, channeled in this case by the "sympathy" of "weird music." Turning Bras-Coupé into sovereignty's subject rather than its object, this scene completes the revision that began with the novel's conversion of the cut arm into a trope for the prince's absolute dominion over his tribe.[42]

Getting to the lower strata of the scene at Congo Square, where the traditional conclusion is still apparent beneath layers of primitivist distortion, takes some effort. The terms of this substitution are concealed in *The Grandissimes*, but they are explained at length in Cable's major historical essays on black performance, "The Dance in Place Congo" (1886) and "Creole Slave Songs" (1886), the former of which literally begins by walking its reader from Place d'Armes to Congo Square. Here is how the essay imagines the relation between the two locations:

> The ancient Place d'Armes . . . stood for all that was best; the place for political rallying, the retail quarter of all the fine goods

and wares, and at sunset and by moonlight the promenade of good society and the haunt of true lovers; not only in the military, but also in the most unwarlike sense the place of arms, and of hearts and hands, and of words tender as well as words noble. The Place Congo, at the opposite end of the street, was at the opposite end of everything. One was on the highest ground; the other on the lowest. The one was the rendezvous of the rich man, the master, the military officer—of all that went to make up the ruling class; the other of the butcher and baker, the raftsman, the sailor, the quadroon, the painted girl, and the negro slave. No meaner name could be given the spot. The negro was the most despised of human creatures and the Congo the plebian among the negroes. The white man's plaza had the army and navy on its right and left, the court-house, the council hall and the church at its back, and the world before it. The black man's was outside the rear gate, the poisonous wilderness on three sides.

This manichaean opposition leaves no doubt that the essay is working overtime to secure the symbolic difference between these two locations, indicating why the transfer of the legend's public climax is necessary for the novel: it preserves the social character of these locations by removing the remainder of each from the other. The unheralded departure of Bras-Coupé from Place d'Armes convenes a polity where the law can stand without racial exceptions, and his on-time arrival at Congo Square commences a cultural performance where race is reproduced without legal mediation. Dedicated to the prospect of a southern future where the racial authority of slavery would be transcended by the rule of law, Cable must imagine a Place d'Armes without a Bras-Coupé at its center. Rather than allowing the legend to puncture the fantasy of the state's potential wholeness, Cable moves its conclusion across town.[43]

In the novel, the stringent contrast between Place d'Armes and Congo Square forms more than the legend's climax. It is structural to its storyline. Consider how Cable represents Bras-Coupé's existence in the cypress swamp. He details the natural landscape: the cypress knees, the vines, the Spanish moss, the pitch-black water, the particular quality of the sunlight. Using a template for natural description that was conventional in his time, Cable catalogs the alligators, turtles, birds, mosquitoes, lizards, spiders,

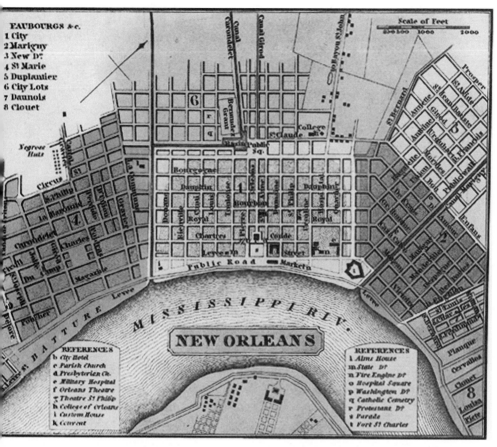

Congo Square is on the municipal boundary (marked "Public Sq."), and the Place d'Armes is the parade ground (marked "s") on the river. Inset from *A New Map of Louisiana with Its Canals, Roads & Distances from place to place, along the Stage & Steam Boat Routes by H. S. Tanner. (with) New Orleans.* Engraved by W. Brose, Philadelphia, 1836. Reprinted with permission from David Rumsey Map Collection.

bats, raccoons, opossums, dragonflies, and centipedes that one might expect to meet in this setting. There are, however, no people other than Bras-Coupé in this swamp. Its "inmost depths" are "clear but lifeless," bereft of almost every sign of humanity: their "endless colonnades of cypresses" and "motionless drapings of gray moss" are kept company by "owls and bats" and "flowers that no man had named," but their "solemn stillness" is "disturbed" by no human presence except for Bras-Coupé. No longer a charismatic leader of the maroons in their battles against the city guard, in the novel Bras-Coupé turns recluse until he arrives at Congo Square, where he is greeted by the people who disappeared from the swamp. By draining the swamp, Cable fills the square, changing the meaning of blackness in the process. In the novel, Bras-Coupé's valor on the battlefield occurs only in Africa, where he was a warrior prince. He never wages war in the swamp, and the only evidence for his past valor is his present prowess in the dance, which is supposed to confirm his natural right to the primitive sovereignty that was taken from him when he was enslaved. If the prince's leadership is measured in Africa by the unbounded loyalty of his subjects, it is expressed at Congo Square by taking center stage at a dance. In the novel, this cultural authority is all that is left from African politics in the New World. This is the force that brings Bras-Coupé to Congo Square.[44]

It is worth remarking, in this connection, that many of the songs Cable offers to substantiate the Congo Square tradition concern the social life of the swamp. Some of their lyrics reference the subsistence practices (gathering "wild berries" and "fishing for perch") and internal economies (collecting and bartering "pokeberries" for "making ink" and "sassafras" for "making tea") that enlivened the swamp. Others are taunts hurled at the militia and the city guard by fugitive slaves ("Oh General Florido. / It's true they cannot catch me!") and elegies memorializing maroon heroes from early campaigns ("Alas! Young men, come, make lament / For poor St. Malo in distress. / They chased, they hunted him with dogs. / They fired at him with a gun. . . . They hauled him from the cypress swamp"). In the essays, Cable notes the history of these songs. Next to the "song of defiance addressed to the high sheriff," he includes a song used as a signal in the "nocturnal prowling" on the "forest-darkened bayous," which calls for people to haul their large and small game for exchange at the boat. Like the legend about Bras-Coupé, Cable gets this signal song directly "from the negroes themselves," but in this case, he remains skeptical about the translation provided by his informants. He admits that the words definitely sound like they are "in some African tongue," but he wonders if a philologist will one day prove that this "strange song" is no "more difficult" to grasp than the "famous inscription discovered by Mr. Pickwick." The reference to Dickens's parody is obviously meant to balance the high seriousness of the ethnographic enterprise, but the allusion also specifies the framework into which the signal song is translated. Cable suggests that it is entirely possible that he is making the same mistake as Mr. Pickwick and confusing a song that is contemporary (and therefore worthless) for a recovered fragment (whose value is predicated on its antiquity). If the song were still in circulation or somehow still relevant to contemporary life, it would not be worth collecting. After making this joke at his own expense, Cable is willing to vouch that, to the best of his knowledge, all the songs he has ascribed to the black tradition are "genuine antiques." In this condensed case, it is easy to tell what is left out when cultural value is forced to imply political irrelevance. In the novel, the stakes of translation are not as clear-cut as they are with Mr. Pickwick. It takes more work to know what is meant by Bras-Coupé's untranslated name, but as the displacement from oral tradition is followed point by point, we find ourselves following the same pattern.[45]

Consider that the scene at Congo Square, for instance, retains the following trace from its antecedents in the oral tradition: it occasions the first and only appearance of the police in the novel. As Bras-Coupé is about to soar in a "more astounding leap than his last," the police throw a lasso around him and bring him "crashing like a burnt tree, face upward upon the turf." Unheralded, this event feels like yet another hiccup in the plot, given that in this case the legend's resolution is provoked not by an agent already introduced in the novel but by an external force that appears only in this singular moment. When a member of the Grandissime family announces that Bras-Coupé is "not exactly taken yet, but they are on his track," the mass rejoinder to this revelation ("Who?") triggers the substitution through which the police enter the novel. The answer to this collective inquiry ("the police") identifies the absent cause that is otherwise left unstated in the story. Because the police are banished from the main line of narrative development, the officers must enter this climatic scene from outside the legend, as the deus ex machina that brings closure to the fugitive's career. Extrinsic to the legend, the police are embedded, like a foreign body, near its close. Recognizable at once as a remnant from the old climax at Place d'Armes or as something left over from the unrepresented history in the swamp, the police's intrusion also indicates something about the history of the square. Congo Square has long been identified as sacred ground, but we will know its whole story only when we have perceived how its sacredness has been distilled from a legend to which it never would have been linked were it not for Cable's mythmaking.[46]

With his characterization of Congo Square in *The Grandissimes* and in his ethnographic essays, Cable has played a key role in casting the language through which later generations have measured the cultural compass of the African diaspora. Because these writings contain not only undeniable evidence but also a language for talking about the historical perseverance of African practices in the New World, they are frequently cited by scholars to exemplify a struggle for cultural conservation that is construed as general to slavery. Congo Square dramatizes the struggle that was happening everywhere, only in secret, through personal exchanges and clandestine meetings whose incidence in the historical record is comparatively slight. This is the reason why Cable has "special significance" for scholars like Melville Herskovits, who were attempting to show that slaves retained considerably more than "scraps of memories" from their homeland. In *The Myth of the Negro Past* (1941), Herskovits specifically cites *The Grandissimes* as "one of the richest stores of data" on black culture in the nineteenth century, suggesting that despite its fictional status, the novel should be taken seriously as a "valid document" and a "real contribution" to ethnographic knowledge.[47]

Cable was influential not only for the claims that he made and the evidence that he gathered but for the way that he brought his claims and his evidence together to make a case for African cultural retentions in the New World. Working with secondhand sources, Cable creatively combined observations made by others to describe the cultural syncretism that he knew was happening at the square whether or not he could say for sure how it looked or sounded. Cable built his writing from antebellum travel books, from the music collections of his acquaintances, and from Mederic Louis Elie Moreau de Saint-Méry's *Description topographique, physique, civile, politique et historique de la partie française de l'isle Saint-Domingue* (1797), which gives reports from dances performed on Saint-Domingue during the 1790s. Seemingly without worry, Cable pasted these scenes onto Congo Square a half-century later, as his philosophy of composition allowed not only Bras-Coupé's passage from the 1830s to the 1790s but also the transfer of the Calinda and its kindred dances from the 1790s to the 1830s. There is no strong reason to doubt whether these dances could have happened at Congo Square given the lively exchange between New Orleans and the West Indies, which made for considerable unity among the slave cultures of the Greater Caribbean. Nevertheless, we need to see that Cable was not representing but reenacting this vibrant syncretism as he reassembled the available archive.[48]

This problem becomes more complex when we consider the police's role in the composition of this history. The only way that Cable was able to write about the mass gatherings at Congo Square, which ended around

THE BAMBOULA.

E. W. Kemble, "The Bamboula," from George Washington Cable, "The Dance in Place Congo," *Century Magazine* 31 (February 1886): 524.

32) a stringed instrument which no doubt was imported from Africa. On the top of the finger board was the rude figure of a Man in a sitting posture, & two pegs behind him to which the strings were fastened. The body was a Calabash. It was played upon by a very little old man, apparently 80 or 90 Years old. — The women squalled out a burthen to the playing, at intervals, consisting of two notes, as the Negroes working in our cities respond to the song of their leader. — Most of the circles contained the same sort of dancers. except One which was

This is the thirty-second page from Benjamin Henry Latrobe's travel journal, containing some of his observations at Congo Square. These notes are the most influential eyewitness account of the square; later writers who have tried to reconstruct some sense of the music and dance there have tended to start with these words and sketches. Benjamin Henry Latrobe, Journal IV, 16 February to 26 February 1819, 32. Reprinted with permission from the Maryland Historical Society.

the time he was born, was by drawing on the written record left by the travelers who visited the square during its heyday, and the only reason that these travelers were able to leave such a record was that the dances were approved by government, contained by a fence, and monitored by police. In the documents that became Cable's primary sources, travel writers like Benjamin Latrobe, John Paxton, and Thomas Nuttall picture the square from a wide angle that captures not only the slaves dancing "barefoot on the grass" and the spectators "pressed round the gate" but also the "civic guard" who survey the scene from a "discreet distance." Cable reproduces the experience of direct observation described in these sources with a direct address to his readers. "See them," he commands, "wilder than gypsies; wilder than the Moors and Arabs whose strong blood and features one sees at a glance in so many of them." Even as these closed imperatives are meant to create the impression of immediate engagement that transcends historical mediation, the second-person construction puts the implied reader literally in the thick of the white tourists who gathered outside the gates to gawk at the slaves dancing on the plaza. This standpoint is maintained throughout the essays, as the reader is told to "see," "hear," "notice," "picture," and "behold" the sights and sounds of the performance, a structure of address that serves the same purpose as the excision of the police from the Bras-Coupé legend. In both cases, the police are structural to the historical documentation of black tradition, and in both cases, they are buried in the background by Cable.[49]

This impact is nowhere more pronounced than in the historiography of jazz. Building on Cable's argument, music historians have often named Congo Square as the birthplace of jazz tradition. Labeled by Henry Kmen as the "first article of faith" in jazz criticism, this origin myth rapidly gained currency in early histories—like Frederic Ramsey Jr. and Charles Smith's *Jazzmen* (1939), Robert Goffin's *Jazz: From the Congo to the Metropolitan* (1944), Rudi Blesh's *Shining Trumpets* (1946), and Marshall Stearns's *The Story of Jazz* (1956)—all of which maintain that jazz begins at Congo Square. To unpack this claim, we must think not only about the weekly goings-on at the square but also about the subsequent conditions that have made the square narratable as a beginning for jazz tradition. Some of these histories are even willing to name the moment when the music came into being. Jazz commenced, they say, when its first great bandleader, Buddy Bolden, heard the drums echoing from Congo Square. "In New Orleans, you could still hear the bamboula on

Congo Square when Buddy Bolden cut his first chorus on cornet," Smith announces in his section preface to *Jazzmen*. Pages later in the same anthology, William Russell and Stephen Smith concur that Buddy Bolden was "in his teens" when the "Congo Dances were discontinued." Rudi Blesh couches the observation as an open question. "Much has been made of the fact that Buddy Bolden was a boy when the Congo Square activity reached its last stages of decline in the 1880s," Blesh remarks. "What, then must have been the effect of this African survival at its height, on the children and youths who, in future years, formed the first street bands? May not some of them have danced and sung, drummed or blown wooden trumpets in the historic square?" Even when the claim does not include Bolden as its dramatic lead, it remains important to these histories that the Congo Dances lasted into the 1880s. Different dates are selected by different scholars—Marshall Stearns says 1885, Barry Ulanov 1890—but the consensus was that the dances lasted for long enough to have "midwifed into existence what we know as jazz."[50]

This origin story is based on a mistake. Drawing upon Cable's writings on Congo Square to make the case for the cultural continuity of the black tradition, these historians assume that Cable was writing about performances that he saw with his own eyes. It would appear that the tense and mood of Cable's imperatives ("See them come!") were even more effective in practice than he likely could have imagined. The impression of an unmediated present fostered by these imperatives was so powerful that it carried over as a working assumption among later researchers who saw Cable not as a fellow researcher but instead as an "observant contemporary" to the scenes he reassembled. This working assumption was common enough to ground not only the anecdote about Buddy Bolden but sustained disagreement about the music's development. Goffin, for instance, takes *Jazzmen* to task for jumping "unknowingly from the primitive period to jazz itself," and thus ignoring the incremental changes in technique and instrumentation that are evident at Congo Square when earlier sources like J. G. Flugel's travel narrative from 1817 are compared to Cable's essays from 1885. The obvious problem here is that Cable himself was depending on sources like Flugel in his own reconstruction of these performances. In other words, Goffin is turning wrinkles in the archive into history. The irony is compounded when we remember that Goffin's critique is largely about *Jazzmen*'s reliance on Herbert Asbury's *The French Quarter* (1936), whose interpretation Goffin finds faulty as it generalizes about Congo Square based on antebellum travel narratives that were "outdated" by the time Cable began writing later in the century. Calling *Jazzmen* to account for going to these primary sources rather than the secondary criticism that Cable derived from them, Goffin misses the fact that *The French Quarter* is crucially informed by Cable. In his chapters on Congo Square, Asbury relates the story of one of its most famous dancers who could "leap higher and shout louder than any of the other slaves who stamped and cavorted in the dance," whose "fame as a Bamboula artist" was rivaled only by the "different sort of renown" that he would come to have as "Bras Coupé . . . the Brigand of the Swamp."[51]

We can confirm that the association Asbury makes between Bras-Coupé and Congo Square starts with *The Grandissimes*. This is something that Cable invented and not something that he inherited from oral tradition. We know this because only one source indicates that the association between Bras-Coupé and Congo Square may have come before the novel. That source is a parallel legend about the New Orleans musician Louis Gottschalk, whose piano compositions, based on creole melodies, attained worldwide popularity in the 1840s and 1850s. It was often said that Gottschalk became inspired to write his syncopated music by hearing the drums at Congo Square. As a boy, he spent weekend afternoons on the third-floor gallery of the family home, dancing to the sounds from down the street. Some versions say that Gottschalk was inspired by the virtuosity of Bras-Coupé. There were hundreds of voices on the plaza but "only one shout about which he could be sure" as there was "no mistaking" the sounds made by "Bras-Coupé." Skepticism eventually overwhelmed this story. There is no solid evidence corroborating its facts, and circumstances including the short duration the family lived in the house (most of which was spent out of town avoiding cholera) and the distance from the house to Congo Square (too far for the music to carry) have cast doubt on its veracity. In his own writings, Gottschalk never makes the link between his music and Congo Square. He also never associates Bras-Coupé with Congo Square, describing the fugitive only as a maroon who battled the police in the swamp. As with other cases, the fanciful connection between Gottschalk and Bras-Coupé appears to derive from Cable, who drew extensively upon the Gottschalk family's knowledge of creole music in writing on Congo Square. The Gottschalks never claimed that their songs were connected to Congo Square, but Cable borrowed them anyway to illustrate the traditions that would likely have been demonstrated in its performances.

He also frequently credited Gottschalk as his source. Improvising upon this retrospective association, it appears that enthusiasts imagined what they considered to be a likely scene on the third-floor gallery. Based on this fantasy, Gottschalk has been venerated for bringing the music of Congo Square to the Paris proletariat in 1848, where his international celebrity detonated with a public concert that introduced his show-stopping Bamboula. The third-floor gallery has also been portrayed as the setting for cultural appropriation, where Gottschalk is established to have stolen his music from slaves. Both interpretations, it seems, derive from *The Grandissimes*. If truth be told, it was not Gottschalk who took songs from Congo Square but Cable who took songs from Gottschalk to make the mythology of Congo Square.[52]

It has become less common than it once was to tell the story about the drums traveling into Buddy Bolden's ears, through his bronchial cavity, to his mouth, and then into his horn. It is a good story, but it cannot stand without its star witness. Even without Cable's first-hand testimony, variations on this story have persisted despite seemingly incontrovertible statements to the contrary by critics who have shown that Bolden never could have heard the drums because the dances were stopped decades before he was born. Even those critics who have dropped not only Bolden but the associated claim about jazz beginning at Congo Square have a hard time doing without the mystique that has become attached to the location. Here are the first seven sentences from Ted Gioia's *The History of Jazz* (1997):

> An elderly black man sits astride a large cylindrical drum. Using his fingers and the edge of his hand, he jabs repeatedly at the drum head—which is around a foot in diameter and probably made from an animal skin—evoking a throbbing pulsation with rapid, sharp strokes. A second drummer, holding his instrument between his knees, joins in, playing with the same staccato attack. A third black man, seated on the ground, plucks at a string instrument, the body of which is roughly fashioned from a calabash. Another calabash has been made into a drum, and a woman beats at it with two short sticks. One voice, then other voices join in. A dance of seeming contradictions accompanies this musical give-and-take, a moving hieroglyph that appears, on the one hand, informal and spontaneous yet, on closer inspection, ritualized and precise.

"The scene could be Africa," Gioia writes. "In fact, it is nineteenth-century New Orleans." As in Cable's essays, it is the structure of this passage that seals the impression of cultural identity. In the opening lines of the book, this scene at first appears without context, and the context supplied after the opening presentation is doubled by the conditional ("could"), which expresses not only the theoretical but the present possibility that these musicians could be in Africa rather than America. The identical scene could be happening on either continent. The fact that it is really happening in one place and not another counts for less than the fact, indicated by the modal auxiliary verb, that there is no way to tell where you are from inside the scene. This disorientation in space (for Gioia) and time (for Cable) is one of the peculiar properties that is imparted to the square as it is converted into myth. It is through this disorientation that the claim for identity—between performances, between peoples—is typically made. Daring readers to tell the difference between this scene and another possible scene somewhere else, Gioia seeks to demonstrate that the two scenes might as well be one for the purposes of the history he is writing. Noting that the force of diaspora is often approached as a "theoretical, almost metaphysical issue," Gioia argues that Congo Square remains fundamental to the history of jazz, because it has allowed historians to ground their claims for cultural continuity in a "real time and place." It is hard to reconcile this view of history with the contrivance that comes before it. Like Cable's direct address, Gioia's opening gambit seems less interested in its historical grounding than in dispensing with historical mediation altogether.[53]

It is in this respect that Gioia exemplifies the continuing influence of Congo Square inside histories of jazz. If Congo Square was created as a myth by misdating and misreading the writings of George Washington Cable, *The History of Jazz* shows how this myth sustains its influence even after it has been merged with the facts. It is possible, moreover, to track this enduring influence even as Bras-Coupé gradually disappears from the archive of jazz history. We first see Bras-Coupé named as the featured performer on the square soon after *The Grandissimes* was published. In *The Historical Sketch Book and Guide to New Orleans* (1885), which shows Cable as a contributor, tourist attention is directed to "Congo Square" where "a long time ago Bras-Coupé danced and sang." In 1936, Asbury says the same thing, naming Bras-Coupé as "one of the famous Bamboula dancers of the early days." The jazz historians who used Asbury as a main source, however, never mention Bras-Coupé by name despite his central-ity to *The French Quarter.* Some later writers recall one dancer who could "leap higher" and "shout louder" than the others, an oblique homage given without elaboration. In Gioia's history, Bras-Coupé is not named, but it can be demonstrated beyond a shadow of a doubt that he is still there.[54]

Bras-Coupé's disappearance from jazz history needs to be grasped as the realization, not the demise, of the revisions introduced by Cable. If Cable rewrote the legend to break its resistance to his vision for legal develop-ment, these historians go one step further by eliminating Bras-Coupé from their storyline altogether. When Cable began to argue in essays like "The Freedman's Case in Equity" (1885) for the formal equality of the ex-slave, his propositions were intensely controversial in the North as well as the South. By the 1940s and 1950s, however, these propositions were becoming increasingly mainstream, as historians began to conceive emancipation as the watershed at which the nation finally began to practice what it preached with regard to liberty and equality. Following Cable, it also be-came common to equate segregation with underdevelopment. Books such as C. Vann Woodward's *The Strange Career of Jim Crow* (1955) made it clear that racial discrimination was a sign of the southern failure to keep up with a national mainstream. These progressive assumptions about na-tional history were also structural to early jazz criticism, which praised the music for its "democratic spirit." Whereas the expansion of the franchise and equal protection from the law remained the standard measures for na-tional progress, jazz was seen as a cultural force for equality that some crit-ics argued had "done more" to advance the cause than the Thirteenth, Fourteenth, and Fifteenth Amendments combined. With Bras-Coupé out of the picture, there was nothing to keep these historians from claiming the music that started at Congo Square as the driving force for a narrative of national progress that was in many respects indistinguishable from Ca-ble's own. As with *The Grandissimes,* the mainspring of this narrative is its integration of law and culture. It is the anthropological approach to black tradition that makes jazz into the cultural property of a nation progressing toward racial equality. These critics departed from Cable in claiming this cultural inheritance as an American rather than an African legacy, but they never could have made this claim in the first place without the prece-dent that Cable established when he moved Bras-Coupé from Place d'Armes to Congo Square. If jazz history requires Congo Square as a sup-plement to complete the unbroken chain of cultural tradition, then Bras-

Coupé is the tradition's missing link, which must be repaired or recovered before it becomes possible to state that African music is America's music.[55]

Among the richest documents produced during this first burst of historical attention to the jazz tradition are autobiographical works such as Mezz Mezzrow's *Really the Blues* (1946), Louis Armstrong's *Satchmo* (1954), and *Mister Jelly Roll* (1950), the book shaped by Alan Lomax from the tape recordings he made with Jelly Roll Morton. And among the richest of these autobiographies is the dense, lyrical, and famously unreliable *Treat It Gentle* (1960), a book about the life and career of Sidney Bechet, who was one of the first important soloists in the jazz tradition. A prodigy who began playing with Bunk Johnson's group at the age of eleven, Bechet adopted the cornet, and then the clarinet, before moving primarily to the soprano saxophone. Renowned for his wide vibrato and his carefully formed but rhapsodic improvisation, Bechet began touring in his early twenties, living between Chicago and New York, and then moving to France in 1950 where he was acclaimed, for the first time in his career, as a genius on his instrument. It was in these secure later years that Bechet and his friends had the idea for *Treat It Gentle* and began assembling its text from Bechet's tape-recorded dictation and from notes jotted by his friend John Reid. Reworked initially by Joan Williams and then by the poet John Ciardi, *Treat It Gentle* was controversial from the moment that its first excerpts appeared in 1952. Bothered by a perceived stylistic excess and a conspicuous inclination to play fast and loose with the facts, Twayne, the book's first publisher, finally shelved the project. As a result, *Treat It Gentle* did not see print until after Bechet's death, when the heavily revised first edition was brought out in Britain by Cassell in 1960.[56]

More than any other musician in his day, Bechet sought to channel his life story through the myth of Congo Square. This was an act of creative appropriation. For some time, Bechet's career had been given support by stalwart traditionalists like Rudi Blesh, who believed that the only authentic jazz was the music played in the traditional style associated with New Orleans, which was purportedly opposed to modern variants, like swing, whose commercialism threatened to corrupt the purity of the tradition. These critics often pointed to Congo Square to explain what made for authenticity in a jazz performance. For Blesh and his cohort, the only real jazz was jazz that was connected to the music that had once happened there—so much so that Blesh was prepared to vouch, for instance, that he could detect the "communal song" from "Congo Square" rumbling inside the opening bars of a recording like "The Chant" from Jelly Roll Morton's Red Hot Peppers sessions. This was the highest praise from critics working in the 1940s to revive the early style of jazz, and Bechet was the perfect candidate for this type of enthusiasm as his style of playing had not evolved significantly since his youth. Bechet was still playing the real jazz, and he was glad to illustrate this point in his autobiography by drawing the line straight to Congo Square. Unlike the critics, Bechet does not summon this mythology to advocate for a particular style of music. He is not sectarian. The intent is not to make himself look good at someone else's expense. It is, rather, to meditate on tradition, authenticity, and the meaning of kinship.[57]

Bechet starts his story at Congo Square. Beginning not with the scene of his birth but with the setting where jazz was being born, Bechet begins this personal history of the music in a conventional way. "It was primitive and it was crude," Bechet admits. Nevertheless, this was how jazz started "in the music they played at Congo Square." The initial scenes of drumming and dancing in *Treat It Gentle* could be mistaken for similar scenes in other jazz histories from the time, except for one key difference. Unlike the other renditions of this origin story, *Treat It Gentle* restores Bras-Coupé to the center of the scene, making him once again into the leader of Congo Square. When the slaves met on Sunday, they gathered around Bras-Coupé, "waiting for him to start things: dances, shouts, moods even." Bechet repeats the claim made by Cable about the fugitive's prowess in the square, even taking things a step farther, making Bras-Coupé not only the leader of the dance but its point of origin. As Bechet describes him, Bras-Coupé is "always ahead of the music, because the music was there in his mind even before he got to the square and began performing it. It was *his* drum, *his* voice, *his* dancing." Bechet accents Bras-Coupé's priority to Congo Square first by repeating the familiar emphasis on natural leadership before turning this narrative priority into a claim about cultural property. Before jazz, there was Congo Square. Before Congo Square, there was Bras-Coupé. As Bechet tells the story, jazz is unleashed from a creative impulse that was already "there" in Bras-Coupé before he arrived at Congo Square.[58]

Bechet presses his luck even further with the amazing suggestion that Bras-Coupé was his own grandfather. "That square," Bechet trumpets, "it was my grandfather's square." Giving Bras-Coupé a new name—Omar—

for the purposes of his autobiography, Bechet is emphatic that his kinship with the outlaw is not the cultural kinship that all jazz players have with the patriarch who invented their music. Bechet is connected to Bras-Coupé by blood. "We are reminded of Alex Haley," Blesh writes in his 1978 preface to the book, "as Sidney's memory takes us back to Omar, who heard in a dream his ancestral music in faraway Africa." Reading black tradition according to a bloodline rather than a cultural inheritance does not settle the problem that others sought to solve when they looked to Congo Square. On the contrary, it intensifies the problem. The problem of origins that was being covered in other historical writings through myth becomes deeper and more complex as soon as Bras-Coupé is readmitted to the tradition. Repeating his desire to "get back" as close as possible to the beginning of jazz, Bechet confirms that Omar is as "far" as he can go. "My grandfather," he determines, "that's about the furthest I can remember back. My grandfather was a slave."[59]

By writing Bras-Coupé back into the history of jazz, *Treat It Gentle* presses against the cultural framework it inherits from critics like Rudi Blesh who were advancing the myth of Congo Square in their writings. But we need to be clear about the nature of this resistance. It would be a mischaracterization to describe this resistance as a well-formed purpose on Bechet's part, pitting Bechet against Blesh as if Bechet were Frederick Douglass and Blesh were William Lloyd Garrison. By all accounts, Bechet had no complaints against Blesh or his varied collaborators in this project. He thought that Blesh paid his musicians well, and he was happy to profit from the revivalist orientation that Blesh advocated in his writings and his radio show. The resistance in *Treat It Gentle* should be deciphered, not as determined opposition, but instead as the involuntary remembrance of rudiments from the Bras-Coupé legend that could not be assimilated by the framework for jazz history that critics like Blesh inherited from Cable. When Bechet decides to put this framework to use in narrating the story of his life, the results are fascinating, as elements from the legend's opening cycle are forced into the frame that Cable devised in his novel. At its most pointed, Bechet's rendition speaks to issues left unresolved by his contemporaries. What does it mean to find, as the absence at the origin of jazz history, a slave maimed by the police? What would it mean to write a history of jazz that includes Bras-Coupé?

Bechet starts his autobiography by accepting the much-vaunted first article of faith in jazz history—the idea that the music started at Congo

Square—only to complicate its received form by reviving the fugitive whose absence had become necessary to its integrity. Revising Cable's revision of the legend, Bechet moves the interpolated climax at Congo Square to the start of the story, alluding to its established role in jazz history. After the panoramic opening, Bras-Coupé leaves Congo Square never to return. As the plot moves forward in time, the legend moves backward in the history of its own evolution, peeling away the layers of narrative that had accumulated following its initial cycle. Returning to the cypress swamp, Bechet narrates the manhunt for Bras-Coupé in a manner that reveals many details from the first cycle that had been covered by accretions from Cable's novel: the "declaration" of outlawry, the "big reward," the "posses working out in all directions," the "wanted posters," the "dogs working the bayou all day long trying to pick up a trail." All of these details come back under the auspices of Bechet's invented genealogy.[60]

The most vital of these details is the loss of the arm. Omar starts at Congo Square with both arms intact (as in *The Grandissimes*) only to lose his arm and flee to the cypress swamp. There he joins the maroons who had been earlier evacuated from their territory after the revisions formed by Cable. Like Cable, Bechet concocts his own love story—in this case, featuring a jealous master—to bridge the plot points left by oral tradition. In *Treat It Gentle*, it is the jealous rival who shoots Omar in the arm. Of all the aspects brought back by Bechet, it is the arm that leaves the most conspicuous stress mark. Whenever Bechet starts to speak about the arm, he interrupts himself. "But I'm ahead of myself here," he says at one point about the arm, swerving back into the main line of plot development. The arm's absence eventually proves essential to his characterization of his grandfather, but references to the arm are always out of place in the story, as Bechet fumbles to find the point where they fit into the mythology of cultural inheritance that has been handed down to him by Cable. The arm always arrives too soon or too late. As Bechet never knows the right time to say what needs to be said about the arm, there are false starts across the book, such as the following:

> He'd have these dreams about things. There was one time he
> had a dream about his right arm, about losing it at the elbow.
> After that, he'd only practice shooting with his left hand. But
> maybe that don't belong here. What I'm saying is that he was a
> musician. No one had to explain notes or rhythm or feeling to

him. It was always there inside him, something he was always
sure of. All the things that was happening to him outside, they
had to get there to be measured—there inside him where the
music was.

If the general pattern of hesitation and uncertainty about mentioning the
loss of the arm communicates the incident's resistance to the narrative
framework inherited from Cable, in this specific instance, Bechet embraces this resistance as an opportunity to bring back something else from
the first cycle: the premonition of the arm's amputation. When it is presented in the first cycle, this portent has a decided purpose. It interrupts
the moment when the law names the fugitive by proposing that Bras-
Coupé already knew his name before it was given to him. It implies, in
other words, that there is something mysterious about the fugitive's point
of view that cannot be explicated in relation to the law. When the premonition is repeated by Bechet, the first thing we can see is that this primary
resistance survives inside the autobiography, whether the book wants it to
or not, posing a problem for the story that Bechet starts to tell about patri-
mony and the cultural goods that he has inherited from his grandfather.
The nature of this problem is dramatized when Bechet interrupts himself
to locate the premonition within an explanatory framework where it does
not belong. The surge of doubt that stutters the arm's return ("maybe that
don't belong here") occasions a discourse upon innate musicianship. This
discourse repeats Cable's translation of the phantom perspective produced from missing arm into a fantasy of innate musical capacity. Blackness slides from a register where it is a remainder of violence to a register
where it is instead characterized, on the model inherited from Cable, as
an intrinsic property of cultural practice.[61]

Replaying almost a century of the legend's development in a few sentences, this non sequitur redacts what Bechet is "saying" from the moment it is said. But the legend backslides into this discourse on natural
musicianship only to embark on a dialectical emergence that integrates
the music on the "inside" with things happening "outside." If this passage
accepts "inside" as the familiar location for musical inspiration, this formulation is complicated as the missing arm becomes the principal occasion for the performance of interiority. Following the pattern in the opening
cycle of the legend, Bechet accepts the loss of the arm as an opportunity
to explore Omar's subjective relationship to his injury. The flickering that

occurs in the early versions when Bras-Coupé is given speech with magical properties, or knowledge that he could never know, is developed in Bechet's autobiography by employing novelistic techniques for establishing psychological depth through self-contradiction and the withholding of expression. Bechet uses these techniques to turn the arm into a prism for identification. When Omar is on the run and his wound starts "giving him trouble," he trusts the "hurt of it" as "a thing to hold on to, a way of knowing what was real." When Omar arrives at the maroon encampment, an identification is formed around the injury. "There was no need of explanation," Bechet writes, adding his own touch to the legend. "Everybody back there, he had his own reason for being there, and every reason it explained every other somehow. . . . He just showed them his arm, and everyone understood everything."[62]

As far as we can tell, Omar's arrival at the maroon camp is a scene that happens for the first time in Bechet. It does not surface in any other versions of the legend. This evident innovation is in the spirit of the other alterations made by Bechet. The steady attention to Omar's thoughts and feelings is what makes *Treat It Gentle* so distinctive in relation to its precursors, where the outlaw's perspective is blurred through primitivism (as in *The Grandissimes*) or structurally barred from consideration (as in the police campaign that launched the first cycle of the legend). Only in the oral tradition are there obvious precedents for the perspective that emerges as the earliest center of consciousness in the autobiography. If the legend's original narrators can be heard as throwing their voices to assume a perspective that had been rendered impossible by the police campaign, Bechet achieves a similar outcome in his writing through different means. The autobiography is reported by Bechet in the first person, but in retelling the legend, the narrative is quick to name the fugitive as its protagonist and to channel emotional intensity into its protagonist's point of view. There are words in the chapter (like "jazz") that Omar never would have used, but the bulk of the prose is focalized from his perspective, meaning that it is narrated not in his own voice but from an objective third-person perspective ("Omar") that is tuned into his thinking and generally constrained to facts that he would have known in the moment. The history behind this strategy is evident when we realize that this focalized perspective is entirely continuous with the perspective that emerged, like a phantom limb, when Bras-Coupé was voiced by his first generation of narrators.

Bechet too resists the police, not by proclaiming his own broadside against their entitlement to firearms, but instead by speaking back to their campaign from the perspective that their rhetoric was attempting to write out of history.[63]

It is fitting in this connection to remember that the police were using the missing arm specifically as a code for dangerous masculinity, a code that was designed to communicate both the fugitive's lack of masculinity as well as his melodramatic overcompensation for that lack. In response, Bechet witnesses Omar's manliness in his capacity to propagate a family—the proof for which is Bechet's existence as the legend's narrator. It is the romance between Omar and an enslaved woman named Marie that begins the patriarchal line whose succession is narrated in the later chapters. The romance comes to completion not within the legend but in the relation between the legend and its frame, a relationship that is recast as a blood connection between its present narrator (Sidney Bechet) and its protagonist (Omar) whose genealogy cuts across the enclosure that Cable uses to convey the legend's obsolescence. In *The Grandissimes*, there is a logical distance between the legend and the setting where it is told. We can evaluate the force of history by the distance that the plot puts (or fails to put) between itself and the legend. In *Treat It Gentle*, this distance is continually bridged by the line of descent that Bechet draws between himself and Bras-Coupé.

We have already observed that this family lineage forms not only Bechet's life story but his history of jazz. "If you're a musicianer," Bechet pronounces, then it is "grandfather's song" that "you're singing." It was Omar who "started the song" that every jazz player has "been singing . . . ever since." Having once repeated the truism that the music comes from Congo Square, Bechet never looks back. He does, however, continue to consider what it means to put an outlaw at the music's origin, converting the inexpressible assumption behind Cable's translation of the legend into the central theme for investigation in his own version. In the process, Bechet creates a new origin story from the raw materials that were available to him. As the patrols cover the swamp in the manhunt for Omar, Bechet describes not only the predicament faced by the fugitives who had been "hiding out in the bayou for all kinds of time" without having to face this kind of difficulty, but also by the slaves back in the city whose regimen changed for the worse as their masters turned increasingly nervous and irritable. "The slaves felt a trouble on them," Bechet writes:

Nights, they was talking low to themselves, trying superstitions to keep away more evil, keeping under cover, trying to stay out of the white man's way. And days, they had their trouble on them. The overseers were being more cruel; the meals had less food to them; the work, they made it harder and there was more and more whip behind it. There was a whole lot more slaves getting beatings these days. The only thing they had that couldn't be taken from them was their music. Their song, it was coming right up from the fields, settling itself in their feet and working right up, right up into their stomachs, their spirit, into their fear, into their longing. It was bewildered, this part of them. It was like it had no end, nowhere even to wait for an end, nowhere to hope for a change in things. But it had a beginning, and that much they understood . . . it was a feeling in them, a memory that came from a long way back. It was like they were trying to work the music back to its beginning and then start it over again, start it over and build it to a place where it could stop somehow, to a place where the music could put an end to itself and become another music, a new beginning that could begin them over again. There were chants and drums and voices—you could hear all that in it—and there was love and work and worry and waiting; there was being tired, and the sun, and the overseers following behind them so they didn't dare stop and look back. It was all in the music.

With a gesture that only becomes imaginable after the previous stages in the legend's development are sketched, this passage finds a new origin for the jazz tradition in the manhunt for Bras-Coupé. Here the historical violence that had been scrubbed from the origin story for the black tradition returns as its unavoidable context: the music rises up from the fields as a retort to the aggression experienced by the slaves by virtue of their involuntary association with Omar. During this meditation, the passage pushes the jazz tradition to a place where it can no longer be plotted according to simple trajectories with clear beginnings and endings. For Bechet, the music expresses an experience of history that refuses the consolation of progress, a feeling that pools instead in feet and stomachs, that suspends time's animation by decomposing its development into longing, waiting, and worry. If history's telos is unavailable, its beginning is not so much known as felt, like the unseen authority of the "overseers following" so closely that these slaves do not "dare stop and look back." By relocating the music's genesis in the violence suffered by these slaves, Bechet revives the question of black tradition enclosed by the myth of Congo Square. Though this substitution injects violence into the very nature of black identity, it also presents the possibility of its unmaking by readmitting the history that must be confronted before freedom is possible. For Bechet, the only way to find the ending for the history of blackness is to start the story over again, rewinding not to a mythical time before history but to the historical setting of slavery.[64]

Bechet's discomfort with the received wisdom about the jazz tradition does not stop there. Even as he hears the violence in the music, he also hears the music evading the violence at its source, starting itself over again, imagining for itself a new ending that is not determined by its onset. He hears the music's beginning in violence, and he knows its struggle to transcend its history. This is the paradox that Bechet sometimes describes as the music's desire to "put an end to itself," or at other times as a desire to "become another music." By naming the threat of slavery's violence as the threat of being beaten in place of Bras-Coupé and then turning that threat into the predication for black music, Bechet opens questions closed by the common understanding of where jazz comes from. Foremost in his mind is the uncertainty about the music's association with blackness. For Bechet, Bras-Coupé holds a key to this question as his legend enfolds a centuries-long argument over what it means to be black, an argument whose stakes are obscured by the appeal to mythical origin. Writing Bras-Coupé back into jazz tradition, Bechet begins a recursive encounter with the music's conditions of possibility. He inches his way into the corners of the archive, retrieving the parts that resist translation into the standard idiom of cultural retention. He pushes into the smallest cracks, the unspoken details, the parts where translation fails, making them into points of articulation where music connects to a history of struggle. In the process, he comes to terms with a core paradox: what defies translation are not those elements most distant in time but those most contemporary. He finds, in other words, that what remains untranslated in the black tradition is its foundation in law. The absences he discovers are precisely those aspects of the tradition that produce his kinship with Bras-Coupé—a kinship predicated not upon the ceremonial continuity of cultural tradition but rather upon the black tradition's negative relation to the law that withholds its name. No longer immured to a progressive narrative where folkways inevitably give way to stateways, Bechet means what he says when he declares, "My grandfather, he was Africa"—a tight phrase that cements the substitution of "Bras-Coupé" for "Africa" in the history of jazz.[65]

There is a strong affinity between Bechet's theory of jazz and the theory that Nathaniel Mackey presents in his *Bedouin Hornbook* (1986), a book that starts with the idea of music as a "phantom limb." For Mackey, this trope names music's capacity to create "a feeling for what's not there." It is a trope that figures as well music's emergence from a situation "in which feeling, consciousness itself, would seem to have been cut off." Music haunts its listeners and its players, writes Mackey, by holding itself apart from the conditions under which it is made—by establishing a feeling for consciousness and connection, that is to say, which by all rights should not be possible. Mackey does not mention Bechet in this formulation, but that does not change the fact that this proposition is about as good a gloss on *Treat It Gentle* as we are likely to get. Not only does Mackey summarize the complexity of the book's kinship claim, he circumscribes the claim in a way that stipulates exactly what Bechet does *not* propose to say through Bras-Coupé. For Bechet, as for Mackey, music is made through alienation. It does not revive a wholeness that has been broken; it embraces brokenness as the reason for its existence and as the only available basis for its "claim to connection."[66]

Mackey is implicitly departing from the prescription that Frantz Fanon furnishes in the famous conclusion to his "L'expérience vécue du noir" (1951), where being black is analogized to losing an arm. Fanon objects to the end of the film *Home of the Brave* (1949), where a black veteran is told by an associate who has lost an arm that it was best to "resign" himself to his race just as the associate had gotten used to his stump. "Nevertheless," Fanon reacts, "with all my strength I refuse to accept that amputation." Among other things, Fanon's refusal is formed as an intervention into the discourse on phantom limbs in Maurice Merleau-Ponty's *Phenomenology of Perception* (1945), which holds that the appropriate way for the amputee to recoup a feeling of personal relation to the world is to accept or trust the phantom part that is felt in the place of the lost limb. Fanon objects to the potential analogy to blackness on grounds that blackness locks its victims into their bodies in a way that bars the potential for self-conscious existence, whether the condition is accepted or not. For Fanon, the path to disalienation begins by rejecting the false consolation offered by the amputee in the veteran's hospital. Though Fanon and Mackey share some ideas about the alienation implied by the trope of amputation, they differ in most other ways. Mackey's thoughts about music as "crippled speech" are very different from the "authentic upheaval" that Fanon prescribes. This divergence is important for Bras-Coupé—both in the sense that it puts a finer point on the question of whether alienation can be overcome, and in the sense that it reopens the legend's critique of violence, which looks like a condition for blackness but not a guarantee of its unmaking.[67]

In many recent histories where Omar is mentioned, critics have maintained, or more specifically have taken for granted, that Omar is a real person. It has long been known that Bechet's paternal grandfather, a free creole named Jean Bechet, was a carpenter, but that has not kept critics, from Rudi Blesh to Martin Williams to Whitney Balliet, from taking Bechet at his word regarding his grandfather, the "great natural musician" who played at Congo Square. For Gioia, it is Omar that compensates for Buddy Bolden's absence from the square. Gioia observes that "traditional accounts" propose that the dances lasted "until around 1885," a "chronology" that suggests that their "disappearance almost coincided with the emergence of the first jazz bands." Gioia begrudgingly admits that "recent research argues for an earlier cutoff date," but he does not bother to mention that the original assumption of a continuous chronology is based upon the misdating of Cable's observations, nor does he mention Bras-Coupé's auxiliary role in the process. But one sentence later, before Gioia has to come to terms with the implications of the earlier cutoff date, Bras-Coupé returns to the narrative. No matter when the dances ended, Gioia declares that the "transplanted African ritual" at the square survived in "collective memory." The evidence for this collective memory is taken from *Treat It Gentle*. "My grandfather, that's about the furthest I can remember back," Gioia quotes Bechet as saying. Memory's implication in this instance hinges on whether we see Omar as an actual person—as Gioia apparently does—or as a legend selected by Bechet to rethink the history of jazz. Once the tale about Buddy Bolden listening to the drums at Congo Square is discredited, a gap opens in jazz history, and it is Gioia's aim to fill this gap by making the connection between Omar and his grandson into the model for the cultural continuity that is fostered by the operation of collective memory.[68]

In recent decades, Omar has also anchored new theories about the cultural compass of the African diaspora. In *The Power of Black Music* (1995),

Samuel Floyd introduces Omar at the outset as the organizing principle for his claims about "cultural memory." Floyd says that the memory in black music "goes back beyond Omar and the slave experience in America to Africa." In language that is completely in tune with Cable's concept of culture, he asserts that the function of this musical memory is to preserve the "mysteries of myth and the trappings of ritual" once they are "no longer functional" in society. Floyd starts thinking about all the people—like Buddy Bolden—who took the music away from Congo Square, citing "preachers" and "conductors on the Underground Railroad" as early carriers and asserting that whenever and wherever these carriers "sang Omar's song" that "all African Americans sang it with them, for Omar's song is a subliminal song, heard by all African Americans who possess the memory." George Lewis similarly conjures "the lesson of 'Omar's Song'" as a context for hearing the Great Black Music made under the auspices of the Association for the Advancement of Creative Musicians (AACM) since 1965. "As people travel, their utterances, their sounds—their musics—move with them, just as Omar's song came with him from Africa and was handed down to his grandson Sidney," Lewis writes, using Bechet to gloss the Art Ensemble of Chicago. Omar, for Lewis, both parallels and proves Lester Bowie's idea that the ensemble's music went back "thousands of years." For Lewis, as for Floyd, Omar is the way to reconnect jazz to Africa, and reconnecting jazz to Africa is the antidote to alienation in America. It is this kinship connection that says where the music has been and what it will become.[69]

By pointing out this misreading, I am not arguing against the kinship that Bechet claims with Bras-Coupé. To the contrary, I am arguing for the truth of this claim, and for the fact that this truth does not need to be sustained by fictions framed in the language of genetics, or cultural property, or continuous contact. To believe in this kinship, we do not have to restore the absent arm as a token of a lost wholeness that might one day be restored. Nor do we have to accept the patriarchal premise that is common to the competing narratives of descent written not only by Sidney Bechet but also by Jelly Roll Morton and W. C. Handy. In Bechet's case, as in the others, the irony is that the claim to connection reveals its meaning only when it is not taken seriously. We need to hear the claim as a claim, in other words, and not as a report of a bloodline, before we can begin to hear Bechet throwing his voice in the style of the legend's first generation of narrators. Treating Omar as somebody related to Bechet by blood, and therefore as an actual person, decontextualizes the gesture that is made in *Treat It Gentle* by abstracting it from the earlier cycles in the legend. The claim's meaning is about its historicity. We cannot hear the claim as a claim without also hearing the echo of Bras-Coupé's dying words from *The Grandissimes*: "To Africa." You have to know that Bechet repeats these words to know how he articulates the historical consciousness in the black tradition. The echo of "To Africa" in *Treat It Gentle* is the theme against which Bechet invents an ancestry for jazz. When Blesh, in *Shining Trumpets*, scoffs at musicians who say that jazz has no African provenance, he anticipates Bechet. "This is like saying," Blesh proposes, " 'I am related to my father but not to my grandfather.' " Yet the seeming impossibility of not being related to your own grandfather is exactly what we need to be willing to contemplate in order to understand *Treat It Gentle*. "My grandfather, he was Africa," Bechet says, and in saying so, cites in the strictest sense what kinship means.[70]

3

UNCLE REMUS AND THE
ATLANTA POLICE DEPARTMENT

Folklore collection was professionalized in the United States during the 1880s and 1890s. In the summer of 1887, letters were circulated proposing an academic society exclusively dedicated to the collection and preservation of the "fast-vanishing remains" of "unwritten traditions" and "rude customs" in the United States. The idea evidently struck a chord. In January 1888, the American Folklore Society held its first meeting at Harvard, with Francis James Child presiding, and the *Journal of American Folklore* published its first issue that April. From the start, the society was able to promote an "esprit de corps" that according to its members had never before existed among antiquarians in the United States. It was largely due to this new-found camaraderie, and the institutional networks it fostered, that ethnographic documentation of the black tradition finally reached critical mass. Attention to black songmaking and storytelling had always been scattershot until these decades, when it was pursued systematically for the first time by collectors who believed they were racing the clock in their effort to salvage the tradition before it was gone for good. This professional interest in black folklore was informed by intellectual precedents going all the way back to Herder and the Grimms, but its immediate inspiration came from Joel Chandler Harris, an editor at the *Atlanta Constitution* who began to produce a weekly column called "Uncle Remus's Folk-Lore" in 1879. Most of Harris's columns were republished as *Uncle Remus, His Songs and His Sayings* (1880), a book that quickly achieved international renown. Although these sketches have been remembered mostly as phenomenally popular children's literature, it is important to recall as well their formative influence upon the transcription of black tradition. There was no doubt in the American Folklore Society that the Uncle Remus stories had "scientific worth." This consensus was apparent all the way from Harris's earliest review in the *New York Times*, which credited him with "the first real book of American folk lore," to his canonization in *The Cambridge History of English and American Literature* (1907–1921), which summarized the long-standing certainty that it was Uncle Remus who "laid the foundation for the scientific study of negro folk-lore." For the *Cambridge History*, the "ethnological value" of the Uncle Remus writings could not be overstated, as it was their enduring achievement to have "typified a race" and therefore "perpetuated a vanishing civilization."[1]

During these decades, there was a surge of enthusiasm for the talking-animal tales exemplified in Harris's fieldwork, and there was keen interest in his handling of black dialect. Ironically, Harris's greatest influence came not from his folklore collection but from the characterization of his native informant. Uncle Remus may have been a fiction, but he was without question the most famous black storyteller in his day, and his preeminence in the minds of collectors made him structurally important to the science of folklore study as it was being professionalized. Collectors went into the field admitting their intention to locate their "own" Uncle Remus in Mississippi, in Jamaica, in the Bahamas, or in the Sudan. But Harris's influence extended beyond those who identified Uncle Remus as their patron saint to the discipline at large, where the early debates over the composition of black culture were necessarily organized around the archive that Harris established, by far the largest of its kind, and necessarily influenced by the framework that Harris invented to explain the folktales that he gathered together. A new generation of collectors frequently summoned Uncle Remus by name in their arguments against the old thinking that said primitive societies had no culture other than the bits and pieces they inherited from neighboring civilizations. Similarly, we can see this new generation trying out arguments, and sometimes even anticipating later anthropological thinking about cultural relativism and intercultural exchange, during the prolonged controversy over the geographical origin of the tales. A great deal hinged upon where the Uncle Remus tales came from—Europe, South America, Asia, Africa—including whether such a thing as "culture" could even have come from Africa. Harris would eventually absent himself from these debates, which are parodied at several points in his later writings, but from 1880 to 1883, he was dedicated to making as strong a case as possible for an African origin. The case remained controversial well into the second half of the next century, and it is good to recognize the extent to which the claim for cultural retentions preserved, across its many permutations, specific steps from Harris's early and influential argument. Long before Melville Herskovits began the research that would become *The Myth of the Negro Past* (1941), the retentions argument was associated with Joel Chandler Harris and even more often with Uncle Remus himself. In his *Fetichism in West Africa* (1904), the self-styled sociologist Robert Hamill Nassau presents the claim as if it required no elaboration. "Uncle Remus's mystic tales," he comments, "are the folk-lore that the slave brought with him from his African home." More than a case in point, Remus communicates *the* folk-lore that made the Middle Passage. Embodying the "survival of African life in America," Uncle Remus was the antidote to the assumption that said the ex-slave had no culture at all.[2]

From the beginning, Harris took it for granted that the tales came from Africa and that they were gradually tailored to the world of slavery as they were passed down through generations. Harris did not have to think too hard about this proposition until it was challenged by professional folklorists who suggested, to the contrary, that the tales told by Uncle Remus were borrowed from American Indians. Provoked by this opposition and by the sudden interest in his work, Harris bought a number of folklore books and subscribed to the *Folk-Lore Journal* from Britain. Though Harris would eventually renounce these professional interests, the critical introductions for *Uncle Remus, His Songs and His Sayings* (1880) and *Nights with Uncle Remus* (1883) tried to introduce this new field of study to the general reader, devoting particular attention to the controversy over the origin of the tales. The controversy commenced with a letter from John Wesley Powell, the head of the Smithsonian Bureau of Ethnology. Powell wrote Harris to tell him about the ethnological importance of the tales told by Uncle Remus and to inform him that the tales were borrowed. Powell remembered some of the tales told by Remus from his fieldwork among the Paiute, explaining that he had no idea that the tales were also told by slaves until he discovered Remus in the *Constitution*. The dispute widened when other scholars began to notice similarities between Remus's storytelling and the tortoise myths collected by Charles Hartt among the Amazonians in Brazil. Harris was glad to acknowledge these connections, but he was also insistent that the tales were invented by slaves. Writing for the *Constitution* in April 1880, Harris drifted between skepticism and sarcasm, listing the "perplexing" and "interesting" issues raised by Powell, among them the matter of language and the restricted potential for "intimacy" between two races whose "tendencies" were so strongly opposed.[3]

Despite his awkward generalizations about racial psychology ("The Indian is reserved and the negro is talkative") and his faulty guesswork about interracial contact ("Has any such intimacy ever existed?"), Harris was surprisingly informed about current thinking in folklore, considering how quickly he came up to speed. Anatomizing the arguments, he was even ready to concede that there was reason for additional research into the origin of the tales. But that was as far as he was willing to go. He remained cynical about what the research would yield:

> It is to be remembered that in some instances, after certain myths have been traced to what is supposed to be a satisfactory origin in one race, they have been discovered to be identical with myths common among a people so remote that contact and transmission are not to be thought of. Similarly, some curious person professes to have traced our whole system of religion to India; so that if investigation as to the origin of affairs proceeds as successfully hereafter as it has heretofore, we shall presently discover that there is nothing modern but antiquity, and that the romances of Uncle Remus are merely modifications of dime novels composed by a desperate Chinese professor millions and millions of years ago.

Harris compares the argument for a non-African origin for Uncle Remus to the philological discovery that the whole family of Indo-European languages developed from Sanskrit. As this thinking was popularized in the late nineteenth century, some scholars even claimed that they could pinpoint on a map the source for all the world's cultures. Harris apparently has in mind the more extravagant variations on this thinking when he lampoons the curious professionals whose search for origins leads them not only to conflate the world's religions but to confuse antiquity for modernity and China for Africa. Harris believes in the difference between traditional and modern culture, but when he breaches this difference, it is more than mere bluster. The Chinese professor is meant to appear absurd but still conceivable as a prescient anomaly in world history. The first movable-type printing press was made in China in 1040; its products were never mass marketed, but there is something about its skipping over the European trajectory that is caught and given a twist when its artifacts are identified as dime novels. If the trope takes a familiar tack in turning China into a society where modernity and barbarism coexist, it also alludes to a contemporary body of scholarship by philologists like Theodor Benfey, who articulated their arguments for an Asian background for European folklore by analogizing the unconstrained flow of oral tradition across continental boundaries to the mercurial transmissibility of print.[4]

When Harris talks about Uncle Remus deriving from an ancient dime novel, he is referring to real positions that were being taken by real philologists, but obviously, his aim is to ridicule the new thinking on cultural diffusion. Scholars like Benfey were getting increasing attention as it was discovered again and again that people belonging to different nations, speaking separate languages, were telling the same stories. The realization that African Americans and Amazonian Indians had culture in common was only one of the many discoveries in the late nineteenth century, generally facilitated by imperialism, that resisted the common assumption that folklore expressed national character. These discoveries led to a new comparative paradigm that envisioned folklore as disconnected from race and nation, an approach that culminated with grand synthetic studies like Sir James George Frazer's *The Golden Bough* (1890). This was a paradigm that rejected the old assumption, inherited from Herder and the Grimms, that every nation had its own tradition (or "folk spirit") that communicated its history and conserved its identity over time. Scholars such as Harris, who remained true to romantic nationalism, continued to assert, contrary to the diffusionists, that folklore remained intact as it moved from place to place. When folklore moved, it followed the people to whom it belonged. Its transmission was diasporic and therefore discernible, across time and space, on the model of heredity. Forced to leave their home, people took their folklore with them, forging a lifeline that tied them to the place they left behind. Harris's tone is different, but otherwise he takes this standard line in binding Remus to Africa through folklore.[5]

As folklorists were professionalizing their new research program during the 1880s and 1890s, Uncle Remus remained a hot topic. The debate over the origin of the tales, which began with Powell's letter to Harris in 1880, was formative for the field. It was the matter most often discussed in the early issues of the *Journal of American Folklore* where it became the lynchpin for theoretical interest in cultural circulation. It did not matter which side you were on, whether you were for diffusion or diaspora, you still had to prove that your methods could account for Uncle Remus. Though research by scholars like James Mooney continued to flow from the Bureau of American Ethnology, making the argument that African Americans had learned these tales from American Indians, diffusionists also began to look elsewhere for origins. Articles such as "Uncle Remus and Some European Popular Tales" (1890) and "Uncle Remus Traced to the Old World" (1893) preferred European sources, often the medieval story cycle about Reynard the Fox, whereas others held that the tales were incubated in the Orient. Joseph Jacobs, the editor at the London-based *Folklore*, argued in his *Indian Fairy Tales* (1892) that "The Wonderful Tar-Baby Story" derived from another tale called "The Demon with the Matted Hair," which he believed was brought from India to Africa by Buddhist missionaries before it was transmitted through the slave trade to the New World. No matter where these arguments turned, they retained the same theoretical stakes. If the legends told by Uncle Remus could be shown to come from somewhere other than Africa, then the strong claim about their connection to racial identity, made by collectors like Harris, did not hold. If you could discover Remus's ancestors in Europe or Asia, then there was no correlation between culture and race.[6]

Uncle Remus also played a starring role in the opposing argument. Tracing the lines of the diaspora, writers went to work looking for analogues to the Uncle Remus tales wherever there were people of African descent. With a frequency that outstripped their diffusionist colleagues, these collectors found tales that were "akin" to those told by Uncle Remus in South Africa, Jamaica, Sudan, Cuba, Angola, the Bahamas, South Carolina, Sierra Leone, the Cape Verde Islands, Hausaland, Louisiana, and Cameroon. Some were even prepared to admit that they embarked on their journeys hoping to locate people who looked like Uncle Remus, and they seem to have had a surprising success rate. Others created their own conceits, putting the stuff they collected into the mouths of fictional storytellers with names like Aunt 'Phrony and Old Jason, using these characters, as Harris used their prototype, to ease readers into the tales. Others, like David Wells in his "Evolution in Folklore" (1892), interpreted the variants that accumulated as the tales traveled from Africa to Atlanta as an index to the "history of the race." The professional organizations where Remus was being debated with such enthusiasm were dominated by white scholars, when they were not for whites only, but Remus was also essential to black folklorists like Fred Wheelock, Robert Russa Moton, Rosa Hunter, Portia Smiley, Charles Herbert, Vascar Barnette, and Charles Flagg.

Working under the auspices of the Hampton Folklore Society and publishing their research each month in the "Folk-lore and Ethnology" column in the *Southern Workman*, these collectors produced an extensive archive that has been mined by twentieth-century historians, like Lawrence Levine, for the story it tells about the black tradition after slavery. Harris is named more often than any other folklorist in the research program followed by Hampton scholars, which proposed to emulate both his approach and his commitment to the conceptualization of folk expression as "the chain that connects the American with the African Negro."[7]

It is sometimes forgotten that Uncle Remus was taken so seriously by the generation of social scientists that laid the groundwork for modern thinking about race and culture. Skepticism about the demeaning characterization of Uncle Remus and the cultural authenticity of his repertoire was being expressed as early as the 1910s and 1920s, but it was not until the release of Walt Disney's *Song of the South* (1946) that Uncle Remus was widely seen as a phony character whose obedience and obsequiousness evidenced the face-to-face indignities that blacks had been forced to endure at the hands of whites since the onset of slavery. As the civil rights movement gathered momentum, Uncle Remus became conjoined with Uncle Tom in the minds of critics whose stated purpose was to liberate black readers from the destructive stereotypes imposed by white writers like Harris. Building on Sterling Brown's landmark study, *The Negro in American Fiction* (1937), critics began to pick apart these stereotypes while delving into the historical lacunae that formed Remus's character from the start, focusing in particular on how its deficiencies were intensified in the film. Whatever the demerits of *Song of the South*, we need to recognize now that one of its effects has been to obscure Remus's enduring influence on prevailing theories of black tradition, in particular those theories that would describe the tradition as a cultural inheritance from Africa. To understand these theories, we must discern that Uncle Remus was not a last-minute additive to the black tradition, like an artificial sweetener, but instead an indispensable ingredient that has structured the archive through which the tradition has been imagined. Reading Uncle Remus this way, we can see better his contribution to the modern declension of the race concept, a declension that we have already begun to demarcate through Bras-Coupé and the range of origin stories for jazz and blues. In this case, as before, our aim is to show not only the difference that Remus made to the new thinking on black culture, but also the difference that the new thinking on black culture made to the theory and practice of statecraft as it developed after slavery.[8]

It is well known that Harris had his own thoughts about the political function of folklore, and it is important to take his thoughts seriously for their own sake and for the influence they have exercised over generations of critics. Following the early cues left by Harris, critics have assumed that Uncle Remus was meant to serve a purpose, which was to assist in national reconciliation after the Civil War. Fifteen years after Lee surrendered at Appamattox, Uncle Remus is said to have brokered the lasting ceasefire that permitted the southern states to win the peace by occupying the hearts and minds of northern readers. In contemporary reviews, there was more-or-less outright agreement that Remus offered a "better method" for settling the conflict than "all the political platforms or merely legal enactments that American statesmanship has yet devised." Along with contemporaries like Irwin Russell, Harris was responsible for converting nostalgia for slavery into the main cultural avenue for national reconciliation. Remus's initial folklore sketches were set after emancipation, but they were still said to preserve, as if in a museum, "the negro as he existed before the war." The talking-animal tales narrated by Remus were advertised as remnants from this bygone time, but Remus was dated most effectively by the quaintness of his characterization in the frame. It was his closeness and his deference to his employers that readers appeared to have in mind when they praised the sketches in these terms. The mood of this reading has changed, especially as critics have come to realize that this reconciliation came primarily at the expense of the ex-slave, but its structure has stayed the same. Critics have continued to appraise the social utility of the tales with terms inherited from Harris, arguing that Remus was responsible for convincing northern elites that southern whites knew best how to manage their former slaves. As northern commitment faltered and Reconstruction wound to its premature conclusion, a downward spiral began that saw ex-slaves and their descendents disfranchised, segregated, swindled, and murdered with impunity. We can still argue about the textual details in the tales, but given the overwhelming evidence, it is hard to deny the force behind this common reading of their early reception.[9]

When critics interpret the sketches this way, they tend to start by considering the backstory in which Harris appears to declare his intentions. When Harris put together his first book, he returned to a sketch he had published in October 1877 and rewrote its conclusion. As printed in the *Constitution*, "Uncle Remus as a Rebel" involves Remus telling about the time during the war when he shot and killed a Yankee soldier to save his own master's life. When it was revised for the book, the sketch was retitled "A Story of the War" and its plot was altered. The northern soldier, who is given the name John Huntington, is not killed by Uncle Remus. Nursed back to health, he survives to marry the sister of Remus's master. This northern ex-soldier ("Mars John") moves with his new wife ("Miss Sally") to Atlanta, taking Remus as a servant. The little boy to whom Remus tells his talking-animal legends is the offspring from this intersectional marriage. As the narratee, the little boy is presumed to personify the political purpose of this storytelling framework. Sired by a northern father and a southern mother, who represent the nation's formerly disunited sections, the boy embodies the national public that the sketches desire for their intended audience. This is a variation on the intersectional marriage plot, a formula traceable to novels such as Caroline Hentz's *Lovell's Folly* (1833) and *The Planter's Northern Bride* (1854), but it did not come into its own until after the war when it was used in scores of novels and short stories, ranging from doctrinaire works like John W. De Forest's *Bloody Chasm* (1881) to imaginative departures like Harris's "At Teague Poteet's" (1883). These works aided national reconciliation with plots where sectionalism was the main obstacle to erotic fulfillment. Waiting for the kiss, in these narratives, was the way to teach northern and southern readers to kiss and make up. It was Harris's innovation to transform this familiar storyline into the prehistory for an ethnographic encounter that would make a new place for the black tradition in the reunited nation, and it was through this particular innovation that his sketches exerted an immediate influence on the cultural politics of national reconciliation.[10]

The bond between Uncle Remus and Atlanta becomes much stronger when we turn back from "A Story of the War" to "Uncle Remus as a Rebel," the version that was published in the *Constitution*. In addition to the change in the ending, there is also an important difference in the setting and situation of these sketches. In the book version, the occasion for Remus telling his story about saving his master's life is a visit from Miss Theodosia Huntington, the sister of John Huntington, who travels from Vermont to stay with her brother's new family. Theodosia Huntington is a skeptical northern visitor who changes her mind about a region she once considered "remote and semi-barbarous" as she hears about its history from Uncle Remus and gradually finds that she feels a new affinity for southern whites. A key character type from the literature of the New South movement, the northern visitor was the stock narratee to whom the ex-slave would give testimony about the good times before the war, a type that was made famous in short stories like Thomas Nelson Page's "Marse Chan" (1884), which in turn were gazing backward to antebellum models from both sides of the slavery debate, the best known being Miss Ophelia from *Uncle Tom's Cabin* (1852). There is no Theodosia Huntington in "Uncle Remus as a Rebel." Instead, the occasion for Uncle Remus to tell his story is his decision to decamp from Atlanta and move back to the country, first to raise cotton and corn, and then after it proves tough to keep people from stealing his crops, to live with his former master, whose life Remus saved in the war. The audience for this version of the story is the editorial team at the *Constitution*, whom Remus visits from time to time. In this rendition, the framework is not geared toward sectional reconciliation. It is, rather, a conventional complaint regarding the fallout from emancipation. One in a long line of apologetics about ex-slaves returning to their masters, a line that culminates in Harry Stillwell Edwards's *Eneas Africanus* (1920), "Uncle Remus as a Rebel" concentrates this tradition by connecting the ex-slave's decision to return to his master with ritual testimony regarding his loyalty in the war. Most importantly, the sketch offers a rationale for Remus's decision to leave the city. "I ain't gwineter be working 'roun' here 'mong dese chain-gang niggers w'en I got a good home down yonder," Remus tells his listeners at the *Constitution*. The contempt expressed here for "chain-gang niggers," a term that is intended to name the entire metropolitan black population and especially its most recent arrivals, demonstrates an approach that is representative in the earliest sketches printed in the *Constitution* between 1876 and 1879, where Remus is a crotchety commentator on the urban scene, before he returns to the country to become, against all odds, an amiable plantation storyteller.[11]

Critics have tended to downplay the significance of the early urban sketches when they have not dismissed them outright as cheap blackface exercises having little to do with the real work that would commence once Remus left the city for the suburbs, swapping his cautionary tales about the urban present for fables from the plantation past. This is a critical approach that extends Harris's own penchant for defining black folklore as an antidote to blackface, an approach that opposes the tales told by

Uncle Remus to the "intolerable misrepresentations of the minstrel stage." This blackface association has kept us from reading the earliest sketches with the attention they deserve. To take these sketches seriously, the first thing we have to do is tighten our timeframe to notice their topical references. We need to pay attention, in other words, to what the early sketches were borrowing from the columns around them. Only when we situate these sketches in the framework of the newspaper does it become possible to notice what they have in common with the folklore that takes their place in the *Constitution*. Going local, in this case, also brings into focus the larger stakes beneath this enterprise. My sense is that there is more to Uncle Remus than we have realized. There is no doubt that Remus was an instrument for promoting a new national consensus about slavery, but it is also true that his influence has outlasted that consensus. We need to address Uncle Remus's continuing influence on our conceptualization of the black tradition, and there is only so much we can say to this issue when we accept "A Story of the War" as our starting point. The marriage plot in "A Story of the War" may frame the ethnographic encounter with Uncle Remus, but it does not explain how ethnographic knowledge of the black tradition became indispensable to the new national narrative of political modernization after slavery. To get to the bottom of this question, we need to see that Uncle Remus was more than a cultural solution to a political problem. The question is not whether Uncle Remus's storytelling is more or less successful than "legal enactments." Instead, it is about Remus's leading role in redefining what counted as culture and what counted as politics. This is a problem that demands an approach unlike the usual protocols in cultural history. It is a problem that compels us to revisit the local scene where Remus had his start—looking closely at the *Atlanta Constitution* where he first appeared, at the journalistic conventions that shaped his character, and at the local controversy over municipal improvement that supplied the content for his sketches.[12]

For Uncle Remus, we will see, Atlanta is something more than a hometown. Down to its grittiest details almost everything about the city is relevant to his characterization, both early and late, and it is only through careful consideration of the city's modernization that it is possible to discern Remus's historical import. Founded in 1837, a full century after Georgia's oldest cities developed on its eastern seaboard, Atlanta was made possible by the forced removal of Indian tribes, mostly Cherokee and Creek, whose blood W. E. B. Du Bois imagines in the redness of the local soil. As the area's long-time residents were being evacuated or eliminated, new railroad lines were extending into the state's interior, and a small settlement was founded at the point where they converged. Atlanta's population exploded with the Civil War as local industries enlarged for wartime production, only to collapse again after the city was burned by William Tecumseh Sherman in 1864. After the war, the railroads were again critical to the city's rise. Almost 20,000 people flooded into Atlanta between 1865 and 1867, and from there the city's total population would more than quadruple by the end of the century. Atlanta took pride in the breakneck development of its transportation networks and in its sudden emergence as a regional center for commerce and industry. With much new construction, the city had a contemporary look that many residents liked, and before long it had an infrastructure to match.[13]

Because of these developments, Atlanta came to symbolize, both to its residents and the nation at large, the promise of the southern future. In March 1874, a newspaper writer named Henry Grady published an editorial in the *Atlanta Daily Herald* titled "The New South," which argued that industrialization was the key to development in the region. Hired as managing editor for the *Atlanta Constitution* in 1876, Grady elaborated this argument in articles and policy speeches during the ensuing decade. His brand of thinking, which came to be known as the New South Creed, proposed a new future for southern history premised on the region's gradual assimilation to the national mainstream. It argued that the path to the future was through economic diversification and reconciliation with the northern states, and it suggested on these grounds that the South needed to build its own factories to process its own natural resources and reduce its dependence on staple-crop agriculture. Acknowledging that the South lacked the capital that was required for this plan to work, Grady and his associates did everything they could to attract northern investment. They staged grand expositions to showcase developments in mining, agriculture, manufacturing, transportation, and technology; those in Atlanta included the 1881 International Cotton Exposition, the 1887 Piedmont Exposition, and the 1895 Cotton States and International Exposition, where Booker T. Washington would deliver his career-making Atlanta Compromise Address endorsing the central tenets of the New South Creed. Newspapers were also crucial to this campaign, and Grady in particular used the *Constitution* for the purposes of promotion, publishing editorials and news about the fast pace of progress in his city. These writings were less interested in correctly reporting the present than in shaping the future, and frequently they were willing to compromise with the facts to make that happen.[14]

In their boosterism, Grady and his associates praised the spirit of enterprise and optimism that reinvigorated local commerce, and they described at great length the civic improvements that were turning Atlanta into a modern metropolis. Between 1868, the year the state capital was moved to Atlanta, and 1880, the year the original Uncle Remus book was published, Atlanta was transfigured. The local population almost doubled during this long decade, and new houses and office buildings were materializing week by week. In these same years, the city fashioned a new infrastructure that brought urban conveniences to much of the city. Streets were paved, and a new house numbering system was installed to facilitate the free mail delivery that started in 1873. New brick sewers were excavated, and sanitation improved markedly as a result. A new dam and waterworks were constructed to supplant the aging maze of wells and cisterns. For the first time in its history, Atlanta also established its own citizen's bank, a public school system, a weather bureau, a professional fire department, and a telephone switchboard exchange. Boosters could not stop talking about these civic innovations and their contributions to Atlanta's progress and prosperity, but it was the new police department that symbolized, better than these other novelties, that the city had moved beyond its archaic commitment to slavery, rising from the ashes in just a few short years as a beacon of southern enlightenment.[15]

At least on the pages of the *Constitution*, the police showed what was going right in Atlanta. They signaled the city's on-time arrival as the capital of the New South—a location where business was booming, patriotism was rampant, and public order was secured by modern state institutions. "Atlanta can take from the records nothing that so much emphasizes its rapid growth and rise into a place among the great cities of the South," a booster committee writes, "as the magnificent showing which has from year to year been made in its affairs of police." We need to see that the police were presented in the *Constitution* not simply as one of the city's many modern features but rather as the requirement for its modernization. By this reasoning, there were no modern societies where individuals retained the right to violence. A state monopoly on violence must be built into a resilient network of institutions before property could be secure and trade could increase without reserve. By these lights, a city could participate as an equal partner

Atlanta Police Day Watch. View of Atlanta police officers standing in front of the Atlanta police headquarters on Decatur Street in Atlanta, Georgia. Image produced after 1893. Reprinted with permission from the Kenan Research Center at the Atlanta History Center.

in the modern world system only after the right to legitimate violence was surrendered to the state, except in exigent circumstances. Among other things, this meant that no slave society could be fully modern.[16]

To make his case, Grady had to take on legal theories that were coined in earlier decades by the pro-slavery writers who came before him. As shown by thinkers like James Henry Hammond, southern jurisprudence displayed a long-standing tendency to champion the slavemaster's "patriarchal mode of administering justice" as a viable alternative to "the whole machinery of public police" in the free states. Hammond, for one, was willing to describe the slavemaster's discretionary authority as wisdom tempered by mercy, and to legitimate this discretion by explicit analogy to the doctrine of the police power that was used in the northern states. Symbolized by the figure of the master but generally practiced as a racial prerogative enjoyed by all whites over all blacks, the restricted right to personal violence was argued to be equally as "indispensable" to any slave society as "armies" and "navies" were to free society. The New South Creed remained opposed to this legal tradition, and it identified the racial entitlement to personal violence not as a bulwark to social order but as an outdated custom that needed to stop before Atlanta could enjoy the benefits of modern living. Grady was willing to admit that "simple police regulations" were the "only type possible under slavery," but he also held that habits from the police system of slavery were now standing in the way of progress. Grady was prepared to indulge in nostalgia for slavery, especially as this nostalgia became increasingly vital to the ethos of national reconciliation, but he remained dedicated at the same time to a gospel of work that saw leisured aristocracy as its enemy and enslavement as its historical antithesis. Slavery was an impediment to a future based on free labor, according to this argument, and it remained obstructive within the domain of the law.[17]

The Atlanta Municipal Police were established by a reform charter in 1874—three years after the military occupation of Georgia ended and the Republicans were swept from statewide office. In an effort to stem corruption and facilitate the department's expansion, the police were removed from the direct control of the mayor and instead governed bureaucratically by a board of police commissioners, a change similar to the reform measures adopted in New Orleans during the 1830s. This board oversaw the construction of a new police headquarters and administered a series of practical reforms within the department, the most notable of which was the adoption of a standard-issue uniform (a badge, tin helmet, and Prince Albert coat) that made officers recognizable on sight. Munitions were also standardized, with each officer issued a pistol and a baton. Police continued to walk their old beats, which were less formal than in many other cities, but for the first time, they also began to patrol on horseback and in wagons. Within a few years, communications were updated, with a new alarm system and then callboxes put to use. Before the new department was established in 1874, Atlanta employed a loosely organized night police, which was strictly voluntary for much of its history before it began to pay fees, but not wages, to its patrol officers. The early force was limited to a marshal and several deputies whose main tasks were capturing stray dogs, removing road obstacles, and calling out the hours of the night ("Nine o'clock and all's well") as they traversed the streets, a tradition that was discontinued when the department was professionalized. Removed from the mayor's direct patronage, the department now had to make a public case when it wanted resources. These demands for increased funding were controversial, especially in a city where the connection between the police and modernization did not sound to most people like common sense, no matter how stringently it was argued in the *Constitution*. Indeed, Thomas Jones, who was introduced with much fanfare as the new chief of police, was abruptly fired in 1875 after advising a raise for his lieutenants and patrol officers. Police, as an idea, remained unsettled in the 1870s, despite the foundation that was laid for the new department.[18]

These police reforms were anticipated by changes to the city's minor judiciary in 1872. The Mayor's Court had been the traditional venue for processing misdemeanants. As was the case elsewhere, in Atlanta the mayor was charged with certain duties that would have been delegated or subcontracted in larger cities: among them managing the police, superintending the streets, and administering petty justice. Originally convened monthly in a room above a popular dry goods store, the Mayor's Court never could have kept up with its potential caseload after the war were it not supplemented by temporary tribunals directed by the Freedmen's Bureau. After the Bureau closed its doors in 1870, there was no choice but to overhaul the court system. The state legislature authorized the city council to select a recorder dedicated to the day-to-day supervision of the city's inferior court, and months later, William T. Newman was the first to take the job. The court's expansion was necessitated by population growth, but it was also a response to slavery's demise. The court was designed to deal with minor offenses—idleness, petty theft, domestic disputes—that were adjudicated extralegally under slavery, typically at the master's discretion. Though slaves were remanded to magistrate's courts for serious infractions, like larceny or assault, and even brought before judges and juries when they were formally charged with offenses punishable by death, like rape or murder, slaveowners did everything they could to keep their slaves away from courts encumbered by procedure, which they felt interfered with their ability to manage their property effectively. After the Civil War, inferior courts across the southern states were established or expanded to process minor charges previously considered within the master's dominion. As behavior that used to be the master's private concern became the public business of the government, court dockets that were once populated exclusively by white defendants became filled with ex-slaves. The *Constitution* was quick to highlight that ex-slaves were the "almost unanimous patrons" of the Recorder's Court. The newspaper went so far as to indicate that the new court would have "little to do" were it not for this "class of offenders," as its schedule was "no sooner delivered one week of its contents than it fills up the next with a new batch," and it was even willing to categorize the recorder as a new kind of overseer, administering a "penal slavery" that was bound to swallow a "large percentage of the race."[19]

With these new police and court systems in place, Atlanta began to enforce misdemeanor laws specifically designed to entrap freed slaves. Discarding the pretense to rehabilitation, the city seized the opportunity to extract as much labor as possible from its convicts. Similar changes were taking place around the state, as a new labor system evolved as an alternative to imprisonment. The procedure varied. When convicts were supposed to be incarcerated, they could be leased to private companies and compelled to labor for the duration of their sentence. When the crime was minor, like vagrancy or trespass, meriting a cash penalty rather than prison time, the court could still impose an exorbitant fine, well beyond the means of almost every defendant, and then allow someone else to step forward, pay the fine, and demand compensation in the form of indentured labor. Other times, when convicts were not sold to the highest bidder, they were easily hitched to the chain gang and forced to work directly for the state. Georgia began to experiment with convict leasing while its state government was still under Republican rule, selling 100 of its black prisoners to the Georgia and Alabama Railroad in 1868. Considered a success by Republicans and Democrats alike, the program was rebid annually, and enlarged year by year, until 1876 when the state legislature decided on a more durable arrangement, granting a twenty-year contract to a conglomerate led by the Dade Coal Company, which paid $500,000 all told for the rights to the state's "able-bodied, long term men." It would be very difficult to overstate the brutality of the resulting labor system. Convicts were beaten, tortured, poorly clothed and fed, pushed daily to their breaking point, morning into night, under unsanitary and exceedingly dangerous circumstances. A large proportion of the state's prison population was literally worked to death, as there was no economic incentive for companies to keep their prisoners alive. The convict lease did not end in Georgia until 1909, when it was supplanted in part by the state-managed chain gang. This decision was prompted by declining profits; the lease's fixed labor costs had begun to make problems for both lessees and the state, no matter how low these costs were driven. Also important was the moral and political pressure brought by muckrakers and congressional inquiries, which categorically condemned the system's inhumanity. There was resistance to the lease from its earliest years, but it was only with crusading exposés like Rebecca Latimer Felton's "The Convict System of Georgia" (1887) and J. C. Powell's *American Siberia* (1891) that effective opposition to the lease commenced. This movement was responsible for originating the sensationalistic iconography of the southern prison, which subsequently provided the typical framework for novels and memoirs like John Spivak's *Georgia Nigger* (1932) and Robert Burns's *I Am a Fugitive from a Georgia Chain Gang!* (1932).[20]

Although the *Constitution* waffled in its support for the lease, the newspaper always counted prison profiteers among its closest allies and investors. Furthermore, there was just no way that the huge industrial and infrastructural development envisioned by the New South Creed would have been possible without the superexploitation permitted by the convict lease. Through the 1870s, the foremost beneficiaries of the lease were the railroad companies, which unlike their competitors in the iron and coal industries, required little investment before they sent convicts to work. Once the roadbeds were graded, getting the money to finish the job was no problem. The astonishing speed of this railroad construction shifted Georgia's economic center of gravity away from its seaboard and cotton belt and toward Atlanta, which became the midpoint connecting the state's iron, coal, and timber industries—all of which similarly came to depend upon convict labor—to the world market. Moreover, the civic improvements that swelled the city's pride were made possible by convict labor. Streets were paved and cleaned by convicts. The bricks that fashioned Atlanta's modern buildings came from the Chattahoochee Brick Company, an adjacent convict-lease operation. For those who preferred stone to brick, the best choice for materials was the granite from Stone Mountain, which had been dug by convicts, then transported on the Western and Atlantic Railroad, which had been lined by convicts. Far from a holdover from a benighted history, or a relic from slavery, convict labor quickly became indispensable to Atlanta's modernization. Its growth was also, therefore, symbolically indispensable to the New South Creed. Prison labor was not an obstacle to historical progress. It was, on the contrary, the force that made history possible.[21]

It is crucial to recall that this new criminal justice system—combining an expanded police department with new inferior courts and a flexible scheme for detention and punishment—would have appeared unfamiliar, and even exotic, to local residents. Even those aspects of the system that we now take for granted, like the state's control over the legitimate use of force, were open to debate in the 1870s. Understanding the vocabulary used by the *Constitution* during this controversy is essential if we want to understand the environment where Uncle Remus first appeared. No matter what the boosters said, there was nothing foregone about Atlanta's eventual route to modernity, and we need to recover that sense of contingency before we can recognize Remus's contribution to the new public understanding of the police power that was beginning to develop after slavery. Police was not a self-evident proposition in Atlanta during the 1870s, and we can learn a lot by monitoring how the principle was explained and justified in these years while it was being turned into majoritarian common sense. The police propaganda appearing on the back pages of the *Constitution* also remains instructive in the material sense that it was being applied to a situation where the state remained extremely weak. "Legitimation" is probably the wrong word to describe the function of this rhetoric, given that the police department had only twenty-six members in the year that it was professionalized. Starting with a ratio of roughly one officer to one thousand residents and limited to the most rudimentary means of transportation and communication, the department could do only so much to keep the peace. To be sure, this point was made repeatedly by vigilantes who declared that the police were too weak, and the courts too capricious, to defend the public welfare on their own. It follows that we should read the *Atlanta Constitution* not as legitimating the state's actually existing powers, but instead as outrunning those powers, by making claims about its capacity to monopolize violence that the state was not prepared to fulfill. The force of these claims, in other words, was not instrumental but constitutive to the idea of the modern state. Making the most of the leverage afforded by this situation, we can begin to distinguish what Philip Abrams calls the "state idea" from the practices of the modern state system, registering in the process how the dividing line between state and society was slowly but surely redrawn after emancipation.[22]

The *Constitution* was vital to this process. Founded in 1868, the newspaper was named to communicate its opposition to federal military rule—which it deemed "unconstitutional"—after the war. The newspaper passed from vendor to vendor, and editor to editor, until Evan P. Howell became part-owner and editor-in-chief in 1876. Straight away, Howell hired Henry Grady and promoted him to associate editor. Formerly Grady had been a chief executive at the *Atlanta Daily Herald* (1872–1876). Grady and his partners at the *Herald* spared no expense in gathering the news and distributing their product, proposing to establish the finest newspaper in the southern states. The editors went so far as to charter an express train to deliver their morning edition to closeby cities and towns. The *Herald* pioneered a new kind of layout, experimenting with new beat reports and urban newspaper genres that had not been tried before in Atlanta, including a satirical column on the happenings at the new recorder's court. These bold experiments were financially disastrous to the *Herald*, but they proved tremendously successful for the *Constitution*, helping to establish the paper's reputation locally and nationally. Among the inclinations carried from the *Herald* to the *Constitution* was Grady's devotion to the New South Creed, which he trumpeted more brashly than ever from its editorial pages. This devotion, as we have already seen, connected with many causes, but none more intensely than police reform.[23]

In addition to the New South editorials that attempted to predicate the city's future on the present condition of its police, the *Constitution* devoted whole columns to individual arrests, usually calling out patrolmen by name in the endeavor to give a human face to the new department. Much of the local news was presented in itemized articles (or "miscellanies") containing assorted items of passing interest: announcements of public events, information about recent arrivals to the city, weather, commodities, and politics. Such columns were typically presented as lists with no internal logic. Evocative of the city's bustle and heterogeneity, these miscellanies exemplify what Richard Terdiman has dubbed the "anti-organicist" structure of the modern newspaper, a structure that makes the city's unity thinkable not by manufacturing an integrated picture of urban life but instead by presenting the spatial contiguity of seemingly unrelated persons, places, and events in the manner of a collection. Through the normal reiteration of this contiguity, these columns connected readers to one another by creating the shared feeling of proximity that in turn produced the city as a social totality. By describing a range of persons, things, and events that a resident might expect to encounter while walking the streets, these miscellanies gave a concrete and visual cast to the imagined unity produced through the purposeful regularity of the newspaper's conventional address to its implied readership.[24]

From the time of the police reorganization, individual police officers were a mainstay in these miscellanies. The *Constitution* even began to dedicate an entire column to the activities of the department. This miscellany (which the editors first entitled "Police Pickings," and then "The Police at Work," before settling on "Police Points") was printed several times a week between 1876 and 1883, combining one-sentence puffs with lesser news items. Entirely forthright about its intention to sing the police's praises, "Police Points" included reports on individual arrests ("Officers Saulisbury and Goodson arrested Wm. Wood yesterday upon suspicion"); on particular work in progress ("The police are after a gang of sneak thieves that infest our city"); on the moral climate around Atlanta ("The city has been on its good behavior for the whole week"); on the happenings at the recorder's court ("There were about thirteen cases before Recorder Milledge yesterday"); and on the progress in the outfitting of the force ("Some of the members of the Atlanta police force carry a pistol in every pocket"). Also commonplace were puffs for individual officers ("Captain Mike White is considered the most fleet-footed member of the police force"; "Captain Connolly recovers more stolen poultry than any other member of the force"; "Patrolmen Veal and Penn are among the most wide-awake men on the force"; "Patrolman McCrary is one of the most gallant men on the force") as well as quaint but always flattering information ("Chief Thomas was a few days ago the recipient of a handsome new hat"; "The average height of the force is 5 feet 11 inches"; "The commissioned officers of the police force pride themselves on their superb moustaches"). As if such reports were not enough, most columns would also take the time to praise the overall efficacy and efficiency of the department. "Our present police system is working admirably," one item says. "The force is now working finely," another says two weeks later. Without exception, these officers were industrious (walking "twenty-five and thirty miles a day"); enthusiastic (performing "their hard work with a cheerfulness that a lazy man cannot understand"); disciplined (with complaints rarely brought "for neglect of duty"); courageous (with "the nerve" required to face down criminals); and honest (with "a regular set of books" containing "a full record of all the business done by the recorder"). "This," the *Constitution* held, is "why they are so active and useful."[25]

At the same time as it was printing miscellanies like the "Police Points" column, the *Constitution* also began to experiment further with an old newspaper genre—the police court report—bending its conventions to suit the characters, conflicts, and spirited recitals taking center stage at the new recorder's courtroom. Police court reporting first appeared as a regular feature in the United States in the 1820s. The *New York Sun* started the police court trend with its popular column written by George Wisner, who was touted as "the Balzac of the daybreak court," and other penny dailies soon followed suit, introducing their own court reports in an effort to keep up in the fierce competition for readers. These facetious columns were based on models in British journalism, which represented the proceedings in the minor judiciary in mock heroic language. They emphasized stock characters—thieves, alcoholics, prostitutes, vagrants— who came before the magistrate to tell their stories and accept punishment for their misdeeds. Although they occasionally indulged in sermons on the dangers of drink and the health benefits of hard labor, these columns aimed for a style of broad humor that depended upon puns, malapropisms, and extended caricature. Police court reporting made its way into the southern states before emancipation, focused on those minor venues where whites were called to account for small crimes, but it would not become a staple in these states until after the war. As the inferior courts across the region were enlarged to process their new constituency of former slaves, the papers began to publish more detailed and outlandish reports that took their cues from southern plantation writings as well as blackface minstrelsy. The bodies of black defendants brought before the recorder were viciously distorted in these police court reports and in the cartoons that eventually accompanied them, with oversized eyeballs and distended lips, their limbs buckled to resemble beasts and inanimate objects. Black speech patterns were similarly stylized ("Sah! May't please Court, I'se hopes sat these Court don spose for single moment that I would insult a lady") according to inherited convention and separated from the standard idiom spoken by the judge, police, and court officers. Whether they were represented as slow-talking and slack-jawed, and correspondingly baffled by the austere complexity of the courtroom, or instead as fast-talking and overreaching, unknowingly making grandiose errors in procedure and pronunciation, it is easy to see what is supposed to be funny about the proceedings. Though most major southern newspapers hired dedicated court reporters at least for a time after the war, none was more keen about the genre than the *Atlanta Daily Herald*, which was flashy in its formal experimentation—prefacing its reports with invocations to the muses and miniature topical limericks, peppering its transcriptions with allusions to Shakespeare and the Bible, and occasionally even rendering the columns typographically as a script for theatrical production, complete with stage directions ("Exeunt Omnes"). The *Constitution* continued to publish the genre into the next century, helping in the process to make city recorders like Nash Broyles and Andy Calhoun into small-time celebrities, known for their wit as much as their wisdom.[26]

The police court column appeared under many titles over its long run in the *Constitution*, ranging from the prosaic ("Recorder's Court") to the salacious ("Police Matinee Pen Shots," "Lively Scenes in the Police Court," "A Busy Session at the Police Barracks"). Like the "Police Points" miscellanies, the court report was doing serious work in spite of its flippant tone, introducing its readers to the city's new venues and procedures for criminal justice. Even more crucial, however, were the paper's crime reports, which were sinister rather than playful in pitch, and routinely splashed across the headlines rather than confined as a regular feature on the back pages. The *Constitution* knew that what it needed to win support for the police was a threat that only the police could handle. Like those who advocated arming the police in New Orleans in the 1830s, the *Constitution* needed an enemy before it could clinch its argument for a stronger and better organized department. The paper found that enemy in the black migrants who were arriving in great numbers throughout the postbellum decades. Rural-to-urban migration appealed to many black families as a strong alternative to life in the country districts where there was scant protection from the terrorist tactics—lynching, whitecapping, sexual assaults—that whites were exercising with increasing coordination and mostly with impunity. This violence was less commonplace in cities, and there was obviously safety in numbers. As a railroad hub, Atlanta was especially accessible to black migrants. Available statistics, as for any floating population, are inconclusive, but we know that the settled black population grew from less than 100 in the 1840s, to around 2,000 in the late 1860s, to around 9,000 in 1880, and finally to more than 35,000 by the end of the century, or 40% of the city's aggregate.[27]

The *Constitution* was insistent that this new migrant population was the primary concern for the police. "A Negro with a bundle on his shoulders," the newspaper guaranteed, "is always an object of suspicion to a policeman."

Such statements were frequent in the crime reporting that tried to win support for the modernization of the police by representing its patrol officers as the absolute last line of defense against the so-called vagrants who were ostensibly threatening to take over the city. These professed vagrants, newly arrived to town without a care in the world, were stock characters in the miscellanies where they were depicted in a matter-of-fact style. A one-line item from an 1877 "Police Points," for instance, notices, without further comment, that "hordes" of migrant "darkies" were being arrested as vagrants. In the police court reports, the black vagrant was often a comedian, by turns preposterous and pathetic. The crime reporting, however, took a very different tack. Alarmist in content, ratcheted up in tone, the *Constitution* organized its news reporting to bring a historical perspective to the problem of vagrancy. "The emancipation of the slaves precipitated a number of worthless vagrants upon us," the *Constitution* eagerly explained, stressing that there was nothing "more dangerous" to public security "than this horde of ruffians" who were said to "infest the by-ways of our land." As the *Constitution* saw it, black vagrants were everywhere in Atlanta: "[blocking] up our doorways," indulging "miserable talk in back alleys," and "[stealing from] houses and yards at night." Indeed, the *Constitution* announced that the vagrants were at times "so thick" as to make the sidewalks "literally impassable for ladies."[28]

As the *Constitution* made a habit of counting the "able-bodied negroes lounging on every street corner," it began to describe black migrants in increasingly menacing terms. Complaints about small-time nuisances gave way to vivid tirades. Black migrants were turned into the monsters that kept residents awake at night, with their character taking a gothic turn at the precise moment that the police were being expanded in the 1870s. "Outcasts and aliens in habit and sentiment, subdued by no fear of local police, and softened by no local attachment," the new migrants who came to town from the countryside were supposed to "skulk . . . like wolves, only harmless when glutted—gathering in gangs when there is crime to be committed." Panic over black migration peaked in summer of 1879 when Martin and Susan DeFoor, an older couple living on the outskirts of the city, were murdered in their sleep. Calling the case the "most horrible murder known to the annals of Fulton county," the *Constitution* demanded swift justice. Based on no reported evidence besides the rumor that there were black men traveling through the neighborhood that week, the police declared an open season on black migrants. As their routine harassment intensified, several men were gunned down by the police and dozens more were arrested, at least three of whom were incarcerated for more than a year as the investigation sputtered and finally went unsolved. This did not stop the *Constitution* from taking the opportunity to pile on its complaints against black migration to the point where even the smallest improprieties would register as a clear signal of violence to come. Small acts were conjoined to more serious crimes—so that loitering, for instance, became the foreseeable precursor to larceny; unlicensed street vending became evidence for future chicken-stealing; failing to yield the sidewalk or avert the eyes became surefire signs that a rape would soon occur. According to this judgment, treating loiterers as if they were already thieves was the best way to prevent crime before it happened.[29]

If vagrancy was the problem for the *Constitution*, more and better policing was the solution. The newspaper stressed the point that the department was expanding at too slow a pace to deal with the influx of potential criminals. The reports on vagrancy policing followed a predictable pattern: they praised the policing that was being done, only to say a week, a day, a column, or a paragraph later that the policing that was being done was not enough. "It is well that our chief of police is making such vigorous warfare on these abandoned parasites," one report stated, noting "a number of cases for vagrancy have been made by the police and will be tried by the city court." Even if the vagrants in question "cannot be convicted" of any crime, the article concluded they should be required to "know that in every neighborhood they will find their course impeded, and find themselves subject to constant investigation." Balancing these affirmative comments were claims that vagrancy ordinances were not being aggressively enforced, a problem that was attributed to the department's lack of resources. "What we need is a stricter application of the vagrant law," the *Constitution* demanded, "Our patrol force is not one-fifth what it should be to properly guard the city." It is time to "place these strolling vagabonds under the strictest surveillance," the paper continued, as their presence "destroys the sense of security that every citizen of a metropolis is entitled to feel, as a sort of compensation for taxes." These commentaries were supplemented in the *Constitution* by anti-vagrancy opinions reprinted from the mayor, members of the city council, the police chief, and the city recorders. Recorder Nash Broyles, in particular, was celebrated for preaching from the bench to vagrants, promising to hand always the "full limit of the law" to anybody unemployed. "We have work which will be given you," Broyles informed his defendants, "and it is in the chaingang." The *Constitution* was at times very candid about what the city stood to gain through these arrests—labor needed in local industries, surely, and also labor needed for local infrastructure. "We need all these loafers, and we need them bad," the paper asserted, remarking that a batch of arrests would supply all the labor required "to develop and perfect the public road system." The paper held that Atlanta would benefit in "two ways" by putting all its vagrants "on the chaingang": it would put a stop to "general lawlessness," and it would "push the work on our roads." At the extreme, the new police operation even seemed like it would become self-supporting. If the force were only "a little larger," a "Police Points" entry suggested in 1879, "the recorder's court could sustain almost all the charges of the police department."[30]

This propaganda created as well as solved problems for the New South Creed. For the police, the assertions embedded in the *Constitution*'s crime reporting were limited by their structural indifference to procedure. When the threat posed to the city reached the point where the city's survival was at stake, it seemed right to protect the city by any means necessary. Legal and extralegal methods of self-defense, from this perspective, were not distinguishable. This flexibility is confirmed when we consider how frequently statements about vagrancy were invoked to vindicate the extralegal recourse to vigilante violence. Lynchings were justified not only as morally appropriate but as socially necessary given the supposed sexual threat that black vagrants posed to white women. In the city and in the country, new terrorist organizations like the Ku Klux Klan represented their violence as the best way to prevent crimes before they could happen. When white mobs murdered dozens of black men and women and burned numerous black homes and businesses during the Atlanta Riot of 1906, they were incited by vagrancy editorials printed by the *Constitution* and competitors like the *News* and the *Journal*, which had continuously raised the stakes in the months leading up to the riot, running headlines inciting readers to "Drive Out the Vagrants" (in the *Constitution*) and "Kill the Vagrants" (in the *Journal*). The tenor of these editorials makes it difficult to tell the difference between banishing vagrants and killing them, but this was a difference that mattered enormously to the editors at the *Constitution*, particularly in the 1870s, when they commenced their campaign to persuade white readers that their traditional entitlement to personal violence should be surrendered to the police. Although the *Constitution* used publicity tactics to back the police that were functionally indistinguishable from those that were used to support the mob, the newspaper's editors remained predominantly, if not always uniformly, committed to separating the legal mechanism from outmoded custom.[31]

Though many improvements requested by the police department had already been implemented elsewhere in older and larger cities including New Orleans, there still existed in Atlanta a residual distrust toward the idea of a permanent uniformed militia on the city streets. This resistance had some predictable contours—including taxpayer skepticism about expense—but in Atlanta, what mattered most was the traditional system of racial policing, which had operated under slavery in a manner that was relatively autonomous from the state. Accustomed to this system, many whites believed that sending ex-slaves into the courts for punishment was tantamount to admitting their own weakness. It did not matter that the courts were controlled by whites and tilted to disadvantage ex-slaves. Going to court meant conceding that the emancipated had legal rights that whites were bound to respect. It made more sense to these skeptics to keep alive the old system through extralegal actions and organizations, which were appreciated as a time-honored response to an unprecedented situation. For the *Constitution*, this rough justice was a throwback to an obsolete stage of history that Atlanta was struggling to leave behind. In an editorial from June 1877 entitled "Law or No Law," the *Constitution* condemned a lynching in a nearby city. Though this editorial expressed greater concern for the state's reputation than for the people who were tortured and then murdered by the mob, it conveyed nothing but scorn for the actions of these "self-commissioned executioners." Lynching, the *Constitution* wrote, was based upon an "easy-going, damaging, and dangerous doctrine." An arrest and conviction for the crime would have been not only more honorable but more efficacious, conveying a "deeper impression" of the "majesty and certainty" of the law, while averting the "disgrace" and "damage" to the state's reputation that came with every lynching. This approach is typical. The *Constitution* was even willing to admit sixteen years later that it remained "hard to draw the line" in these cases, only to plead with its readers that lynchings should not become "too common" in the state. How common is too common? The willingness to beg this question, which cannot be answered in the terms in which it is posed, shows how tenuous the state's presumptive monopoly on violence remained, even for its most ardent advocates.[32]

The line separating would-be vigilantes from law-and-order champions is so blurred in these cases that it is tempting to disregard it altogether were it not for the fact that it was taken so seriously not only by white factions but by some black leaders and their organizations as well. Analyzing local conflicts over what the law could mean after slavery, we can expand what we already know about politics as it was practiced in Atlanta's black neighborhoods, in its black-owned newspapers, and in the campaigns that promoted black candidates for city office. There was nothing monolithic about the black response to the new criminal justice system in Atlanta. From the start, the system had its critics, but there were some who had their own reasons to sign onto the claims made by the *Constitution* concerning the purported scourge of vagrancy. Some members of the self-styled black vanguard were devoted to a strategy that made the case for racial equality by pointing to their own moral and material success. Knowing that the language of anti-vagrancy, as it was used in the white press, was meant to condemn the entire race, some elites chose to combat this charge through selective, rather than thoroughgoing, rebuttal. They accepted the idea that the black masses were degraded only to name themselves as the exception that proved the race's potential for progress in the long term. In practice, this meant that leaders like Atlanta's Henry Hugh Proctor countenanced the racial tirades in the white press only to exempt themselves from the rules that otherwise governed the race. As Kevin Gaines says, this is how some members of the black middle class forged their self-image: they defined their economic rationality against the race's shiftlessness, their propriety against its licentiousness, their power to defer gratification against its self-indulgence, their autonomy against its dependence, their evolution against its degeneration, and their idyllic homelife against its homelessness — defining their own moral authority, in the process, as a philanthropic obligation to uplift the masses. Confident in their entitlement to speak for the race and eager to impart the secret of their success, they phrased their philosophy in rigid parallelism. "The silly, uneducated, shiftless Negro puts his pay on his back," Washington says, "the business Negro puts his pay in the bank." "Sacrifice to-day's indulgence," he hastens to add, "for tomorrow's independence." Such phrases aimed to explain the ex-slave's propertyless condition, whether waged or unwaged, in the emerging system of agricultural production as evidence that the majority of the race was still developing toward freedom. These phrases hold to precedent not only in their syntax and implied timeline but also in their ethics, which derives the possibility of political consent from property ownership. Property comes before politics in these writings. Work hard today, keep your nose down, and worry later about winning back your civil rights. According to many of its critics, this was the reason why the Racial Uplift Movement could be so quickly integrated with the New South Creed.[33]

Many of these race leaders tried their hardest to avoid confrontation over the blanket condemnations issued by the white press, preferring to lecture their constituencies on temperance, hygiene, housekeeping, sexual restraint, and square dealing. Even those, like Du Bois, who counseled engagement on problems like segregation, began their careers with a capacity to see both sides when it came to the state's role in administering the black masses. Du Bois took a basically moralistic approach in studies like *The Philadelphia Negro* (1899), which generated a rough agenda for generations of sociologists by bringing cutting-edge quantitative methods to bear upon the apparent problems of urban blight and black family disorganization. This moralism, which is so brazen in the writings of Washington and Du Bois, was powerful among the new generation of race leaders that came of age near the turn of the century, but there was great variation in this general pattern. In Atlanta, both the black-owned *Independent* (1903–1933) and the *Voice of the Negro* (1904–1907) were committed in principle to racial uplift. But J. Max Barber, editor at the *Voice*, praised the upward mobility of the black middle class without pathologizing the rest of the race. Barber, in fact, condemned the vagrancy propaganda printed in white publications, reserving special scorn for those black leaders who were willing to buy into the hype. Barber went so far as to document cases where white lawbreakers had painted their faces black to throw the police off their trail. Many leaders who made such direct claims, including Barber, were forced to flee for their lives, and thus it was the case that some of the most unstinting arguments were dispatched from the relative safety of northern cities — examples would include books like T. Thomas Fortune's *Black and White* (1884), D. A. Straker's *The New South Investigated* (1888), and Ida B. Wells's *A Red Record* (1895). There was, however, a well-developed black public sphere in Atlanta that fostered critical thinking about the evolution of criminal justice. There are limits to what we can know about this oppositional culture, as so many records have been lost, but we can get some feeling for the arguments that were being made and the actions that were being taken by looking to the few issues that have been preserved from local black newspapers, like the *Atlanta Weekly Defiance* (1881–1889), as well as to black newspapers published concurrently in neighboring cities, like the *Savannah Tribune* (1875–1960).[34]

In majority-black districts in Atlanta such as Shermantown and Diamond Hill, there was quick resistance to the new police department. Already in the 1860s, before the department's reorganization, black political associations had been pointing to due process violations and protesting against police brutality, in some cases even winning cases against officers in the judicial system. In the 1870s, these associations put forward their own policy solutions, asking specifically that the city hire some black officers. Though this would not solve all the problems that were endemic to the justice system, it was felt that including blacks on the police would at least improve the situation, and at the same time, it would transform the police's symbolic role in the city. This demand was consistent with other campaigns run by black organizations that demanded their fair share from the stock of patronage appointments, but something more was being contested as well: the purpose of the police, their place in history, and the nature of "the people" that consents to the new monopoly on violence. Every one of these petitions was denied, for reasons that are easy to tell when we remember that the *Constitution* and its allies had to have an all-white police to represent the department as a modern institution that was destined to improve upon the kind of security that had previously been provided by slavery.[35]

Grady, for one, argued that modern policing was compatible with white supremacy. He asked the southern states to commit to the rule of law, but he maintained at the same time that the only way for the law to prevail in the region was by honoring the color line. For Grady and the *Constitution*, there was nothing color blind about the state or its police powers. Of course, black Atlanta did not wait for Grady to make this point. For two decades previous, its newspapers and political associations had been arguing that the law was being enforced unequally on the streets, that the rights of black residents were ignored by the police, that hiring in the schools and public works projects was discriminatory, that black neighborhoods were being forced to live with unpotable water and unpaved roads even as white neighborhoods were receiving indulgences like electric streetlamps. The complaints against the police became even louder as these movements gained strength at the end of the 1870s—with black candidates very nearly winning local offices in 1879, anti-lynching leagues organizing in 1880, and the city's washerwomen striking in 1881. While black activists were making advances on several fronts, the campaign to win concessions from the police failed year after year, and progressively, individuals began to take matters into their own hands, claiming sovereignty over their neighborhoods. One prominent example of this resistance came in 1881, when a black youth named John Burke was clubbed after he pushed past a white woman as he was trying to enter the Opera House. After the police threw Burke onto the ground and started to beat him with their clubs, a crowd of black onlookers tried to intervene. As Burke was walked to the police station, the crowd followed behind, shouting for his release and pelting the officers with debris. "This thing is becoming too common," the *Constitution* announced the next morning. "Almost every day something of the kind occurs. The negroes, whenever an arrest is made in an 'out of the way' part of the city, try every way to obstruct the officers." Reports on organized resistance against the police were indeed common in these years. Black bystanders were willing, to a degree they had not been before, to intervene in arrests and offer asylum to individuals chased by police, whether or not they knew the person, whether or not they knew the rationale for the arrest.[36]

Following a line similar to the *Constitution*, some black leaders saw this resistance as absolute lawlessness. It was instinctual, resulting from bad impulse control. It was action without form. The challenge, then, if we want to read this action historically, is not only to detect its form but to find what it was about its form that was indiscernible to its critics. This can be done, I will propose, by augmenting the remarkable research of historians like Tera Hunter with a fresh look at black newspapers like the *Defiance* and *Tribune*. Because only a few issues of the *Defiance* have survived, the *Tribune* is the best available source for local reporting in the black press on the criminal justice system. Although it was published in Savannah, its editors were in contact with the most outspoken neighborhood leaders in Atlanta and were closely aligned in spirit with publications, like the *Defiance*, that were able to contemplate direct action. The *Tribune* published its own crime reporting, but equally important to its mission was its critical engagement with the crime reporting in the white press. Often its editors appeared less concerned with beating their competitors to the story than with playing the watchdog, insetting long quotations from other newspapers, and critically analyzing their unspoken

assumptions, line by line. The *Tribune* even published occasional paro-
dies on the police court reporting in the white press, inverting its mock
heroic idiom to the point where the proceedings began to look distinctly
unfunny. Sometimes the *Tribune* supplemented this second-order explanation by returning to the scene of a crime to look for evidence that the
police did not collect, and other times it published letters from eyewit-
nesses to lynchings and from convicts trapped on the chain gang. In noticeable contrast to muckraking narratives like Powell's *American Siberia*,
the *Tribune* took a systematic approach to criminal justice that integrated
its interpretations of convict leasing with reporting on the police and the
courts. It could condemn convict leasing and the chain gang as scandalous survivals from slavery without losing sight of their historical character as institutions for the state's modernization. By joining muckraking
columns with titles like "Chain Gang Outrages" and "Horrors of the
Chain Gang" to regular reports on the police, the *Tribune* built its case
that the criminal justice system was driven, in the final instance, by the demand for labor. "Speaking of the placing of the convicts around the city on
the drainage work," the *Tribune* ventures in a typical aside, "the *Savannah
Press* . . . said fifty of them will be put to work and just as many more can
be secured." Then the point is made: "Now just where the extra fifty men
can be secured is the question. Will word be sent to the recorder and the
judge of the city court for these extra men?" In such cases, nothing more
is needed but a short gloss. By stating the obvious when it came to the
means, incentives, and profits that structured the criminal justice system,
the *Tribune* established its point of entry into a controversy that it could
then subject to extended analysis.[37]

Among the most noticeable aspects of the *Tribune*'s regular layout was
its decision to report lynchings and police brutality alongside the rest of
its crime coverage. In articles with titles like "Murder! Murder! A Colored Man Literally Riddled with Bullets" and "Blood! Iago! Blood!" the
Tribune reported on vigilante actions around the state, at once examining
the informal criminal allegations made against the people who were
lynched, evaluating the facts made available by coroner's inquests, and
vowing that these murders, like any others, deserved to be investigated by
the police. "If the authorities make no effort to enforce the law, and protect the rights of life," the *Tribune* professed, "they become as morally guilty
as the murderers." For the *Tribune*, this reluctance to prosecute lynching
was wholly continuous with the police actions that were pursued by the

state. In miscellanies such as "Georgia Justice" and "No Justice in Georgia Courts," the *Tribune* cut through the endless discussion over legal versus extralegal prevention in the white press, identifying the violence that was happening week after week, whether committed by the police or by the mob, not as rough but substantial justice, nor as primitive retribution, nor as the law overreaching its bounds, but instead as itself a crime. "Another Murder" announces one headline, with a lede explaining that "the victim is Willie Smith and the murderer policeman Bradley." Another headline makes the assertion even more succinctly ("Criminal Policeman") before moving on to narrate a case where two officers were fined ten dollars for killing someone named Eddie Harris after mistaking him for a fugitive. The *Tribune* also depicted more routine encounters with the police—when, for instance, an unnamed man was clubbed, arrested, and fined after obeying an order to secure his umbrella; when a light-skinned woman named Gertie Cherry, mistaken for white, was imprisoned for appearing in public with a black man; when individuals were stopped without cause on the street, searched, and arrested for carrying articles they bought earlier in the day. These reports were sometimes made into object lessons for expository articles on due process (explicating the law of domicile) and equal protection (tallying the wildly disproportionate penalties handed down by the recorder's courts). As in those articles where the *Tribune* was concerned to prove the state's complicity in mob violence, these police reports also devoted careful attention to the law's underenforcement. When the victim was black, the police were often unwilling to take the time for an inquest, no matter the race of the alleged assailant, a point that the *Tribune* emphasized by printing letters from black men and women who were snubbed by the police after their homes or businesses were burglarized, their paychecks were withheld, or their persons were violated.[38]

The *Tribune* also spoke directly to the anti-vagrancy editorials that appeared in the white press. Sometimes this meant reprinting articles from other newspapers and responding point by point. Breaking one editorial from the *Morning News* into six inset quotations, for example, the *Tribune* asked readers to compare its claims to their own observations of the city. One extract taken from the *News* says: "Accost, if you please, any number of the crowd of idle blacks and ask if he wants work, and he will say yes. But if the work requires any exertion worth mentioning he will not show up at the time agreed upon." In its gloss on this quotation, the *Tribune* reminded readers that the "most laborious work" in Savannah had always been done, and was still being done, by black labor. Walk on the river-front, the *Tribune* challenged its readers, and the truth will appear before your eyes. Against the *News's* assertion that ex-slaves were wandering into the cities for no reason in particular, the *Tribune* described what it saw as the reasons for this rural-to-urban migration. "In recent years the cities and towns of nearly all of the southern states have been flooded with our peo-ple," it noted. Admitting that it was a "wonder" that people would "leave their homes" in such "large numbers" and "come to a place where em-ployment is scarce," the *Tribune* offered the following thoughts:

> We concede that there is work for them, yes, great need for them in the country, and that there are millions of acres waiting to be cleared of their primeval forest and by the ladened fertility of their soil enrich the south untold millions. If this be true, as it certainly is, why the constant gathering of these black men and women who presume to have heart and souls in them like other men and women, into the cities? It is because they are too often cheated of what they have made year after year; it is because they are absolutely denied all participation in the forming of the laws and almost never granted the protection of the law; it is be-cause they are lynched and murdered and without even an at-tempt of protection throughout the rural districts of the south. This is the cause. Now let the *News, Press, Journal* and other pa-pers that have been so anxious to see these colored men sent to the gang do justice once in their existence by using their influ-ence to have these causes removed, and this influx of colored men will surely stop.

To the newspapers raising the alarm about black vagrancy, the *Tribune* re-sponded that it was necessary to remember that "these people have hu-man feelings." Being "harassed and cowed by those who have everything in their power," it was only natural to "seek some clime that is more con-genial for their safety and protection." Listing them week by week, the *Tribune* kept an informal tally of cases where people were beaten, killed, and arrested under questionable pretenses. From this evidence, the news-paper explained why there could exist reasonable cause to interfere with the police, noting cases where officers had beaten people to the point of senselessness before taking them to the station. "Naturally," it added, "any one standing by and seeing the injustice would try to stop it." The *Tribune* went so far as to stake its reputation on its claim that this interference would immediately cease were the city to commence policies to "discountenance" police brutality. In the absence of these policies, what was most striking was not the occasional resort to self-defense but instead the restraint within the black community. The "lawfulness" of the black community was demonstrated by its moderation in a situation where so many of its members were "being unlawfully treated."[39]

The *Tribune* was always willing to raise its voice against this mistreatment—as shown in an editorial on a lynching in Columbus, Georgia. Describing how the mob went unpunished although it acted "unmasked" in "broad daytime" on a main thoroughfare, an editor pressed a series of rhetorical questions: "I ask the Negro can he stand it? I ask the entire white race, who boasts of their superiority to my race in every particular, can they stand it? I ask our honorable governor can he stand it? And with my knees to the ground, with one hand on my heart and the other on my Winchester, I ask my God how long will he stand it?" Recalling the victim's mutilation and the mob's jubilation, the editorial continues: "Where is the state militia that these demons still defy the purpose of the law? I ask where is the protection of a state when a handful of men can run to slaughter and defy the law?" Calling for a law that is still to come while clutching a Winchester rifle to the breast, these questions bring together their indictment of the state's complicity with a second line of argument, keyed to the common sense in papers like the *Constitution*, that says the only modern people in the southern states are those who speak out against this barbarism. Through this sequence of rhetorical questions that build from self-recrimination, to confrontation, to something like despair—or more likely a dramatized breaking point—this article assumes a posture that was occasionally embraced in the *Tribune* but which appears to have been more common in the *Defiance*. "We have lived in Atlanta twenty-seven years," the *Defiance* announced in 1881, "and we have heard the lash sounding from the cabins of the slaves, poured on by their masters. But we have never seen a meaner set of low down cut throats, scrapes, and murderers than the city of Atlanta has to protect the peace." The potential for direct action in collective self-defense, left implied in the rifle at the *Tribune*'s shoulder, becomes overt in the *Defiance*, which was set to call its readers to action: "Are we going to be murdered like dogs right here in this community and not open our mouths?" As best we can tell, this style of argument shows the formative intellectual background for the direct resistance—the praxis—that was being tested in Atlanta's black neighborhoods, and reported with alacrity in the *Constitution*, when Uncle Remus was first going to press.[40]

It is important to understand the arguments made by the *Tribune* and the *Defiance* as historical claims and not merely as normative indictments. They are criticizing injustice, for sure, under the most dire circumstances, but this only makes it all the more important to understand how their claims are calibrated. By tuning into the historical consciousness embedded in these arguments, we can find more than lawlessness in the call for direct action. As we can discern from the *Defiance*, it was possible to confront not only the mob but the police by asserting the similarity between slavery and freedom. The complexity to this claim, which equates the law with the lash in practice but not in theory, becomes accessible when we follow its critical engagement with the New South Creed. In this statement, the *Defiance* directly contradicts the historical narrative of legal development that was proposed in the *Constitution* by representing the transfer of sovereignty from the slavemaster to the state as continuous rather than discontinuous. It is necessary to observe, in the first place, that this argument moves in two directions at once: it insinuates continuity by analogizing the present to slavery, but it also proposes its own concept of slavery by analogizing enslavement to the warfare that was presently happening on the streets between the police and the city's black population. Through this double analogy, warfare turns into a consistent explanatory framework for understanding both past and present. By making warfare into their own historical frame of reference, these black newspapers could begin to question the new understanding of sovereignty promulgated by the *Constitution*. This does not mean that they were speaking for lawlessness or against the police. Rather, it means that they were suggesting that the new mythology of public right was inadequate to the recent history of their region. Henry Grady and his cohort were getting the story wrong.[41]

It is possible to see how this critical approach was substantiated in daily reporting when we recall that these black newspapers were producing their own distinctive system of historical explanation by engaging, sometimes line by line, the rhetoric in the white press. Warfare was invented as an historical topos not by these black journalists but by the police's early supporters, who invoked its violence not as an explanatory principle but instead as a vague and ever-present threat, a symbol for what would happen were the state refused the authority and the resources it needed. In the *Constitution*, this threat became embodied in the black vagrant, which made the policing of the black migrant imaginable as a preemptive necessity, as something that had to be done to defend against the ever-present possibility that society would fall into the chaos of warfare. In this scenario, warfare has no truth. It is not a historical principle so much as a reminder that history is vulnerable to disruption. This wholly disruptive force is what the *Constitution* described as the lawlessness in the black community. Black newspapers borrowed these terms directly from the white press without capitulating to their characterization as lawlessness or conceding their irrationality. Warfare became for the black press a way to explain patterns and intentions that otherwise remained unavailable to representation. It became a way to introduce what others were not prepared to admit—the black migrant's human feeling—as a basis for political action. When we consider that warfare was required not only for the mythology of modern government, where warfare propels the people to create the state, but also for the classical concept of slavery, where warfare precedes the fateful scene where the captive chooses slavery over death, the stakes appear even higher. The claim that is made in the black press, that the war is not over, that the war has never been over, that the war has been going on all along, encompasses not only the recent history of emancipation but the entire history of slavery that comes before it.

This argument, in other words, speaks not only to the state's projected monopoly on violence but to history. Acknowledged here is that the New South Creed can only monopolize historical truth by transforming black politics, whether or not it involves direct action, into lawlessness. Black politics is something that is extrinsic to the historical process. It is a category of incidents that cannot be explicated according to the laws of history. As soon as warfare is permitted to operate as a speculative principle for understanding history and these lawless events become intelligible as a series, it becomes possible to speak all at once to the continuum of the black tradition and to the current struggle organized around the state. The *Defiance* could do both these things at once only because its intervention was staged within a situation where the primary language of politics was historical in orientation. With one decisive gesture, the paper could take this language as its own to criticize not only how society was currently being managed by the state but also how society's history was being misinterpreted and thereby turned into a negative force inside local politics. This theoretical generalization also meant that warfare could be conceptualized not as an exception to the norms that governed society but instead as determining those norms. The *Defiance* took a broad view of war that could account not only for the brutalizing of the black migrant by the mob or police but also for the symbolic violence that was done to the migrant's body in the white press. It could integrate the mob's violence and the cruelty of convict leasing into a general theory that included every feature of society within its purview, such that withholding funds from a school or potable water from a neighborhood could be reasonably described as an act of war. Law existed for this argument not as an enemy but as a standard that did not yet apply. Labeling state action against black migrants as warfare is a way to say that we are still living with the struggle that is supposed to end when the state is established. Describing police actions as crimes is a way to take this argument a step further, building upon the rhetoric of warfare to indict policemen as criminals according to a law that can only exist conditionally or in the future tense. The *Tribune* often pointed to the fact that the laws that were broken with impunity by white mobs were written by white governments. Barring black participation in lawmaking, white governments drafted rules that they then refused to enforce against themselves. This point was often made to convey the hypocrisy in southern law enforcement, or to question whether the southern states were fit for self-government, but it also goes to show what the *Tribune* and the *Defiance* intended to say when they said "law." In a limited sense, they were talking about the laws on the books, but in a profound sense, they were also referring to a law that had not arrived, a law whose history was still being written, a law still to come, whose long-delayed advent would bring an end to the warfare that was still raging across their cities and towns.[42]

These, then, are the combined circumstances that structured Uncle Remus's appearance in the *Constitution*. The New South Creed with its ethos of national reconciliation and its relegation of slavery to historical romance, the brass tacks of infrastructural development, the symbolism of police reform, the expansion of the minor judiciary, the spread of convict labor, the stigmatization of black migration, the debate over lynching, the Racial Uplift Movement with its prescriptions for self-improvement and its hedging diplomacy, the second-order accounting within the black press, and the turn to direct action—all of these local forces and factions left their marks on Uncle Remus. Equally as significant for the early sketches were newspaper genres (editorial boosterism, city miscellanies, dialect hu-mor) that gained increased prominence in the *Constitution* thanks to its new associate editors, Henry Grady and Joel Chandler Harris. True to the form that Harris inherited from the antebellum humorists, Remus oper-ated in these early sketches mainly as a mouthpiece for editorial opinion. As the resident expert on race issues, Remus repeated the newspaper's standard line on hot-button matters like migration. Even as Remus's exas-peration at the current state of the city was played for laughs and his ver-nacular language was embroidered for entertainment purposes, the newspaper saw the serious opportunity that was afforded by these sketches to represent its own thinking as if it had the moral authority of insider knowledge. All this goes to show that Uncle Remus was not merely con-tiguous to the newspaper's campaign for the police—he was part of it. His early sketches treated many of the same topics as the crime and court re-porting that appeared in adjacent columns, and a strong plurality of the early sketches directly addressed the local controversy over the newly strengthened circuit connecting the police department, the inferior courts, and convict leasing.

Harris was steeped in newspaper culture from the time he was an ado-lescent, when he worked as a printer's assistant for the *Countryman*, likely the only plantation newspaper ever produced in the history of the United States. From there he took a job as typesetter at the *Macon Telegraph*, then as sketch writer at the *Monroe Advertiser*, before landing with the *Savan-nah Morning News*, where he worked as an editor and humorist, produc-ing a daily miscellany called "Affairs of Georgia." When he commenced as associate editor for the *Constitution*, Harris continued writing a miscellany called "Roundabout in Georgia," which listed local news and events from around the state. The boundary separating Harris's miscellany from others in the *Constitution*, like the "Police Points," was porous. Harris would is-sue puffs for the police, and he freely combined blackface humor with un-gainly wordplay ("A negro pursued by an agile Macon policeman fell in a well the other day. He says he knocked the bottom out of the concern") in a mode similar to the police court column. His early editorials were simi-larly keyed to the newspaper's common concerns, pressing for a third way in southern politics, even sounding at times more like George Washington Cable than Grady. When the *Constitution* hired Harris, it already had a humor column, written by Sam W. Small, featuring a sardonic dialect speaker, Old Si. Harris was twice tapped to replace Small: first in 1876, when Small left briefly after Howell purchased the newspaper, and again in 1878, after Small left for good to accept a political appointment. After trying a character called Uncle Ben, Harris settled upon Uncle Remus. Like all the rest of Harris's journalistic writing from the 1870s, Remus's sketches were hardwired into the newspaper where they appeared. Uncle Remus's concerns were the *Constitution*'s concerns. Opinions discussed with gravity in editorials were inflected differently, to be sure, when they were voiced by Remus as cantankerous cynicism or spontaneous philosophy, but even so these sketches would become meaningful for their original readers only in relation to the newspaper's general advocacy: for industry, for investment, for the police.[43]

The early Uncle Remus sketches are topical. They often get started with salutations like "What's de news?" or "You ain't heerd de news is you?" or with bracing statements about contemporary politics that become fodder for conversation. Remus speaks to national problems like the silver trade dollar and the Hayes-Tilden dispute though he is mostly interested in local issues. No matter the particular topic, the aim in these sketches is to give a comical spin to a political argument seriously advocated by the *Constitution*, as in an installment like "Uncle Remus as a Weather Prophet" from August 1878, where Remus tells a group of black men gathered at the car-shed he has learned that the Freedmen's Bureau is sending down some experts to regulate the weather. Sharing scenery and characters with other local news, these sketches were tightly integrated into the *Constitution*, partly because they were set in real locations like Whitehall Street, or the intersection of Broad and Alabama, or Maddox's Corner, or the National Hotel. Remus has several meetings at the refurbished depot where passengers were dropped from the new Georgia Air-Line Train, a recently finished rail project whose initial miles were laid by prisoners leased by Grant, Alexander, and Company. The mere mention of new train lines, bustling avenues, and fancy hotels is significant given how easily these details could be assimilated into the newspaper's historical orientation, but this scene-setting is only the beginning.[44]

It did not take Harris long to realize that the Uncle Remus sketches were an ideal medium in which to work out the newspaper's editorial arguments on black vagrancy. These arguments appear, for instance, in sketches where Remus speaks to (or about) recent arrivals to Atlanta: excursionists, or inbound migrants, or people passing through town. Remus has little patience for the strangers who accost him on the streets. In "Uncle Remus and the

Emigrants" from August 1878, Remus encounters "an old negro man, a woman and two children sitting in the shade" who claim to be on their way to "Tallypoosy." Responding to Remus's inquiries, the father explains that their plan is eventually to travel to Mississippi, where they hope to make a better life, though they have no contacts or family there. Remus learns the migrants have no provisions, having eaten all their food before they started, and no train ticket even for the first leg of their journey. Remus is indignant, and he declares that the family's fate is foregone. Inevitably, the father is going to "rob somebody," then he will be put "on de chain gang." His wife and children will be stranded in a town where they have no friends. It is hard to tell if Remus is joking when he proposes that it would be better for the man to go to jail before he commits a crime: "Yo' best holt is de chain-gang. You can make yo' livin 'dar w'en you can't make it no whar else." For these migrants, as for so many others, going to prison is a better choice than going on the road. "I'me talkin' wid de bark on," Remus persists, "I done seed deze yet Arkinsaw emmygrants come lopein back, an' some un 'em didn't have rags nuff on 'em fer ter hide der nakidness." Remus sees no difference between people traveling on their own initiative and those who are planning for organized mass emigration to Africa, Mississippi, or Kansas. Extending from "Uncle Remus as an Emigrant" (1878) to late sketches like "Views on the African Exodus" (1892), emigration is shown as a scam meant to prey upon the desire to live without working. "I know d re's plenty er loafers w'at oughter go, but I dunno who ter inwite," one would-be emigrant pronounces on the corner. Living in Liberia could not be easier, he promises Uncle Remus. "Dey say coffee grows in de frunt yard, an' de sun pa'ches it an' de rain wets it, an' it falls in a hole in de groun' an' dar's yo coffee." Remus laughs off the idea that Liberia is a land where coffee is automatically dispensed by the earth, and he ties this utopianism to the empty promises (Forty Acres and a Mule) and failed projects (the Freedmen's Bank) that were already worsening the lot of ex-slaves.[45]

There is a similar approach in sketches where Remus addresses people who try to live without labor contracts. In "Turnip Salad as a Text" from November 1880, Remus speaks with a group of black men that "knocks 'roun an' picks up a livin'" rather than sign an annual contract with an employer. Sounding something like the recorder at the police court, Remus is quick to pass judgment over these men: "Hit's agin de mor'l law fer niggers fer ter eat w'en dey don't wuk, an' w'en you see um 'pariently fattenin' on a'r, you k'n des bet dat ruinashun's gwine on some 'rs." Remus even goes so far as to say that he can "count up right yer in de san' en number up how menny days hit 'll be 'fo' you'er cuppled on ter de chain-gang." In "Uncle Remus Makes a Confession" from August 1879, Uncle Remus corners the sporting editor at the *Constitution* to complain about black street vendors "'lopin' roun' town wid cakes 'n pies fer ter sell." Declaring that "some niggers ain't gwine ter work nohow," Remus says these vendors will never resist the temptation to eat the pies and so will soon find themselves on the chain gang. Although it could conceivably take some empathy to realize how much work it would have taken for the men in "Turnip Salad as a Text" to knock around and pick up a living, Remus's take on street vendors is untenable based on internal evidence alone. Even the sporting editor objects that selling pies is "just as honest and just as regular" as "any other kind of work."[46]

Sometimes Remus talks to his vagrants and sometimes he talks about them, but the effect remains the same whether the address is direct or indirect. Like the police court report, the Remus sketches sift indiscriminate charges about black vagrancy from the *Constitution*'s editorial pages and enlarge them into narrative situations. This goes to show, again, not only how these sketches were formed by the newspaper's programmatic commitments but also how fast those commitments could bloom into farce. Uncle Remus's moralizing is what makes these sketches humorous, allegedly. This means that Remus can consistently overreach in his claims about life in the city without jeopardizing the reader's provisional identification with his perspective. The point is not whether his claims are true or false; it is the pleasure in their projected delivery that matters. Because the sketches suspend the reader's ability to evaluate his claims as claims, Remus is permitted to lapse into self-contradiction, and indeed, he is obliged to lapse given that the situational irony in the sketches often banks on things he does not know or words he cannot pronounce. The pleasure in the sketches is intensified, that is to say, when editorial claims made in all seriousness elsewhere in the newspaper are allowed to fall apart. Notably, these claims fail on points that are also depicted in the critical analysis in the black press. If Remus's disposition was supposed to remain compelling for readers despite (or even because of) its capacity for performative contradiction, the black press was on a parallel course, leveraging these sticking points for critique.

Harris does more than put editorial opinions in Uncle Remus's mouth. He crafts interlocutory scenes where the repetition of these opinions becomes meaningful in relation not only to their speaker but also to their listeners. Harris makes his decisive intervention when he turns Uncle Remus into a spokesperson for the anti-vagrancy campaign, but he is also able to augment this rhetorical framework in individual sketches through his choice of interlocutors. When Remus's interlocutors are black, they are typically left nameless and portrayed as social types: "a colored politician" or a "lazy looking negro." His white interlocutors, by contrast, are real people identified by name. Whether Remus is stopping by the *Constitution* to chat with the editors, or hitting up Lewis Clarke, the foremost hatter in Atlanta, for a dime, he is speaking with individuals who were known by reputation, if not recognizable on sight, by most residents. The effect is strongest when Harris has Remus articulate his caustic opinions about black migrants to police officers. When the sketches were placed in his first book, the names of the officers were withheld, but in the original versions in the newspaper, the names are included. In "Uncle Remus as a Murderer" from August 1878, Remus's interlocutor is Officer Jarrel. In "Uncle Remus in the Role of a Tartar" from July 1878, Remus complains to Officer Willis King, known from the crime reports as a brave defender of the public peace and from "Police Points" as an aspiring actor and a newlywed. When Remus gets into a scuffle, he knows he can count on Chief Tige Anderson, shown elsewhere as "calm and collected under all circumstances" with "a heart as bold as a lion." Learning from the crime reports that Anderson was "fit to marshal armies," regular readers of the newspaper would also recall from "Police Points" that he slept as little as three hours a night, that he could tell an escaped convict from the palm of his hand, and that he had three dogs. In a later sketch, Remus even testifies as a defendant in recorder Andy Calhoun's courtroom.[47]

The police officers sympathize with his frustration, but Remus invariably complains more loudly and more bitterly than his blue-coated counterparts. If the police advocate moderation, Remus calls for violent reprisals. These are standard good cop–bad cop routines where Remus plays the bad cop. Sometimes Remus not only speaks for the police, or to the police, he also acts as their surrogate. He literally takes over the bad policeman's role, bragging about his quick trigger finger, sprinting after petty thieves, and hitting anyone who steps out of line. In a few sketches, he even reenacts the archetypal cases, rehearsed over and again in court and crime coverage, where the drifter lounging on the corner, the migrant just come to town, or the thief escaping the chicken coop is collared by the police officer. Even the language spoken by the police ("You don't mean to tell me that you have killed a colored man, do you?") sounds principled in contrast to the peculiar turns in Remus's talk. The function of these routines is not to prove that Remus is wrong and the police are right. It is, instead, about enjoying the newspaper's temporary capacity to sustain itself in relation to a conceptual problem that it could not otherwise resolve. The sketches are so telling because they present these cases as if police action required no legitimation. Remus is not subjected to the constraints that the law would place on the state. He is unreasonable, and his surrogacy establishes a disposition from which police violence can be pictured without worrying about the principle at stake. When Remus takes action, there is no point to asking whether he is inside or outside the law. The distinction between legal and extralegal action does not trouble the sketches, as it did trouble the *Constitution*, which struggled mightily in its editorials to explain the difference this distinction made, even as its reporting continued to rely on anti-vagrancy language that barred this distinction from consideration.[48]

It was on 20 July 1879 that Harris published, without fanfare, a new column with the heading "Negro Folk Lore." This was the first time that Uncle Remus assumed his station as plantation storyteller. The new sketches were a hit with Georgia readers within their first six months, and before long, they were syndicated nationally. Though he would republish the urban sketches in his first book, Harris was quick to insist on the difference between those first trials and the mature work in which Remus was a mouthpiece, not for the newspaper, but for the black tradition. Harris had found a serious mission, which was to "to preserve as far as possible" the "characteristics" of a vanishing vernacular tradition with as much precision as possible. Critics have always admitted that the dialect in the later tales is consistent with the blackface tradition that informs the earlier sketches, but otherwise they have taken Harris at his word when he argued these new works functioned in a new mode. There are some instances where the contemporary association is undeniable, like "The Story of the Deluge" from December 1879, which concerns a political assembly where the animals congregate, make ridiculous speeches, and write preambles only to get into a brawl that unleashes a flood. "The Story of the Deluge" prolongs its allusion to Reconstruction for the duration of the installment, making it hard to miss the connection to urban sketches like "Uncle Remus's Politics" and "Uncle Remus and a Democratic Christmas," from November and December 1876, respectively, where Remus talks current events with black would-be politicians who seem to have no clue what they are talking about. Remus admits that he knows nothing about politics either, but he supposes knowing about politics matters less than knowing where his next meal is coming from. If the folklore in "The Story of the Deluge" looks backward, it also looks one column over in the same day's newspaper to an article saying that the "colored people" who prosper are those who are "not actively engaged in politics."[49]

There is frequently a topical orientation even in the folklore sketches that would appear most removed from contemporary politics, such as "The Wonderful Tar-Baby Story," which was originally printed in the *Constitution* as "Brer Rabbit, Brer Fox, and the Tar-Baby" in November 1879. In the succeeding decades, anthropologists would go to work tracing "The Wonderful Tar-Baby Story" to points throughout Africa as well as to Lithuania, Spain, Greece, Portugal, India, Cuba, Guatemala, Louisiana, and North Carolina. An influential theory proposed by none other than Franz Boas held that the tale was taken from Asia to Africa by Portuguese and Spanish traders. Whatever trajectory is drawn for the Tar Baby, the tale's prior evolution matters less for the *Constitution* than the cues that Harris inserts to orient readers to what may have been an unfamiliar tradition. These cues frame the tale by anchoring its narrative in conventions that were already functioning in the urban sketches and in the newspaper's local coverage of city life. This is true of the dialect. Following the promise to preserve every discernible inflection in the black voice, Harris is quick to abandon even the slightest pretense to phonetic realism to play for laughs, using the most hackneyed forms available to him, such as eye dialect ("duz" for "does" or "stummuck" for "stomach"), malapropism ("segashuate"), and the substitution of closed for open syllables ("innercent"). More telling are the allusions that draw the encounter between Brer Rabbit and the Tar Baby into the blackface tradition, such as the moment when the rabbit heads down the road "sassy ez a hotel nigger" toward the fox's trap. Anticipating the rabbit's comeuppance, the epithet implies not only a type but a whole character system, orienting the reader to the comedy of manners that is to come with the tar baby, a comedy that defines the porter-putting-on-airs even further by tying the trope to the perceived social problem of sidewalk etiquette. When the rabbit strikes the tar-baby for failing to show respect to strangers in public, he plugs into the role that Remus plays in urban stories like "Uncle Remus

ally isolate Greenville and
ecution of this edict of os-
irit of bigotry and intoler-
he early Christians, which
he middle ages like wild
imes tortured protesting
very age of darkness has
ht. It is a very slight re-
ne thumb-screw and the
it the spirit of American
teenth century.

eenville are not slandered
ie state of South Carolina.
They are giving the ene-
leadly weapon of attack.
this one organization will
ent of the southern people,
nent. It will keep away
the south stands so much
c new homes are not going
ler an absolute and merci-
Where freemen cannot
n they will not settle.
because of his political
which no community can
g upon itself the contempt
ving people everywhere.
nville who do not indorse
ought to be heard from,
,s been misrepresented by
ght to make haste to con-
t has been outraged.

the Law.

and Advertiser.

in Atlanta has furnished
rion of the fallacy of the
he governor the appoint-
plicitors, and placed the
es in the hands of the leg-

e field for political ma-
the crime of lobying, and
t of temptation men, who
ions, should be free from
litical contests. If a man
of the executive chair, he
to sway the appointing
good that this new order
h. The offices have been
s of men than the gov-
ccustomed to appoint;
scramble for the
red members of the legis-
e state, who know nothing
plicants, detracts consid-
of the offices. It's a game
manipulation is more pow-
and the most expert politi-
eed. We do not mean by
at all the officers elected
this manner, but we mean
is well calculated to pro-
ences.
y the legislature in dispos-
been considerable, and the
ess has been monstrous.
e can render no better ser-
ie state than to repeal this
y, and we may say, evil

Sentiment.
Republican, rep.

Display advertisement for Joel Chandler Harris, *Uncle Remus, His Songs and His Sayings: The Folk-Lore of the Old Plantation*, from the *Atlanta Constitution*, 29 November 1880.

and the Fourth," which opine against the offensive manners of black migrants met on the streets. Where Remus throttles the black excursionist who dares to bump into him, Brer Rabbit tries the same when he thinks that the Tar Baby is being rude to him, recouping these prior associations while forging a new type of connection to the contemporary world of the news. This connection is only strengthened by the rumor, floated at the end, that Brer Rabbit remained stuck until he was freed by Judge Bear.[50]

These allusions anchor the tales in the newspaper. They do not produce allegory, but they do make the war between the rabbit and his adversaries conceivable in relation to the battles that were being reported from the streets of Atlanta. Warfare is motivated in the tales in several ways. Sometimes it is sexual competition, as in "Brer Rabbit Again Grossly Deceives Brer Fox" from December 1879, in which the rabbit puts a saddle on the fox and rides him by Miss Meadows's house. This tale follows the archetypal pattern in which the sexual desire between male rivals is triangulated through their shared object of affection, in this case the "ladies" on the porch, whom the rabbit tells, presumably with a straight face, that he has turned the fox into his "ridin'-hoss." Characteristically, however, war in the tales means war over food. From the first "Negro Folk Lore" sketch in July 1879, "The Story of Mr. Rabbit and Mr. Fox, as Told by Uncle Remus," in which the fox asks the rabbit to his house for dinner with the intention of eating the rabbit for dinner, warfare is coordinated around subsistence. There are tales about beef, honey, butter, sugarcane, peanuts, greens, milk, roast corn, cabbage, fish, chicken, and calamus root. War often starts when one animal makes a plan to eat another. When they are not trying to eat each other, they are warring over provisions. In "The Fox Goes a Hunting, but the Rabbit Bags the Game" in February 1880, the rabbit plays dead to trick the fox into dropping his hunting bag. Banking not only on Brer Fox's greed but on his vanity, the rabbit changes himself into game in order to steal some game for himself. Similarly in "How Brer Rabbit Saved His Meat" from March 1880, Brer Rabbit nabs a string of fish from Brer Wolf, and then offers to make amends by slaughtering a cow. He tells the wolf that a slave patrol is approaching and then hides the meat when the wolf is concealed in the underbrush. In "The Sad Fate of Mr. Fox" from July 1880, Brer Rabbit and Brer Fox join forces to steal meat from the cow owned by Mister Man. When they are caught stealing, the rabbit double-crosses the fox, and the man beats the fox to death. The rabbit persuades the man to give him the fox's head and takes the head to the fox's family, telling Miss Fox not to look at it, but that it is "nice beef" for dinner. When the fox's son peeks into the pot, he discovers his own father's head stewing.[51]

In certain sketches, the contemporary reference for this warfare gets even more specific. In the first tale, the rabbit fixes a "smashin' dinner" after raiding "a gyarden like Miss Sally's out dar." In the third tale, the possum and the raccoon begin a night together by filling their bellies: the possum eats persimmons off the trees, and the raccoon catches and eats frogs and tadpoles. In a song from October 1879, Remus discourses on pan-toting ("Hi my rinktum! Black gal sweet/Same like goodies w'at de w'ite folks eat/Ho my Riley! don't you take'n tell 'er name/En den ef sumpin' happen you won't ketch de blame"), recording for posterity an early example of a theme that would become even more prominent in later decades as it was assimilated into blues and vaudeville. In the same installment, Uncle Remus also sings about workplace theft ("Hi my rinktum! better take'n hide yo' plum/Joree don't holler eve'y time he fine a wum"), a theme that was also magnified in later decades. As with the blackface hints in the Tar Baby, these references connect to the urban sketches, where scarcely a week went by without a fight with burglars-in-the-making or a chase with crop-thieves. Recall, as well, that Remus returns to his master in "Uncle Remus as a Rebel" because he cannot stop people from taking the cotton and corn that he tries to grow on his own. These references connect just as strongly to the news reported in neighboring columns. Livestock-stealing, rag-picking, and pan-toting were major concerns in the police court. One report, from January 1902, went so far as to acknowledge the degree to which the recorder shared this fixation with Uncle Remus. With the title "Brer Rabbit in the Collard Patch," the report features a defendant, Hunter Bailey, who gets caught taking collards from a neighbor's yard. Addressed as "Brer Rabbit" by Judge Broyles and the arresting officer, and drawn as such in the accompanying cartoon, Bailey testifies that he was owed the collards by his neighbor. Queried about his employment, Bailey replies that he is working irregularly ("At furs one place an den annudder") rather than on contract, and that he takes payment in kind ("Fuss one t'ing an' den annudder") rather than wages. Hearing this testimony, Judge Broyles sends Brer Rabbit to the chain gang.[52]

Regular readers would not have needed this guidance to catch the contemporary reference in Remus's tales. Clearly this reference has not been lost on some of their most astute twentieth-century critics, including June Jordan, who has no sympathy for Brer Rabbit. For Jordan, the rabbit is a "pathological hustler." He is a deadbeat who needs to "grow his own darn cabbages and carrots." We do not have to subscribe to the idea that Brer Rabbit's subsistence practices are pathological to realize that Jordan is right about their historical reference, both in her own time and in the time of slavery. Brer Rabbit refers directly to the hustling that had to happen under slavery. Although they were not thrilled about it, many slaveowners accepted it as a fact of life that slaves were going to help themselves to milk, eggs, chicken, and meat from the smokehouse—some of them even admitted to reducing their standard rations to below subsistence on the grounds that slaves were going to be stealing food anyway. In most jurisdictions, it was against the law for slaves to head out at night hunting, or to release their livestock for open-range grazing, but these practices were also tolerated by planters who saw that this self-provisioning worked to their own advantage. It made sense to permit slaves to hunt, fish, forage, keep livestock, and tend gardens for their own subsistence, as it reduced the expenditure that was required to sustain a bound workforce. In an economic downturn, slaves's capacity to feed themselves relieved some of the pressure on their owners, and sometimes it became a make-or-break contribution, keeping farms viable that would have otherwise gone under. Generally, it was custom in the southern states to treat unfenced lands, even when they were privately owned, as available for hunting, fishing, and grazing. Because most of the acreage on southern farms was unfenced, there was a tremendous quantity of land available to the public, and the customary right to access this land for subsistence purposes was shared with the enslaved.[53]

These subsistence practices persisted even as their context changed after emancipation. Ex-slaves continued to contribute to their own livelihood by hunting, fishing, and gardening, and they continued to subscribe to the moral economy of slavery, which said that they had customary rights to some small portion of the harvest that they worked to produce. If planters knew that these customs may have been beneficial under slavery, they also knew they were now contrary to their interests. Few ex-slaves managed to evade the wage market altogether, but many realized that their ability to supplement their income through these traditional subsistence practices gave them leverage in labor negotiations and potential flexibility in their work schedules. Employers fought back with legislation that restricted access to the land and criminalized subsistence practices accepted under slavery as customary rights. There were new laws on criminal trespass, laws against grazing and the gathering of wood from un-enclosed land, laws restricting weekly and seasonal access to waterways, and laws mandating wildly disproportionate penalties for petty larceny, in-cluding the notorious five-year mandatory minimum for pig stealing. After Reconstruction ended in Georgia in 1871, new game laws were introduced for three counties in 1872, then six more counties in 1875, eighteen in 1876, six in 1877, and six in 1878. There was also aggressive prosecution for "larceny after trust" brought against tenants in disputes over shared crops, and vagrancy laws were rewritten to include hunting and fishing "on the land of others" as legitimate cause to arrest. The *Constitution* represented this campaign as an important step against vagrancy. By the newspaper's lights, it was only proper for the state to block access to the resources that enabled vagrants to live without working. In the urban sketches, Remus feels the same way: it is just wrong to knock around and pick up a living. The results, however, are different when the practices criminalized by the government, and pathologized in the *Constitution*, are projected into the vernacular tradition, and the first step to perceiving this difference is look-ing to the form of the new sketches.[54]

To understand how the folklore sketches interact with the news stories around them, we need to think about how they are framed. It is the frame narrative, where Remus speaks to the little boy, that mediates between the world of the tales and the world of the news. The frame is not the reality that counts here. It is, instead, a formal device that fits the fantasy in the tales into the *Constitution*. In this context, there is no question that a world where animals talk, croon, and smoke cigars is a mythical world; it is also, unequivocally in this case, a mythical past. Remus explains at sev-eral junctures that the tales are set in "dem days w'en de creeturs wuz san-ter'n 'roun' same like fokes" with "lots mo' sense dan dey got now." This chronology is asserted, but it is also a formal necessity. The events within the tales must occur, if they occur at all, before they can be narrated. Any tale relates to the scene in which it is told through a chronology that is structural and irreversible. You cannot report an event before it occurs: this applies even when the event appears to be unreal. Framed as a tale-within-a-tale, the black tradition is recast as an unsettling fantasy that is engaged and reworked in the interlocutory encounter until it is relegated to the past. In the transference, the problem of legal development is dramatized by repeating everyday scenarios from the newspaper's crime and court coverage with surrogate actors—rabbits, foxes, wolves, terrapins, and cows. As the tales reset again and again to their starting point, the expectation is that their tension will eventually be assimilated into the frame and thus resolved as folklore. This explains why the timing of the encounter does not matter as much as we might assume. Harris adjusts "A Story of the War" in his first book to locate the encounter after emancipation, but he does away with this timing before his second book, *Nights with Uncle Remus* (1883), in which the encounter is backdated to slavery. Nothing is lost in the process as the frame's main purpose is to make the events in the tales narratable in the situation of the news, and the frame does not require fixed historical coordinates to make that happen. The fact that the news often looks more like the bellicose world inside the tales than like the peaceful world where the tales are told only confirms that something is happening here, that the therapeutic work in the frame is ongoing, that there is something still to be achieved.[55]

Another way to describe this process is to say that the *Constitution* treats these tales as if they were parables about the world as it once existed. Brer Rabbit lives in a state of nature that is hanging at the moment when a strong central government begins to seem like a reasonable idea. As it is represented in the tales, nature is coextensive with warfare. This is a world where isolated individuals battle against one another for survival. Brer Rabbit is a fine guide to this natural world. Famously, he is amoral. He is without loyalties. He is happy to torture and kill his enemies and willing to sacrifice innocents to preserve himself. He is dishonest, selfish, vengeful, destructive, and cruel—as much malicious as mischievous— and yet it is hard to condemn these actions given their circumstances. The battle between the rabbit and his adversaries is conditioned by the confusion that reigns in this world. It is a world in which nothing is known for certain. You can have a truce with someone, but you never can tell how long the truce will last as nobody has the power to limit breaches of contract. Moreover, there is no naturally discernible right to property. Self-preservation is an absolute imperative in these tales; it follows that you can seize another's property or violate another's person when your own survival is at risk. The struggle that arises under these conditions is exacerbated by the fact that it is impossible to say for sure whether such claims are made under exigent circumstances, as there is no objective criterion for evaluating their legitimacy. It is wrongheaded to try to decide whether the fox needs to eat the sparrow to survive, or whether the rabbit goes too far when he traps the cow to milk her dry, as the tales are arranged to eliminate these questions from consideration. As the natural right to property is overwritten, so is the potential for treating persons as self-possessed individuals. The indistinction between person and property is no less foundational to the tales than it is to slavery, only in the tales it registers specifically as an anthropomorphism that permits talking animals to substitute for humans in a political equation where the capacity to speak equals the capacity to deceive.[56]

In the *Constitution* generally, warfare is a threat. It shows what life would be like without an effective state. It is a chronic condition, inherent to society, a condition that can return at any moment if you do not guard against it. This view of warfare is the crux of the newspaper's case for the police. The police should be adequately supplied to prevent society from sliding into the chaos of warfare. It follows that Brer Rabbit's world is not confined to the distant past. It is a world that is always potentially still with us. It relates to the present day. This threat, however, is managed differently in the folklore sketches than the urban sketches. Rather than pathologizing the survival tactics of street vendors and pan-toters, Remus superannuates them. Rather than merely ridiculing the politics of black civil society, Remus imagines a mythical world where these politics are still prescient, only to witness that world slipping away. While the tales sustain a connection to the news that keeps them from slipping into the past tense, their frame nevertheless implies that history has a direction. Moral progress toward law is felt, although it is never named, in the movement from the tales to the world of the news. This is inescapable. War is never gone completely, but it is always going. It is obsolescent. It insinuates a chronology. History, at least as it was written in *Constitution*, depends on this.

This historical movement is also described in the *Constitution*'s promotional materials about Uncle Remus. In an editorial from April 1880, Harris speaks plainly on the matter. Directing the editorial to anyone who had failed to understand the "purpose of the legends" that had been "appearing in THE CONSTITUTION," Harris explains that their solitary aim is "to preserve in permanent shape those curious mementoes of a period that will no doubt be sadly misrepresented by the historian of the future." Harris goes on to insist that the tales were invented by slaves, and that they encapsulated everything that one could ever know about the slave's point of view. Readers picked up both these arguments. The *New York*

Times praised Harris for depicting the "subtle characteristics" of a tradition that would be "practically unknown" but for "the historian Uncle Remus." Walter Hines Page, the celebrated editor and publisher, pushed the point even further, writing that Uncle Remus was "so great a piece of literature" that "if all histories and records of slave-life" were "blotted out," a "diligent antiquarian" could reconstruct its "essential features" even "thousands of years hence" from the body of trickster legends that Uncle Remus narrates to the little boy.[57]

These statements are reckless, and even macabre, but they are also historically representative. Analytically, they are important for how they elucidate the symbolic action in the frame narrative. Specifically, they demonstrate how the frame narrative was made to serve the campaign for the police. By superannuating the trickster tradition, the *Constitution* reinforced an old mythology about the origin of modern government by threading it through a new idea about black culture. Demonstrating the tradition's obsolescence became a means to explain not only "black culture" (or the black tradition's reduction to culture) but also why it was sensible to have a state with enough muscle to keep the peace. All this happens at once in Remus's tales, which are enclosed by interlocking frames of political allusion that only become integrated when they are cross-referenced with contemporary thinking about cultural difference. It was commonplace in 1879 to believe that there was one track for world history. Societies differed from one another only insofar as they were more or less advanced along this single track. Difference meant difference in development. There was no chance that some other society would have its own way of doing things that was different but equally as good as your own. One result of this assumption was that collectors, who considered themselves more developed than the people they studied, believed that it was possible to discover their own prehistory within the lives of others. In the *Constitution*, this meant that the world within Remus's tales could stand at once for Africa and for a period in world history that Atlanta had left behind. By borrowing this assumption from current anthropology, the newspaper could do two things at the same time. It could offer a hypothesis about the modern state, and it could make the black tradition into folklore. To understand the tales, we need to realize that these are two parts to the same social process.[58]

It can be difficult to reconstruct the relation between the Uncle Remus folklore sketches and contemporary legal thinking, given how quickly the sketches covered their own tracks. But consider for a moment a comment by Theodore Bacon in his commencement address for Yale Law School in 1896. Bacon told the graduating class that "jurisprudence" was the engine that moved civilization forward. Remarking that this "growth" was evidenced not only in common law but in statute books, he hastened to add that he did not mean to reference legislation as a class, nine tenths of which, in his estimation, had "no more relation to jurisprudence than a tale of 'Uncle Remus.'" This is a throwaway line, whose casual inclusion indicates its condition as common sense. Nothing has less to do with the law than Uncle Remus. This is an idea that the *Constitution* worked hard to indicate to its readers, and one measure of its success is this application two decades later in New Haven. It was important to the *Constitution* that Remus mattered to the current events in the adjacent columns only in an attenuated sense as their obscure prehistory. Black tradition was prepolitical. It came from a time before the law. It was static, in contrast to the law's development, or changing only to the extent that it was disintegrating moment by moment. This is an idea that Uncle Remus helped to produce.[59]

By reading the folklore sketches in relation to the news, we can see how their sense of history is produced. The best guide to Remus's vernacular storytelling is the urban commentary given by Uncle Remus himself, which candidly addresses the topical themes that are refracted into the vernacular tradition in the folklore sketches. This is especially noticeable with the police. More-or-less oblique references to slave patrols and judges and imprisonment appear throughout the folklore, but the police register most powerfully not at the level of allusion but as the historical agency that connects the tales to their frame. The urban cycle culminates with "Uncle Remus and the Fourth," a sketch that was published in July 1879, only two weeks before Harris's initial "Negro Folk Lore" experiment. More than any other installment, "Uncle Remus and the Fourth" is explicit about the imperatives that formed both the urban and the folklore sketches. As such, it is a bellwether for Uncle Remus's great transformation. This sketch resembles others that came before it. Recalling previous installments like "Uncle Remus and the Emigrants" and "Jeems Rober'son's Last Illness," which focus upon black migration, the occasion for "Uncle Remus and the Fourth" is a complaint about black excursionists who take the train into Atlanta on holidays. The sketch is conventional, as well, in its subject matter: it addresses the daily battle over public manners on the sidewalk, a topic that was already familiar to loyal readers from sketches like "As to Education" and "Uncle Remus in the Role of a Tartar" and from the *Constitution's* editorial page. Finally, the sketch feels familiar in its choice of interlocutors. Remus makes his complaint to the editorial staff at the newspaper, evoking the other sketches where he converses with the society editor, the sporting editor, the politics editor, and the police court reporter. Inside the complaint, there is the direct address to the offending excursionist and then dialogue with a policeman, following a pattern where Remus polices and then speaks to the police about what he has done.

"Uncle Remus and the Fourth" starts with Remus entering the *Constitution* offices with one arm bandaged. Noticing the injury, one of the editors asks what happened. Remus confesses that he was fighting at the July Fourth celebration, and the editor begins to chastise him. Remus says it was not his fault. He explains that he was standing on the sidewalk minding his own business when an excursionist from Mobile bumped into him, not once but three times. On the final pass, the man even dared to touch a watermelon rind against Remus's left ear. Losing his temper, Remus throttled the man and broke his own arm in the process. Remus's reaction to the Mobile excursionist at once reenacts and supersedes the greeting that many black migrants received from the police upon arriving in Atlanta. As in the other sketches where Remus plays police, it is evident here that he is exceeding his self-imputed authority, but in this case, the effect is different. Usually Remus's immoderation is contained by situational irony. The sketches do not identify the legal distinction between personal violence and police violence as a matter for consideration. Rather, they leave the distinction unspecified, turning its application into a joke — as in "Uncle Remus's Church Experience" where Remus decides to bring his "hoss pistol" to church to quiet the rabble he finds there, or in "Uncle Remus as a Murderer" where he fires his rifle point-blank at someone trying to make off with his chickens. For the joke to work, the distinction has to remain sensible to the friendly officers and uneasy editors even as it is disobeyed by Remus.[60]

In "Uncle Remus and the Fourth," by contrast, the distinction between personal violence and police violence is named, and it immediately becomes a topic for conversation. In the encounter with the excursionist, Uncle Remus's surrogacy for the police is indistinguishable from personal violence. When he strikes the excursionist, Remus becomes the "criminal policeman" censured by the *Savannah Tribune*. His action looks like retribution though its occasion recapitulates the *Constitution*'s rationale for the preventative maintenance of the public peace. The *Constitution* often wrote as if the rationale for police violence in this situation were self-evident, but in this sketch, Remus's act is obviously unfounded. It derives not from public necessity but from personal prejudice. As the story unfolds, the situation looks more and more like a he-said-he-said affair. In the end, it is not clear who started it. By taking the law into his own hands, Remus appears lawful (like the police) and unlawful (like a criminal) all at once. Unlike in earlier sketches, in this case this problem is understood by everyone. In the exchange with the editors, Remus is called a bad citizen for failing to concede violence to the state, and in the exchange with his policeman interlocutor, the consequences of this conversation are even more dramatic.[61]

In this final urban installment, Remus talks not just to any police officer but to the Chief of Police, George T. "Tige" Anderson. A Confederate veteran who had led his army brigade into thirty-eight battles and served on the Atlanta police force since 1872, Anderson had a powerful public image. The *Constitution* was even willing to suggest that the police would have folded in their struggle for the city were it not for their "great regard" for Anderson, who "aroused a desire in their hearts to aid him in policing the city." Inspired by Anderson's model, the police under his command were alleged to toil with an intensity "that would honor them anywhere on the globe." More than anyone else on the force, Anderson would seem to fit the profile for the "good cop" to whom Remus speaks in counterpoint. Though this expectation is fulfilled in every other one of the early double acts, here it is not. Remus explains to the editors that Anderson arrived on the scene while he was beating the excursionist, but this was just fine. Because of their long-standing acquaintance, Anderson is willing to "shet one eye" whenever Remus "gits mixed up in a racket." He knows why Remus feels "bleedged ter drap on dese outside cullud people," and he is shown signing onto the cause. From here, the sketch is forced to continue without recourse to the interlocutory framework that formerly structured Uncle Remus's relationship to the police. Anderson can no longer play good cop to Remus's bad cop, which means that the division of labor that otherwise obtains in the urban sketches, where the good cop speaks for how the law is practiced under normal circumstances and the bad cop speaks for the exceptional instances, breaks down as soon as Anderson steps onto the scene and discards the role that he had been assigned elsewhere in the *Constitution*.[62]

General George T. "Tige" Anderson—interlocutor to Uncle Remus, Confederate veteran, chief marshall for the Atlanta police from 1872 to 1879, Atlanta police chief from 1879 to 1881. Pictured here around 1889, when he was the police chief for Anniston, Alabama. Courtesy Jerry M. Cook.

The resulting allegory is clearly defined. Consider, for instance, the sketch's setting. July Fourth was a contested holiday in the southern states. Enthusiastically celebrated by blacks, southern whites were gradually beginning in the 1870s to resume their own patriotic pageants and parades, which had been suspended since the war. This trend was praised in northern newspapers like the *New York Times* and was supported by progressive southern newspapers like the *Constitution*. This particular sketch addresses national reconciliation through its setting, and it is instructive for the extent to which it manages to think more deeply by training its attention upon local circumstances. Responding to the tale about the excursionist, one of the editors tells Remus that he has desecrated July Fourth with his violence. "It is really singular," the editor intones, "not even an ordinary holiday—a holiday, it seems to me, that ought to arouse all the latent instincts of patriotism in the bosom of American citizens can occur without embroiling some of our most valuable citizens." Remus is a failed citizen, but he fails for different reasons than the excursionist. The excursionist fails for a reason that is already conventional: he misconstrues the meaning of freedom. Coming to the city for a good time, he confuses liberty with excessive license, showing with his bad manners and big spending (like other interlocutors he wears an expensive brass watch) that his emancipation came too soon. The case with Remus is different. He desecrates July Fourth not as a vagrant but as a double for the police. He makes problems for July Fourth for the same reason he makes problems for the newspaper's lobby for the department. From the moment that he strikes the excursionist, Remus wipes away the legal distinction between personal and police violence. In this situation, policing is indistinguishable from ordinary fisticuffs. The people look like any other crowd, and the Fourth of July seems like any other day. "Hit may be de fote er de fif' er July," Remus announces to the editors, "er hit may be de twelf' er Jinawerry, but w'en a Mobile nigger gits in my naberhood right den an' dar trubble sails in."[63]

The *Constitution* faced a clear-cut problem with its advocacy for the police. It tried to show the need for the police by raising the stakes on its anti-crime argument to the point where it became difficult to witness the distinction between police violence and mob violence. As criminal policeman, Remus embodies this problem. His action cannot be explained according to the advent of law. It breaks away from the myth of legal development that was propagated by the *Constitution* and commemorated on the Fourth of July. "Uncle Remus and the Fourth" intensifies the problem only to offer some notes toward a solution. When the editors convey their surprise at his aggression, Remus scoffs at them. Remus claims that he is "es fon' er deze Nunited States as de nex' man," only to note that on this occasion his patriotism was overcome by his raw instincts. "Well, you des oughter see me git my Affikin up," he tells the editors, "Dey useter call me er bad nigger 'long 'fo' de war, an' hit looks like ter me dat I gits wuss and wuss." Conceivable at first as an off-duty police officer, Remus leaves that position behind to become an outlaw. No longer the bad cop, Remus is the "bad nigger." This brings a new parity to the encounter with the excursionist. When Remus challenges the excursionist like a policeman confronting a vagrant, there is an asymmetry to the encounter that disappears after Remus is outlawed. As far as the *Constitution* is concerned, both of them are criminals. This is key for the entire sketch. So long as Remus looks like a policeman, his violence makes July Fourth look like any other day. It is only after his violence becomes African (or "Affikin") rather than American that the rite is revived. Using Africa to motivate this violence, the sketch appeals to rivalry and retribution (the politics of "naberhood") as an alternative explanation for the war on the streets. It is this gesture that turns July Fourth back into July Fourth again by marking the difference between the warfare in the sketch's foreground and the ceremony of the law in its background. Perspective remains unstable, but there is enough clarity at the ending to reveal the new meaning that Africa could hold for America. By the sketch's conclusion, Remus's encounter with the excursionist begins to seem like mere tribalism. This change is registered even in the offhand insults that Remus hurls at his enemy. The sketch starts with one of Remus's favorite put-downs from the early urban sketches: "Show me a Mobile nigger," he boasts, "and I'll show you a nigger dat's marked for de chain-gang." By the end, things are different: "[T]urn a Mobile nigger loose in dis town, fote er July or no fote er July," Remus says in the last sentence, "an' me er him one is got ter lan' in jail. Hit's proned inter me." As far as the sketch is concerned, Remus has become indistinguishable from the excursionist. Both are recognizable at once as belonging to that "certain class" whose continuing violence indicates their alienation from the state.[64]

Placed on an equal footing in the foreground of the sketch, their fight starts to look not like police brutality but like a face-off between equals, something like the natural warfare that must have existed between people before there was a state to intervene in their disputes. As it initially appears in the sketch, the fight might as well have been excerpted from the *Savannah Tribune*, which was citing this kind of police brutality to support its claim that law had not yet arrived in the southern states. Remus's violence may not be explicable in terms of the ritual it interrupts, but it could be explained, in the terms of the *Tribune*, as a brand of warfare. This explanation is like Remus in that it sees no difference between January Twelfth and July Fourth. It says that any day of the year can be like July Fourth, if the right pressure is applied, just as any crowd can lay claim to being "the people" by representing the natural justice in their cause. It is this open feeling for history that connects the *Tribune's* critical resistance to the legacy of radical abolitionism, which never hesitated to claim the slave as the true successor to the revolutionary republican, a legacy that was given its most powerful expression when Frederick Douglass declared his intention to represent the Fourth of July from "the slave's point of view." This claim registers obliquely in the sketch itself. Listening to the story, an editor asks the obvious question: "And where were the police all this time?" This question is compelling, in the first instance, because it marks the time of the sketch as a time when the police are absent, or a time when the police have not yet arrived, or a time when they have arrived only to disappear. When Remus replies that the police were on the scene the whole time, pointing to Chief Anderson's complicity in his attack on the excursionist, he forces the sketch to consider something it would rather suppress: how the police could exist in this scene and remain police. Really all that it should have taken was this one image—Anderson's shut eye, the shut eye of the law—to spur the *Constitution* to create a supplementary rationale for its modernization campaign. As it happened, a new rationale was introduced two weeks later, in the same section of the newspaper, where Remus suddenly resurfaced as a folk storyteller.[65]

In contrast to "Uncle Remus and the Fourth," which quickly gestures to this tribalism at its conclusion, the folklore sketches treat the topos of warfare quite systematically as cultural memory. On July Fourth, Remus is black because he is warlike. In the folklore sketches, Remus is black because he tells warlike tales that have come through generations. On July Fourth, black violence is prepolitical. It is violence that precedes or exceeds the social contract. In the folklore sketches, this political association is maintained even as the interpersonal rivalry between Brer Rabbit and his enemies is depicted as a disappearing tradition deserving the most painstaking preservation. Filtered through Uncle Remus's storytelling, the black tradition became apprehensible to its readers in the *Constitution* as vernacular expression that was culturally significant but manifestly irrelevant to the near-present tense of the newspaper.[66]

From the standpoint afforded by "Uncle Remus and the Fourth," we can begin to understand how the scholarly controversy over the cultural origin of Remus's folklore was structured by political imperatives. When professionals told Harris that Uncle Remus was telling stories that came from places other than Africa, Harris felt compelled to respond. It simply seemed outrageous to him that the tales could have come from Europe or India. It belied common sense. We want to think specifically about how Harris parsed this common sense, but it is worth observing that we already know everything that we need to know to say why Africa was indispensable to his understanding of the tales. Harris needs a theory about African cultural retention to preserve folklore's political function. He could not bear the idea that the tales were borrowed from somebody else, because his allegorical interpretation for the tradition—where Brer Rabbit equals the slave—depended on their being original to the black tradition. Harris needs an African origin because he needs this political allegory, and he needs this political allegory because he needs to convert the black tradition into the prehistory that leads into the New South Creed. The professionals were prepared to agree that the tales came from a primitive time in world history, but that was not sufficient for Harris, who had not only to superannuate the tradition but also to demonstrate to his readers that the tradition he was superannuating was an entirely black tradition.

The impact of this interpretation has been extraordinary. By the 1890s, a strong ethnographic movement followed Harris's lead in connecting the tales to Africa and in claiming that the rabbit was adapted by storytellers to personify the "obscure ideals" of the race under slavery. The rabbit has been permitted, in other words, to stand as an emblem for slave subjectivity in general. This ethnographic assumption shaped much of the early writing about black cultural kinship. Black activists and thinkers were always interested in their connection to Africa, but it was not until the 1880s and 1890s that they started to represent this connection as a kinship based on cultural inheritance rather than blood, spirit, or common interest. Uncle Remus was the first real test case for this new cultural paradigm, and very soon, a related debate developed around the spirituals after Richard Wallashek's *Primitive Music* (1893) argued that the spirituals were "borrowed" from whites. The case for the spiritual's African source was powerfully made in Edward Krehbiel's *Afro-American Folksongs* (1914) and in James Weldon Johnson's *The Book of American Negro Spirituals* (1925), but already the argument was associated, indelibly in many minds, with the closing chapter from Du Bois's *Souls of Black Folk* (1903). Du Bois traces the spirituals back to Africa through his own bloodline. He tells about a song that was passed down by his family, whose meaning had been forgotten. Despite this loss of meaning, or maybe because of the displacement that registers as loss of meaning, the song conveys kinship: "The child sang it to his children and they to their children's children," Du Bois writes, "and so two hundred years it has travelled down to us and we sing it to our children, knowing as little as our fathers what its words may mean, but knowing well the meaning of its music." Filiation is the primary function of the spirituals, according to Du Bois's early formulation. They are songs that attach their singers to their ancestral homeland. With an "undoubted Negro origin," it can be safely assumed that this music is "peculiarly characteristic of the slave."[67]

Du Bois takes the same position in the debate on the spirituals that Harris takes on the trickster tales. Their affinity is striking. Although it is possible to trace lines of influence between them, we need to realize that the similarity is predominantly accidental. It would be an overstatement to cast their similarity in any other way, not least because there was very little in this line that Du Bois could have learned from Harris. Before he wrote his concluding chapter on the spirituals, Du Bois was professionally trained, at the leading universities in the world, to practice in the fields where Harris was dabbling as an interested amateur. If Du Bois and Harris have a common commitment to romantic nationalism, Du Bois had no need to go through Harris to get to Herder, given that he was already reading Herder in the original, which we know for sure that Harris was not. Nonetheless, Harris came to stand in Du Bois's mind for a specific approach to the black tradition he had taken in some early work, most notably in "Of The Sorrow Songs." Harris became a character through which Du Bois could inquire into the historiography of the black folk tradition. When Du Bois summons Harris in his autobiographical writings, the thing that he wants to know is what gets lost when your inheritance comes packaged as a folk tradition, but what he learns by way of his own missed connection to Harris is something different. Through Uncle Remus, Du Bois learns that the missing links in the black tradition had, by his time, already become its primary ligatures.[68]

There is something grotesque about inheriting your tradition from somebody like Uncle Remus. Nevertheless, it was typical for African American intellectuals of Du Bois's generation to applaud Harris for calling public attention to the cultural value of black vernacular expression. Booker T. Washington was willing to say that there were "few higher authorities" on "the Negro" than Harris, and Anna Julia Cooper went so far as to equate Harris with Chaucer. According to Cooper, Chaucer's glory was that "he justified the English language to itself" by changing the "homely and hitherto despised Saxon elements" into a literature that "even Norman conceit . . . might be glad to acknowledge and imitate." Cooper held that Harris was doing for black folklore what Chaucer had done for English, pausing only to lament that Harris was "not to the manner born." The most famous piece of praise came from James Weldon Johnson, who listed Uncle Remus first in the register of accomplishments demonstrating the race's capability to make art with universal appeal. "The status of the Negro in the United States is a question of national mental attitude," Johnson deduced, only to go on to say that the best way to "change that attitude" was to prove the race's "mental parity" through "the production of literature and art." On this basis, Johnson suggested that Uncle Remus was elementary to the fight against racism. In his mind, the Uncle Remus stories were "the greatest body of folk lore" in the United States, and publicizing their "greatness" was an effective way to strengthen the argument for political equality. For a time, Du Bois agreed.[69]

This dominant impression changed as the note of ambivalence, first struck by Cooper, started to develop as scholars like Benjamin Brawley objected to the characterization of Uncle Remus in the frame narrative. "The day of Uncle Remus," Brawley announced in 1921, "is over." Remus was a "relic." He was a sycophant, glad to rely on the guidance of his white employers. He represented the Old Negro, who was already superseded by the new generation. Some critics, like Arthur Huff Fauset, disparaged both Remus and his storytelling, but more frequently, the approach was to sanction the tales while regretting their packaging, thereby reversing the trend among nineteenth-century readers, like Mark Twain, who were lukewarm about the tales themselves but charmed by the characterization of their storyteller. In the 1920s, black critics often sought to minimize the role that Harris played in framing the tales. Alain Locke, who agreed with Johnson that Uncle Remus was "a national asset of the first rank," portrayed Harris as an "amanuensis." It was not that Harris created Uncle Remus, according to Locke, but rather that Uncle Remus "created himself" from an "imaginative background" that was African. William Stanley Braithwaite shared the opinion that "the race was its own artist" in these stories and that Harris was merely a "providentially provided amanuensis." Du Bois had reached the same conclusion. In his *Gift of Black Folk* (1924), Harris is depicted as nothing more than "successful translator" for a vernacular tradition, which had been "transplanted from Africa and developed in America."[70]

The change of opinion about Uncle Remus's characterization was crucial, not only to the reassessment of the black vernacular tradition, but also to the new claims made by black artists about the avant-garde ambitions of their own work. The transition from Old Negro to New Negro was decisive for the stories that black artists and intellectuals were telling about themselves, and it has remained foundational to the cultural histories that have since been written about them. If the new interpretation of Uncle Remus is rightly valued for contributing to the self-definition of a generation of black artists and writers, it is also vital to observe that there is a subsidiary cost associated with this new critical tendency: the disavowal of Uncle Remus has made it hard to distinguish the ways in which his character has continued to shape our thinking about the black tradition. From the time Remus returned to the *Constitution* as a plantation storyteller, he was playing a role in the modern declension of the race concept. By disparaging or minimizing the importance of the frame narrative where Uncle Remus speaks to the little boy, we have not done away with its influence. Rather, we have tended to naturalize its effect on the tradition. This influence is apparent in landmark writings like Sterling Brown's "Negro Folk Expression" (1950), an essay that first rejects the ethnography that makes the "favored house servant" into a native informant before proceeding to apply the same canons of authenticity that Harris dramatized through Uncle Remus to the tradition that Harris transcribed, including assumptions about the black folk tradition's obsolescence, its opposition to mass culture, and its African provenance. Easy to perceive in works like "Negro Folk Expression," Uncle Remus's lasting influence can be tracked via the ambivalence that later thinkers like Brown and Du Bois felt as they returned to Harris, time and again, struggling to rid themselves of his legacy.[71]

In the 1930s, Du Bois began telling one particular anecdote about Harris. The anecdote appears many times in his published writings—in pamphlets and essays like "A Pageant in Seven Decades" (1938) and "My Evolving Program for Negro Freedom" (1944), in interviews with William Ingersoll (1960) and Ralph McGill (1965), and in books including *Dusk of Dawn* (1940) and *The Autobiography of W. E. B. Du Bois* (1968). It concerns the time Du Bois was walking from his office at Atlanta University to the *Constitution* to see Harris and ask him to intervene in the case of Sam Hose, an accused murderer who would be lynched if something was not done. In every variation, Du Bois is consistent in representing his near-encounter with Harris as a turning point in his own career. The canonical version is from *Dusk of Dawn:*

> At the very time when my studies were most successful, there cut across this plan which I had as a scientist, a red ray which could not be ignored. I remember when it first, as it were, startled me to my feet: a poor Negro in central Georgia, Sam Hose, had killed his landlord's wife. I wrote out a careful and reasoned statement concerning the evident facts and started down to the *Atlanta Constitution* office, carrying in my pocket a letter of introduction to Joel Chandler Harris. I did not get there. On the way news met me: Sam Hose had been lynched, and they said his knuckles were on exhibition at a grocery store farther down on Mitchell Street, along which I was walking. I turned back to the University. I began to turn aside from my work. I did not meet Joel Chandler Harris nor the editor of the *Constitution.*

Later in life, Du Bois told Ingersoll that it was this event more than any other that made "the most abrupt change in my thought." Interviewed by McGill for the *Atlantic* at his home in Ghana, six months before he died, Du Bois told the story for the last time, insisting in this final instance that he had seen the fingers with his own eyes. "I saw those fingers," Du Bois vowed, his voice shaking. "I didn't go to see Joel Harris and present my letter. I never went!"[72]

To understand the meanings that this story accrued as it was told over the course of Du Bois's career, we need to realize that Du Bois never looks away from the plight of Sam Hose even as he makes Hose's fingers into an abstraction for contemplating the "race concept." Although the story quickly takes on these broad associations in Du Bois's retelling, it never loses touch with its victim. Indeed, it is only by bringing these associations into the story that Du Bois ultimately realizes how to encompass the totality of his commitment, not only to Hose, but to the others like him whose lives are carefully numbered in the sociology that Du Bois was producing at the turn of the century. To access these broad associations, we must start not with Hose but with Harris, or more specifically, with Du Bois's rationale for approaching Harris. Du Bois decides to approach Harris because Harris has a reputation for political moderation, a reputation based largely on his opposition to lynching and mob violence. Throughout his career, Harris believed the state should remain the only arbiter where race was concerned; this explains why, for instance, his opposition to lynching was entirely consistent with his support for segregation. Du Bois, in other words, approaches Harris based on Harris's advocacy for the police. Du Bois expects Harris to side with Hose because he knows Harris believes in the law.[73]

We have already observed that the strict opposition between police and personal violence collapses when we think about how people like Sam Hose were represented in the *Constitution*. And in fact, one thing we can say for sure about Sam Hose is that he was one of the people who was pathologized in the *Constitution* as a lazy and depraved vagrant. A migrant laborer, born in Macon, Hose spent time working irregularly around Atlanta before signing onto a full-time arrangement in Coweta County. The rhetoric used by the *Constitution* in the 1870s and 1880s to advocate for the police came back with a vengeance during the years when Hose lived in Atlanta. In addition to the editorials encouraging the police in their "war on the tramps and vagrants," and the short news items describing the good roads paved by the chain gang, the *Constitution* expanded its police court coverage to three columns—granting its beat reporter, Gordon Noel Huotel, the license to include frills not seen since the days of the *Daily Herald*, including cartoons and his own doggerel. At the turn of the century, the anti-crime rhetoric was intensified by many factors, including the competition between the *Constitution* and more overtly negrophobic outlets like the *News* and the *Journal*. During the 1906 governor's race, pitting Clark Howell (the *Constitution*'s editor) against Hoke Smith (former publisher of the *Journal*) in a battle to see who could most effectively demonize the state's black population, the law-and-order propaganda intensified to the point where it inspired thousands of whites to inundate Atlanta's streets, wanting revenge for crimes that they were led to believe had occurred, shouting slogans like "Kill the Negroes!" as they injured scores of people and destroyed property.[74]

The *Constitution* had always tried to draw the line when it came to explicit advocacy for lynching, and this was an appreciable position in a state where many newspapers argued, for instance, that someone such as Sam Hose was too dangerous to be left to the "laggard processes of the courts." On this point, the *Constitution* was ambivalent. Following its usual approach, the newspaper did not advocate lynching, but it did demonize Hose to the point where there seemed no reason to go with the courts rather than the mob. With her pamphlet, *Lynch Law in Georgia* (1899), Ida B. Wells took aim at the *Constitution*'s ambivalence. In her writing, she repeatedly quotes from the *Constitution* to refute the suggestion that lynchings were "condemned by the best white people." Poring over its double headlines and the $500 reward posted by the editors, Wells singles out the *Constitution* in a day-by-day breakdown, pitting its legal philosophy against its matter-of-fact predictions that Hose would soon be captured, tortured, and burned at the stake. Wells magnifies the resulting tensions until it becomes apparent that the distinction between the *Constitution* and its pro-lynching competitors is not a distinction that makes a meaningful difference.[75]

In the anecdote, Du Bois's approach to Harris is destabilized by this ambivalence. Du Bois approaches Harris based upon a commitment to the law that Harris can express only by abandoning people like Sam Hose. This shows what is wrong with Du Bois's approach to Harris, and it also shows why turning away from Harris tends to register in the anecdote not as resignation but as renewed commitment to Hose. Because Du Bois approaches Harris on terms that force him to leave Hose behind, turning away from Harris means turning back to Hose. Du Bois reads this turn as a realization about the false optimism that motivated his journey in the first place, the dawning awareness that there was "no use" in going to someone like Harris for help in these cases. But as the story is retold, and the turning backward becomes coincident with the major turn in Du Bois's thought, we can see the loyalty that is communicated here. It is vital that Hose stays invisible in the story even after this commitment has been made. There is a way in which the whole story turns on the hard truth that Du Bois is returning (like Ida B. Wells to Robert Charles) to someone who is not there. It is a commitment that is made to someone who is literally unseen, someone that, in this specific instance, was known to Du Bois only through rumors and the newspapers where Hose was represented as a "monster" and a "fiend." It is through this mediation—not despite it—that Du Bois's commitment to Sam Hose opens outward to acknowledge all the people who were abandoned, whether pathologized or superannuated, in the history made by the *Constitution*.[76]

In the anecdote, this turn arrives at the climax when Du Bois learns Sam Hose's fingers are on display in a store window further down the street. When Du Bois imagines this part of Hose's body, carried away from the scene of its dismemberment, he confronts a fragment that opposes everything that he could have learned from Harris about how fragments relate to history. As a fragment, the fingers do not serve an ethnographic purpose. They stop Du Bois in his tracks, blocking the sublimation that would enable him to experience their form as he experienced his family's song. For Du Bois, these fingers are not a remnant from a departed past. On the contrary, they represent the violence that remains all too present, no matter how much time passes between the experience and its retelling. Like the arm that is missing from Bras-Coupé, these fingers signal the point in the black tradition that does not reduce to folklore. They are a remainder, not from an original condition where the body was whole, but from the ethnographic practice that made connection to an absent wholeness into the paradigm for conceiving racial kinship. As the story is retold, the fingers become a sticking point that forces Du Bois to consider what was left unaccountable in his ethnographic approach to the spirituals. They point the way to a new mode of kinship—a kinship that Du Bois would encapsulate in *Dusk of Dawn* not as the continuity of cultural inheritance but as the experience of a common disaster.[77]

Du Bois bonds to Sam Hose not through the badge of their skin or the soulful songs they may have known, but through their common experience of statelessness, which forms their perspective and their message to the world. This is what Du Bois learns about the race concept. It is a lesson that he learns continuously as he turns backward to someone who appears to him only when he is claimed as kin. It is this same kinship that Du Bois attempts to record in his early ethnographic expeditions in the Black Belt. Through the tale about Sam Hose, we find Du Bois returning to the strangers he meets in *The Souls of Black Folk* but does not know well enough to name: "ragged black man," "peasant girl," "tall bronzed man," "ragged, brown, and grave-faced man," "sunken-cheeked old black man." *Souls* was published in the same year that W. C. Handy purportedly met his ragged songster on the train platform in Tutwiler, but the would-be informants that Du Bois waylays will not sing for him despite their demographics. Their staccato speech does not disclose their hidden depths, nor does it break the oppressive silence that Du Bois attributes to the landscape. Their stories remain "untold." Their words feel worthless, like "cheap" socialism. Du Bois departs from the standard ethnographic script only when he is unable to turn this persistent withholding into evidence for authenticity or into the narrative prelude for delayed gratification. He leaves these encounters no less alienated than when he arrived. He works his hardest to turn these vagrants into native informants, but he cannot do it. He tries to get them to sing his family's song, but they do not know what he is talking about. It is appropriate, then, that Du Bois worked through his unresolved relationship to these people by retelling a story about Joel Chandler Harris, a person who could stand in his mind as the symbolic source for the ethnographic expectations that were disappointed in the Black Belt. Returning to these encounters and recasting them so it is not Harris who stands between himself and his would-be informants, but instead the resisting informant who stands between himself and Harris, Du Bois makes his turn, discovering a new line of descent.[78]

4

THE BLACK TRADITION FROM
GEORGE W. JOHNSON TO OZELLA JONES

Probably the biggest star in the first decade of the phonograph business, George W. Johnson was also one of the first black musicians to record commercially. It seems that Johnson cut his first cylinders for the New Jersey Phonograph Company in 1890 before heading to work for other outfits—including Edison, Columbia, and Berliner Gramophone. He usually stuck to his signature songs, "The Whistling Coon" and "The Laughing Song," during an era when most musicians were developing big repertoires to maximize profits. As affordable spring-driven phonographs suitable for household use would not become widely available until the turn of the century, Johnson's records were first marketed to commercial operators whose coin-in-slot machines were placed among the novelties at carnivals and expositions and in the automated phonograph parlors in commercial districts. For a penny, patrons could put their ear to a tube and listen to Johnson's songs. Given that his records were sold chiefly to exhibitors and not individuals, the reported statistics on Johnson's most popular songs—over 25,000 sold in their first four years—are all the more remarkable. These figures are also extraordinary given limitations on production. There was no reliable technology for copying recordings before the Edison Company began to work with negative metal molds at the turn of the century, and so every cylinder had to be waxed individually. When a vocalist such as Johnson had a powerful voice, cylinders could be manufactured in batches by recording with as many as six machines at once. Paid twenty cents for a two-minute performance, Johnson performed the same songs over and over to meet demand.[1]

"The Laughing Song" appears to have been the best-selling recording in the 1890s, and for a time, Johnson was the only black performer whose music was widely distributed by the phonograph industry. Johnson was one of many performers in the opening decades of the record business specializing in so-called coon songs, capitalizing on a fad boosted by big-time numbers like "All Coons Look Alike to Me," written in 1896 by black ragtime composer Ernest Hogan and covered three years later for Edison Records by Arthur Collins and banjo virtuoso Vess Ossman. Johnson's records were notable in the estimation of his contemporaries, not for his material, but for his style. It was the realistic grain of Johnson's voice that supposedly set him apart from white singers who performed in black dialect like Arthur Collins. Johnson was marketed with a focus on how gracefully his songs proved the technological potential of their medium. At a time when most singers were bellowing or overenunciating into the horn, straining to the point of stilting their words in their attempts to register unambiguously on the needle, Johnson was dropping his closing consonants and slurring between words, sometimes with discernible vibrato, all the while remaining entirely comprehensible to listeners. Other singers sounded projected and deliberate at best, but Johnson was able to stretch his syllables to obtain a texture that was unlike anything else on record. If the press releases can be believed, this texture is what attracted listeners to Johnson. Promising that canned music could sound like it came straight from a black singer on the street, the marketing for "The Laughing Song" in particular stressed the record's fidelity to its source, turning the novelty of laughter's reproducibility into the song's greatest selling point. Speculating upon Johnson's charisma, the first industry publication, *The Phonogram*, went so far as to suggest that mechanical reproducibility was a racial dispensation. Like a "barking dog" or "neighing horse," the distinctive voice of the black performer made for "good repetition on the phonograph." Concertinas record better than organs, and men better than women, it was presumed, and "negroes take better than white singers" as the black voice has a "harshness" that a "white man's does not."[2]

When people listened to Johnson's records, they testified that they were hearing a voice that was "exactly like" what they expected to hear. The accuracy of the recordings, their fidelity to their source, was paramount, and it was this amazing accuracy that made the recordings so important to the phonograph's early commercial application. Johnson's songs were marketed as demonstration pieces. The need to show the phonograph's competence influenced not only the advertising but also the selection of the songs that Johnson recorded. It is no coincidence that "The Laughing Song" and "The Whistling Coon" are organized around vocal sounds that do not reduce to speech. The songs tackle sounds difficult to reproduce

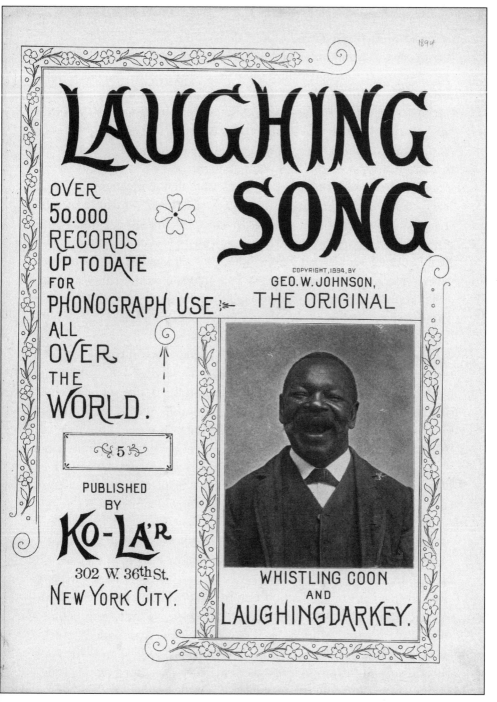

George W. Johnson, "The Laughing Song" (New York, 1894). Reprinted with permission from the Rare Book, Manuscript, and Special Collections Library at Duke University.

on paper to show what was distinctive about the phonograph. By staging the successful reproduction of nonspeaking sounds, the songs drew listeners, changing in the process how these listeners imagined the black voice. As far as these listeners were concerned, Johnson's records were *about* their fidelity to their source. They were *about* the surprising fact that recorded laughter could sound "like a carefree darky." For collaborators like session pianist Fred Gaisberg, it was Johnson's capacity to sound "like" a "darky" that made his career. Johnson was habitually praised in these terms: for manufacturing "deep-bellied" and "lazy" songs that sounded unmistakably like themselves when mechanically reproduced. Advertisements depicted a voice that was true to life, a genuine instance of something that had been imitated for decades by others. Much as readers flocked to the writings of Paul Laurence Dunbar after their interest was trained by white-authored verse in black dialect, consumers came to Johnson wanting the real thing, and it seems that they felt they were getting what they wanted. His music sounded like something they already knew before they heard it. The pleasure in the music was the pleasure of anticipation fulfilled.[3]

Almost everything we know about Johnson's life is filtered through a murder trial in 1899. When Johnson was accused of killing his third common-law wife, newspapers ran features on the singer, some of which described his "itinerant" years as a "traveling musician" drifting from town to town. The trial coverage undoubtedly distorted Johnson's history, making a singer who was by most first-hand accounts sober and industrious into a character who would have fit into the most outlandish coon songs. Depraved (already on his third wife), irrational (preternaturally talented yet still living amid squalor), and oblivious (unconcerned by the goings-on at trial) according to the papers, Johnson was a cause célèbre for many New Yorkers. He was given legal counsel by a benefactor, and at the peak of interest, his trial was being reported simultaneously by the *Times*, the *Herald*, the *Evening Telegram*, the *World*, and the *Sun*. The newspaper coverage paid as much attention to Johnson's colorful character as to his alleged crime. The "Whistling Coon" has "suffered little from confinement and suspense," the *Times* wrote. Rather than worrying about his case, Johnson spent "his time in jail whistling for his own and other prisoners' diversion." Furthermore, he could "keep from bursting into music in the courtroom" only "by keeping his mouth firmly closed." The trial closed after a day for lack of evidence, and Johnson is alleged to have bounded down the courthouse steps, belting out for the occasion, "I don't care if you never come back," a parody of the song titled "I Don't Care If I Never Come Back." "Whistled Out to Freedom," read the headline in the *World*. "Clear of Murder, Negro Sang," echoed the *Times*.[4]

By the time his career ended around 1910, Johnson's songs were falling out of favor. Since then they have mostly been known, when they have been known at all, through anecdotes rather than careful listening. Many details from these anecdotes have not been confirmed. Apocryphal or not, they have been key to how his songs have been remembered. According to one version of the mythology, Johnson was an ex-slave who migrated to New York City from Virginia following the Civil War. A local character celebrated for his pitch-perfect renditions of popular tunes, Johnson made his living performing for spare change on the sidewalks. He led an unexceptional life until one day he was discovered by a record producer—some believe the producer was none other than Thomas Edison—while he was singing near the Hudson River Ferry Terminal. Impressed with what he heard, Edison invited Johnson to produce a song for his fledgling phonograph company, and the rest was history. Whether the man who stumbled upon Johnson at the ferry was Thomas Edison, or as others have advocated, Victor Emerson, a relative unknown attached to the New Jersey Phonograph Company, matters less than the existence and popularity of the Edison version of the legend. Like the story about T. D. Rice stumbling upon the stablehand, or the myth about W. C. Handy awaking to the ragged songster, the celebrated encounter between Edison and Johnson has been employed to explain a historical transition in retrospect, in this case the transition to commercial recording. We are interested here not with the actual facts of the matter, most of which are unconfirmed, but with how the myth about Edison and Johnson shaped the reception of Johnson's novelties, placing them out of kilter with the black tradition.[5]

It is my sense that this mythology becomes most revealing at its stress points. In particular, I am interested in Edison's appearance inside the encounter story, which is almost certainly fabricated. The timing is unlikely given Edison's initial skepticism about recording music, and the circumstance implausible given that Edison was near-deaf since childhood. But there is more than phonemic drift (Eme-Edi-who?) or a predictable substitution of an illustrious for a lesser-known character at work here, as it is Edison who transforms the encounter into a fable, making the kind of sense that could only have been made retrospectively about the phonograph's long-term influence on black music. Edison's appearance is the most jarring inconsistency in the story, and as such, it can be thought to indicate its point of greatest necessity. It is at this juncture that storytellers would appear to have had no choice but to add an element, if they were to strengthen rather than break the expectations previously established for the song. Here we can discern these storytellers inventing something they cannot do without. They needed Edison to say what had to be said about the phonograph's impact on the black tradition. We can safely say that the encounter never occurred, but this does not mean it can be ignored. On the contrary, its explanatory power derives from the happenstance of its composition, from the retrospective necessity that prompted those who told the story to introduce Edison where he was almost certainly absent.

It is not hard to guess what Edison would have represented to the people who included him in the story. By the 1890s, Edison was already on his way to becoming a folk icon celebrated for inventions like the phonograph and the incandescent light bulb. A personification of better living through technology, Edison was eventually lionized in textbooks and on postage stamps for his ingenuity, running second to Benjamin Franklin in the race to be recognized as the nation's number-one inventor. Embodying the spirit of invention, Edison stands in the encounter with Johnson for his invention. He stands for the phonograph and for the phonograph's necessity to the transformation encoded by the legend. This necessity is figured at the instant when Edison first observes Johnson's talent. The story states that when Edison passes Johnson on the docks, he is struck by the sound of a voice that is uncommonly suited to replication by the phonograph. Edison does not hear the voice intimately, not exactly. He hears in the moment the possibility of hearing the voice intimately after it had been committed to record. According to the legend, this instant recognition is what gave birth to mass culture in the form of the recording industry's first-ever musical sensation.[6]

It is worth asking exactly what it means for Edison to hear music friendly to the phonograph. Edison's gift in this case is to predict the fidelity that would make Johnson's records appealing to consumers. He hears the black voice in the moment as if after the fact—that is his stroke of genius. In the process, Edison resolves the problem that had been haunting collectors of black folksongs for some time, but not in a manner they had thought possible. Collectors had long wondered at the sublimity of a voice that resisted every effort at transcription, but Edison discovers the secret to reproducing its grain. Although he fails to locate the face-to-face intimacy necessary for full transcription, he finds instead that he can hear in the live performance how the music will sound after it is recorded. This sixth sense runs against the conventional wisdom that says fidelity is possible only after sound is reproduced, because only then can sound be measured against its source. Sound reproduction, the distribution of a signal over time and space, would seem to be a prerequisite for the possibility of sound fidelity. This prerequisite is overwritten by the epiphany that links Edison to Johnson. Edison hears fidelity before the voice is reproduced. He hears fidelity where there is no discernible gap between a sound and its source, and therefore where there is no source at all, given that a source only becomes a source, in this proper sense, after it is reproduced. Time turns imperceptibly out of joint at this moment in the encounter, a fact that the story minimizes by invoking Edison's genius to cover the improbability and generalize the scale of the insight. The point here is not that blackness is reproducible by a genius. Blackness is reproducible by anybody who possesses the appropriate technology, and Edison's genius is to have discovered this general truth.[7]

Most relevant to our concerns, however, is how Edison impacted the collectors who adapted the phonograph to cultural preservation. Even before he is alleged to have discovered Johnson on the docks, Edison was promoting the phonograph in a way that would leave an important but delayed impression on the recording of folk tradition. Edison patented a tin-foil phonograph in 1878, but he neglected the technology for nearly a decade while he worked on the light bulb. At the start, Edison was picturing the phonograph as a tool, not for entertainment, but primarily for office dictation. He also proposed that the machine would allow for the posthumous preservation of human speech. Listing the sounds that one could hear again "one year or one century later," Edison named the public addresses of political leaders or the last words of "a dying man" or "mistress." It was left to folklorists like Jesse Walter Fewkes to extend this line of thinking not only to dying individuals but to dying cultures, or more precisely, cultures that were thought to be dying by collectors. This preservationist approach descended directly from Edison to Fewkes, who brought an Edisonphone to Maine and the American Southwest in 1889–1890 to record the Passamaquoddy and Zuni, respectively. Based upon cylinders he deposited at the Peabody Museum at Harvard, Fewkes published an article for the *Journal of American Folklore* asserting that the way to preserve "dying" cultures for posterity was through the phonograph. Interpretation could wait, Fewkes argued, but collection could not: time was running out, and these voices had to be "rescued from oblivion" before it was too late. According to Fewkes, the phonograph supplied the only means to preserve primitive cultures beyond their natural life cycle. This was a minority opinion among folklorists, but there were other forward-thinkers, like Franz Boas, who agreed with Fewkes, and some even expressed their support in terms that could easily have been applied to "The Laughing Song." In "Canning Negro Melodies" (1916), for instance, George Miller confirms the standard line about black music being "so elusive in character" as to be "almost impossible to reduce it to notation," only to hold out the possibility that the "talking-machine" would prove equal to the task of reproducing its "peculiar characteristics." But most folklorists were slow to see the promise in the wax cylinders and steel wires and aluminum discs whose fragility and dubious fidelity made transcription seem attractive in contrast. Rather than sustaining the elusive aura of the music, the new technology was thought to exemplify the modernizing currents that were making the folk tradition into a thing of the past. Even early adaptors like Howard Odum, who was recording in the field by the first decade of the century, saw the cylinders he was making not as artifacts in their own right but as aids to transcription. Once the words were written down, Odum had no qualms about reusing the cylinders. It was not until 1928 that Robert Winslow Gordon, the first curator at the Archive of American Folk Song at the Library of Congress, inaugurated the first programmatic effort to apply the phonograph to the preservation of folk traditions, an effort that would founder until the archive and its resources were turned over to John Lomax six years later.[8]

I think that it is safe to say that Edison's influence in this sphere is even greater than we have assumed. The catch here is that we can only gauge this influence by giving Edison credit for something that he did not actually do. It is not what Edison actually did but what he is rumored to have done—listening in the moment as if after the fact—that models the listening that enthusiasts for black music would soon be practicing in the field. Having been touched by the phonograph, these later collectors could take for granted the principle of live fidelity. If fidelity is supposed to presume a gap between sound and source, for collectors like Howard Odum and John Lomax—as for the apocryphal Edison—it does not. The sense that there were voices that were true to themselves in the moment of their expression was vital to these collectors. Under its aegis, the Lomaxes managed to find their way to some of the most celebrated examples of black music ever recorded. Reading forward from the fable about Edison and Johnson, we can note how folklorists gleaned their new ideas about cultural authenticity from the phonograph, whether they knew it or not.[9]

This influence is easily discernible not only in work by technophiles (like the Lomaxes) but also in work by technophobes who held that nothing good would come from bringing machines into the field. Collectors committed to pen and ink may have sworn against the phonograph and its role in propagating mass culture, but their orientation to the folk artifact was imprinted by the new technologies for sound reproduction long before field recording became standard practice. The coherence criterion used to say whether a given object belonged to black culture borrowed its conceptual structure from the technologies for sound reproduction, an adaptation that finally turned signal-to-source fidelity into the new standard for discerning cultural authenticity. Without the special standpoint afforded by Edison, this chain of reasoning would be hard to reconstruct given that collectors were quick to rename authentic voices that sounded true to themselves as voices that were—literally—untouched by the phonograph. Only by disavowing the phonograph, it appears, were these collectors able to translate the concept of live fidelity from a technological into a cultural idiom. Maintaining that the phonograph was antithetical to black expression, collectors disowned the means that had enabled them to imagine a source for the tradition. What collectors were doing to the black songs they were reproducing in the field is not unlike what record companies and early listeners were doing to "The Laughing Song" when they praised the record's fidelity to the voice of its singer. The difference is that listeners to Johnson remained immured to a technological definition of fidelity, whereas folklorists, following in Edison's apocryphal footsteps, began to perceive fidelity, not after a song was reproduced, but in the moment. They began to hear songs in the moment as if they were already recorded, but they did not put it that way. They claimed no genius for telling what would sound good on record. In fact, they claimed no special powers at all, preferring to attribute the fidelity they were hearing to the performances themselves. If Johnson's listeners were taking a song focalized through the impossible perspective of a ragged street singer and turning its sound into a technological marvel, later collectors like the Lomaxes began to propose a strong alignment between the perspective inside the music and the person doing the singing. Based on this perceived alignment, collectors began to annotate the remarkable effects in black performance, which followed from the willful assumption of a legally impossible perspective, as if they were properties inherent to cultural practice.

By teaching everybody involved in the performance circuit to orient their listening to a source that could be thought but not physically seen, the phonograph established a framework for hearing the fidelity of a voice that had never before been realized, by collectors or performers, as true to itself. The phonograph offered a new explanation for why the black voice sounded not only disenfranchised but disembodied, as if it came from nowhere. The voice's disembodiment, once called its sublimity, registered on record only to be reconnected to a source whose primacy could not have been imagined before the invention of sound reproduction. Once they were recorded, these effects, which had always been noticeable in black performance, became undifferentiated from their medium. What encrypted the black voice was not primarily the fact of the groove, not in the sense that record grooves can be "read" or decrypted by a phonograph needle. Rather, blackness was encrypted by the fact that it could only be decrypted by technology that made the voice appear as if it were already thrown. From the point of reproduction, the black voice's primary effects became indistinguishable from their technological condition of possibility, and this led to a situation where, for the first time in its history, the music could be commonly considered as folklore on the grounds that it was indexed directly to the individual consciousness of its producer. Alienating the voice from the body, in this instance, creates rather than disrupts speech's capacity to stand for subjectivity, producing a new opportunity for face-to-face immediacy between collector and informant. The aura is made, not destroyed, by the phonograph.

George W. Johnson can help us to think differently about the phonograph's impact upon the black tradition for two reasons: first, because the story about his discovery anticipates the selection criterion of live fidelity that was soon to be applied by leading folklorists in the field, and second, because the songs that Johnson recorded for the phonograph have been anathema to the ethnographic norm that his legend helped to form. Despite his unprecedented accomplishments in the recording industry and a demographic profile that would appear ready made for inclusion in the vernacular tradition that would be reconstructed in his wake, Johnson has been remembered as a curiosity. Although Johnson was an itinerant and perhaps ragged musician, he has never been drawn into line with the threadbare singer who accosted W. C. Handy in Tutwiler, nor has he been seen as a precursor to street corner players like Blind Lemon Jefferson and Charley Patton, who were discovered under parallel circumstances by record industry scouts. Johnson is excluded from this privileged company based upon his erstwhile status as a mass-cultural icon and his willingness to perform minstrel caricature, tendencies that are intuitively opposed to the wrenching immediacy that is thought to distinguish the folk blues tradition. Traveling songsters, the more ragged the better, were seen as the best sources for traditional songs, because their marginality protected them from the corrupting influence of mass culture. During the period when the phonograph was allegedly eroding whatever remained in the vernacular reserve, the ragged songster was seen as the last living connection to a tradition that would soon be extinct. The rags, the soul, the ratio of rags to soul, the cracked voice with its unaccountable grain, the belief that black music is a mode of self-consciousness or a way of talking to yourself about yourself, the assumption that black music enters history not when it is invented but when it is discovered—all these elements have been decisive to the conceptualization of the tradition. If the tradition is routed instead through Johnson's perceived inauthenticity, it becomes possible to think again about this presumed baseline. By considering what "The Laughing Song" has in common with canonical examples from the black vernacular archive, especially the field-defining prison recordings made by the Lomaxes in the 1930s, we can think again about what it is that holds the black tradition together, what binds Johnson to his relatives whether they have claimed him or not.

To reconsider Johnson's exclusion from the tradition, we need to dispense with those explanations that would oppose black tradition to mass culture. These explanations shortchange the tradition by eliminating some of its most important participants, and they hide what is really at stake in their own conception of racial authenticity. What bars examples like "The Whistling Coon" and "The Laughing Song" from the tradition is not their association with blackface, or incipient mass culture, or the new technologies for sound reproduction. These songs are excluded, because they embrace the racial epithet—darky, coon, nigger—as their occasion, and that acceptance makes it impossible to hear in Johnson's laughter any deep-rooted originality that is not predicated, at some level, on racial convention. In other words, Johnson's songs remain indebted to the epithet to an extent that makes them unavailable to the program that would claim the ragged songster as a primary source for black folklore. Johnson's big hit "The Whistling Coon" was written by Sam Devere, but it appears that Johnson wrote "The Laughing Song" for himself, at least according to the sheet music published in 1894. "The Laughing Song" in particular asks listeners to take the epithet seriously, to think through the epithet, rather than dismissing its occurrence inside the music as self-inflicted stereotyping, or internalized racism, or unfortunate artistic compromise allowable only to make a buck.[10]

Recorded over and over again, adapted for stage productions like *The Inspector* (1890), a cops-and-robbers comedy in which Johnson made a cameo, featured in abbreviated minstrel routines put on record by contractors like Len Spencer, for whom Johnson also worked as a valet, "The Laughing Song" had a great run over its initial decade. Later, there was a best-selling adaptation by Burt Shephard from 1910 and a few less notable covers. Among extant recordings of "The Laughing Song," the following is an undated but early rendition, likely from around 1894. Others have only slight variations from this version, which for the purposes of our analysis will be treated as standard:

> As I was coming round the corner, I heard some people say,
> "Here comes the dandy darky, here he comes this way.
> His ears are like a snowplow, his mouth is like a trap,
> And when he opens it gently you will see a fearful gap."
> And then I laughed . . . [Laughs in time with the music]
>
> I just can't help from laughing . . . [Laughing in time]
> I just can't help from laughing . . . [Laughing in time]
>
> They said, "His mother was a princess, his father was a prince,
> And he'd been the apple of their eye if he had not been a quince.
> But he'll be the king of Africa in the sweet by and by."
> And when I heard them saying it, why, I laughed until I cried.
> And then I laughed . . . [Laughing in time]
>
> I just can't help from laughing . . . [Laughing in time]
> I just can't help from laughing . . . [Laughing in time]

So now, kind friend, just listen to what I'm going to say.
I've tried my best to please you with my simple little lay.
Now, whether you think it's funny, or quite a bit of chaff,
Why all I'm going to do is just to end it with a laugh
And then I laughed . . . [Laughing in time]

I just can't help from laughing . . . [Laughing in time]
I just can't help from laughing . . . [Laughing in time]

Following the label "dandy darky" are similes that associate the singer's ears and mouth with simple lever-based and spring-based machines (a snowplow and coil trap) before settling into metaphor ("fearful gap"), a series that imitates theatrical convention in its deformation of the singer's facial features. On stage the distortion was accomplished with make-up. According to *The Amateur Negro Minstrel's Guide* from 1880, all it took was "three quarters of an inch of lipstick" to make the face "look all mouth when opened to its full extent." There is no lipstick here, but the song still manages to mime by other means the conventional exaggeration of the orifice in blackface, an exaggeration that puts the singer in a state that is vulnerable to sexual penetration by the crowd he meets on the corner.[11]

The epithets in "The Laughing Song" take their coordinates from blackface, but their meaning is discernible only when this history is understood as the foundation for a formal structure of address. The epithet synchronizes the encounter between the singer and the crowd he meets on the corner. In the initial two verses, the singer is situated in relation to the epithets thrown at him by this group of strangers. A blind intersection between adjacent perpendicular paths, the corner connects two standpoints represented as first-person singular ("I") and third-person plural ("they"). Besides their readiness to insult the singer, all we are given about the "they" that challenges the singer is the ad hoc designation as "some people," suggesting a loose affiliation typical of a crowd. Because the crowd notices the singer before the singer notices the crowd, there is a slight torque after the first line. As soon as it is established, the song's first-person perspective ("I was coming round the corner") is usurped from its outside ("I heard some people say"). Although it is subordinated as quoted expression, this unexpected address overwhelms the singer with its magnitude (taking three lines to his one) and its aggression (hurling epithets that trap the singer in the third person). The second verse repeats this pattern, resetting the context of the encounter ("They said") to cite the singer as a would-be prince in an African setting derived from imperial romance. Even this second time around, the crowd's address catches the singer off guard, arriving too suddenly to register fully in consciousness. From out of the blue, the crowd places the singer as a latecomer to his own performance. Blindsided by an address that begins before the beginning of the song, the singer cedes the pretense to self-definition. This is important to the song: the singer can open his mouth to speak only after his name is called by another. The only name he can give to himself is the name he has been given by the crowd, and the name he is given by the crowd is the epithet ("darky") that would revoke his right to speak at all.

It is a peculiar property of this framework that the epithet at all times seems to preempt the singer no matter the order in which the exchange is presented. Even as the song enters its second and third cycles, the epithet appears again too soon and too quickly, striking before the singer is ready. It would be right to say that this use of the epithet alienates the singer from the terms that are used to describe him, producing a kind of critical consciousness, but that cannot be the whole story, because the epithets, even when alienated, continue to define their object. Johnson sounds like a minstrel man. It would be impossible to hear him otherwise; the sound of his voice would be inaudible without the framework that the epithet provides. This is what is most strange about the performance: how its singer cannot help but sound like he is a minstrel character, even as he performs the racial conventions of minstrelsy as epithets that are externally imposed upon him. These conventions, marked as conventions, are still there in the grain of his voice.

Given the epithet's general character as a figure of speech, this framework is formally appropriate. Classically, an epithet (meaning "imposed") is a phrase that attaches to its object as if it were an analytic appositive or literally a part of the object's name. Whether demeaning or not, epithets tend toward metaphor, bringing their object into focus by highlighting one of its aspects (as in the phrase "wine-dark sea"). What makes an epithet potentially demeaning is its capacity to delineate its object according to a single concentrated or exaggerated feature, implying not only possession of that feature but the converse that the object can be denoted, or labeled, by that feature alone. It is the epithet's capacity for exemplification that abstracts its object to the point where its dominant aspect can abbreviate its identity. Judgment here is not synecdochic: the flattened nose or the enlarged lips do not substitute for the person. Rather, they are acknowledged in a manner that renders all other parts of the person irrelevant to consideration. The epithet refuses its object the capacity to display any qualities that it might possess besides those that are symbolized in its dominant aspect. The epithet claims to say everything that needs to be said about somebody. It does not modify or describe its object; rather, it structures the field in which the object is perceived. The epithet thereby renders its object supernumerary in two senses: in the sense that the object becomes superfluous to the situation in which it appears, and in the sense that its superfluity forecloses the capacity for speech. The epithet does not banish its object from the world; rather, it includes the object in the world without acknowledging its perspective. The object appears within the world, but it does not speak.[12]

In this sense, the song represents a specific instance of the general problem of subjectivity. It is a version of the dilemma that Jean-Paul Sartre has termed being-for-itself, a dilemma that was soon after inverted and elaborated by Frantz Fanon. If "The Laughing Song" can tell us something that we do not already know about this condition, the way to get to that knowledge is by considering the song's historical specificity. When the singer is walking alone along a street and is stopped by a hostile crowd shouting racial epithets, he is feeling something other than the general burden of self-consciousness. He is confronting a present threat to his life, a threat that had a precise meaning in 1894 when 134 blacks were lynched by mobs that must have looked to their victims much like the crowd looks to the singer in this song. There were more than 1,969 black men and women lynched during the course of the twenty years when Johnson was recording "The Laughing Song," a figure that does not account for an exponentially greater number of informal acts of violence that were committed with impunity over these same decades. Obviously, these numbers do not even start to measure the weight of an existence lived under the continuous threat of violence. None of these facts are incidental to the song; they impart both force and form to its epithets. As the song returns to the scene on the corner, its epithets are distinguished not only by their continual erasure of the singer's point of view but also by the immediate threat of violence that they are meant to communicate. Or to put it more concisely, this erasure follows from the threat of violence. The singer has no standing in the scene on the corner as there is nothing that can be known about him, besides the fact of his blackness, that is relevant to the mob's decision as to whether he should live or die. Just being at the wrong place at the wrong time is enough to erase everything about the singer that could ever be substantial enough to cast a shadow. His personal history, his state of mind, his blameworthiness, the profile of his ears and his mouth are irrelevant as far as the mob is concerned. The epithet requires no corroboration.[13]

To understand everything that we might understand through the lynching scenario in "The Laughing Song," we need to extract its form from the standard terms through which the history of vigilantism in the United States has been portrayed, terms that would treat the irrationality of lynching as an exception to the national line of legal development. The scene on the corner is distorted when it is read under the assumption that the mob is opposable to the rule of law. Part of the problem here is that this reading comes with its own recipe for redress. According to this interpretation, what the singer needs is legal recognition. Only the law can save him from the mob. Only the law can establish or revive the rights-bearing personhood that the mob seeks to take away. Because this resolution comes so easily, it forecloses the critical reflection that is opened by the song before it has effectively gotten started. To follow this reflection further, we need to ponder not only "The Laughing Song" but a variant by a British comedian named Charles Penrose. In 1922, Penrose altered the words to Johnson's already-forgotten classic and accelerated its tempo to fashion a routine that became a favorite on children's radio and television in the United Kingdom. "The Laughing Policeman" thrived for long enough to be used in advertising cars and video games both in Britain and the Americas and to inspire other copycat variations like "Giggling Gertie the Laughing Traffic Warden" in the 1970s.[14]

By following "The Laughing Song" through its declension in "The Laughing Policeman," we can say more about the historical context in which both songs locate the sound of their laughter. Here is Penrose's version:

> I know a fat old policeman
> He's always on our street

A fat and jolly red-faced man
He really is a treat
He's too kind for a policeman
He's never known to frown
And everybody says he is
The happiest man in town [Laughing in time]

He laughs upon point duty
He laughs upon his beat
He laughs at everybody
When he's walking in the street
He never can stop laughing
He says he's never tried
But once he did arrest a man
And laughed until he cried [Laughing in time]

His jolly face, it wrinkled
And then he shut his eyes
He opened his great mouth
It was a wondrous size
He said "I must arrest you"
He didn't know what for
And then he started laughing
Until he cracked his jaw [Laughing in time]

So if you chance to meet him
When walking round the town
Just shake him by his fat old hand
And give him half a crown
His eyes will beam and sparkle
He'll gurgle with delight
And then you'll start him laughing
With all his blessed might [Laughing in time]

Revising the encounter between the singer and the crowd in "The Laughing Song" as a series of exchanges between the policeman and the strangers he meets on the street, this version absorbs the epithet, reconstituting and redirecting its violence. The scene differs from "The Laughing Song." The verses are addressed not by the primary character in the song—the policeman—but by an unspecified speaker who claims to know the policeman well. Furthermore, the main character here is the source of the violence, rather than its victim, and the specific type of violence is legitimate (licensed by the state) rather than illegitimate (performed by a mob). As the song's elements are shuffled, it becomes possible to see things about the original situation in "The Laughing Song" that are otherwise obscured by the song's severance of retribution (violence) from pretext (criminality), might ("some people") from right ("we the people"), and expression (laughter) from predication (the epithets that not only confront but form the singer's perspective).

Just as it remains possible to situate the lynching scenario in "The Laughing Song" in space and time, so it is possible to specify the on-the-street activities in the "The Laughing Policeman." The police officer who is "always on our street" abbreviates a particular stage in the modern history of police organization, especially associated with the United Kingdom and with the so-called golden age of police legitimacy, which spans the middle decades of the twentieth century. At this stage, police emphasized face-to-face interaction between the public and an officer, known by name, on a regular beat patrol. In the United States, this type of police organization was adopted then dismantled in the 1960s and 1970s when campaigns against corruption drew police from their beats into a bureaucracy designed to solve crimes after they occurred. The foot patrol later returned to favor, subsequent to the publication of "Broken Windows" (1982), an article from the *Atlantic Monthly* by George Kelling and James Q. Wilson that recommended aggressive enforcement of so-called quality-of-life laws as the strategy for preventing crimes before they happened. It would be hard to overstate the influence of Kelling and Wilson's essay, which set the blueprint for the community policing movement, which has succeeded in overhauling the management of police departments in the United States and elsewhere, beginning most famously with New York City. The return to this informal style of policing has often been expressed through nostalgia for the institutional arrangement lampooned in "The Laughing Policeman."[15]

In contrast to Penrose's satire, Kelling and Wilson represent the informal authority of the police officer on the beat patrol as a panacea. The officer's discretion, they emphasize, is mandatory to law enforcement.

Describing what it was like to follow a white officer through a black neighborhood in Newark, New Jersey, Kelling and Wilson provide the following synopsis, which furnishes a practical rationale for a power typically framed as procedural necessity:

> The officer—call him Kelly—knew who the regulars were, and they knew him. As he saw his job, he was to keep an eye on strangers, and make certain that the disreputable regulars observed some informal but widely understood rules. Drunks and addicts could sit on the stoops, but could not lie down. People could drink on side streets, but not at the main intersection. Bottles had to be in paper bags. Talking to, bothering, or begging from people waiting at the bus stop was strictly forbidden. If a dispute erupted between a businessman and a customer, the businessman was assumed to be right, especially if the customer was a stranger. If a stranger loitered, Kelly would ask him if he had any means of support and what his business was; if he gave unsatisfactory answers, he was sent on his way. Persons who broke the informal rules, especially those who bothered people waiting at bus stops, were arrested for vagrancy.

The intimacy between the policeman and the regulars, which is extended to the reader with the invitation to call the policeman by his first name, is tendered here as reason enough to accept that the officer is acting in good faith even when his actions are not legally sanctioned. "Sometimes what Kelly did could be described as 'enforcing the law,'" Kelling and Wilson confess, "but just as often it involved taking informal or extralegal steps" that "probably would not withstand a legal challenge." What Kelly does half the time is illegal, but that is okay by the authors, who intuit those illegal acts as essential to the police function. Policing becomes ineffective, in their view, when the police are restrained from performing certain illegal acts. When police officers act illegally in the course of their duty, they are doing what is needed to check the "disreputable or obstreperous or unpredictable people" that negatively affect the lives of "regular" people. Policing is keyed not to crime but to the difference between "regulars" and "strangers."[16]

Although the legitimacy of police action is warranted in this passage by the police officer's intimacy with the community, under the presumption that status knowledge is the kind of knowledge you can only have when you are always on the street, the distinction between formal and informal, or legal and illegal, policing is collapsed by the passage's conclusion, where we are told that those who break the informal rules are arrested as vagrants. From this moment, the discretion the authors describe as extralegal in its basic orientation is performed as a legal prerogative, a specific prerogative that is designated across its history generically as the police power. It is no coincidence that Kelling and Wilson formalize this discretion as the law against vagrancy, given that vagrancy, since Blackstone, has been understood as the paradigm example for the legitimacy of the police power. This remained the case into the era of "Broken Windows." Even after the U.S. Supreme Court greatly narrowed the authority of vagrancy laws in 1960s and 1970s, they remained one of the most severe uses of the police power. The innovation in "Broken Windows" is the suggestion that the discretion exemplified in vagrancy laws should be embraced once and for all as necessary to the ordinary activities of police on the street. Kelling and Wilson propose that "selection, training, and supervision" internal to police institutions should be coordinated to curb abuse, but even as they acknowledge the inevitability of corruption, they are adamant that the law should admit no "outer limit" to the police's "discretionary authority."[17]

Like "Broken Windows," "The Laughing Policeman" features the image of a policeman who is "always on our street." But in this case, the pastoral description of the friendly officer passes into hyperbole ("never known to frown," "happiest man in town") and overcompensation ("too kind"), which is glossed by the insinuation that all of this undue affability comes from habitually drinking on the job ("red-faced"). The strong discretion that Kelling and Wilson claim as indispensable to law enforcement appears from this point in the song to corrupt the law, turning its enforcement into a joke. A demeanor too good to be true becomes downright bad across the second and third verses, as the compulsion fathomed as alcoholism and expressed as laughter is connected to the discretionary authority that the officer inherits from the lynch mob in the original version of the song. Laughter arrives not when the mob traps its quarry but when the policeman wrongfully arrests. Laughing is what the police officer does when he is left to his own devices, when on point duty, or on his beat. It is indiscriminate (for "everybody") as well as indispensable (so unstoppable that the officer has "never" thought to try). Occasioned by the license that exists on the beat, laughter is expressed through personal decisions that are represented as nonintentional commitments that "must" be upheld for reasons that are unknown or unknowable to the individual policeman. There is a principle at stake here.

As both "Broken Windows" and "The Laughing Policeman" are ready to admit, the difference between the mob and the police is not the difference between illegal and legal violence. The discretion enacted by the policeman on his beat is not opposed to the mob's violence. It is, rather, a new version of the same problem that is presented by George W. Johnson, a new version that offers certain advantages insofar as it enables us to connect the interlocutory encounter in "The Laughing Song" with the history of the police power. This connection is forged through a trope that "The Laughing Policeman" inherits from the original: the extra-large mouth. When the mouth passes from the singer (in "The Laughing Song") to the officer (in "The Laughing Policeman"), it says something that it is left unspecified in the source. "I must arrest you," the mouth calls to its object, a statement that depicts the force of the epithet better than any epithet could, in the formal sense that what matters most about these words is that they have no meaning for their addressee. There is no certainty about what the big mouth says, as its speech is tagged and direct, but its speech does not issue a command to halt or move along, nor a solicitation, nor an identification, that would make it possible to turn around in response to the police officer's words (as in the counterexample "Hey, you there!"). The individual that the policeman threatens to arrest in the third verse, like the individual arrested for no reason in the second verse, is like the singer in "The Laughing Song" to the degree that the only thing that registers about him in these verses is the fact that he is caught in the wrong place at the wrong time. Nothing else about him materializes in the song; even the gendered baseline ("man") furnished in the second verse has disappeared by the third, where the officer's "eyes" are "shut" when the arrest occurs. There is no word in the verse, no sound in the song, where the target of this arrest is positively designated. The object flickers into its hypothetical existence only at the moment when it is struck.[18]

Like "The Laughing Song," "The Laughing Policeman" closes with a direct address to the implied listener that recomposes the interlocutory framework of the preceding verses. In "The Laughing Policeman," the concluding address comes from an unmarked position, apparently an authoritative speaker who breaks the frame to reassure the listener that the officer is actually friendly, especially if he is offered a bribe. The song concludes not by reaffirming its own skepticism but by separating its implied listener from the unnamed individuals who are beaten and arrested in the other verses, effectively dividing its audience between those who are able to accept this reassurance and those who are barred from such acceptance. Limiting law's corruption to small-time bribery means restricting the song's address to those who feel confident about their own entitlement to the goodwill that the officer is not legally bound to provide. The implied listener is someone who can look straight at the unregulated threat posed by law's violence but feel at the same time that its target is other people. Separating this implied listener from the violated object, "The Laughing Policeman" tells the difference between two kinds of people: between those who hear the direct address at the song's conclusion as confirming their membership in society and those who feel instead like the object battered by the officer, despite the fact that the song closes every opening that would potentially allow for this identification. The line here is the same one that is asserted in "Broken Windows," between regulars and strangers, and the attempt at reassurance is indistinguishable from the lesson about the police that is communicated by Kelling and Wilson.[19]

There is nothing innovative in how the distinction between regulars and strangers is made either in the song or in the essay. This distinction is basic to the police power, and it is built into the language of the police statutes that we have been reading in this book. When you read a police statute, whether slave code, vagrancy law, or an ordinance on intrastate commerce, one thing is clear: the law's object is distinguishable from its audience. Police statutes do not address the people to whom they apply. Their audience does not include the people who will pay the price if the law is broken. Slave statutes mostly cover the actions and station of slaves, but they are addressed not to slaves but to their masters or society at large. Vagrancy codes speak not to vagrants but to citizens who believe they are citizens, in part, because they know they are not vagrants. Laws governing liquor, wharves, and counterfeit coins are addressed not to the objects they regulate but to the population those objects could potentially harm. It is possible to have an association with the objects named in these laws (they might be your property, for instance), but it should not be possible to feel addressed by these laws and at the same time to believe that you are their object. To the degree that this identification is possible, the law in question fails to qualify under the police power and is open to constitutional challenge. Police is for other people. It is not for regulars who already know their name before they are hailed by the law, but for those left nameless by the law. Police does not operate as a commandment ("Thou shalt not"), as it avoids at all times the direct address that would distinguish anything about its object. Represented in one sense (as existing) but not in another (as participating in the state), the police power's object is included but never named in law, just as the objects in the middle verses of the "Laughing Policeman" are arrested but not seen by the police officer. It is this peculiar condition that is objectified in "The Laughing Policeman" from the point of view of the unlawful arrest.[20]

Like the moral tendered at the end of "The Laughing Policeman," the legal theory proposed by Kelling and Wilson assumes this structure of address. In their writing, the distinction between regulars and strangers rationalizes the inconsistency internal to law with the argument that police must perform illegal acts if they are to remain police. What the essay does not see is that, according to its own broad interpretation of the police power, these illegal actions are not only lawful but necessary before any of the rights granted to regulars (like equal protection and due process) can be imagined in opposition to the exceptional treatment that is reserved for strangers. The point is not that Officer Kelly is a bad cop, as bad as the Laughing Policeman. Rather it is that Officer Kelly's discretion can be insulated from principled scrutiny only on the grounds that it applies to people besides ourselves. In the essay, like in the song, the point is not about two types of people (black and white) who are outsiders and insiders to law. Instead, the point is that the law's address is inconsistent no matter its recipient. The closing address in "The Laughing Policeman" is stabilized by the idea that some people, some *other* people, are black. Only when the inconsistency in this address is color-coded as a racial exception is it possible for anyone to feel acknowledged by the law. It is not that whites are subject to one address and blacks to another; the law's inconsistency is felt in every case. Rather it is that every identification confronts a point where law stops making sense, a point where identification can proceed only through racial fantasy. This is a fantasy that allows some people to make the law their own by passing its burden, its ever-present insecurity, to someone else. Through the operation of this fantasy, blackness becomes an object lesson whose existence makes it possible for anyone (including black people) to manifest a normal relationship to authority.

"The Laughing Policeman" reveals this ambivalence even as it projects its significance back toward "The Laughing Song." When the officer accepts the half-crown and starts to gurgle and beam and sparkle, he looks like a coin-operated toy. Giving the officer this extra connotation by hinting at his resemblance to a plaything whose only function is flailing its arms or rolling its eyeballs in exchange for a pittance, "The Laughing Policeman" ends by recoding the laughter that it had been decoding from its outset. Folding back into itself, the adaptation ends by returning to its source, naming its source for the first time in terms consonant with its popular reception. Making the officer into a toy when he is bribed, "The Laughing Policeman" knows that what consumers were hearing when they put their coins in the slot and their ears to the tube was something other than the machine's amazing fidelity to its source, something that was instead amazing, or unimaginable, because it had crossed over the law.[21]

With these points established, we are at last ready to listen to the celebrated sound of George W. Johnson's laughter. Contemporary listeners clearly experienced the verses in "The Laughing Song" as ancillary to its laughing refrains. Taking a roughly equivalent number of bars to the sung verses, the refrain dominates the music with its volume and its insistence. Johnson's talent for laughing in time with near-perfect pitch is a virtuoso example of this technique at the peak of its popularity. Laughing-in-time songs, beginning with the "L'eclat de rire" in Daniel François Auber's *Manon Lescaut*, were popular in the 1890s, and Johnson's debt to this tradition is instantly recognizable. Johnson's laugh sounds at times forced or mechanized, and at other times impulsive, a texture that is not adequately explained with the terms (realistic, faithful, infectious) most often used to validate its distinctiveness. Lacking a strong explanation for why the singer is laughing so hard for so long, we are left with sound whose excessiveness feels undermotivated, socially out of tune, disproportionate to its occasion, accidental, even compulsive, as something he "just can't help" doing. This uncertainty is reinforced as the laughter continues to adhere to the melody, making it impossible to distinguish intention behind its inflections. This strict patterning eliminates even the slightest pretense to expression by suppressing aspects of laughter that might serve as a surrogate for speech. Like whistling or humming, laughing can imitate a range of phonemes that can be combined and accented through rhythm and stress to simulate original utterances. Because laughter (like grunting) is already constrained as it results from the force of exhalation, and not from moving the tongue or the mouth, its potential for linguistic novelty is reduced to near-zero when it is tied to a recurring melody. These constraints explain not only the fascination with Johnson's technical accomplishments but also the unshakable sense that we cannot know what his laughter means. For sure, there are times during his extended exhalations when Johnson seems to take a quick breath while holding a fixed mouth posture, bringing on a choking sound that cuts across the melody with what threatens to become a sob, but the dominant impression remains blank, even automatic, a feeling that is undoubtedly shaped by the mixed conditions of production—part artisanal and part industrial—imposed upon Johnson by the nascent mass medium that would make him into a modern celebrity.[22]

It is at this point, where the black singer seems about to merge with the machine, where laughter becomes most perfunctory and least capable to substitute for speech, that the commitment to the near-minimum of patterned regularity becomes the obstacle, rather than the vehicle, for reducing laughter to a nonexpressive medium. Finally, it is rhythm's regularization that keeps the sounds escaping the singer's mouth from seeming formless. The irony is that once the song hammers away laughter's usual resources for signification, the remaining sounds emphasize with greater cogency than before the irreducible difference between laughter and noise. The laugh's strong segmentation does not sound like Morse code exactly, but its rhythm does manage to approximate the pulse of a prisoner hitting a rock against a wall. Admittedly, the idea that there may be something encrypted inside the singer's laughter remains impressionistic at best. But it is hard to shake the sense that its rhythm could, at any instant, without warning, muster enough coherence to transmit a message to anybody who is listening. This impression is bolstered as laughter begins to imitate the melody, first by alternating between two snorts with different pitches, and then by ascending the scale in repeated increments. Foreign to laughter in its ordinary state, the performance of laughing tones involves not only regulation of breath but movement of the tongue and lips, the kind of movement that someone laughing would make if he or she were starting to speak. This patterning presses laughter as far as it can be pressed toward speech without allowing for its semanticization. Whether speech's incipience in laughter is felt in time (as not yet ready to happen) or in space (as beyond the listener's earshot), its insistence, half-perceived and perhaps inadvertent, still manages to suggest somebody whose speaking registers but only scarcely on the wax surface of the cylinder, somebody whose natural expression for some reason resists reproduction. As a sound that does not, or does not yet, register as speech, laughter inscribes its meaning in the realm of possibility. A placeholder for expression that cannot appear as the sign for subjectivity, laughter sounds like noise that is continually threatening to become speech, or to flip and extend the terms, like speech from a self that exists only in a future whose contours are specified only in the context that is revealed through the song's declension as "The Laughing Policeman."

In its substance and its dramatized context, the laughter in "The Laughing Song" evinces certain characteristics, not least a resistance to speech-based metaphysics, that for some time had been seen as general attributes of the black voice. Collectors had long complained that the trajectory of black speech could not be stabilized to allow for transcription in the time when they were face to face with an informant. In an ethnographic exchange, black voices did not sound like they could be indexed to their speakers. This was a voice whose "odd turns" broke the diatonic scale and whose speech had to be transcribed in tortured syntax and effusive misspelling if its timbre were even to be approximated. By 1929, when Dorothy Scarborough noticed that it was not possible to write down the "unusual" sounds made by black songsters, she was echoing not only Charles Peabody, who thought the worksongs he was hearing at the turn of the century were "impossible to copy," but earlier words by antebellum eavesdroppers like Frances Kemble (who felt that slave songs were "wild and unaccountable") and Mary Chesnut (who held slave music was "all sound" with "no meaning at all"). This assumption was also indispensable to the first book-length collection of black folk music, *Slave Songs of the United States* (1867), which held that black music was "as impossible to place on the score as the singing of birds or the tones of an Æolian Harp." The idea that black music was to some degree ineffable dates to the late eighteenth century. Before that time, enthusiasts for exotic music had always assumed that the inconsistencies in their field notes were not mistakes in transcription but mistakes in performance, which were to be expected given the primitive condition of the songs they were studying. Once collectors began to consider the possibility that they could be responsible for these mistakes, they began to lose faith in their notational systems' ability to represent music from outside the European tradition. This seed of doubt bloomed into full-blown fascination as collectors early in the next century became increasingly preoccupied with transcription's impossibility. This moment of self-absorption coincided with the new interest in slave music. Resistance to representation was named as the hallmark that accounted not only for slave music's tonal and rhythmic distinctiveness but also for its essential blackness, a lament turned around by later anthologists like James Weldon Johnson, who heard in this resistance an "elusive" essence that proved black songs "in their very nature" were not "susceptible to fixation" and were consequently only complete in performance.[23]

Across the nineteenth century, the black tradition appears to have frustrated every ethnographic expectation that would treat its songs as a kind of speech. By the ordinary measures of communication, where speech is taken as the sign for the self's evidence, the black voice was deemed either sublime or ridiculous. It retained either too much or not enough to count as discourse. Many tried to explain this disparity by reading black singing as a bad imitation of white speaking. Collectors heard "queer, fanciful, and awkward" turns in black music as the inevitable distortion that occurred when "words from fairly educated people" cast "shadows" into "the minds of almost totally ignorant people." The opinion that folksongs in general were bad copies of received traditions found support among researchers like Louise Pound, who maintained that anyone looking for folk music in a penitentiary would be sorely disappointed as "prisoners in stripes and lock step" had neither the time nor the inclination to "invent songs." Black expression could not be reproduced, according to this line of thinking, because it was already a reproduction, and a bad reproduction, of the language in which collectors were struggling to render its particular inflection. This theory found increasing approval near the turn of the twentieth century, reversing the trend started a hundred years earlier by once again blaming the informant for oversights and inconsistencies within the collector's transcription.[24]

These ethnographic precedents can tell us two things about Johnson's laughter. First, they explain why the reproduction of the black voice was an especially amazing feat for the phonograph: it was something that could not be accomplished by other means, according to conventional wisdom. It was something that collectors had long been trying and conspicuously failing to accomplish with pen and ink, and it was therefore the best possible evidence for the distinctive utility of the phonograph in comparison to existing technologies. Second, they help us to discern the general significance of the theory of black expression that is represented in "The Laughing Song." The laughter in the song, always tending toward speech but never resolving itself semantically, reproduces the dominant thinking about black expression only to place that thinking in a historical framework where it can be tracked according to its evolving connection to the law. Embedded within the song, in other words, is a critical framework that can displace the predominant explanation of the song as a technological marvel. Not only does framework pressure the technical criterion of fidelity that is brought to bear on "The Laughing Song," it also can help us think through the criterion for cultural authenticity that was subsequently derived by collectors like the Lomaxes from this technical precedent. When the vernacular tradition that was assembled by these collectors is revisited through the standpoint preserved in "The Laughing Song," rather than defined in opposition to its inauthenticity, it becomes much easier to access what Ralph Ellison famously called the "lower frequencies," where black speaking is continually being invented in response to its awkward occasion. Because "The Laughing Song" is immune to mystification as folk consciousness, the song remains a compelling point from which to rethink the broad spectrum of black performance, especially those aspects that have frequently been mischaracterized as cultural properties. "The Laughing Song" functions like an *ars poetica* for the black tradition, pronounced from the point of its technological transformation. Although it has been heard as a song about technology, "The Laughing Song" is more about what was passing, or what was being carried forward from the past, than what was unprecedented in its recording. Its service is to preserve and exemplify precisely those live strategies in the black tradition that were destined to become encrypted by the phonograph.[25]

My intention in the remainder of this chapter is to apply the insights that have derived from "The Laughing Song" to some of the writings and recordings made by John and Alan Lomax in the 1930s. The Lomaxes are an important case to consider, because it was their fieldwork that turned the ethnographic impressionism of previous collectors like Howard Odum into a system. The Lomaxes agreed with their predecessors about where to look for authentic black expression, but they were the first to frame the assumption as a scientific rationale. Just as important, it was the

Lomaxes who made the phonograph vital to the recording and documentation of black expression. After John Lomax became Honorary Consultant and Curator to the Archive of American Folk Song at the Library of Congress in 1933, he spent a decade working with associates assembling the most notable collection of field recordings ever produced in the United States. The influence of these field recordings on the development of popular music throughout the world has often been represented in superlatives; for some, it is incalculable. These recordings provided a research base for scholars, a resource for writers putting together the so-called folklore treasuries popular at midcentury, as well as the raw material for commercial long-playing records. With his son and collaborator Alan, Lomax also published his own best-selling folklore collections, including *American Ballads and Folk Songs* (1934), *Negro Folk Songs as Sung by Lead Belly* (1936), *Our Singing County* (1941), and *Folk Song: U.S.A.* (1947). The content in these collections was diverse, featuring not only cases of the Anglo-American folksongs canonized by James Francis Child but vaquero songs from the Rio Grande and Acadian dance tunes from Louisiana. As cultural nationalists, the Lomaxes celebrated a folk tradition indigenous to the United States, and they held that one of the strongest currents in that national tradition came from black performers, who produced "the most distinctive of folk songs."[26]

The contents of the archive are remarkable, and equally important to Lomax's legacy is how those contents were collected. Through his advocacy for sound recording in the field, Lomax permanently changed the practice of folklore collection by eliminating whatever anti-technological prejudice remained from earlier decades. Lomax was far from the first to assert the phonograph's advantages over transcription in preserving the "tonal, rhythmic, and melodic characteristics" of music, but his fieldwork was still innovative for his time. No matter how collectors were thinking about the compatibility between technology and black music, there were financial and practical obstacles to getting recording equipment into the field. Those obstacles were overcome for good by the blend of self-promotion and ingenuity that inspired Lomax to build a 315-pound acetate disc recorder into the backseat of his Ford for a summer of field research on the road with his eighteen-year-old son Alan. That original trip in 1933, followed by many more in the next decades, yielded results that forever changed the minds of skeptics who felt the phonograph was ill-adapted, if not antithetical, to folklore collection. No longer vulnerable to skepticism, recording on location stole the aura that was once reserved for paper and ink. Packing a machine into your car and lighting out to record almost-forgotten music is a fantasy—for some at least—with a proven resilience that is only partly explained as a romantic fascination with outsider culture, a predilection that was with folklore collection since its inception.[27]

To get this project moving, Lomax needed money. He needed money to support his family, and he needed money for state-of-the-art recording equipment and for expensive recording blanks on which his discoveries were to be preserved for posterity. Before he took his position at the Library of Congress, Lomax wrote a series of proposals to funding agencies and phonograph manufacturers requesting support. Those proposals name the principles behind Lomax's research program, bringing an unprecedented clarity to the scattershot intuitions—about where to go, whom to find, what to record—that had been guiding negrophile collectors as a group since the turn of the century. These proposals garnered support not only from the Library of Congress but from external agencies including the American Council of Learned Societies, the Carnegie Corporation, and the Rockefeller Foundation. To an unacknowledged extent, these proposals capitalize on certain propositions made by Edison fifty years earlier by combining them with other propositions Edison never made that nevertheless became associated with his legacy through his connection, both real and apocryphal, to George W. Johnson. Basically Lomax proposed to stage the very same conditions that were retrospectively composed in the apocryphal encounter between Edison and Johnson as a narrative explanation for the phonograph's impact upon black music. Represented as a chance encounter, the exchange between Edison and Johnson is shaped by retrospective necessity insofar as it is obliged to account for the technological transition that happened between the time when the story takes place and whenever the story was being told. Lomax did not labor under any such obligation to name what was already under way; the proposals he wrote in the early 1930s are prospective in orientation. Their purpose was to stipulate ahead of time the right conditions for recording the black voice. Those conditions were to be engineered, not explained after the fact via effects they were already supposed to have produced. Lomax brought a new coherence to the documentation of the black vernacular tradition, because he needed to rationalize a research hypothesis to subsidize the equipment he wanted to bring into the field. Rather than intuitions about singers who were the subjects of their songs,

Lomax needed a system with justification. In response, he drafted a comprehensive theory that made criminality into a baseline criterion for black cultural authenticity.

Besides Edison, the encounter between Edison and Johnson has only one other ingredient: Johnson himself. In addition to an impossibly astute inventor who embodies the technological potential of the phonograph, the story needs Johnson—a street singer, an ex-slave, an accused murderer—because he is someone who can be mistaken for the subject of "The Laughing Song," which like the tradition for which it stands, is focalized through its lawlessness. The only singer to whom such a tradition can be faithful is the criminal. This is Johnson's purpose in the legend: to anchor black tradition to a street-level perspective defined by its incipient criminality. The inventor and the criminal are both required for the song that passes between them to sound faithful to its source. Where the inventor suggests ahead of time the breach that occasions fidelity, the criminal repairs that breach with his similarity to what he sings. Matching this narrative formula point for point, Lomax proposed to various funding sources—including Edison's own recording company—that the only way black tradition would ever be preserved in the absence of slavery was through a structured series of encounters between black lawlessness and modern technology. He proposed, in other words, that the most appropriate place to record the black tradition was in prison. By recording in a place where the singer is guaranteed to *sound like* a criminal even before the song starts, Lomax aligned his research, ahead of time as it were, with a tradition whose perspective is defined by its criminalization. This impression holds whether or not there were appropriate cues in a song's words or whether a song had words at all. This research paradigm has been responsible not only for canonizing certain musicians (Leadbelly) and settings (Parchman Farm) but also for establishing a listening framework that has powerfully influenced how the black tradition has been packaged ever since.

Earlier collectors, like Howard Odum, made offhand comments about the "prison" and "chain gang" as the "best setting" in which to gather true-to-life black folksongs, but none conceived a project on anything like the scale suggested by Lomax. Proposing to build a substantial archive from field recordings produced on location at southern penitentiaries, Lomax made a case in 1933 to the Library of Congress that black music in its "primitive purity" was obtainable "as nowhere else from Negro prisoners."

His supposition was that in visiting southern penitentiaries he would discover "unsophisticated ballad-singing Negroes in considerable numbers."
Insulated from modern lifestyles and the corrupting influence of the radio, black prisoners suffered an enforced isolation whose tightly circumscribed conditions were "practically ideal" for folklore collection.
Whether or not he was correct in this assumption, Lomax assured his
would-be benefactors that poor black men had a known tendency to "get
into serious trouble" that was enough to ensure that every penitentiary
they visited on their journey would prove "a repository of folk songs." The
idea that prisons were cloisters and prisoners were the last folk singers
proved compelling not only to the agencies to whom it was addressed but
also to the individuals and institutions that archived, printed, and commercially packaged the prison recordings deposited by the Lomaxes.
These recordings came from places like West Columbia and Clemens
State Farm in Texas, Cumins State Farm in Arkansas, Parchman Farm in
Mississippi, Angola State Penitentiary in Louisiana, Reid Farm in South
Carolina, Raiford Penitentiary in Florida, Bellewood Prison Camp in
Georgia, the Nashville Municipal Workhouse in Tennessee, and the
Milledgeville and Raleigh Penitentiaries in Virginia—to name a few of
the locations visited by the Lomaxes and their associates with the Library
of Congress during the 1930s and 1940s. The abundant results from these
expeditions were tendered as irrefutable evidence for the theory proposed
at their outset: that prisons were the last remaining repositories for black
cultural authenticity.[28]

Essentially, Lomax's hypothesis was that penitentiaries preserved black
culture. He would freely admit that the "sinister iron bars" and "crowds of
men in dismal-looking grey stripes" augmented the "impression that a
tone of sadness runs through the songs," but primarily he linked the perceived "purity" of these songs with their prison context in the collateral
sense that prisons were, apart from their punitive functions, culturally
conservative. "The Negro in the South is the target for such complex influences that it is hard to find genuine folk singing," he begins. It was the
influence of the radio and phonograph, in particular, that was "killing the
best and most genuine Negro folk songs" by prompting songsters to imitate mass-produced melodies from big cities rather than making the only
music that would ever be true to their own tradition. But it was not too
late, Lomax emphasized, as there were still places where blacks were "almost entirely isolated" and the tradition was being preserved, but it was vi-

tal to get there and record the songs that were left before they were gone for good. Because segregated penitentiaries were probably the places most isolated from corrupting influences—"without books or newspapers, the radio or the telephone"—it followed that they would prove the "last retreat" for the truly black music that was "formerly sung all over the South." Lomax was also quick to say that penitentiaries were advantageous not only for their isolation but for the positive pressures they exerted on the folk tradition. Penitentiaries not only stopped but reversed the tradition's deterioration. Black prisoners "slough off the white idiom they may have once employed in their speech and revert more to the idiom of the Negro common people." "Naturally," it was also the situation that "long-term Negro convicts" resorted "to the songs they sang before coming to the penitentiary. Thus the old songs are kept alive and growing as they are passed along to successive generations of convicts." For these reasons, Lomax proposed, the only blacks who continued "to create what we may rightly call folk-songs" were those who were imprisoned. In "almost complete isolation," their singing was guaranteed to be "practically pure." Prisons, it followed, were the antidote to modernization.[29]

By proposing that prisoners were the last folk singers and prisons were the only remaining repositories for black authenticity, Lomax transformed the legal imperatives that defined black tradition into cultural properties. He offered a systematic explanation for the privilege accorded to criminals in his ethnographic program without talking about the law. Prisons do not function in Lomax's proposals in terms of law. They function in terms of culture. The positive reason to visit the prison is not to find outlaws or miscreants. It is to find people untouched by mass culture. Just as Lomax replaces the appeal to Edison's genius with a claim for the phonograph's value to folklore collection, so he dispenses with the idea that Johnson had some special "talent" for recording. Where the mythology of Edison and Johnson has no excuse for this special talent besides occasional speculation that it may be a racial dispensation, Lomax offers a reasoned explanation for why songs made in prison were uncommonly true to themselves.

This explanation deserves to be taken seriously and not dismissed as an alibi for a hidden agenda. Although it led to misattribution and mischaracterization in certain instances, it is important that in an empirical sense, Lomax was right about what he would find in the prison. He was right that prisons, like the lumber camps, were populated disproportionately by

Left: prisoner with guitar at compound no. 1, Angola, Louisiana. *Right:* African American prisoners at compound no. 1, Angola, Louisiana (Lead-belly in foreground). Alan Lomax, photographer. Created between 1934 and 1940. Courtesy Lomax Collection at the United States Library of Congress.

migrant laborers who came from far away, and he was right that prisons consequently became cultural junctions where song traditions that had developed apart from one another were exchanged between players. He was right that the preference for gang labor in prison preserved worksongs that were rapidly disappearing in the outside world as agricultural industries became increasingly mechanized, and he was right as well that the patterns of call-and-response in these worksongs derived from Africa. These circumstances help us to appreciate the music that was being made in the penitentiary system, but they should not be taken as confirming the cultural proposition that facilitated its preservation. Simply pointing to the songs or cataloguing their inherited attributes cannot get us to the bottom of what it means to describe a prison as a "repository of folk songs" or what it means to characterize prisoners as people untouched by the phonograph. It cannot tell us what it means to say that penitentiaries increase the cultural store of blackness, returning whatever they absorb with interest, through their structural intensification of folksong tradition. Cultural historians have been right to attribute something like world-historical importance to the Lomaxes, but they have mistaken what makes them so important. When close attention is paid to the examples, in particular the legal precedents, for their research, we can see the larger stakes embedded in their enterprise.[30]

Just as indispensable to this project was the technology that the Lomaxes brought into the prison. Without their portable recording machine, it would have been much more difficult, if not entirely impossible, to reconstruct the ethnological purity of the black voice. Another way to put this point is to say that the purity of the black voice, its self-evident relation to its source in the black body, only becomes imaginable when the voice is separated from any situation that could be construed as its native context. The phonograph, again, does not disrupt the face-to-face intimacy of the ethnographic encounter. Rather, it makes the illusion of that intimacy possible. This explains, in part, why the low fidelity of field recordings served as proof of their authenticity. The hisses, pops, and clicks, the warped passages where the acetate yielded to summer heat, the songs that break off abruptly or begin late due to equipment malfunction—these distractions augment the music's authenticity by recalling the live encounter in the field. They are essential to its raw sound, facilitating a fantasy of immediate access that puts the listener in the collector's place. The irony here is that cultural fidelity becomes inversely proportional to acoustic fidelity. The noise on the record is not experienced as degrading the music's fidelity. It is, rather, its best evidence. Having less noise on these records would not make them sound more true to life. This is the case because the machine marks the gap between the copy and the source in a manner that allows listeners to hear breaks inside the music as if they were inadvertent effects of its reproduction. Scratches on the record, in other words, were a focusing device for listeners, because they fostered the illusion that the only obstacles standing between the listener and the black musician were technological. The result is the idealization of modern ethnography, an idealization that claims blackness can be reproduced under the right conditions if the right tools are employed. The incommensurability between the singer and the perspective in the song is reconstructed by the Lomaxes as a remediable problem of technological mediation, a problem whose solution promises to leave the folklore collector alone at last with the voice he had been trying to hear all along.

Through this idealization of the ethnographic encounter, the most essential aesthetic strategies of the black tradition become indistinguishable from their medium of reproduction. The noise on record, in other words, screens the noise that would otherwise be apparent in the music as the rasping sound of a voice thrown into existence. This technological screen was operating not only for archivists and enthusiasts who were listening months or years later but also in the field. One of the new-fangled features of Lomax's "music-reproducing apparatus" was its "play-back arm," which made it possible to "play back at once any song recorded." Continually recording and replaying music in the field, the Lomaxes first split their attention between the live performance and their notoriously temperamental portable phonograph, which required constant adjustments. Only within the playback was their attention to the black voice undivided. Lomax may have lacked the strange genius that enabled Edison to hear music in the moment as if after the fact, but still he managed to shrink the window between performance and playback to the point where the music no longer existed apart from the means of its reproduction. This deferred listening was a necessity, but it was also named as a distinct advantage in the reports Lomax drafted for his patrons. Recalling the record-now-interpret-later program advocated by Jesse Walter Fewkes in 1890, Lomax stressed that he had no musical training and claimed this made it easier to stay detached during collection. He promised not "interpretation" but "sound-

African American prisoners working outside Reed Camp, South Carolina; portraits of Ernest and Paul, Jennings, Louisiana; portrait of Sam Ballard, New Iberia, Louisiana; views of a baptism near Mineola, Texas. Created 1934. Courtesy Lomax Collection at the United States Library of Congress.

photographs of Negro songs, rendered in their own native element, unrestrained, uninfluenced and undirected by anyone who had his own notions of how the songs should be rendered." Interpretation would be left to the experts, and experts were unwanted in the field. This chronological division of ethnographic labor, separating interpretation from the sound of live performance, helped Lomax to define his role in the field by inserting a delay into the meaningful apprehension of the music, and in a stronger sense, indefinitely deferring the moment when the real listening, the listening with the authority to give meaning to the black voice, would be done.[31]

By orchestrating a series of technologically mediated encounters with black singers who had no choice but to look like the perspective in their songs by virtue of their imprisonment, the Lomaxes performed programmatically an equation that was engineered retrospectively for Edison, with the addendum that the fidelity in their encounters was something cultural rather than technological. With these preconditions in place, Lomax had serious leverage on the black tradition. Bringing together the black criminal and the phonograph, Lomax was poised to complete the process begun decades earlier by collectors like George Washington Cable and Joel Chandler Harris. He was poised, in other words, to reinvent black tradition as a folk tradition. Based on the apparent association between these prison songs and their singers, Lomax was ready to claim that these field recordings came from a traditional world where artistic expression was still indexed directly to its producers, before the corrupting influence of the phonograph and its kindred technologies. Unaccountably self-expressive, the songs made by black prisoners were heralded as the last living remnants from a disappearing world, valued for their increasing scarcity, demanding full protection to prevent further contamination from the outside world. In Lomax's words, these folksongs were nothing less than "the natural emotional outpouring of the black man in confinement." Prisons, it follows, had become the natural habitat for black songmaking. According to Lomax's system, black is to prison as bird is to tree—literally. "It is well known that the Negro is fond of singing," he writes. "He is endowed by nature with a strong sense of rhythm. His songs burst from him, when in his own environment, as naturally and as freely as those of a bird amid its native trees." The tension in these formulations comes from their attempt to conceal the connection between confinement and nature by ignoring how confinement conditions what sounds natural to the collector. It comes, in other words, from citing the prison's isolation (hence its naturalness) as a reason for the signal-to-source fidelity that is catalyzed in the reaction between recording technology and the bricks, guns, and barbed wire that keep the prisoner uncontaminated.[32]

By making the black prisoner into the conduit that channels the black tradition into the modern world, Lomax could base his entire theory of the tradition on a few representative informants whose life stories guaranteed the authenticity of their songs. In addition to having the requisite hard luck, these informants were supposed to have made the most of the cultural opportunities afforded by the prison. Commenting on one such informant, Mose "Clear Rock" Platt, the Lomaxes observed that he "seemed to have caught in his capacious memory every floating folk-song that had been current among the thousands of black convicts who had been his only companions for fifty years." The most prized informant of them all, of course, was Huddie Ledbetter, whom the Lomaxes represented as the embodiment of the African American folk song tradition. A convict imprisoned in Angola State Penitentiary for murder, talented on the twelve-string guitar, Leadbelly first met the Lomaxes in 1933 while he was still incarcerated. He greatly impressed the collectors with his extensive repertoire. Released for good behavior the next year, Leadbelly was hired by the elder Lomax as an assistant in the field. Both Lomaxes helped spread the myth that Leadbelly gained his release by singing an appeal so emotionally powerful that it moved Louisiana governor O. K. Allen to grant a pardon—a myth that sounds like the sentimental return of the farcical ending to George W. Johnson's trial, when Johnson is liberated and sings his way down the courthouse steps. That is not the only connection, however, between the singer who was the record industry's first great sensation and the singer advertised as the greatest of all the ragged songsters.[33]

The kinship between George W. Johnson and Leadbelly can be reconstructed by examining the rhetorical techniques responsible for making Johnson (a ragged man who became a recording star) and Leadbelly (a ragged man who became a recording star) into seeming opposites. Once it is granted that Leadbelly's status as "living link" to the past is determined not directly by "his eleven years of confinement," which were in Lomax's estimation enough to "cut him off both from the phonograph and from the radio," but instead by his ability to personify the themes about which he sang, we can tell not only what connects Johnson to Leadbelly—the law—but why Leadbelly had to be marketed as he was for that legal inheritance to become discernible as cultural property. We can tell, for instance, why Lomax promoted Leadbelly as he did when he took him on tour for exhibitions and benefit appearances. The barrage of publicity that was timed to coincide with Leadbelly's arrival in New York City included the notorious headline in the *Herald-Tribune*, "Sweet Singer of the Swamplands Here to Do a Few Tunes Between Homicides," phrasing that was later disowned by Lomax that nonetheless shows the tone of the promotion. Lomax introduced Leadbelly to reporters as "a 'natural' who had no idea of money, law, or ethics." Infamously, he forced Leadbelly to wear his convict clothes during public appearances. Lomax said the clothes were for "exhibition purposes"—not to exhibit the clothes themselves, we can presume, but to frame the exhibition of the singer. The clothes were necessary, because they helped listeners to transform the singer into the subject of songs like "Matchbox Blues" and "Angola Blues" and to turn his repertoire, no matter its individual contents, into the unaffected expression of a criminal consciousness. Leadbelly could leave prison, but Lomax sensed that he needed to take the prison with him for his music to retain its integrity. The appearance that Leadbelly was singing music that *belonged* to him was essential to the claim that he embodied a disappearing folksong heritage. It was his capacity to personify his own singing that gave his music the aura that was supposedly being lost everywhere else in a world where culture was becoming standardized and there was no longer a clear connection between the songs you sang and who you were.[34]

The conflicts that arose between Lomax and Leadbelly over the course of their increasingly strained relationship are too well known to rehearse here, but I do want to pause over one line that Leadbelly reportedly spoke to Lomax in conciliation after one of their disagreements. "A nachul rambler, boss, dat's what I am," Leadbelly says. There is little surprising about the content or manner of Leadbelly's address to his white employer, but there is more than convention to his words. Literally, they are quotation. Variations on the line appear in songs and sayings transcribed in various locations. Lomax himself published the following one:

> I'm a na'chul bo'n reacher,
> Oh, I'm a na'chul bo'n reacher,
> I'm a na'chul bo'n reacher
> An' it ain't no lie.

When Lomax printed this verse in an essay published in 1917, he did not mention the variants that had already been transcribed by collectors, where the speaker confirms his natural-born condition as a rounder, rambler, or Eastman. Curiously, however, Lomax does invent his own verse. "Certainly," Lomax says, if the singer were "self-conscious" about "his skill" he would have also included in his song the following variation on the well-known verse:

> I'm a na'chul bo'n singer,
> Oh, I'm a na'chul bo'n singer,

> I'm a na'chul bo'n singer
> An' it ain't no lie.

This is a verse that existed nowhere in the vernacular tradition, so far as Lomax knows, a verse however that Lomax considers so obvious and so essential that he invents the words himself. The movement from the original verse, which allegedly celebrates "a raid on a chicken roost," to the interpolated verse, which is tendered to confirm the singer's capacity for "spontaneous lyric expression," repeats in miniature what Lomax was doing all the time to informants, including Leadbelly. In an article on Lomax and Leadbelly's arrival in New York, *Time* observes: "John Lomax's protégé was a murderer, but he was also a natural-born minstrel." The reason that Lomax's early and awkward substitution ("singer" for "reacher") is valuable for us is that it preserves access to the connection between criminality and musical capacity, a connection that remained structural to later writings on Leadbelly, such as the *Time* article, even as it was covered over in those contexts by ambiguous conjunctions ("but") that obstruct analysis.[35]

What is revealing about Lomax's early gesture is how it scripts the term "singer" as a foreign word entered into the vernacular registry. If the gesture first teases us with the possibility that removing the collector's prejudice from the ethnographic transcript could be as simple as drawing a line through a word, finally it has the opposite effect. It is as if Lomax crosses out the word for us, and in the process announces that it remains his organizing principle. It is not a word that can be cleanly struck from the record, because the tradition that Lomax gathered would still be structured around this natural-born character even after the additive ("singer") is removed.

Yet Lomax's awkward substitution is enough to interrupt the common sense that says that black criminals are natural singers, putting enough distance between the singer and the song to permit us to ask what it means, in the first place, to call yourself a natural-born reacher. Consider the following variation:

> Well, they call me a rounder if I stay in town,
> And they say I'm a rounder if I roam aroun';
> I got it writ on the tail of my shirt:
> "I'm a nachel-bo'n rounder and don't need to work."
> And so I ain't bothered; no I ain't bothered.

This was transcribed from an anonymous informant by Gates Thomas in Texas in 1905. The first thing to observe is that its fifth line samples the same phrase that Leadbelly speaks to Lomax and that Lomax assigns to his natural-born singer in the essay from 1917. This coincidence is not surprising. Lines were always being passed from song to song. Making "rounder" into "reacher" is also standard practice; there are variations on the phrase that refer not only to reachers and rounders but to ramblers, travelers, creepers, eastmen, and thieves. What is remarkable about this verse are the quotation marks that locate the words, "I'm a nachel-bo'n rounder and don't need to work," not in the singer's mouth but on his back. Usually sung in the first person, the line is reassigned to a third-person interlocutor, a public identified only by its plurality and its abstraction ("they") and by its inclination to harass the singer no matter where he goes. The singer knows the words on his back, he knows what they say, he knows others can see them, but he cannot see them or say them himself. He has no choice but to identify with the name he is called by the public, but he cannot take the name as his own.[36]

In contrast to Lomax's ideas about natural-born singing, here the line reduces the singer's public name to an epithet scrawled on his shirt-tail, dramatizing its diminished power to determine his point of view. By highlighting the tenuous relation between his voice and the "I" on his shirt-tail, the singer unscrews the connection between seeing and being seen to the point where his song is shown to issue from a place that is different from the position that he is assigned in society. The public may nullify his choice to stay or go, but the choice that counts in the song, if it can be properly named as a choice, is the choice not to be bothered. The phrase "I ain't bothered" in the last line notches the gap between the name the singer is called by the public and the perspective in the song, making their distance indelible.

Moreover, the singer in this version appears to learn what is written on his back, not from watching the police or the public, but from listening to other songs. The words—"I'm a nachel-bo'n rounder and don't need to work"—are quoted not from a vagrancy law, or from a police officer, but from elsewhere in the black tradition. Or to be exact, they are borrowed from the tradition, which at some previous moment had borrowed them from the law. This type of lineage is only intermittently evidenced in verses like this one, which take the time to reflect on the tradition as a whole. More frequently, the action is truncated in verses like the one—"I'm a na'chul bo'n reacher/An' it ain't no lie"—that Lomax reprints for his essay. That verse is not elaborated to the same degree as the earlier one collected by Gates Thomas, but its trajectory is similar. When Lomax changes the verse, substituting singing for reaching, we catch him struggling to account for the surprise he feels when confronted by a performance that, for all intents and purposes, seems to arrive from nowhere. It is the song's apparent excess to its occasion that Lomax identifies as an unaccountable yet intrinsic characteristic of the black voice, a quality that is undeniably there in the voice even as it feels mysterious, like something that could not be taught or learned or explained, something that could only have been naturally born.

If Lomax's strategies for cultivating natural-born singing are apparent in his characterization of marquee informants like Leadbelly, they also inform how he handles relative unknowns. Among his best strategies was asking a prisoner to sing about how he or she got into the penitentiary. Lomax found some remarkable music with this request, including performances by Reese Crenshaw (from Milledgeville State Farm in Georgia), Blind Joe (from Central Prison in Raleigh, North Carolina), and Jesse Wadley (from Bellwood Prison in Atlanta). Replying to Lomax's request, Wadley explained his presence in Bellwood with these lines:

> Judge read my verdict, rocked in his easy chair;
> Judge read my verdict, rocked in his easy chair.
> Said, "I'm sorry, Jesse Wadley, you can't have no mercy here."

When Lomax asked for a song about getting into prison, he was asking his informants to allocute to their crimes. He was asking for confession, in other words, casting himself all at once as judge to accused, priest to confessor, analyst to patient. Based on how Lomax described the ensuing performances, we can tell that his main purpose in coaxing confessions from convicts was not to affirm the convict's guilt in order to endorse the penitentiary system that held them in thrall. The penitentiaries were flawed but necessary according to Lomax, and they were abominable according to his son Alan, but the system's legitimacy was never the predominant concern for either of them. By recording these performances as confessions, Lomax was banking on a romantic convention that treated the personal admission of wrongdoing as speaking in its purest and most private sense. Confessional singing played a special role in Lomax's collecting. Certainly he wanted to obtain as many traditional songs as he could, but he held the convict's verbal performance of self-recognition as his gold standard, as it exemplified the unalloyed self-expression that brought him to the penitentiary in the first place.[37]

Like in "The Laughing Song," when the singer is preempted even as he speaks before the crowd, these confessional verses cannot help but sound like a response to the direct address of the law whether or not that prior address is dramatized in the music. Consider, for example, the following song performed for John Lomax by Ozella Jones at Raiford State Farm in 1936:

> I been a bad, bad girl, wouldn't treat nobody right,
> I been a bad, bad girl, wouldn't treat nobody right,
> They want to give me thirty-five years, someone wanted to take
>   my life.
>
> Judge, please don't kill me, I won't be bad no more,
> Judge, please don't kill me, I won't be bad no more,
> I'll listen to everybody, something I never done before.
>
> Now I'm so sorry, even the day I was born,
> Now I'm so sorry, even the day I was born,
> I want to say to all you bad fellows that you are in the wrong.
>
> Now I'm sittin' here in prison with my black cap on,
> Now I'm sittin' here in prison with my black cap on,
> Boys, remember this, even when I'm gone.
>
> Now I'm so sorry, even the day I was born,
> Now I'm so sorry, even the day I was born,
> I want to say to all you bad fellows that you are in the wrong.

"I Been a Bad, Bad Girl," an unaccompanied blues, appears to have been sung following a request for a confession, and the performance is most notable for how it frustrates the prurient expectations that are raised by such a request. The words needed to create the depth that Lomax desires—"I did it"—are not forthcoming. Jones resists the demand for narrative, withholding the depth that only narrative can provide. She stymies expectation by proposing to pay not for something she has done but for being born "in the wrong." Jones treats criminality not as a bad action performed in the past for which she must atone in the present but as an inherited condition that structures her petition to the judge. This departure from the narrative baseline for confession upsets the song's future tense: the repentance, absolution, and reintegration that is supposed to follow from confession hinges upon the identification of an action that one can renounce and choose not to repeat. Moreover, the song takes away the satisfaction that might come from questioning her motives, whether those motives are understood as fully intentional (admitting to the wrong crime in order to hide something worse) or involuntary (inventing a crime to receive the punishment she unconsciously feels she deserves). The song's withholding of the ethical baseline for confession is not the same as telling listeners that they might as well perform bad works because it pays the same. The point is not about good or bad works but about their irrelevance to the only salvation the song can offer. We should take seriously what Jones means when she says she was born sorry. Not doing wrong but being born in the wrong—bearing the Mark of Cain as original sin—motivates her confession. Criminality, in the case of this performance, is prior to individuation. It comes before action and intention. Refusing to narrate her sins, Jones neither romanticizes her guilt nor presupposes her innocence. Rather, she makes an appeal that is conditioned neither by guilt nor innocence but by their irrelevance. She points continually to the wrong place from which she speaks, outlining the curve to her voice as it rebounds to the opening address that comes before she is ready to begin.[38]

These aspects in the song are intensified in the ethnographic archive by Lomax's failure to account for them. Based upon what appeared to him like an authentic confession from somebody who looked like an authentic criminal, Lomax turned this song into the standard by which others should be evaluated. Printing "I Been a Bad, Bad Girl" in *Our Singing Country* (1941), the Lomaxes are quick to note the song's fidelity, its truthfulness to its singer, as something that was lacking in commercial recordings manufactured for the phonograph. "If Bessie Smith enthusiasts," they propose, "could hear Ozella Jones or some other clear-voiced Southern Negro girl sing the blues, they might, we feel, soon forget their idol with her brassbound, music-hall throat." When blues is "sung by an unspoiled singer in the South, sung without the binding restrictions of conventional piano accompaniment or orchestral arrangement," it sounds unlike the factory product. The blues, sung in prison by someone like Ozella Jones, is "a wild flowering vine in the woods." Its melody "bends and then swings and shivers with the lines like a reed moving in the wind." We have already seen that the Lomaxes are doing more with these gestures than drawing the line between organic tradition and mass production. The blues sung by Ozella Jones is unspoiled not because it is insulated from technology but because her imprisonment creates the impression that she embodies the music's perspective. The reason Ozella Jones seems unadulterated and Raiford Penitentiary looks like the woodlands is not that there are no phonographs there. To make black tradition into a folk tradition, you need the threat of cultural contamination. Disavowing convention, whether blackfaced or brassbound, is the only way to describe the tradition in positive terms apart from the law that is broken whenever black speaking begins. When you disavow convention, you strike the law from the ethnographic record, and this leaves the tradition sounding soulful or natural or supernatural, terms that are supposed to identify the elusive thread within the tradition that remains intrinsically black even as it resists every possible attempt at cultural explanation.[39]

The irony in this specific example has been frequently noted: "I Been a Bad, Bad Girl," touted by the Lomaxes as a paradigm for vernacular authenticity, derives from a phonograph record. The song is nearly a word-for-word cover of "Bad Boy," recorded by Ed Bell, under the name Barefoot Bill, for Columbia in 1930. This often happened in the field. Collectors went to great lengths to explain to informants what songs were authentic, and objected strenuously when informants gave them pop songs anyway, including on several occasions, "The Laughing Song." Much of the time, as in this case, it appears that collectors did not know what they were getting. Dispensing with Lomax's artificial distinction between authentic and inauthentic blackness is the first step to acknowledging the kinship between Ozella Jones and Bessie Smith, or between Huddie Ledbetter and George W. Johnson, and it is also a step that has to be taken before we can tell what Jones is singing about. After Ed Bell is identified as the source for the song, Lomax's explanation becomes untenable. Any attempt to circumvent the song's structure of address by supplying a crime where none is specified, for instance by calculating that a jury trial with a penalty from thirty-five years to life is likely for murder, only repeats Lomax's mistake in forgetting that the judge, jury, and the penalty phase of the trial are not merely references to people and events in Ozella Jones's own experience but lines inherited from Ed Bell. We can be certain that the prison where she sits with her black cap on is not (or not only) Raiford Penitentiary where Jones was recorded. The prison is a hereditary convention that frames black speech in song.[40]

The aspect of her performance that bears the brunt of Lomax's misreading is its celebrated "holler" quality. Field hollers were usually performed solo while at work, with an unhurried tempo and long melismatic phrases built upon minor intervals and so-called blue notes. Unlike the prototypical field holler, which was rhythmically free, "I Been a Bad, Bad Girl" sustains a tenuous relationship to the implied beat it takes from "Bad Boy." Following Ed Bell, Ozella Jones sings in blues stanzas, twice repeating an end-stopped line with a medial caesura, with a third line responding that, in this case, also rhymes. Bell's rhythm (a beat that starts most lines trochaic and turns iambic) and pitch (a dependable vibrato that accentuates every stressed syllable) turns more adventurous in Jones's version, which is unconstrained by instrumental accompaniment. Much of the tension in her singing, it is true, comes from how she stretches her phrases as if performing a field holler. Starting late or holding a note a bit too long, coloring the melody with pitches that change as they are sung, Jones gives a distinctive inflection to her prison confession that is finally what matters most about her performance.

The Lomaxes point to this holler aspect as evidence for the "family connection" between Ozella Jones and the authentic blues tradition. The field holler, many critics have proposed, began in Africa. Whether the holler is taken on its own as the wellspring for the blues, or as an ingredient that combined with harmonic accompaniment patterns from the ballad tradition, the idea that there is a direct line of descent from the holler to the blues has long been a guiding principle for informed listeners. This analysis is borne out in the music and hard to deny in a general sense, but there is no question that these formal continuities in cultural practice, especially those much-vaunted blue notes, have been forced to bear too much weight in defining the family connection that constitutes the black tradition. This is nowhere more apparent than in the moment when the Lomaxes use this family resemblance to tell the difference between Ozella Jones and Bessie Smith. The interpretive problem presented when Ozella Jones is used to banish Bessie Smith from black tradition, or when Bessie Smith is used to make Ozella Jones sound like she is drawing a confession from deep inside herself, is resolved only when it is understood that what makes their singing black as well as blue is not its provenance but its application. When Jones pulls her phrasing from the ground beat, simulating the cross-rhythms traditional to many styles of African music, or lifts a single syllable through a full interval as in the "Ju-u-udge" that begins the second verse, she is making sounds whose history can be traced backward through the diaspora. But the blackness of those sounds is not inborn to the cultural practices that produced them. Their blackness inheres, rather, in their mnemonic capacity to entice the friction of expression from an otherwise blocked or forbidden point of address.[41]

Ozella Jones's singing is black not because of where it has been but because of what it is doing, and what it is doing is reducing the conventional language of the law to a material cause. By taking the law at its word, literally taking the law's words, and repeating them, bending them, taking them as close to mere phonemes as possible and then rebuilding their sense, Jones finds a place for herself inside a legal framework that refuses her capacity to speak even as it requires her confession. This is an amazing procedure, something like finding a new person in the conjugation of an ordinary verb, but it is entirely conventional to black tradition. By taking the terms that make blackness from the law and coarsening their timbre, growling and stuttering and spitting their leads and off-rhyming their ends, singers in this tradition—including not only Ozella Jones but Bessie Smith and Barefoot Bill—manage to loosen the state's language. Singing this language in a way it was never meant to be spoken, Jones sounds out her perspective in response to the implied direct address from the judge that comes before the song starts. This is a musical strategy that has been called overvocalizing, or the "effacement of text by voice," a strategy based on choral embellishments such as melisma, which are supposed to interrupt the prearranged lines of identification in a given composition. This speech effect does not imply consciousness with music as its vehicle. The sense that there is a consciousness to the music begins with the vague impression that its sounds are shaped. It begins with the lengthening and molding of words that are not your own. This shaping consciousness has little in common with what is ordinarily insinuated by speaking; it is a consciousness that appears only belatedly as the suggestion of someone who by all rights should not be there but is anyway. This is what it means to say that black speech only exists inside the music—or only in the split seconds when the epithet's drift is arrested by the music. Understood by collectors, including the Lomaxes, as untranscribable, these stretched or bent tones are the very same sounds that are represented metonymically in recordings by George W. Johnson as laughing, hooting, grunting, and whistling.[42]

"I Been a Bad, Bad Girl" is especially revealing, because the song pays such close attention to its own predication. Like "The Laughing Song," it is an example of the black voice's coming into existence being the main event in the performance. Jones appears only as a projection of her voice, and she allows the activity of self-projection, apart from the proceedings or propositions that might follow, to exhaust the song's resources. This activity is completed when the singer turns in the middle verse away from the authority that is variously represented as the judge, the world outside the prison, and the "everybody" whose orders must be obeyed by the penitent. Turning to speak directly to the "boys" who are identified as her listeners, the singer takes on the didactic posture that is previously assumed by her imposing interlocutors. This serial reconstitution of direct address—from judge to singer, singer to judge, and finally singer to implied audience—replicates the movement in "The Laughing Song" where the singer is preempted by the crowd, only to speak back to the crowd from the impossible position to which he is consigned by their epithets, finally holding that position while turning for a concluding address to his "kind friend" the listener. If "The Laughing Song" permits its listeners a choice that is not really a choice about whether or not to hear the song as chaff, "I Been a Bad, Bad Girl" offers an object lesson without a cautionary tale—an object lesson, that is to say, without a lesson. It may sound like she is telling the boys to change their evil ways, but the song offers no way to imagine the difference that repenting could possibly make either in this world or the next. There is no sense that acting differently will bring worldly or otherworldly rewards in a situation where your past actions have no bearing on your present position in the world.

The warning to the boys is cast in an imperative mood that projects a future even as it is kept from drawing on the narrative resources of the past. For the line "Boys, remember this, even when I'm gone," there is no lesson to be remembered and thus no antecedent for "this" besides the song itself. This future concerns the boys, but it is also the singer's future, her own life in song, that matters. The trope of artistic immortality is certainly not an improbable conclusion to a gallows address, with its familiar implication that the sinner's only chance to survive is as an object lesson to the community, but here there is no promise that the community can return to glory or rise to new heights. Without narrative there can be no jeremiad offering future glory as a reward for repenting; the transformation that is promised in this warning hinges instead upon the power of the voice alone. What is reproduced in the song is not a morality tale but the false memory of having been born in the wrong—false because the memory is not linked to an event that can be recalled to the mind. It is indexed, rather, to an occasion that needs to be invented or bequeathed to you. The gift that is given by Jones to the boys in the song stands both for the future and for the past. It is a figure for the reproduction of tradition, a figure standing simultaneously for the gift that Ozella Jones gives to her listeners and for the gift that Ed Bell gave to Ozella Jones. With this gift, Jones inherits a right to speak that is not hers by law. Kinship entails passing this right to others. This is why telling the boys that they are in the wrong is not the same as telling them to change their ways. Once salvation gets detached from the demand to act differently, what remains is the claim to likeness. It says: "You are like me." This is a claim that is linked to "The Laughing Song" and to "The Laughing Policeman." Unlike "The Laughing Song," which concludes by transposing the enmity between the singer and the crowd onto the relation between the singer and his listener, "The Laughing Policeman" concludes with the creepy promise that a bribe makes everything fine. If this reassurance divides listeners between those who feel recognized by law despite its corruption and those barred from such reassurance, effectively including the former group and excluding the latter group from the song's address, "I'm a Bad, Bad Girl" imagines the exact same line through its audience, only to turn finally not to the law's friends but to its enemies. This song is not for those who think they are born in the right; it is for those who are born in the wrong.

Making herself into an object lesson, Jones lifts her song from the individual lifespan into the time of the tradition. The song starts before she was born and it persists after she dies. By widening its timeframe beyond the scale of the individual, the song emphasizes its own address to the black tradition. It is the tradition that bequeaths to the ex-slave and her descendents a life that is not positively apprehensible as life, that is rather a proximate condition or an afterlife lived in the present tense, which is sustained, in large part, by the power of song. Because this afterlife is the only life that can be experienced from the foreclosed perspective that is represented at the song's outset, it appears not only where it is explicitly demarcated at the song's conclusion but wherever it is enacted as the blue sound of the black voice. With that sound, as with Johnson's laughs, Jones announces what the tradition has been doing all along.

It has been my aim in this chapter to show that this approach is applicable not only to Jones's singing but to all of the works recorded by collectors like the Lomaxes. Consider, as one final example, the odd track that opens Alan Lomax's *Roots of the Blues* compilation. To prove a proposition about the African diaspora, Lomax spliced together two separate field recordings, "Louisiana" by Henry Ratcliff, a prisoner in Mississippi, and an untitled song by Bakari-Badji, an agricultural worker in Senegal. Both songs are hollers, and Lomax believed that their similarity was striking enough to convert anyone who might otherwise remain skeptical about the cultural continuity of the African diaspora. In his liner notes, Lomax says that the composite track should be accepted as "positive aural evidence that, in spite of time and change of language and setting, the whole spirit of West Africa still flourishes in the United States and that the roots of the blues are African." Spliced together, the two songs sound "like a conversation between second cousins over a backyard fence."[43]

Lomax is explicit about the presumption that is made by this composite recording, which leaps more than 5,000 miles between the Senegalese rice field to the Mississippi penitentiary, but he is less than forthcoming about the components that link this late experiment to the early field recordings he made with his father. As we have seen, the two components that galvanized those early field recordings are the imprisonment of the informant and the modern technology of the phonograph, both of which are disavowed by the ethnographic enterprise that they are made to serve. The same disavowal occurs in the later case when the double recording is described by Lomax as a backyard conversation between cousins, a description that once again turns prison into pastoral and once again recovers the fading world of face-to-face communication by opposing the song's aura to the technological mediation, in this case the splicing, without which the song could never exist. The challenge, again, is not only to expose but to peer through this sleight-of-hand to discover, in the song that it makes possible, the broken connection between strangers that Lomax likens to the kinship of cousins. It is this same kinship that is revealed in the "holler" aspect of Ozella Jones's song, a quality that John Lomax was right to intuit as a "family connection" but wrong to reduce to a categorically exclusive cultural property.

Following the trace of this open-ended and elective kinship, it becomes possible to describe these songs without prejudicing the question of how their descent should be sequenced, liberating analysis from the burdensome assumption that tradition flows only in one direction. This problematic assumption is literally built into the cases that I have been considering in this book, all of which assume the priority of orality to literacy, enchantment to enlightenment, folk culture to mass entertainment, face-to-face performance to its mediation by the mechanical reproduction of image and sound. I have not tried to offer anything like my own theory about the temporality of the tradition, but I have sought to stress connections that run counter to the standard timeline: moving from the newspapers to the oral tradition, for example, or from the ancient dime novel to the folktale, or from art's reproducibility to its aura. I have also tried to mark small gestures that float free from the common sense of chronology, traveling across time to find connection with strangers—moving backward, for example, from Ida B. Wells-Barnett to Robert Charles, from Sidney Bechet to Bras-Coupé, from W. E. B. Du Bois to Sam Hose, and from Ozella Jones to all of the people that she has left behind.

This type of recursive gesture, which remains time bound even as it obstructs the perception of progress, often accompanies the tradition's attenuated claims to first-person perspective. It is a gesture that appears, for instance, at the start in Nathaniel Mackey's epistolary fiction, *Bedouin Hornbook* (1986), when the writer recounts a dream in which he assembles and begins to play a bass clarinet, only to realize that the music he is playing "already existed on a record." He can hear this well enough to name the original (Archie Shepp's solo in "Cousin Mary" on *Four for Trane*) and also well enough to hear the sound of the record's scratches "coming from somewhere in back and to the left" as he plays. It is this realization that ends the dream, provoking his first waking meditation in the book on how music can feel like a phantom limb. Mackey prompts his opening meditation on the broken connection facilitated by black music, in other words, by saying the one thing that John Lomax would never allow himself to hear from Ozella Jones: the one fact that is structurally prohibited from consideration at Raiford State Farm is the fact that Jones's song existed before on record. By focusing our listening through this fact, we can break open the ethnographic framework that has too often limited the meaning of the black tradition to discover something else that is still there in her words: the possibility of hearing the sounds of others in your own voice. The ambition of this book has been to write a history of this possibility, and therefore a possible history of the black tradition. My feeling is that all of the speculation, and even the presumption, involved in this enterprise will have been worth it, if the book succeeds in making otherwise unimaginable connections appear indelible, even for a moment.[44]

NOTES

Introduction

1. Robin Blackburn, *The Making of New World Slavery: From the Baroque to the Modern, 1492–1800* (London, 1997). Ira Berlin, *Many Thousands Gone: The First Two Centuries of Slavery in North America* (Cambridge, Mass., 1998). Sidney Mintz, *Sweetness and Power: The Place of Sugar in Modern History* (New York, 1985). Barbara Jeanne Fields, "Slavery, Race, and Ideology in the United States of America," *New Left Review* 181 (1990): 95–118. Michael A. Gomez, *Exchanging Our Country Marks: The Transformation of African Identities in the Colonial and Antebellum South* (Chapel Hill, N.C., 1998). Gwendolyn Midlo Hall, *Slavery and African Ethnicities in the Americas* (Chapel Hill, N.C., 2005). Winthrop Jordan, *White over Black: American Attitudes toward the Negro, 1550–1812* (New York, 1968). Eric Williams, *Capitalism and Slavery* (Chapel Hill, N.C., 1944). A contrasting approach is Molefi Asante, *The Afrocentric Idea* (Philadelphia, 1987). Huddie Ledbetter [Leadbelly], "You Don't Know My Mind" (Library of Congress 129-A). Frantz Fanon, "L'expérience vécue du noir," *Esprit* 179 (1951): 657–679. Ralph Ellison, *Invisible Man* (New York, 1952).

2. Frantz Fanon, "The Fact of Blackness," in *Black Skin, White Masks*, trans. Charles Lam Markmann (New York, 1967), 109–140. The phrase "fact of blackness" is a famously controversial translation, seemingly without any direct correlation to the original chapter title in French, "L'expérience vécue du noir." U.S. senator Joseph Biden used the words "clean" and "articulate" to describe Barack Obama, a rival presidential candidate. Jason Horowitz, "Biden Unbound: Lays into Clinton, Obama, Edwards," *New York Observer*, 4 February 2007. W. E. B. Du Bois, *The Souls of Black Folk* (Chicago, 1903). *Somerset v. Stewart*, 98 Eng. Rep. 499 (1772). Frederick Douglass, *Narrative of the Life of Frederick Douglass, an American Slave. Written by Himself* (Boston, 1845), 65–66. *The Politics of Aristotle*, trans. Ernest Barker (Oxford, 1957).

3. Fred Moten, *In the Break: The Aesthetics of the Black Radical Tradition* (Minneapolis, 2003). Robin D. G. Kelley, *Freedom Dreams: The Black Radical Imagination* (Boston, 2002). Harryette Mullen, "African Signs and Spirit Writing," *Callaloo* 19 (1996): 670–689. Roger D. Abrahams, *Singing the Master: The*

Emergence of African-American Culture in the Plantation South (New York, 1992). John W. Roberts, *From Trickster to Badman: The Black Folk Hero in Slavery and Freedom* (Philadelphia, 1989). Sterling Stuckey, *Slave Culture: Nationalist Theory and the Foundations of Black America* (New York, 1987). Cedric J. Robinson, *Black Marxism: The Making of the Black Radical Tradition* (Chapel Hill, N.C., 2000; first published 1983). Lawrence Levine, *Black Culture and Black Consciousness: Afro-American Folk Thought from Slavery to Freedom* (New York, 1977). Eileen Southern, *The Music of Black Americans: A History* (New York, 1971). Sterling Stuckey, "Through the Prism of Folklore: The Black Ethos in Slavery," *Massachusetts Review* 9 (1968): 419–420. Amiri Baraka [LeRoi Jones], *Blues People: Negro Music in White America* (New York, 1963). Melville Jean Herskovits, *The Myth of the Negro Past* (New York, 1941).

4. Alan Watson, *Slave Law in the Americas* (Athens, Ga., 1989), 76–77. Jonathan A. Bush, "Free to Enslave: The Foundations of Colonial American Slave Law," *Yale Journal of Law and the Humanities* 5 (1993): 417–470. Bradley Nicholson, "Legal Borrowing and the Origins of Slave Law in the British Colonies," *American Journal of Legal History* 38 (1994): 38–55. William M. Wiecek, "Somerset: Lord Mansfield and the Legitimacy of Slavery in the Anglo-American World," *University of Chicago Law Review* 42 (1974): 86–146.

5. Bush, "Free to Enslave," 420–428.

6. Many have pointed to the uncertain status of slave codes in the colonies as one strong reason not to found a theory of slavery on a genealogy of its laws. Because there was no jurisprudence on slavery for the English colonies, only inconclusive measures concerning theft and assembly and flight risks, we have no precise sources stating where legislators were looking as they wrote laws responding to perceived local exigencies. In later centuries, abolitionists would point to this disorganization, declaring that it proved the system's illegitimacy, noting especially the failure to name precedent or positive foundation for holding persons as property. "Search the statute books," Theodore Dwight proposes in 1794, "and tell me where is the law which establishes such an inhuman privilege." Others have said that the laws on the books fail to elucidate anything that is innovative and truly essential to racial slavery, especially new conventions governing testimony, kinship, and sexual behavior. Historians have worked to fill these gaps. Some have held that slaves were maneuvered by the existing common laws of property, while others have minimized the importance of the law altogether, pointing instead to the prevalence of anti-black racism in the later sixteenth century, professing that it was these cultural conventions, rather than legal precedents, that were decisive for English slavery. It has been argued as well that by looking to culture rather than precedent we can guard against the inclination to overemphasize parochial characteristics of one slave system, expanding interpretation instead to attitudes shared around

the Atlantic and Mediterranean basins, drawing their overlapping and inter-connected societies into comparative consideration. Bush, "Free to Enslave," 417–420, 420–428. Theodore Dwight, *An Oration, Spoken before the Connecticut Society, for the Promotion of Freedom and the Relief of Persons Unlawfully Holden in Bondage* (Hartford, Conn., 1794), quoted in Wiecek, "Somerset," 123. For an early, influential, and unstinting version of the argument that "slavery had no legal meaning" in the English colonies, see Oscar and Mary F. Handlin, "Origins of the Southern Labor System," *William and Mary Quarterly* 7 (1950): 199–222. For a synopsis of this argument, see Morris, *Southern Slavery and the Law, 1619–1860* (Chapel Hill, N.C., 1996), 37–57.

7. William Blackstone, *Commentaries on the Laws of England*, 4 vols. (Chicago, 1979; first published 1765–1769), 4:161–175. Patrick Colquhoun, *A Treatise on the Police of the Metropolis* (London, 1806). Fortunatus Dwarris, *A General Treatise on Statutes: Their Rules of Construction, and the Proper Boundaries of Legislation and Judicial Interpretation* (Albany, N.Y., 1885), 467. On the list and Blackstone's police, see Marcus Dirk Dubber, *The Police Power: Patriarchy and the Foundations of American Government* (New York, 2005), 47–62. On the lists in early police measures adopted in the United States, see William J. Novak, *The People's Welfare: Law and Regulation in Nineteenth-Century America* (Chapel Hill, N.C., 1996). On the list as the "knowledge format of police powers" in general, see Mariana Valverde, *Law's Dream of a Common Knowledge* (Princeton, N.J., 2003), 141–166.

8. South Carolina legislature, quoted in Bush, "Free to Enslave," 437. Christopher Waldrep, *Roots of Disorder: Race and Criminal Justice in the American South, 1817–80* (Urbana, Ill., 1988). Alex Lichtenstein, *Twice the Work of Free Labor: The Political Economy of Convict Labor in the New South* (London, 1996). Saidiya V. Hartman, *Scenes of Subjection: Terror, Slavery, and Self-Making in Nineteenth-Century America* (New York, 1997), 164–206. *Plessy* held that racial segregation was within the "exercise of the police power." In response to the claim that this would allow the application of arbitrary rules—forcing railways, for instance, to have separate cars for people with specific hair colors, or compelling blacks to walk on one side and whites on the other side of the street—the Supreme Court cautioned that "every exercise of the police power must be reasonable, and extend only to such laws as are enacted in good faith for the promotion of the public good." Segregation laws met this standard according to the court's definition of public necessity. On the basis for *Plessy's* police thinking in antebellum police cases, see Leonard W. Levy, *The Law of the Commonwealth and Chief Justice Shaw* (New York, 1957), 109–117. Even more explicitly than *Plessy*, Collins Denny Jr. names the association between police and the perception of racial threat. "It has been very fortunate for that section," Denny writes about the South, "that the Supreme Court has given the

police power such a wide range, and due to this power the South has so far been able to ward off the danger arising from her large Negro population." Collins Denny Jr., "The Growth and Development of the Police Power of the State," *Michigan Law Review* 20 (1921): 201.

9. My genealogy of the police power borrows frequently from the extraordinary research of Marcus Dirk Dubber. See especially Dubber, *Police Power. Slaughter-House Cases*, 83 U.S. 36, 49 (1873). "Police, n.," *Oxford English Dictionary*, 2nd ed. (New York, 1989). Cesare Beccaria, *On Crimes and Punishments*, trans. Henry Paolucci (New York, 1963). Jeremy Bentham, *Introduction to the Principles of Morals and Legislation*, ed. J. H. Burns and H. L. A. Hart (London, 1996). Blackstone, *Commentaries on the Laws of England*. Chancellor James Kent, *Commentaries on American Law* (New York, 1971). *Commonwealth v. Alger*, 61 Mass. 53 (1851). *Gibbons v. Ogden*, 22 U.S. 1 (1824). *License Cases*, 46 U.S. 504, 583 (1847).

10. As Dubber has observed, the defining characteristic of the police power appears to be its resistance to definition. For its most influential commentators, police is indeterminate and unbounded. It is indispensable to sovereignty, and it is therefore impossible to differentiate police from sovereignty, as there can be no sovereignty without police. According to Jeremy Bentham, the police power is "too multifarious to be susceptible of any single definition." For Lemuel Shaw, it remains "easier to perceive and realize the existence of the power than to mark its boundaries or to prescribe limits to its exercise." According to Roger Taney, the "police powers of a state" are "not susceptible of an exact limitation" as they are "nothing more or less than the powers of government inherent in every sovereignty to the extend of its dominions." For Thomas Cooley, police is the "most comprehensive branch of sovereignty, extending as it does to every person, every public and private right, everything in the nature of property, every relation in the State, in society, and in private life." For William Packer Prentice, the police power is "difficult of exact definition," because "the generality of the terms employed by jurists and publicists in defining this power, while they show the breadth and universality of its presence, nevertheless leave its boundaries and limitations indefinite." According to W. G. Hastings, the police power remains a "catch word" for the "vast and vague notion of the powers of the state" whose formulation as "a definite word in popular discussion" is owed to the "very indefiniteness of the conception." For Fortunatus Dwarris, police is "commensurate with the sovereignty of the state" and so "must be regarded in this state, to be settled, and founded upon principles which are above and beyond the reach of constitutional restriction." For Ernst Freund, police is "indispensable in the vocabulary of American constitutional law." It remains in "constant use" despite the fact that it has no "authoritative or generally accepted definition." Bentham, *Introduction to the Principles*, 198.

Commonwealth v. Alger (1851). *License Cases* (1847). Thomas Cooley, *The General Principles of Constitutional Law in the United States of America* (Boston, 1898), 250. W. P. Prentice, *Police Powers Arising under the Law of Overruling Necessity* (New York, 1894), 1–2, 6. W. G. Hastings, "The Development of Law as Illustrated by the Decisions Relating to the Police Power of the State," *Proceedings of the American Philosophical Society* 39 (1900): 371. Fortunatus Dwarris, *A General Treatise on Statutes: Their Rules of Construction, and the Proper Boundaries of Legislation and Judicial Interpretation* (Albany, N.Y., 1885), 450–451. Ernst Freund, *The Police Power: Public Policy and Constitutional Rights* (Chicago, 1904), iii. On the police power and racial prerogative both under and after slavery, see Hartman, *Scenes of Subjection*, 198–200, 204–206.

11. Dubber, *Police Power*, xi–xvi, 120–138. Pasquale Pasquino, "Theatrum Politicum: The Genealogy of Capital-Police and the State of Prosperity," *Ideology and Consciousness* 4 (1978): 41–54. Dorothy Roberts, "Race, Vagueness, and the Social Meaning of Order-Maintenance Policing," *Journal of Criminal Law and Criminology* 89 (1999): 775–836. See also Ruth Wilson Gilmore, "Terror Austerity Race Gender Excess Theater," in *Reading Rodney King/Reading Urban Uprising*, ed. Robert Gooding-Williams (New York, 1993), 23–37.

12. On these cases leading up to *Lochner*, see Hastings, "Development of Law," 359–554. Alfred Russell, *The Police Power of the State and Decisions Thereon as Illustrating the Development and Value of Case Law* (Chicago, 1900). Denny, "Growth and Development of the Police Power," 173–214. On Mill's harm principle, see Ray A. Brown, "Police Power—Legislation for Health and Personal Safety," *Harvard Law Review* 42 (1929): 866–898. On police power after *Papachristou*, see Bernard Harcourt, *Illusion of Order: The False Promise of Broken Windows Policing* (Cambridge, Mass., 2001). For comparison, see Debra Livingston, "Gang Loitering, the Court, and Some Realism about Police Patrol," *Supreme Court Review* 141 (1999): 141–202.

13. [Thomas Paine], *Common Sense* (Philadelphia, 1776). Alexander Hamilton, James Madison, and John Jay, *The Federalist Papers* (New York, 1788). The police power is not named in the United States Constitution. The relevant portions of the document for subsequent jurisprudence on the police power are those that address the division of the powers of domestic regulation between federal and state governments, especially in Article I, Section 8. Blackstone, *Commentaries on the Laws of England*, 4:161–175. On Blackstone's impact in the United States, see Freund, *Police Power*, 2–3. Walter Wheeler Cook, "What Is the Police Power?" *Columbia Law Review* 7 (1907): 332–336. See also Dubber, *Police Power*, 47–62.

14. *Brown v. Maryland*, 25 U.S. 419 (1827). *State of New York v. Miln*, 36 U.S. 102 (1837). Hastings, "Development of Law," 366–389. Dubber, *Police Power*, 143–145, 198–200. William J. Novak, "Common Regulation: Legal Origins of State Power

in America," *Hastings Law Journal* 45 (1994): 1061–1097. In addition, see Russell, *Police Power of the State.*

15. *License Cases,* 46 U.S. 504, 578 (1847). *Commonwealth v. Alger,* 61 Mass. 53 (1851). On the context for *Alger,* see Levy, *The Law of the Commonwealth,* 229–265.

16. Thomas M. Cooley, *A Treatise on the Constitutional Limitations which Rest upon the Legislative Power of the United States* (Boston, 1868). Christopher G. Tiedeman, *A Treatise on the Limitations of Police Power in the United States* (St. Louis, 1886). Freund, *Police Power. Lochner v. New York,* 198 U.S. 45 (1905).

17. The improper storage of gunpowder is introduced as a paradigm case for the police in *Brown v. Maryland,* when it was suggested to Marshall in an argument that was made by Taney. It recurs in *Miln, Alger,* and the *License Cases.* Concerning this recurrence, see Hastings, "Development of Law," 359–378. Bentham's fragment on torture, unpublished in his lifetime, first appeared as W. L. and P. E. Twining, "Bentham on Torture," *Northern Ireland Legal Quarterly* 24 (1973), 305–356. Michael Walzer, "Political Action: The Problem of Dirty Hands," *Philosophy and Public Affairs* 2 (1973): 160–180. Niklas Luhmann, *Law as a Social System* (New York, 2004), 464–490. Lincoln Diamant, *Dive! The Story of David Bushnell and His Remarkable 1776 Submarine* (Fleischmanns, N.Y., 2003).

18. Dwarris, *General Treatise,* 455–456, 449. Prentice, *Police Powers Arising,* 6. William Stevens, *The Unjust Judge: Or, the Evils of Intemperance on Judges, Lawyers, and Politicians* (Mansfield, Ohio, 1854), 312–314. In his principal work on the police power, Johann Fichte puts the distinction in this way: criminal laws "prohibit merely the *actual violation* of the fundamental compact" whereas "police laws are made to prevent the *possibility* of such violation." J. G. Fichte, *The Science of Rights,* trans. A. E. Kroeger (London, 1889), 377.

19. Hugo Grotius, *The Rights of War and Peace,* ed. Richard Tuck (Indianapolis, 2005). Thomas Hobbes, *Leviathan,* ed. Richard Tuck (Cambridge, U.K., 1991). Samuel Pufendorf, *On the Duty of Man and Citizen according to Natural Law,* ed. James Tully (Cambridge, U.K., 1991). Richard Tuck, *The Rights of War and Peace: Political Thought and the International Order from Grotius to Kant* (New York, 2001), 78–165.

20. Tuck, *Rights of War and Peace,* 78–165. Twining and Twining, "Bentham on Torture," 305.

21. *License Cases.* Prentice, *Police Powers Arising,* 4. In a capsule summary, George Wickersham figures the "entire doctrine of the police power" in these decisions as pronouncing "the necessity of harmonizing provisions of written constitutions of states and nation with the imperative needs of civilized society." George W. Wickersham, "The Police Power, a Product of the Rule of Reason," *Harvard Law Review* 27 (1914): 297.

22. Tuck, *Rights of War and Peace*, 1–15. John Locke, *Two Treatises of Government* (Cambridge, 1967), 341–342, 302, 291–292, 295. Bartolomé de Las Casas, *Short Account of the Destruction of the Indies* (New York, 1999). G. W. F. Hegel, *The Phenomenology of Spirit*, trans. A. V. Miller (New York, 1979). Alexandre Kojève, *Introduction to the Reading of Hegel: Lectures on the Phenomenology of the Spirit* (Ithaca, N.Y., 1980). Orlando Patterson, *Slavery and Social Death* (Cambridge, Mass., 1982). David Brion Davis, *The Problem of Slavery in Western Culture* (New York, 1966). Charles Mills, *The Racial Contract* (Ithaca, N.Y., 1999). Claude Meillassoux, *The Anthropology of Slavery: The Womb of Iron and Gold*, trans. Alide Dasnois (Chicago, 1991). For one example of how Hegel has been adapted to frame the historical analysis of modern slavery, see Guyora Binder, "Mastery, Slavery, and Emancipation," *Cardozo Law Review* 10 (1989): 1435–1480. For skepticism about this type of application, see Jonathan Bush, "Hegelian Slaves and the Antebellum South," *Cardozo Law Review* 10 (1989): 1517–1563.

23. Fichte, *Science of Rights*, 374, 261, 364.

24. Fichte, *Science of Rights*, 367, 365, 374–387.

25. Samuel Pufendorf, *The Law of Nature and Nations*, trans. Basil Kennet (London, 1749), 7:769, quoted in Tuck, *Rights of War and Peace*, 159. Fichte, *Science of Rights*, 377. "Society," Isaac F. Redfield writes, "in all these cases and many others, has the right to anticipate, in order that it may prevent, the injury, which is thus threatened. If it were not so, men, in a social state, would be far more powerless, for purposes of defence, than in a natural state." *Spalding v. Preston*, 21 Vt. 9 (1848). "The exigencies of the social compact," William Prentice concurs, "require that such laws be executed before and above all others." Prentice, *Police Powers Arising*, 14. Dwarris cites Pufendorf on the law of necessity to back the claim that the police power "is an exception to all human ordinances and constitutions, and that therefore it gives a right of doing many things otherwise forbidden." Police, Dwarris summarizes, "is the application of the personal right or principle of self preservation to the body politic." Dwarris, *General Treatise*, 447–450.

26. Fichte, *Science of Rights*, 366. On the theory and the practice of vigilante violence after slavery, see Philip Dray, *At the Hands of Persons Unknown: The Lynching of Black America* (New York, 2002). For an influential study stressing both the passivity (unequal protection) and the activity (unequal enforcement) that is licensed by legal abandonment, see Randall Kennedy, *Race, Crime, and the Law* (New York, 1997).

27. *Wilmington Messenger*, 22 July 1898. Making the same point as the *Messenger* but applying it to legal doctrine, Fortunatus Dwarris notes that "the evil arising from nuisances, and from pestilential diseases" would be unbearable if "authorities were obliged to wait the slow progress of a prosecution" instead of taking them as a police matter. Dwarris, *General Treatise*, 447.

28. Kent, *Commentaries on American Law*, 2:275. The passage draws on the model of outlawry, a precedent that is the root of the police power, which we will consider subsequently in the cases of Robert Charles and Bras-Coupé. Here suffice it to say that outlawry presents the negro's lack of standing as a self-inflicted condition, suggesting that the negro was not outlawed by the government but that the negro "had outlawed himself." *Wilmington Messenger*, 22 July 1898.

29. Primo Levi, *The Drowned and the Saved*, trans. Raymond Rosenthal (New York, 1989). Gayatri Chakravorty Spivak, "Can the Subaltern Speak?" in *Marxism and the Interpretation of Culture*, ed. Cary Nelson and Lawrence Grossberg (Urbana, Ill., 1988), 271–313. Giorgio Agamben, *Homo Sacer: Sovereign Power and Bare Life*, trans. Daniel Heller-Roazen (Stanford, Calif., 1998). Giorgio Agamben, *Remnants of Auschwitz: The Witness and the Archive*, trans. Daniel Heller-Roazen (New York, 1999). Achille Mbembe, *On the Postcolony* (Berkeley, Calif., 2001). I am referring here to a tradition of commentary that extends from the discussion in the fifth chapter from Hannah Arendt's *The Origins of Totalitarianism* (New York, 1951), "The Decline of the Nation State and the End of the Rights of Man." Arendt's chapter is concerned not specifically with slavery but with statelessness, a condition where every quality that could potentially lead to political recognition is stripped away. "The fundamental deprivation of human rights," Arendt proposes, "is manifested first and above all in the deprivation of a place in the world which makes opinions significant and actions effective." Arendt, *Origins of Totalitarianism*, 292–293. As background, see Carl Schmitt, *The Concept of the Political*, trans. George Schwab (Chicago, 1996). Du Bois, *Souls of Black Folk*, 1–12. On this problem, as it is framed by Du Bois, I have learned from the extraordinary assessment in Nahum D. Chandler, *The Problem of Pure Being: Annotations on the Early Thought of W. E. B. Du Bois and the Discourses of the Negro* (New York, forthcoming).

30. Hortense J. Spillers, "The Idea of Black Culture," *New Centennial Review* 6 (2007): 25.

31. John William Burgess, *Political Science and Comparative Constitutional Law* (Boston, 1891), 136. John William Burgess, *The Reconciliation of Government with Liberty* (New York, 1915), 28–29. Colin [Joan] Dayan, "Held in the Body of the State: Prisons and the Law," *History, Memory, and the Law*, ed. Austin Sarat and Thomas R. Kearns (Ann Arbor, 1999), 183–247. Colin [Joan] Dayan, "Legal Slaves and Civil Bodies," *Nepantla* (2001), 3–39. Colin [Joan] Dayan, "Legal Terrors," *Representations* 92 (2005): 42–80.

32. For a polemic against the culture-based approach, specifically in literary studies of the black tradition, see Adolph Reed Jr., *W. E. B. Du Bois and American Political Thought: Fabianism and the Color Line* (New York, 1997).

33. Sidney W. Mintz and Richard Price, *An Anthropological Approach to the Afro-American Past* (Philadelphia, 1976). Eric Hobsbawm and Terence Ranger, eds.,

The Invention of Tradition (Cambridge, U.K., 1992). Paul Gilroy, *The Black Atlantic: Modernity and Double Consciousness* (Cambridge, Mass., 1992). David Morley and Kuan-Hsing Chen, eds., *Stuart Hall: Critical Dialogues in Cultural Studies* (London, 1996). Michael A. Gomez, *Exchanging Our Country Marks: The Transformation of African Identities in the Colonial and Antebellum South* (Chapel Hill, N.C., 1998). David Scott, *Refashioning Futures: Criticism after Postcoloniality* (Princeton, N.J., 1999). Brent Edwards, *The Practice of Diaspora: Literature, Translation, and the Rise of Black Internationalism* (Cambridge, Mass., 2003). Michelle Wright, *Becoming Black: Creating Identity in the African Diaspora* (Durham, N.C., 2004). Gwendolyn Midlo Hall, *Slavery and African Ethnicities in the Americas: Restoring the Links* (Chapel Hill, N.C., 2005).

34. Baraka [Jones], *Blues People*. Moten, *In the Break*, 24. Robinson, *Black Marxism*, 73.

1. The Black Tradition from Ida B. Wells to Robert Charles

1. Paul Oliver, *The Story of the Blues* (Boston, 1969). Albert Murray, *Stomping the Blues* (New York, 1976). Jeff Todd Titon, *Early Downhome Blues: A Musical and Cultural Analysis*, 2nd ed. (Chapel Hill, N.C., 1995). David Evans, *Big Road Blues: Tradition and Creativity in the Folk Blues* (Berkeley, Calif., 1982). Bruce Bastin, *Red River Blues: The Blues Tradition in the Southeast* (Urbana, Ill., 1985). William Barlow, *"Looking Up at Down": The Emergence of Blues Culture* (Philadelphia, 1989). Ferdinand "Jelly Roll" Morton, "I Created Jazz in 1902, Not W. C. Handy," *Down Beat* 5 (August 1938): 3, 31. An earlier version of this letter was printed as "Handy Not Father of Blues, Says Jelly Roll," *Baltimore Afro-American*, 23 April 1938. For Handy's response, see W. C. Handy, "I Would Not Play Jazz If I Could," *Down Beat* 5 (September 1938): 5. The letters, written in Morton's voice, to the *Afro-American* and *Down Beat* were produced collaboratively by Morton and his advocate, Roy Carew. For Handy's treatment in the black press, see "Father of Jazz Does His Stuff over Radio," *Chicago Defender*, 18 December 1926, 4. For a contrasting illustration, see Edmund Wilson, "Shanty-Boy Ballads and Blues," *New Republic* 47 (14 July 1926): 227–229.

2. W. C. Handy, *Father of the Blues*, ed. Arna Bontemps (New York, 1969; first published 1941), 99, 74. Abbe Niles, "Introduction," in *Blues: An Anthology*, ed. W. C. Handy (Bedford, Mass., 2001; first published 1926), 12–13. Robert Palmer, *Deep Blues: A Musical and Cultural History of the Mississippi Delta* (New York, 1981), 44–47. Evans, *Big Road Blues*, 34–45, 174–175. Houston A. Baker Jr., *Blues, Ideology, and Afro-American Literature: A Vernacular Theory* (Chicago, 1984), 3–5. Oliver, *Story of the Blues*, 27–30. Sidney Finkelstein, *Composer and Nation: The Folk Heritage in Music* (London, 1989; first

published 1960), 306–308. Eileen Southern, *The Music of Black Americans* (New York, 1997; first published 1971), 332–333. William Ferris, *Blues from the Delta* (New York, 1978), 36–37. Giles Oakley, *The Devil's Music: A History of the Blues,* 2nd ed. (New York, 1997; first published 1977), 9–10. Alan Lomax, *The Land Where the Blues Began* (New York, 1993), 163–167. Titon, *Early Downhome Blues,* 23–25. Francis Davis, *The History of the Blues: The Roots, the Music, the People* (New York, 1995), 24–25. Greil Marcus, *The Dustbin of History* (London, 1996), 48.

3. On the historiography of this character, see the following: Clyde Woods, *Development Arrested: Race, Power, and the Blues in the Mississippi Delta* (London, 1998). Angela Davis, *Blues Legacies and Black Feminism* (New York, 1998). Benjamin Filene, *Romancing the Folk: Public Memory and American Roots Music* (Chapel Hill, N.C., 2000). Marybeth Hamilton, "Sexuality, Authenticity and the Making of the Blues Tradition," *Past and Present* 169 (2000): 132–160. Adam Gussow, *Seems Like Murder Here: Southern Violence and the Blues Tradition* (Chicago, 2003). Elijah Wald, *Escaping the Delta: Robert Johnson and the Invention of the Blues* (New York, 2004). Marybeth Hamilton, *In Search of the Blues: Black Voices, White Visions* (London, 2007). Patrick Mullen, *The Man Who Adores the Negro: Race and American Folklore* (Urbana, Ill., 2008). These works frequently draw upon an earlier critical exchange between anthropology and literary studies. Edward Said, *Orientalism* (New York, 1978). Johannes Fabian, *Time and the Other: How Anthropology Makes Its Object* (New York, 1983). Eric Hobsbawm and Terence Ranger, eds., *The Invention of Tradition* (Cambridge, U.K., 1983). James Clifford, *The Predicament of Culture: Twentieth-Century Ethnography, Literature, and Art* (Cambridge, Mass., 1988). Mary Louise Pratt, *Imperial Eyes: Travel Writing and Transculturation* (London, 1992). An important landmark for this critique within African American literary studies is Hazel Carby, "The Politics of Fiction, Anthropology, and the Folk: Zora Neale Hurston," in *New Essays on* Their Eyes Were Watching God, ed. Michael Awkward (Cambridge, U.K., 1991), 71–93. In this line of thought, I have also learned from Gina Dent, "Flowers and Colored Bottles: The Anthropology of Culture in Twentieth-Century African American Writing," PhD diss., Columbia University, 1997.

4. Handy, *Father of the Blues,* 74. The claim that the black folk were "at once singers and subjects" of their songs is a commonplace among collectors in the first decades of the twentieth century. Howard W. Odum and Guy B. Johnson, *Negro Workaday Songs* (Chapel Hill, N.C., 1926), viii. Among collectors of Odum's generation, one influential source for this idea was William Graham Sumner, *Folkways* (Boston, 1906). On folk expression as distinguished by the natural alignment of the producer's "words, soul, eye, and hand," see Walter Benjamin, "The Storyteller," trans. Harry Zohn, in *Illuminations* (New York,

1969), 83–109. On the institutionalization of the assumption in folklore studies, see Regina Bendix, *In Search of Authenticity: The Formation of Folklore Studies* (Madison, Wis., 1997). On its currency in U.S. culture, see Miles Orvell, *The Real Thing: Imitation and Authenticity in American Culture* (Chapel Hill, N.C., 1989).

5. John Jacob Niles, "Shout, Coon Shout!" *Musical Quarterly* 16 (1930): 516–530. Charles Peabody, "Notes on Negro Music," *Journal of American Folklore* 16 (1903): 148–152. Joel Chandler Harris, *Nights with Uncle Remus: Myths and Legends of the Old Plantation* (New York, 1883), xv–xvii. The most commonly cited source for the story about T. D. Rice learning how to Jump Jim Crow is Robert P. Nevin, "Stephen C. Foster and Negro Minstrelsy," *Atlantic Monthly* (November 1867): 608–616. It is worth recollecting that although this story is most likely apocryphal, it was taken very seriously by folklore collectors as a model for their own practice. Rice's version of the song is often reprinted in folklore collections from the early decades of the twentieth century, in some cases supplemented by evidence of its absorption into the folk tradition. Thomas W. Talley, *Negro Folk Rhymes*, ed. Charles K. Wolfe (Knoxville, Tenn., 1991; first published 1922), 11. Dorothy Scarborough, *On the Trail of Negro Folk-Songs* (Cambridge, Mass., 1925), 125–127. Newman I. White, *American Negro Folk-Songs* (Cambridge, Mass., 1928), 162–163. Robert Duncan Bass, "Negro Songs from the Pedee Country," *Journal of American Folklore* 44 (1931): 427–428. John Lomax and Alan Lomax, *Folk Song U.S.A.* (New York, 1947), 78. On the Rice legend and the ambivalence of cultural appropriation, see Eric Lott, *Love and Theft: Blackface Minstrelsy and the American Working Class* (New York, 1993), 38–62.

6. Odum and Johnson, *Negro Workaday Songs*, 6. Howard W. Odum, "Folk-Song and Folk-Poetry as Found in the Secular Songs of the Southern Negroes," *Journal of American Folklore* 24 (1911): 259. Will H. Thomas, *Some Current Folk-Songs of the Negro* (Austin, Tex., 1936; first published 1912), 5, 3. Howard Odum, *Rainbow Round My Shoulder: The Blue Trail of Black Ulysses* (New York, 1928), 253. For elaboration of Odum's theories on race and moral character, see also Howard W. Odum, *Social and Mental Traits of the Negro* (New York, 1910).

7. Although there was a preference for spirituals among collectors during the late nineteenth century, interest in secular songs and sayings became intense during the first half of the twentieth century, and frequently this interest was focused through characters who looked exactly like Handy's ragged drifter. Like the sources named above, the following list is merely illustrative with regard to this new ethnographic approach. W. E. B. Du Bois, *The Souls of Black Folk* (Chicago, 1903). Kelly Miller, "The Artistic Gifts of the Negro," *Voice of the Negro* 3 (1906): 252–257. John W. Work, "The Songs of the Southland," *Voice of*

the Negro 4 (1907): 51–54. Harris Barrett, "Negro Folk Songs," *Southern Workman* 41 (1912): 238–245. Robert R. Moton, "Negro Folk Music," *Southern Workman* 44 (1915): 329–330. John W. Work, *Folk Song of the American Negro* (Nashville, 1915). E. C. Perrow, "Songs and Rhymes from the South," *Journal of American Folklore* 25 (1912): 137–155; 26 (1913): 123–173; 28 (1915): 129–190. Henry E. Krehbiel, *Afro-American Folksongs* (New York, 1914). Anna Kranz Odum, "Some Negro Folk-Songs from Tennessee," *Journal of American Folklore* 27 (1914): 255–265. Walter Prescott Webb, "Notes on the Folk-Lore of Texas," *Journal of American Folklore* 28 (1915): 290–299. John A. Lomax, "Self-Pity in Negro Folk-Songs," *Nation* 105 (1917): 141–145. Josh Dunson, "Enigmatic Folksongs of the Southern Underworld," *Current Opinion* 67 (1919): 165–166. John Harrington Cox, "John Hardy," *Journal of American Folklore* 32 (1919): 517–528. Natalie Curtis Burlin, *Negro Folk-Songs: Hampton Series* (New York, 1919). Nettie McAdams, "Folk-Songs of the American Negro," M. A. thesis, University of California at Berkeley, 1922. Howard W. Odum and Guy B. Johnson, *The Negro and His Songs: A Study of Typical Negro Songs in the South* (Chapel Hill, N.C., 1925). R. Emmett Kennedy, *Mellows: A Chronicle of Unknown Singers* (New York, 1925). Alain Locke, ed., *The New Negro* (New York, 1925), 7. Gates Thomas, "South Texas Negro Work Songs," in *Rainbow in the Morning*, ed. J. F. Dobie (Hatboro, Penn., 1965; first published 1926), 154–180. Newbell Niles Puckett, *Folk Beliefs of the Southern Negro* (Chapel Hill, N.C., 1926). Newbell Niles Puckett, "Race Pride and Folklore," *Opportunity* 4 (1926): 82–84. Don C. Seitz, "Ballads of the Bad: Colored Chain Gang Chansons Collected at Chapel Hill," *Outlook* 143 (4 August 1926): 478. Robert Winslow Gordon, "Negro 'Shouts' from Georgia," *New York Times*, 24 April 1927. Langston Hughes, *Fine Clothes to the Jew* (New York, 1927). Edward C. L. Adams, *Congaree Sketches* (Chapel Hill, N.C., 1927). Guy B. Johnson, "Double Meaning in the Popular Negro Blues," *Journal of Abnormal and Social Psychology* 22 (1927–1928): 12–20. Howard Odum, *Wings on My Feet* (Indianapolis, 1929). Phillip Schatz, "Songs of the Negro Worker," *New Masses* 5 (May 1930): 6–8. Howard Odum, *Cold Blue Moon* (Indianapolis, 1931). Sterling Brown, *Southern Road* (New York, 1932). John A. Lomax and Alan Lomax, *American Ballads and Folk Songs* (New York, 1934). Lawrence Gellert, "Negro Songs of Protest," *New Masses* 5 (1931): 6–8. John Lomax, "'Sinful Songs' of the Southern Negro," *Musical Quarterly* 20 (1934): 177–187. Alan Lomax, "'Sinful' Songs of the Southern Negro," *Southwest Review* 19 (1934): 105–131. Nancy Cunard, ed., *Negro* (New York, 1934). Zora Neale Hurston, "Characteristics of Negro Expression," in *Negro*, ed. Cunard, 39–46. Zora Neale Hurston, *Mules and Men* (New York, 1935). John A. Lomax, *Negro Folk Songs as Sung by Leadbelly, "King of the Twelve-String Guitar Players of the World," Long-Time Convict in the Penitentiaries of Texas and Louisiana* (New York, 1936). Lawrence Gellert and Ellie Siegmeister, *Negro Songs of Protest* (New York, 1936). Zora Neale Hurston, *Their Eyes Were Watching God* (Philadelphia, 1937). Lawrence Gellert, *Me and My Captain: Chain Gang Songs of Protest* (New York, 1939). Muriel Davis Longini, "Folk Songs of Chicago Negroes," *Journal of American Folklore* 52 (1939): 96–111. Zora Neale Hurston, "Turpentine," in *Go Gator and Muddy the Water*, ed. Pamela Bordelon (New York, 1999), 61–67. H. C. Brearley, "Ba-ad Nigger," *South Atlantic Quarterly* 38 (1939): 75–81. John W. Work, *American Negro Songs and Spirituals* (New York, 1940). John A. Lomax and Alan Lomax, *Our Singing Country* (New York, 1941). Sterling Brown, ed., *Negro Caravan* (New York, 1941). Mary Wheeler, *Steamboatin' Days* (Baton Rouge, La., 1944). Sterling Brown, "Negro Folk Expression: Spirituals, Seculars, Ballads, and Work Songs," *Phylon* 11 (Autumn 1953): 45–61. Langston Hughes and Arna Bontemps, *The Book of Negro Folklore* (New York, 1958). Harold Courlander, *Negro Folk Music, U.S.A.* (New York, 1963). Harry Oster, *Living Country Blues* (Detroit, 1969). Bruce Jackson, *Wake Up Dead Man: Afro-American Worksongs from Texas Prisons* (Cambridge, Mass., 1972). An extensive collection of noncommercial field recordings from the 1930s and 1940s has been reissued as Document Records 5575–5580, 5598–5600, 5614, 5621, 5629–5630, 5672, 1998–2002. Commercial albums featuring music recorded by the Lomaxes and others between 1933 and 1946, first released by the Library of Congress, are reissued by Rounder Records in the series *Deep River of Song* (Rounder 1821–1832).

8. Paul Oliver, "Special Agents: An Introduction to the Recording of Folk Blues in the Twenties," *Jazz Review* 2 (1959): 20–25. R. M. Dixon and John Godrich, *Recording the Blues* (New York, 1970). Gayle Dean Wardlow, *Chasin' That Devil Music: Searching for the Blues* (San Francisco, 1998). Robert Cantwell, *When We Were Good: The Folk Revival* (Cambridge, Mass., 1996). On the form of the collection, see Susan Stewart, *On Longing: Narratives of the Miniature, the Gigantic, the Souvenir, the Collection* (Durham, N.C., 1993).

9. Thomas, *Some Current Folk-Songs*, 5, 7. Gellert, *Me and My Captain*, n.p. On the schema employed for Hurston's collecting, see Zora Neale Hurston, "Proposed Recording Expedition into the Floridas," in *Go Gator and Muddy the Water*, ed. Bordelon, 61–67. Hurston, "Characteristics." On the culture concept and the Boasian turn in anthropology, see George W. Stocking Jr., *Race, Culture, and Evolution: Essays in the History of Anthropology* (Chicago, 1982; first published 1968).

10. John A. Lomax, "Self-Pity," 143. Odum and Johnson, *Negro Workaday Songs*, 6, 71, 55. Odum, *Rainbow Round*, 253–254. As is shown in these quotations, the new interest in secular songs by assumed ne'er-do-wells was influenced by and intertwined with ethnographic thinking about the spirituals. William Francis Allen, Charles Pickard Ware, and Lucy McKim Garrison, eds., *Slave Songs of*

the United States (New York, 1955; first published 1867). Du Bois, *Souls of Black Folk.* Krehbiel, *Afro-American Folksongs.* James Weldon Johnson and J. Rosamond Johnson, *The Books of American Negro Spirituals, Including The Book of American Negro Spirituals and the Second Book of Negro Spirituals* (New York, 1969; first published in 1925 and 1926). Dena J. Epstein, *Sinful Tunes and Spirituals: Black Folk Music to the Civil War* (Urbana, Ill., 1977). Jon Cruz, *Culture on the Margins: The Black Spiritual and the Rise of American Cultural Interpretation* (Princeton, N.J., 1999). Ronald Radano, *Lying Up a Nation: Race and Black Music* (Chicago, 2003).

11. Odum and Johnson, *Negro Workaday Songs*, 55. Newman White has the most elaborate version of the claim that black folksongs are "solidly based on what are subconsciously the real interests of the singer." White, *American Negro Folk-Songs*, 250–254, 290–292, 311–312, 341–346, 356–358, 376–378, 387–390. For a variation on this idea, see Zora Neale Hurston, "Spirituals and Neo-Spirituals," in *Negro*, ed. Cunard, 359–361.

12. Francis James Child, *The English and Scottish Popular Ballads*, 5 vols. (Boston, 1882–1898). Thomas Percy, *Reliques of Ancient English Poetry* (London, 1765). Joseph Ritson, *A Select Collection of English Songs* (London, 1783). Webb, "Notes on the Folk-Lore of Texas," 292. Johann Gottfried von Herder, *Outlines of a Philosophy of the History of Man*, trans. T. O. Churchill (London, 1800). Roger D. Abrahams, "Phantoms of Romantic Nationalism in Folkloristics," *Journal of American Folklore* 106 (1993): 3–37.

13. Among the costs associated with this rhetorical violence has been the long-standing confusion about the relationship between black vernacular expression and mass culture. If collectors needed to claim informants who looked like the perspective in their songs to corroborate the idea that their music was folk music, they also needed to abide by a corollary to this claim, which said that any singer who did not satisfy this criterion was faking it. Saying you were a lonesome drifter while singing for a paying crowd in your dapper suit, or in sequins and jewels and feathers, would not cut it. Performing a song you learned from a traveling show, from a printed score, or from a phonograph record was also a problem, as it implied you were performing something that did not belong to you. To wear blackface, as many performers including W. C. Handy and Jelly Roll Morton were doing on the vaudeville circuit, was to admit the history of your performance in a popular culture alien to your own. When musicians who did not look like ragged drifters sang about being stateless, their work was often greeted by folklorists with disdain. In fact, it was typical for folklorists to talk about these popular artists not as singers in their own right, but instead to discuss them only in the negative, as a threat to the folk, reiterating the standard lament about the folk's inevitable contamination by mass culture. Many collectors were loud in their condescension when it came to blues queens like

Ma Rainey, Ida Cox, and even Marion Harris, who were too closely associated
with commercial recording (they dominated the phonograph) and with vaudeville (they were the most popular headliners on Fred Barrasso's Tri-State Circuit
and the Theater Owners Booking Association). Male performers who played
medicine shows and vaudeville circuits were also maligned, despite the fact
that many of them (like Skip James) would be repackaged by record labels as
folk artists. The problem is not with the songs made by these professional musicians, which often had enough nitty gritty to spark controversy in the recording
industry, but with the singers themselves, whose glitz was not assimilable by the
ethnographic procedure that would have made their music into folk music.
Paul Oliver, *Songsters and Saints: Vocal Traditions on Race Records* (Cambridge, U.K., 1984). Lynn Abbott and Doug Seroff, "'They Cert'ly Sound Good
to Me': Sheet Music, Southern Vaudeville, and the Commercial Ascendancy
of the Blues," *American Music* 14 (1996): 402–453. Nick Tosches, *Where Dead
Voices Gather* (Boston, 2001). Lynn Abbott and Doug Seroff, *Out of Sight: The
Rise of American Popular Music 1889–1895* (Jackson, Miss., 2002). Wald, *Escap-
ing the Delta.* Tim Brooks, *Lost Sounds: Blacks and the Birth of the Recording
Industry 1890–1919* (Urbana, Ill., 2004). Lynn Abbott and Doug Seroff, *Ragged
But Right Black Traveling Shows, "Coon Songs," and the Dark Pathway to Blues
and Jazz* (Jackson, Miss., 2007). Richard Middleton, "O Brother, Let's Go
Down Home: Loss, Nostalgia and the Blues," *Popular Music* 26 (2007): 47–64.
Hamilton, *In Search of the Blues,* 125–160, 161–197. Bruce Bastin, "From the
Medicine Show to the Stage: Some Influences upon the Development of a
Blues Tradition in the Southeastern United States," *American Music* 2 (1984):
29–42.

14. Gellert, *Me and My Captain,* n.p.
15. Criminalizing irregular patterns of labor, vagrancy laws held that individuals
    who could not prove that they were currently working were subject to a fine
    (sometimes as much as fifty dollars). If you could not pay the fine, someone
    could advance the money and demand compensation through indenture. If
    you were imprisoned, somebody could purchase rights to your labor through
    the convict-lease system. Or you could be hitched to the chain gang and go to
    work for the state. In practice, these laws turned police into de facto labor
    agents able to arrest sturdy men as needed to meet the changing demands of
    agriculture and industry. Edward L. Ayers, *Vengeance and Justice: Crime and
    Punishment in the Nineteenth-Century American South* (New York, 1984), 141–
    276. Amy Dru Stanley, "Beggars Can't Be Choosers: Compulsion and Contract
    in Postbellum America," *Journal of American History* 78 (March 1992): 1265–
    1293. Alex Lichtenstein, "Good Roads and Chain Gangs in the Progressive
    South: 'The Negro Convict Is a Slave,'" *Journal of Southern History* 59 (Febru-
    ary 1993): 85–110. Saidiya V. Hartman, *Scenes of Subjection: Terror, Slavery, and*

Self-Making in Nineteenth-Century America (New York, 1997), 115–163. James D. Schmidt, *Free to Work: Labor Law, Emancipation, and Reconstruction 1815–1880* (Athens, Ga., 1998), 1–6, 93–235.

16. William Blackstone, *Commentaries on the Laws of England*, 4 vols. (Chicago, 1979; first published 1765–1769), 4:161–175. *State of New York v. Miln*, 36 U.S. 102 (1837). *Prigg v. Pennsylvania*, 41 U.S. 539 (1842). *Moore v. People of the State of Illinois*, 55 U.S. 13 (1852). William J. Novak, *The People's Welfare: Law and Regulation in Nineteenth-Century America* (Chapel Hill, N.C., 1996), 153–171. Mark Neocleus, *The Fabrication of Social Order: A Critical Theory of Police Power* (London, 2000), 16–21. Marcus Dirk Dubber, *The Police Power: Patriarchy and the Foundations of American Government* (New York, 2005), 120–138. Mark E. Kann, *Punishment, Prisons, and Patriarchy: Liberty and Power in the Early American Republic* (New York, 2005), 21–85. On the analogy between police and slavery, see John Codman Hurd, *The Law of Freedom and Bondage in the United States*, 2 vols. (Boston, 1862), 2:342–375.

17. Christopher G. Tiedeman, *A Treatise on the Limitations of Police Power in the United States* (St. Louis, 1886), 120, 124.

18. Tiedeman, *Treatise on the Limitations*, 120, 122, 124, 117. On the dangerous classes manifesting characteristics that cannot be named as characteristics, see the chapter "The Recognition of Habitual Criminals as a Class to Be Treated By Itself" in Simeon Baldwin, *Modern Political Institutions* (Boston, 1898), 290–315. In his anatomy of southern life at the nadir, Ray Stannard Baker comes to a strikingly similar conclusion about the specific application of vagrancy laws to black workers in southern states. Baker considers the laws "excellent in their purpose" but observes both their racially disproportionate enforcement and the striking fact that "a Negro arrested for vagrancy" is forced to "prove that he is not a vagrant." In this situation, for Baker as for Tiedeman, the "old rule of law" that a man is innocent until proved guilty "is . . . reversed for the Negro so that the burden of proving that he is not guilty of vagrancy rests upon him, not upon the state." Ray Stannard Baker, *An Account of Negro Citizenship in the American Democracy* (New York, 1908), 81. For a more recent application of Tiedeman's claim that "infractions of the law would be reduced to a surprisingly small number" if "vagrancy could be successfully combated," see Justice Clarence Thomas's dissent in *Chicago v. Morales*, 527 U.S. 41 (1999). See also the standard commentary on vagrancy policing and social necessity in Ernst Freund, *The Police Power: Public Policy and Constitutional Rights* (Chicago, 1904), 97–100, 230, 478–479. In 1871, the *New Orleans Picayune* offered a practical assessment of police discretion in vagrancy cases that would remain relevant to the case of Robert Charles. "It is scarcely possible," the *Picayune* reminded its readers, "that penal law on the subject of vagrancy can be so framed as to distinguish between those who are merely

unfortunate and those who are committedly vicious. Much must be left to the discretion and limits of the constabulary who make arrests and of the magistrates before who vagrants are brought for examination." *New Orleans Picayune*, 21 January 1871.

19. Tiedeman, *Treatise on the Limitations*, 118–119.
20. Tiedeman, *Treatise on the Limitations*, 117–118.
21. Handy, *Father of the Blues*, 99. Tiedeman, *Treatise on the Limitations*, 125. Blackstone, *Commentaries on the Laws of England*, 4:161–175.
22. Clifford Geertz, "Thick Description: Toward an Interpretive Theory of Culture," in *The Interpretation of Cultures* (New York, 1973), 3–32. "Lumpenproletariat, n." *Oxford English Dictionary*, 2nd ed. (New York, 1989). On this absence of characteristics, described as an excess of submultiples over terms, see Alain Badiou, *Being and Event*, trans. Oliver Feltham (London, 2005), 81–120. Another way to express this is to say that vagrants are unrecognizable in the context they inhabit. They lack the baseline legibility needed to represent themselves to others. They exist in society, but they have no perspective that matters as far as society is concerned. Marx brushes against this point in his account of the vagrant's political unreliability. For Marx, producing value is essential to developing political self-consciousness. Because the lumpenproletariat is engrossed in the circulation not the production of goods, as Marx sees it, there is no opportunity for political consciousness to develop among this population. What holds true for the urban rabble also holds for the small-holding peasants, who similarly lack the capacity for politics, in their case due to their marginality to industrial organization. "They cannot represent themselves," Marx famously writes, "they must be represented." Antonio Gramsci would develop Marx's commentaries on these nonpolitical classes into a general theory of folklore. Gramsci thought Marx was right about the peasantry: its members have "no cohesion among themselves" and "as a mass they are unable to give a centralized expression to their aspirations." According to Gramsci, folklore is what nonpolitical populations have rather than political consciousness. Folklore is disorganized for the same reason that a catalogue of vagrants is disorganized: neither has a genuine relationship to the world as it is presently organized. Folklore's disorganization confirms that it has been made by people who have fallen behind or outside history. Combined from bits and pieces in fits and starts, with no governing principles to focus its composition, folklore is a junkyard. For Gramsci, it is the "residue of traditional conceptions of the world," conceptions that may have once been effectual but have since been superseded by the "modern outlook" that is now required for political thinking. Folklore needs to be eliminated from the minds of the masses before politics can commence. For Gramsci, this is why education remains important. Marx, "Eighteenth Brumaire," 378. Antonio Gramsci, *The Southern Question*, trans. Pasquale Verdicchio (West Lafayette, Ind., 1995), 36, 34.

23. Handy, *Father of the Blues*, 87. Niles, "Introduction," 1. Odum and Johnson, *Negro Workaday Songs*, viii–ix. Carl Sandburg, *American Songbag* (New York, 1927). Walt Whitman, *Leaves of Grass* (Philadelphia, 1891–1892). Karl Marx, "The Eighteenth Brumaire of Louis Bonaparte," in *Marx and Engels: Basic Writings on Politics and Philosophy*, ed. Lewis Feuer (New York, 1959; first published 1852), 358–388. Henry Mayhew, *London Labour and the London Poor* (London, 1861). On the lumpen as a figure in black politics, see Stuart Hall, Chas Critcher, Tony Jefferson, John Clarke, and Brian Roberts, *Policing the Crisis: Mugging, the State, and Law and Order* (London, 1978), 348–397. On the reception of Fanon's writing on the lumpenproletariat, and its adaptation by the Black Panther Party, see Eldridge Cleaver, *On the Ideology of the Black Panther Party* (San Francisco, 1970); Eldridge Cleaver, "On Lumpen Ideology," *Black Scholar* 3 (1972): 2–10; Kathleen Cleaver, *On the Vanguard Role of the Black Urban Lumpenproletariat* (London, 1975). For a critique of this formula, see Clarence J. Munford, "The Fallacy of Lumpen Ideology," *Black Scholar* 5 (1973): 47–51. On the specific form of the lumpen in Marx, see Gayatri Chakravorty Spivak, *A Critique of Postcolonial Reason: Toward a History of the Vanishing Present* (Cambridge, Mass., 1999), 259–276.

24. On the implications of this non-inhabitable social position, see Badiou, *Being and Event*, 52–80.

25. Morton, "I Created Jazz in 1902." Alan Lomax, *Mister Jelly Roll: The Fortunes of Jelly Roll Morton, New Orleans Creole and "Inventor of Jazz"* (New York, 1950). Howard Reich and William Gaines, *Jelly's Blues: The Life, Music, and Redemption of Jelly Roll Morton* (New York, 2003), 131–163.

26. Note, for instance, the scare quotes around the term "Inventor of Jazz" in the subtitle to *Mister Jelly Roll*. Handy, *Father of the Blues*, 99.

27. Sidney Bechet, *Treat It Gentle* (New York, 1960), 55–56. Delisle's rendition and a redaction of Morton's version appear in the book that Alan Lomax based on his 1938 interview with Morton. Lomax, *Mister Jelly Roll*, 91–92, 56–57. Jelly Roll Morton and Alan Lomax, "Aaron Harris, His Hoodoo Woman, and the Hat that Started a Riot," "The Story of the 1900 New Orleans Riot and the Song of Robert Charles," and "The Story of the 1900 New Orleans Riot, continued," in *The Complete Library of Congress Recordings* (Rounder 1888). William Ivy Hair, *Carnival of Fury: Robert Charles and the New Orleans Race Riot of 1900* (Baton Rouge, La., 1976), 178–179. William Schafer, "Further Thoughts on Jazz Historiography: That Robert Charles Song," *Journal of Jazz Studies* 5 (1978): 19–27. Leon F. Litwack, *Trouble in Mind: Black Southerners in the Age of Jim Crow* (New York, 1998), 409–410. Gussow, *Seems Like Murder Here*, 176–177.

28. Ida B. Wells-Barnett, *Mob Rule in New Orleans: Robert Charles and His Fight to the Death, the Story of His Life, Burning Humans Alive, Other Lynching*

Statistics (Chicago, 1900), 33–42. Hair, *Carnival of Fury*, 3–93. Dale Somers, "Black and White in New Orleans: A Study in Urban Race Relations, 1865–1900," *Journal of Southern History* 40 (1974): 19–42.

29. Benjamin Brawley, *A Social History of the American Negro* (New York, 1921), 315–317. Hair, *Carnival of Fury*, 94–120. Wells-Barnett, *Mob Rule*, 5–23. On the intellectual backgrounds for Charles's advocacy, see Wilson Jeremiah Moses, *The Golden Age of Black Nationalism, 1850–1925* (New York, 1988).

30. Wells-Barnett, *Mob Rule*, 33. Proceeding point by point, Wells-Barnett examines the evidence provided by the press that "Charles was a desperado," including the claim made by the *Times-Democrat* that his "wearing apparel was little more than rags," a claim begging the question about rags counting as evidence that we have already seen developed by Tiedeman. On Charles's rags, see *New Orleans Times-Democrat*, 25 July 1900. The innovations in Wells-Barnett's criminology are well known. In contrast to contemporary journalism in the muckraking mode, *Mob Rule in New Orleans* is distinctive for its commitment to nominalism and therefore for its anticipation of the school of criminological thought known as labeling theory, which maintains that crime becomes meaningful only through state action. Arthur Weinburg and Lila Weinburg, eds., *The Muckrakers* (Urbana, Ill., 2001). On labeling theory, see Frank Tannenbaum, *Crime and the Community* (New York, 1938).

31. Dubber, *Police Power*, 157–189.

32. Wells-Barnett, *Mob Rule*, 5. Dubber, *Police Power*, 157–189. Francis Bowes Sayre, "Mens Rea," *Harvard Law Review* 45 (1932): 974–1032. Randall Kennedy, *Race, Crime, and the Law* (New York, 1997), 29–167.

33. On summary inquiry, see "Police Power to Stop, Frisk, and Question Suspicious Persons," *Columbia Law Review* 65 (1965): 848–866.

34. Wells-Barnett, *Mob Rule*, 5–6, 9–10.

35. Wells-Barnett, *Mob Rule*, 6–9, 10, 12–16, 17–18, 19–22. For a parallel procedure, see Ida B. Wells, *A Red Record: Tabulated Statistics and Alleged Causes of Lynchings* (Chicago, 1895). Tiedeman, *Treatise on the Limitations*, 116–136. On forcing, see Badiou, *Being and Event*, 391–430.

36. Morton and Lomax, "Hat that Started a Riot." Morton and Lomax, "Story of the 1900 New Orleans Riot."

37. Alan Lomax, *Land Where the Blues Began*, xi. For the litany of spurious excuses that were regularly featured in the Lomaxes's collections, see Alan Lomax, "'Sinful' Songs of the Southern Negro." Note that this essay, published in the *Southwest Review* when Lomax was still a teenager, is not the same as the essay of the same title (punctuated slightly differently) by his father. Commenting on this reticence, William Ferris Jr. has noted that black musicians have a particular racial repertoire for all-black audiences. Ferris, "Racial Repertoires among Blues Performers," *Ethnomusicology* 14 (1970): 439–449.

38. Alan Lomax, *Mister Jelly Roll*, 141, 185. Morton and Lomax, "The Story of the 1900 New Orleans Riot." Morton and Lomax, "The Story of the 1900 New Orleans Riot, continued." Morton, "I Created Jazz in 1902," 3.

39. On the of idea of apostrophe adapted in this paragraph, see Jonathan Culler, "Apostrophe," in *The Pursuit of Signs* (Ithaca, N.Y., 1981), 135–154. For contrast, see Sianne Ngai, *Ugly Feelings* (Cambridge, Mass., 2005), 89–125.

40. Morton, "I Created Jazz in 1902," 3.

41. Samuel B. Charters, *The Country Blues* (New York, 1959). Frederick Ramsey Jr., *Been Here and Gone* (Athens, Ga., 2000; first published 1960), 95, 55. Robert Johnson, *King of the Delta Blues Singers*, Columbia CL1654, 1961. Samuel B. Charters, *The Poetry of the Blues* (New York, 1963), 110.

2. The Strange Career of Bras-Coupé

1. Jacquelyn Dowd Hall, "'The Mind That Burns in Each Body': Women, Rape, and Racial Violence," in *Powers of Desire: The Politics of Sexuality*, ed. Ann Snitow, Christine Stansell, and Sharon Thompson (New York, 1983), 329. On the early development of southern exceptionalism, see Jennifer Rae Greeson, "The Figure of the South and the Nationalizing Imperatives of Early United States Literature," *Yale Journal of Criticism* 12 (1999): 209–248.

2. Roger Lane, *Policing the City: Boston, 1822–1885* (Cambridge, Mass., 1967). James F. Richardson, *Urban Police in the United States* (London, 1974). Wilbur Miller, *Cops and Bobbies: Police Authority in New York and London 1830–1870* (Chicago, 1977). Roger M. Fogelson, *Big-City Police* (Cambridge, Mass., 1977). David Ralph Johnson, *Policing the Urban Underworld: The Impact of Crime on the Development of the American Police, 1800–1887* (Philadelphia, 1979). Samuel Walker, *Popular Justice: A History of American Criminal Justice* (New York, 1980). Sidney Harring, *Policing a Class Society: The Experience of American Cities, 1865–1915* (New Brunswick, N.J., 1983). Eric H. Monkkonen, *Police in Urban America, 1860–1920* (Cambridge, U.K., 1981). Allen Steinberg, *The Transformation of Criminal Justice, Philadelphia, 1800–1880* (Chapel Hill, N.C., 1989).

3. The work that frames this historiographical problem is Dennis C. Rousey, *Policing the Southern City: New Orleans, 1805–1889* (Baton Rouge, La., 1996). See also Michael Hindus, *Prison and Plantation: Crime, Justice, and Authority in Massachusetts and South Carolina, 1767–1878* (Chapel Hill, N.C., 1980). Edward L. Ayers, *Vengeance and Justice: Crime and Punishment in the Nineteenth-Century American South* (New York, 1984). Sally E. Hadden, *Slave Patrols: Law and Violence in Virginia and the Carolinas* (Cambridge, Mass., 2001). This interest in the links between slavery and the modernization of policing in southern cities is anticipated by John Hope Franklin and Richard Wade. John Hope Franklin, *The Militant South* (Cambridge, Mass., 1956). Richard

Wade, *Slavery in the Cities* (New York, 1964). On comparative timelines for police development and population ratios, see Rousey, *Policing the Southern City*, 11–39.

4. Hadden, *Slave Patrols*, 1–5, 167–220. For a recent work that repeats the idea about the unmediated relation between master and slave, see Andrew Fede, *People without Rights: An Interpretation of the Fundamentals of the Law of Slavery in the U.S. South* (New York, 1992). For slavery and police activities in New Orleans, see Stacy K. McGoldrick, "The Policing of Slavery in New Orleans 1852–1860," *Journal of Historical Sociology* 14 (December 2001): 397–417.

5. Rousey, *Policing the Southern City*, 1–10. Primary sources on Bras-Coupé include the following: Lafcadio Hearn, "The Original Bras-Coupe," *New Orleans Item*, 27 October 1880. Louis Gottschalk, *Notes of a Pianist*, ed. Clara Gottschalk (Philadelphia, 1881), 11–12. Marion Baker, ed., *Historical Sketch-Book and Guide to New Orleans and Environs* (New York, 1885), 21–22. Henry Castellanos, *New Orleans as It Was* (New Orleans, 1895), 209–215. Grace King, *New Orleans: The Place and the People* (New York, 1895), 340–342. George Washington Cable, "[How I Came to Write the Episode of Bras-Coupé]," George W. Cable Collection, Manuscripts Department, Howard Tilton Memorial Library, Tulane University. John Smith Kendall, *History of New Orleans* (Chicago, 1922), 131–132. Marcus Christian, "Bras Coupé," Marcus Christian Papers, Archives and Manuscripts Division, Earl K. Long Library, University of New Orleans. Herbert Asbury, *The French Quarter* (New York, 1936), 180–192. Hodding Carter, *Lower Mississippi* (New York, 1942), 178–179. Lyle Saxon, Edward Dryer, and Robert Tallant, *Gumbo Ya-Ya: A Collection of Louisiana Folk Tales* (Boston, 1945), 253–254. B. A. Botkin, ed., *A Treasury of Southern Folklore* (New York, 1949), 328–330. Vernon Loggins, *Where the World Ends: The Life of Louis Moreau Gottschalk* (Baton Rouge, La., 1958), 13–14, 27–28, 64, 71–72. Jay Robert Nash, "The Legend of a One-Armed Murderer," in *Almanac of World Crime* (New York, 1986), 310–311. Attempts to transform, rather than transcribe, the legend into narrative (short story, novel, autobiography, poetry) include the following: Armand Garreau, "Bras Coupé," *Les cinq centimes illustrés*, 29 March 1856, 122–126. Armand Garreau, "Le Nègre marron," *Les cinq centimes illustrés*, 2 February 1856, 57–59. George Washington Cable, *The Grandissimes: A Story of Creole Life* (New York, 1880). Sidney Bechet, *Treat It Gentle* (New York, 1960). Frank Yerby, *The Foxes of Harrow* (New York, 1946). Tom Dent, *Magnolia Street* (New Orleans, 1976). Kalamu ya Salaam, "Bras Coupe," in *Dark Dreams: A Collection of Horror and Suspense by Black Writers*, ed. Brandon Massey (New York, 2004), 37–65. There is also a blackface opera based upon the legend, whose performance history extends from London (1899) to Port-of-Spain, Trinidad (1995), where it was presented for the first time with an all-black cast. The earliest complete libretto is Frederick Delius and Charles F.

Keary, *Koanga, Opera in Three Acts* (1897), rev. by Sir Thomas Beecham and Edward Agate (London, 1935). Distinctive elements from the legend were re-composed by Robert Penn Warren, who renamed the fugitive Rau-Ru and ex-tended his career to encompass an unlikely stint in the Union Army; Robert Penn Warren, *Band of Angels* (Baton Rouge, La., 1983; first published 1955). The role of Rau-Ru is played by Sidney Poitier in the film adaptation: *Band of Angels* (dir. Raoul Walsh, 1957). Writings on Bras-Coupé as a character in his-tory include the following: Frederick W. Turner III, "Badmen, Black and White," PhD diss., University of Pennsylvania, 1965, 158–165. Lawrence Levine, *Black Culture and Black Consciousness* (New York, 1977), 388. John W. Roberts, *From Trickster to Badman: The Black Folk Hero from Slavery to Free-dom* (Philadelphia, 1989), 134–136. Robert O. Stephens, "Cable's Bras-Coupé and Merimeé's Tamango: The Case of the Missing Arm," *Mississippi Quarterly* 35 (1982): 387–405. Barbara Ladd, "'An Atmosphere of Hints and Allusions': Bras-Coupé and the Context of Black Insurrection in The Grandissimes," *Southern Quarterly* 29 (Spring 1991): 63–76.

6. Gwendolyn Midlo Hall, *Africans in Colonial Louisiana: The Development of Afro-Creole Culture in the Eighteenth Century* (Baton Rouge, La., 1992), 99–100, 119–155. Jerah Johnson, "Colonial New Orleans," in *Creole New Orleans: Race and Americanization*, ed. Arnold R. Hirsch and Joseph Logsdon (Baton Rouge, La., 1992), 12–57. On slavery and state formation in the colonial period, see also Thomas N. Ingersoll, *Mammon and Manon in Early New Orleans: The First Slave Society in the Deep South, 1718–1819* (Knoxville, Tenn., 1999). For background, see Herbert Aptheker, "Maroons within the Present Limits of the United States," *Journal of Negro History* 24 (1939): 167–184.

7. Midlo Hall, *Africans in Colonial Louisiana*, 120–121, 143–155, 203–236. For background and comparison, see Judith A. Carney, *Black Rice: The African Origins of Rice Cultivation in the Americas* (Cambridge, Mass., 2002).

8. Midlo Hall, *Africans in Colonial Louisiana*, 343–380. Rousey, *Policing the Southern City*, 11–39. Joseph Holt Ingraham, *The South-West: By a Yankee*, 2 vols. (New York, 1935), 1:95, 111–112, quoted in Rousey, *Policing the Southern City*, 13. *A Digest of Ordinances, Resolutions, By-Laws, and Regulations of the Corporation of New Orleans and a Collection of the Laws of the Legislature Rel-ative to the Said City* (New Orleans, 1836), 105–115.

9. *New Orleans Mercantile Advertiser*, 17 February 1834. For an overview of these determinants, see Rousey, *Policing the Southern City*, 11–39. On patronage and the scuffle between political parties for control of police appointments, see Stacey McGoldrick, "Not at Liberty to See: Police, Party Politics and Violence in New Orleans, 1852–1880," PhD diss., The New School for Social Research, 2003. For a quite extraordinary synopsis of civil-law slavery in Louisiana and a discussion of the difference that this legal heritage made, particularly in the

appellate courts, to the criminal prosecution of slaves, see Judith Kelleher Schafer, *Slavery, the Civil Law, and the Supreme Court of Louisiana* (Baton Rouge, La., 1994). On the stigmatization of civil law in the language of the abolitionists, see Thomas D. Morris, *Southern Slavery and the Law, 1619–1860* (Chapel Hill, N.C., 1996), 37–57. On contrasting police development in France (whose heavily armed republican gendarmerie dates to 1790) and England (whose lightly armed metropolitan police did not appear until 1829), see Raymond B. Fosdick, *European Police Systems* (New York, 1915). Concerning the new ethnic groups that unsettled this conflict and fundamentally altered the debate over police services (especially with regard to languages spoken by the police), see Rousey, *Policing the Southern City*, 25–31, 59–64.

10. *Louisiana Advertiser*, 17 February 1834; also reprinted in *New Orleans Bee*, 15 February 1834. On the following day, the *Advertiser* goaded Mayor Denis Prieur, a supporter of the police. "Our worthy mayor," the paper proposed, "is a wise and observing man," and "he will not stand in the way of the removal of such a foul stain upon the laws." *Louisiana Advertiser*, 18 February 1834.

11. It is striking that the pressure for demilitarization was powerful enough to overrule the general trend to increased policing in southern states following the publication of David Walker's *Appeal* (1829) and the Southampton Slave Revolt led by Nat Turner (1831). See Judith Kelleher Schafer, "The Immediate Impact of Nat Turner's Insurrection on New Orleans," *Louisiana History* 22 (1980): 361–378. A point of comparison for the demilitarization campaign is the less organized resistance to the London Metropolitan Police Service at its founding in 1829. See Michael Ignatieff, "Police and People: The Birth of Mr. Peel's Blue Locusts," *New Society* 30 (1979): 433–455.

12. *Louisiana Advertiser*, 18 February 1834. Police violence, the reformers said, was driving the city backward in time by compelling citizens to "wear arms for their own protection"; in the "custom of an age of barbarism, 'when every man's hand had to keep his own head,'" *New Orleans Bee*, 15 February 1834. Related diatribes against the "flinty-hearted guard" include *Louisiana Gazette*, 8 December 1810; *Louisiana Advertiser*, 10 May 1830; *Mercantile Advertiser*, 25 June 1831; *Louisiana Advertiser*, 14 February 1834; *New Louisiana Advertiser*, 17 February 1834; *Mercantile Advertiser*, 17 February 1834. These claims grew stranger (and more bitterly ironic) at the points when proposed reforms are cast not as opposition to tradition, or despotism, or barbarism, but specifically as opposition to slavery. There is a tendency within the reform campaign to represent the police as a "badge of slavery in a free and enlightened community." The irony of representing a slave society as "free and enlightened" is compounded when "slavery" is invoked not to refer to the actual slaves but to the oppression suffered by the city's free citizens at the hands of its police. Obviously, there are strong precedents for this kind of doubletalk about slavery, extending to the

revolutionary republican rhetoric surrounding the establishment of the United States as a free nation of slaveholders and to the writings of earlier pro-slavery reformers like John Locke. Edmund Morgan, *American Slavery, American Freedom* (New York, 1975). On the trajectories of the social contract tradition in the slave states, see Michael O'Brien, *Conjectures of Order: Intellectual Life and the American South, 1810–1860* (Chapel Hill, N.C., 2004), 781–876.

13. *Mercantile Advertiser*, 17 February 1834. Denis Prieur, "Message from the Mayor to the City Council," 21 January 1836, City Archives, New Orleans Public Library. See also Prieur's repeated assertions that demilitarization would render the police "inadequate." Denis Prieur, "Message from the Mayor to the City Council," 17 May 1836, City Archives, New Orleans Public Library. The counteroffensive against the reform campaign was led by Prieur, the eighth mayor of New Orleans, a Jacksonian Democrat who was first elected in 1828 and then to four subsequent terms, whose administration was marked by its recurrent battles with the city council. If the police were ineffective, Prieur allowed, it was not because they were too military, it was because they were not military enough. This was a common refrain among supporters of the police, who invoked Charleston, South Carolina, as a counterexample. "Are we the only city having an armed police such as our city guard?" the *Mercantile Advertiser* elaborated in their editorial from the 17th of February in the heat of the reform. "No—look at Charleston, we there find an armed police of tenfold extent to our own, yet there we hear no murmurs—there we do not see the people on every little occasion arrayed against the police, and yet it is armed in every respect as ours." On the Charleston City Guard, established in 1783, consult Edward Cantwell, *A History of the Charleston Police Force from the Incorporation of the City* (Charleston, S.C., 1908).

14. *New Orleans Bee*, March 26, 1830. Prieur, "Message from the Mayor," 21 January 1836. Disputing the allegation that "l'equippement des gardes de ville soit anti-republican" [the equipment of the city guard is anti-republican] or "desagreable à tout homme libre" [unpleasant to any free man], the *Bee* pointed to the farce of demilitarization, wondering if the reformers expected police to offer criminals an "honnête invitation" [honest invitation]: "Pardon Monsieur le bandit, j'en suis bien faché mais je viens pour vous arrêter" [Pardon Mister Bandit, I'm very annoyed by it, but I come to arrest you]. *New Orleans Bee*, 21 July 1835.

15. For the arrests in 1834–1835, see New Orleans City Guard, Reports of the Captain of the Guard, 1826–1836, City Archives, New Orleans Public Library. For the sheriff's notice to claim a captured maroon called Squire, see *New Orleans Bee*, 11 November 1834. This sheriff's notice is available in the Marcus Christian Papers, Archives and Manuscripts Division, in the Earl K. Long Library, University of New Orleans.

16. *The Liberator*, 2 July 1836. *New Orleans Picayune*, 19 July 1837.

17. *New Orleans Picayune*, 19 July 1837. Another obituary is in the *New Orleans Bee*, 20 July 1837. There is controversy over the amount of the reward offered for the fugitive. Most often quoted is $2,000, but other estimates range from $1,000 (Hearn, "Original Bras-Coupe"), to "6000 piasters" (Garreau, "Bras Coupé"), to speculation about a massive sum (Castellanos, *New Orleans*). The $2,000 estimate appears to have been transposed in later renditions into the sum paid to purchase Bras-Coupé in the slave market. Loggins, *Where the World Ends*. The *Bee* reported that the "impression" that "very high rewards" had been offered by the mayor was a "mistake" and that the bounty was a mere $250. The idea that the reward was false advertising also became standard to the legend. Garreau, "Bras Coupé." The failure of the proposed "scouring" of the swamp is mentioned in a later complaint about "runaway slaves who are known to infest the swamps." *New Orleans Bee*, 9 October 1839. For a concurrent firsthand account of banditry on the city's riverfront, see *Trials and Confessions of Madison Henderson, alias Blanchard, Alfred Amos Warrick, James W. Seward, and Charles Brown, Murderers of Jesse Baker and Jacob Weaver: As Given by Themselves . . . Taken in Jail Shortly after Their Arrest* (St. Louis, 1841).

18. Harriet Beecher Stowe, *Dred: A Tale of the Great Dismal Swamp* (Boston, 1856). Ida B. Wells-Barnett, *Mob Rule in New Orleans* (Chicago, 1900), 10. Although "customary usages" under slavery were usually enough to "supersede the necessity of any formal proclamation," magistrates were sometimes asked to outlaw escaped slaves in order to suspend the protections guarding the slave as property. This meant that the slave could be killed without reimbursing the owner. See William Goodell, *The American Slave Code in Theory and Practice: Its Distinctive Features Shown by Its Statutes, Judicial Decisions, and Illustrative Facts* (New York, 1853), 230–237. One example of the abolitionist claim that outlawry is a fundament to slavery; see *The Anti-Slavery Record* 3 (1837): 154–155. "To take his body into his own keeping," the *Record* states in the case of the slave, "is *insurrection*, and incurs outlawry." For an expansion on this standard argument, see Harriet Beecher Stowe, *A Key to Uncle Tom's Cabin* (Boston, 1853), 83–87.

19. Heinrich Brunner, *The Sources of the Law of England: An Historical Introduction to the Study of English Law* (Edinburgh, U.K., 1888). Frederick Pollock and Frederic William Maitland, *History of English Law before the Time of Edward I*, 2nd ed., 2 vols. (Cambridge, U.K., 1898), 1:303–304. These sources are discussed in Marcus Dirk Dubber, *The Police Power: Patriarchy and the Foundations of American Government* (New York, 2005), 14–21.

20. *Mercantile Advertiser*, 17 February 1834.

21. On Calhoun and the police power, see W. G. Hastings, "The Development of Law as Illustrated by the Decisions Relating to the Police Power of the State,"

Proceedings of the American Philosophical Society 39 (1900): 359–554. *New York Times*, 7 November 1857. On slavery and police, see also Dubber, *Police Power*, 3–46.

22. William Burdett, *The Life and Exploits of Three-finger'd Jack, the Terror of Jamaica* (London, 1801). Pollock and Maitland, *History of English Law*, 2:460–461, 490–491.

23. David Brion Davis, *The Problem of Slavery in Western Culture* (New York, 1966), 58–59. The claim that slaves are registered as persons only through criminal liability is familiar from the abolitionists. Consult, for example, Goodell, *American Slave Code*, 309–318. *The Politics of Aristotle*, trans. Ernest Barker (Oxford, 1957), 13–14. Harriet Beecher Stowe, *Uncle Tom's Cabin; or, Life among the Lowly* (Boston, 1852). Eugene D. Genovese, *Roll, Jordan, Roll: The World the Slaves Made* (New York, 1974). Morgan, *American Slavery, American Freedom*. A. E. Keir Nash, "Reason of Slavery: Understanding the Judicial Role in the Peculiar Institution," *Vanderbilt Law Review* 32 (1979): 7–218. A. Leon Higginbotham, *In the Matter of Color: Race and the American Legal Process* (New York, 1978). Mark Tushnet, *American Law of Slavery 1810–1860: Considerations of Humanity and Interest* (Princeton, N.J., 1981). James Oakes, *Slavery and Freedom: An Interpretation of the Old South* (New York, 1990). Fede, *People without Rights*. On the legacies of this formulation in intellectual property, see Stephen Best, *The Fugitive's Properties: Law and the Poetics of Possession* (Chicago, 2004).

24. J. G. Fichte, *The Science of Rights*, trans. A. E. Kroeger (London, 1889), 366. *License Cases*, 46 U.S. 504, 583 (1847). *Commonwealth v. Alger*, 61 Mass. 53 (1851). *Spalding v. Preston*, 21 Vt. 9 (1848). *Prigg v. Pennsylvania*, 41 U.S. 539 (1842). On the police power in *Prigg*, see Don E. Fehrenbacher, *The "Dred Scott" Case: Its Significance in American Law and Politics* (New York, 1978), 43–54. I am drawing again here on Dubber, for whom one of the defining characteristics of police is "the ahumanity of its objects." Dubber, *Police Power*, xv, 115–119.

25. On amelioration as the registration of the slave as person in law and the technicalities that obstructed this process, see Morris, *Southern Slavery*, 161–368. On amelioration as social science, see Seymour Drescher, *The Mighty Experiment: Free Labor versus Slavery in British Emancipation* (New York, 2004). The phrase "unoffending and unresisting" is taken from a case from South Carolina in 1840, *State v. Wilson*, quoted in Morris, *Southern Slavery*, 185.

26. For illustrative battle sequences and exhibitions of superpowers, consult the following: Castellanos, *New Orleans*. Baker, *Historical Sketch-Book*. Gottschalk, *Notes of a Pianist*. Loggins, *Where the World Ends*. Christian, "Bras Coupé." For an afterthought, we can look to Charles Chesnutt's prescription for black self-representation in literature, which credits Cable with inventing these su-

perpowers. "If there are no super-Negroes," Chesnutt says, "make some, as
Mr. Cable did in his *Bras Coupé*." Chesnutt, "The Negro in Art: How Shall He
Be Portrayed?" *Crisis* (November 1926): 28–29.

27. The sequence where "Squier" is shot by police and his arm amputated is related in Saxon et al., *Gumbo Ya-Ya*. Kendall, *History of New Orleans*. Castellanos, *New Orleans*. Christian, "Bras Coupé." Gottschalk, *Notes of a Pianist*.
Garreau, "Bras Coupé." Asbury, *French Quarter*. The police officer who shot
Bras-Coupé is occasionally identified as a "Monsieur Flietas." An alternative
sequence in the legend's opening cycle proposes Bras-Coupé's arm was shat-
tered during an altercation with an overseer. Hearn, "Original Bras-Coupe."
See also the discussion of this aspect of the oral tradition in Stephens, "Cable's
Bras-Coupé," 389–393. Regarding speech and political ontology, see Jacques
Rancière, *Disagreement: Politics and Philosophy* (Minneapolis, 1998). The political distinction between speech (which can name justice and injustice, advantage and disadvantage) and voice (which can distinguish merely pleasure
and pain) derives from Aristotle. See Barker, trans., *Politics of Aristotle*.

28. "We do not know . . . what gave birth to Squier's plans. Later he told of how he
had practiced his marksmanship until he became an expert shot, not only with
one hand, but with both. He said that he knew he was to eventually lose an
arm, that one day he would become Bras Coupé." Christian, "Bras Coupé," 2.

29. One way to put this point is to say that the legend's labor, in Alain Badiou's language, takes the form of an illegal operation. By staying true to an event that
never should have happened, which in the strictest terms means any event as
such, the legend introduces a new rule into the system in which it unfolds. Another way to put this point is to take an initiating cue from the leap that Frantz
Fanon proposes at the conclusion to *Black Skins, White Masks*, a leap that is
about "introducing invention into existence." Without collapsing the differences between these radical approaches to the problem of historical ontology,
I would insist that they have something crucial in common, which is resistance
to the dialectical resolution proposed by Jean-Paul Sartre in his introduction to
Léopold Senghor's *Anthologie de la nouvelle poésie nègre et malgache* (1948), in
which blackness becomes not itself a mode of universality but instead a particu-
larism, or an identity politics that is a necessary stage in the political process
that can, however, only realize its universality through self-negation. Alain Badiou, *Being and Event*, trans. Oliver Feltham (New York, 2005), 201–261. Frantz
Fanon, *Black Skin, White Masks*, trans. Charles Lam Markmann (New York,
1967), 229. Sartre's preface has been reprinted in translation as Jean-Paul Sartre,
Black Orpheus (Paris, 1963).

30. The countingroom anecdote is related in Cable, "[How I Came to Write the
Episode of Bras-Coupé]." Hearn claims to the contrary that Cable learned
about Bras-Coupé from Alexander Dimitry, a white bookseller in Exchange

Alley. Hearn, "Original Bras-Coupe." Concerning Cable's work with the legend, from his early efforts to sell his story "Bibi" (now lost) during 1872–1873 to the legend's incorporation into *The Grandissimes* during 1876–1880, see Arlin Turner, *George W. Cable: A Biography* (Durham, N.C., 1956), 54–55, 94–100.

31. Cable's interest in Bras-Coupé coincided with his awakening to a political program of racial equality, usually dated to a letter written in 1875 for the *New Orleans Bulletin* on school segregation, which is described in Arlin Turner, "George W. Cable's Beginning as a Reformer," *Journal of Southern History* 17 (1951): 135–161. This was a time of intense turmoil in New Orleans politics, encompassing interracial experiments in local government (the new metropolitan police), street warfare incited by the Crescent City White League (the Battle of Liberty Place in 1874), and the return of white supremacists to political power in 1877. Cable had close ties on both sides of this conflict. George Washington Cable, "The Convict Lease System in the Southern States," *Century Magazine* 27 (February 1884): 582–599. George Washington Cable, "The Silent South," *Century Magazine* 30 (September 1885): 674–691. George Washington Cable, "The Freedman's Case in Equity," *Century Magazine* 29 (January 1885): 409–418. George Washington Cable, "The Dance in Place Congo," *Century Magazine* 31 (February 1886): 517–532. George Washington Cable, "Creole Slave Songs," *Century Magazine* 31 (April 1886): 807–828.

32. For Cable's characterization of his native informant, see "[How I Came to Write the Episode of Bras Coupé]." On the ethnographic assumptions implied by Cable's evocation of a black voice outside history, see Ronald Radano, *Lying up a Nation: Race and Black Music* (Chicago, 2003). On the boundary thinking that demarcates Cable's conception of the political sphere, see Saidiya V. Hartman, *Scenes of Subjection: Terror, Slavery, and Self-Making in Nineteenth-Century America* (New York, 1997), 164–169.

33. Edward B. Tylor, *Primitive Culture*, 2 vols. (1871; reprint, New York, 1977). Cable mostly avoids the disdain (soon to be associated with Richard Wallaschek) that frames African music as expressing a guttural propensity for rhythm and imitation. His essays also eschew the tradition of Romantic nationalism (inherited from Johann Gottfried von Herder and subsequently applied to black music by Antonín Dvořák and W. E. B. Du Bois) that finds folklore's relevance to politics by staking national independence upon reconnection to indigenous roots. Richard Wallaschek, *Primitive Music: An Inquiry into the Origin and Development of Music, Songs, Instruments, and Pantomimes of Savage Races* (London, 1893). Antonín Dvořák, "Music in America," *Harper's Monthly* 90 (February 1895): 428–434. W. E. B. Du Bois, *The Souls of Black Folk* (Chicago, 1903).

34. On Cable and culturalism, see Gavin Jones, "Signifying Songs: The Double Meaning of Black Dialect in the Work of George Washington Cable," *American Literary History* 9 (1997): 244–267. For contrast on the novel's politics, see

Louis D. Rubin Jr., "The Division of the Heart: Cable's *The Grandissimes*," *Southern Literary Journal* 1 (1969): 27–47.

35. Cable, *Grandissimes*, 219. This does not mean, however, that the novel stops all traffic between "politics" and "culture." Cable is not so rigid as to refuse all nonsynchronous engagements between past and present. What is most brilliant about Cable's adaptation, in fact, is its insinuation of the legend into the present, which is achieved through the mediation of characters like Palmyre Philosophe, who play a role on both sides of the frame. Bras-Coupé loves Palmyre, but Palmyre does not love Bras-Coupé as she loves another character. She, in turn, is loved by someone else and is the mortal enemy of yet another. These character-driven connections turn the legend into a determinant for the plot, bridging the chasm between past and present. Palmyre's plan to kill her enemy goes wrong when her accomplice Clemence is caught in a bear-trap while placing voudou charms by the Grandissime mansion. Things get worse when the Grandissimes find that she is holding a diminutive coffin with an "image, in myrtle-wax, moulded and painted with some rude skill, of a negro's bloody arm cut off near the shoulder—a Bras-Coupé—with a dirk grasped in his hand" (Cable, *Grandissimes*, 314). Finding the arm, they shoot Clemence (their former nursemaid) in the back as she flees. If Palmyre commands respect as a voudou, her magic not only fails to accomplish its purpose, it gets Clemence killed. All that is left from her voudou is the arm, packaged in a tiny coffin, whose wax-and-paint suggests the depleted aura of an enchanted politics nearly disintegrated into curiosity. Cable trades on the charisma of superstition, but he never takes its politics seriously. The present may be haunted by uneven development, but the novel never doubts that its past will be exorcised. On the disenchantment of the arm, see Jenny Franchot, "Unseemly Commemoration: Religion, Fragments, and the Icon," *American Literary History* 9 (1997): 502–521.

36. Cable, *Grandissimes*, 219, 221.

37. Cable, "[How I Came to Write the Episode of Bras-Coupé]." Bras-Coupé is also mutilated in the novel though not by the loss of an arm. His punishment comes not at the story's start but at its end, and his mutilation results not from the discretionary power of the police but from the *Code noir*, which dictates the punishment for striking his master. Displacing the formative violence of the police into a legal code associated with colonial prehistory, this revision refigures the consciousness that is generated by putting the identifying injury at the start of the legend, breaking at the same time the analogy between the Louisiana Purchase and Reconstruction that is supposed to form the novel's political intervention. "We have a Code Noir now," Cable writes parenthetically in the novel, "but the new one is a mental reservation, not an enactment." Cable, *Grandissimes*, 235.

38. Cable, *Grandissimes*, 221. Saxon et al., *Gumbo Ya-Ya*, 253–254. Thomas Hobbes, *Leviathan* (London, 1651).

39. Cable, *Grandissimes*, 220, 221. On the precedents for representing enslaved royalty, see Wylie Sypher, *Guinea's Captive Kings: British Anti-Slavery Literature of the XVIIIth Century* (Chapel Hill, N.C., 1942). The tradition is extended within the United States by works such as William Cullen Bryant's "The African Chief" (1839), Henry Wadsworth Longfellow's "The Slave's Dream" (1842), and Herman Melville's "Benito Cereno" (1856).

40. Cable, *Grandissimes*, 221, 236, 221. Franz Boas, "On Alternating Sounds," *American Anthropologist* (January 1889): 47–53.

41. The exhibition of the fugitive's body at Place d'Armes is described in *New Orleans Picayune*, 19 July 1837. Christian, "Bras Coupé." Gottschalk, *Notes of a Pianist*. Baker, *Historical Sketch-Book*. Castellanos, *New Orleans*. Hearn, "Original Bras-Coupe." Kendall, *History of New Orleans*. Saxon et al., *Gumbo Ya-Ya*. Asbury, *French Quarter*.

42. Cable, *Grandissimes*, 248, 247. An analogue and possible source for Cable's version of the capture of Bras-Coupé at Congo Square is the legend of François Macandal, the San Domingan revolutionary, who was also captured by his enemies at the Calinda while he was drunk. See Ladd, "Atmosphere of Hints," 69–71.

43. Cable, "Dance in Place Congo," 518. It is worth noting that Cable's writing on Congo Square emerged, in part, through a debate with Joel Chandler Harris over whether slaves played the banjo. Harris's contention that slaves did not play the banjo appeared in "Plantation Music," *The Critic* 3 (1883): 505–506. Cable knew from multiple sources, including drawings by Benjamin Henry Latrobe, that slaves were playing something like a banjo at Congo Square.

44. Cable, *Grandissimes*, 236–237.

45. Cable, "Creole Slave Songs," 812, 823. Charles Dickens, *The Posthumous Papers of the Pickwick Club* (London, 1836–1837). On some of the struggles expressed in these songs, see Midlo Hall, *Africans in Colonial Louisiana*, 201–236.

46. Cable, *Grandissimes*, 246–248. For similar descriptions of the swamp's emptiness, see King, *New Orleans*.

47. Melville Jean Herskovits, *The Myth of the Negro Past* (New York, 1941), 246. See Lorenzo Turner, *Africanisms in the Gullah Dialect* (Chicago, 1949). Richard Alan Waterman, *Acculturation in the Americas* (Chicago, 1952). Janheinz Jahn, *Muntu: An Outline of the New African Culture*, trans. Marjorie Grenee (New York, 1961). Amiri Baraka [LeRoi Jones], *Blues People: Negro Music in White America* (New York, 1963). Sidney W. Mintz and Richard Price, *An Anthropological Approach to the Afro-American Past* (Philadelphia, 1976). Sterling Stuckey, *Slave Culture: Nationalist Theory and the Foundations of Black America* (New York, 1988). For an excellent synopsis of the "inaugural

problematic" inherited from Herskovits, see David Scott, "That Event, This Memory: Notes on the Anthropology of African Diasporas in the New World," *Diasporas* (1991): 261–284. Scott has helped to consolidate a new approach to black internationalism that acknowledges diaspora as a political strategy for affiliation as well as an ongoing debate about the meaning and history of blackness. Much of the resulting research has been pathbreaking. See, especially, Michael A. Gomez, *Exchanging Our Country Marks: The Transformation of African Identities in the Colonial and Antebellum South* (Chapel Hill, N.C., 1998). Brent Hayes Edwards, *The Practice of Diaspora: Literature, Translation, and the Rise of Black Internationalism* (Cambridge, Mass., 2003). Stephanie Smallwood, *Saltwater Slavery: A Middle Passage from Africa to American Diaspora* (Cambridge, Mass., 2007).

48. Mederic Louis Elie Moreau de Saint-Méry, *Description topographique, physique, civile, politique et historique de la partie française de l'isle Saint-Domingue* (1797–1798; reprint, Paris, 1958). Concerning Cable's use of this source, as well as his debts to the Gottschalks, see Turner, *George W. Cable*, 227–242. References to Bras-Coupé's genius at Congo Square include the following: Asbury, *French Quarter*. Christian, "Bras Coupé." King, *New Orleans*. Bechet, *Treat It Gentle*. Saxon et al., *Gumbo Ya-Ya*. Delius and Keary, *Koanga*. Loggins, *Where the World Ends*. Barbara Ladd notices Cable's use of the *Description topographique* in her argument that the Bras-Coupé legend draws from Carribean models, including the maroon leader François Macandal, who was executed in Saint-Domingue in 1758. See Ladd, "Atmosphere of Hints."

49. Benjamin Henry Latrobe, *The Journal of Latrobe, Being the Notes and Sketches of an Architect, Naturalist and Traveler in the United States from 1796 to 1820* (New York, 1905), 180–181. Thomas Nuttall, *Journal of Travels into the Arkansas Territory* (Philadelphia, 1821), 245. John A. Paxton, *Paxton's Directory of New Orleans* (New Orleans, 1822), 40. Cable, "Dance in Place Congo," 522, 523, 525. The dances at Congo Square only peaked after 1817, when an ordinance was passed banning such assemblies except in places and times designated by the mayor. It was decided that slaves could "gather in a crowd" only in Congo Square and only on Sunday afternoon, under the supervision of a police officer who would designate with a gunshot when the dancing was to begin and end. Slaves "assembled" elsewhere would be "arrested by the police" and punished with "ten to twenty-five lashes." "Ordinance Concerning the Slaves of the City, Suburbs and Places Adjacent to New Orleans," Conseil de Ville, Resolutions and Ordinances, 4 January 1817 to 27 December 1817, City Archives, New Orleans Public Library. Such gatherings had been happening for decades before this law was passed in the urban interface with the swamp. Travelers reported viewing "vast numbers of negro slaves" around the "skirts of the city" engaged in "drumming, fifing and dancing in large rings." After the Louisiana Purchase,

there were at least a dozen dances happening every weekend on levees and embankments, by the lake, and in vacant lots across the city; Fortescue Cuming, "Cuming's Tour to the Western Country," in *Early Western Travels*, 32 vols., ed. Rueben Gold Thwaites (Cleveland, 1904), 4:363, 366. Jerah Johnson, "New Orleans' Congo Square: An Urban Setting for Early Afro-American Culture Formation," *Louisiana History* 32 (1991): 117–157. Gary A. Donaldson, "A Window on Slave Culture: Dances at Congo Square in New Orleans, 1800–1862," *Journal of Negro History* 69 (1984): 63–72. David C. Estes, "Traditional Dances and Processions of Blacks in New Orleans as Witnessed by Antebellum Travelers," *Louisiana Folklore Miscellany* 6 (1990): 1–14. Following the research of scholars like Kimberly Hanger, Ned Sublette has even argued that the early references to "Place Congo" in the historical record may have been, not to the site that was later called Congo Square, but instead to any site in the city where slaves gathered to dance and make music—including the Place d'Armes. Ned Sublette, *The World That Made New Orleans: From Spanish Silver to Congo Square* (Chicago, 2008), 119–121. Kimberly S. Hanger, *A Medley of Cultures: Louisiana History at the Cabildo* (New Orleans, 1996). It is worth noting that the tourism at Congo Square was important to the history of blackface minstrelsy. Delineators, such as E. P. Christy, who said that their blackface acts were based on first-hand observation of slaves' performances frequently named Congo Square as a site where they had done their field work. See Robert Toll, *Blacking Up: The Minstrel Show in Nineteenth-Century America* (New York, 1974), 45–50.

50. Frederic Ramsey Jr. and Charles E. Smith, eds., *Jazzmen* (New York, 1939), 5, 9. Rudi Blesh, *Shining Trumpets: A History of Jazz* (New York, 1946), 157–158. Russell Roth, "On the Instrumental Origins of Jazz," *American Quarterly* 4 (Winter 1952): 305–316. Marshall Stearns, *The Story of Jazz* (New York, 1956). For the the claim that jazz starts at Congo Square, see also the following: Asbury, *French Quarter*, 185. Rudi Blesh, *This Is Jazz* (San Francisco, 1943). Robert Goffin, *Jazz: From the Congo to the Metropolitan*, trans. Walter Schaap and Leonard Feather (New York, 1944). Robert Goffin, *Horn of Plenty: The Story of Louis Armstrong*, trans. James F. Bezou (New York, 1947). Rex Harris, *Jazz* (1946; reprint, London, 1956). Barry Ulanov, *A History of Jazz in America* (New York, 1952). Eric Hobsbawm [Francis Newton], *The Jazz Scene* (London, 1959). Baraka [Jones], *Blues People*. Gunther Schuller, *Early Jazz: Its Roots and Musical Development* (New York, 1968). Ishmael Reed, *Mumbo Jumbo* (New York, 1996; first published 1972), 4. Albert Murray, *Stomping the Blues* (New York, 1976). Ted Gioia, *The History of Jazz* (New York, 1997). The standard work on the square is Johnson, "New Orleans' Congo Square." See also Joseph Roach, *Cities of the Dead: Circum-Atlantic Performance* (New York, 1996), 63–68. The problems with this "first article of faith" in jazz criti-

cism were first broached by Henry Kmen in "The Roots of Jazz in Place Congo: A Re-Appraisal," *Inter-American Musical Research Yearbook* 8 (1972): 5–17. Kmen's historiographical insights remain valuable despite the unnecessarily hard line he takes with his claim that "it was as an American rather than as an African" that "the Negro" formulated the jazz tradition. See Kmen, *Music in New Orleans: The Formative Years, 1791–1841* (Baton Rouge, La., 1966), 245.

51. Cable, "Dance at Place Congo," 522. Marshall Stearns and Jean Stearns, *Jazz Dance: The Story of American Vernacular Dance* (New York, 1968), 19. Goffin, *Jazz*, 22–30. Asbury, *French Quarter*, 244–245. J. G. Flugel, "Pages from a Journal of a Voyage down the Mississippi to New Orleans in 1817," ed. Felix Flugel, *Louisiana Historical Quarterly* 7 (July 1924): 427.

52. Loggins, *Where the World Ends*, 13–14, 27–28, 64, 71–72. Gottschalk, *Notes of a Pianist*, 11–12. This paragraph summarizes insights that are communicated in S. Frederick Starr, *Bamboula: The Life and Times of Louis Moreau Gottschalk* (New York, 1995), 32–45, 62–77. For a later work showing some of the research done by the Gottschalk family, see Clara Gottschalk Peterson, *Creole Songs from New Orleans in the Negro Dialect* (New Orleans, 1902).

53. Gioia, *History of Jazz*, 3–6.

54. Baker, *Historical Sketch-Book*, 21–22. Asbury, *French Quarter*, 244–245.

55. Goffin, *Jazz*, 1. Rudi Blesh says, with a similar inflection, that jazz is a "laboratory" for "democracy." *Shining Trumpets*, 12. Gunnar Myrdal, *An American Dilemma: The Negro Problem and Modern Democracy* (New York, 1944). C. Vann Woodward, *The Strange Career of Jim Crow* (New York, 1955). Stanley M. Elkins, *Slavery: A Problem in American Institutional and Intellectual Life* (Chicago, 1959). On some of the uses to which jazz was put during the Cold War, see the following: Penny M. Von Eschen, *Satchmo Blows Up the World: Jazz Ambassadors Play the Cold War* (Cambridge, Mass., 2004). Scott Saul, *Freedom Is, Freedom Ain't: Jazz and the Making of the Sixties* (Cambridge, Mass., 2005). John Gennari, *Blowin' Hot and Cool: Jazz and Its Critics* (Chicago, 2006).

56. Mezz Mezzrow, *Really the Blues* (New York, 1946). Louis Armstrong, *Satchmo* (New York, 1954). Alan Lomax, *Mister Jelly Roll: The Fortunes of Jelly Roll Morton, New Orleans Creole and "Inventor of Jazz"* (New York, 1950). John Chilton, *Sidney Bechet: The Wizard of Jazz* (New York, 1987). The likeness between Omar and Bras-Coupé is identified in Levine, *Black Culture and Black Consciousness*, 388. For contrast, see also Jürgen E. Grandt, *Kinds of Blue: The Jazz Aesthetic in African American Narrative* (Columbus, Ohio, 2005), 1–22.

57. Blesh, *Shining Trumpets*, 247. Jelly Roll Morton, "The Chant," Victor 36241-1, 1926.

58. Bechet, *Treat It Gentle*, 8, 6, 8.

59. Bechet, *Treat It Gentle*, 8, 4, 6. Rudi Blesh, "Preface" in Bechet, *Treat It Gentle* (New York, 1978; first published 1960).

60. Bechet, *Treat It Gentle*, 18, 26, 27, 28, 31, 34, 39, 41, 42, 43.

61. Bechet, *Treat It Gentle*, 18, 6.

62. Bechet, *Treat It Gentle*, 6, 33, 17.

63. Bechet, *Treat It Gentle*, 1, 2, 3.

64. Bechet, *Treat It Gentle*, 202, 17, 30.

65. Bechet, *Treat It Gentle*, 30, 45.

66. Nathaniel Mackey, *Bedouin Hornbook* (Los Angeles, 1997; first published 1986), 7–9, 12, 42. Mackey's formula alludes to Wilson Harris, "History, Fable and Myth in the Caribbean and Guianas," in *Selected Essays of Wilson Harris*, ed. Andrew Bundy (London, 1999), 152–166.

67. Frantz Fanon, "The Fact of Blackness," in *Black Skin, White Masks*, 140, 8. *Home of the Brave* (dir. Mark Robson, 1949). Maurice Merleau-Ponty, *Phenomenology of Perception*, trans. Colin Smith (New York, 1962). Mackey, *Bedouin Hornbook*, 194. One way to understand Mackey's apparent departure from Fanon is through Fred Moten's discussion of the "rhythm" of abjection. For Moten, the refusal of recognition that occasions the authentic upheaval, or the refusal of amputation, has already been broken prior to this assertiveness by the "oscillation" that is always there in the "prior connection between self and other." Because "radical break of the self from the other" is "never not contained by the continuity that it would sever," it follows that there is "no possibility of the formation of a wholly internally generated identity that would somehow come as the function of such a break." See Fred Moten, "Knowledge of Freedom," *New Centennial Review* 4 (2004): 307–308. On the totality said to preexist this encounter, see Cedric J. Robinson, *Black Marxism: The Making of the Black Radical Tradition* (Chapel Hill, N.C., 2000), 167–171.

68. Bechet's grandfather, a free creole named Jean Bechet, was a shoemaker. See Chilton, *Sidney Bechet*, 1. Critics who describe Omar as Bechet's flesh-and-blood, either explicitly or implicitly, include the following: Gioia, *History of Jazz*, 3–6. Rudi Blesh, *Combo U.S.A.: Eight Lives in Jazz* (Philadelphia, 1971), 35–36. Martin Williams, *Jazz Masters of New Orleans* (New York, 1967), 140. Whitney Balliet, *Jelly Roll, Jabo, and Fats* (New York, 1983), 39–40. Raymond Horricks, *Profiles in Jazz: From Sidney Bechet to John Coltrane* (Piscataway, N.J., 1991), 1–3. Grace Lichtenstein and Laura Dankner, *Musical Gumbo: The Music of New Orleans* (New York, 1993), 41. Samuel A. Floyd Jr., *The Power of Black Music: Interpreting Its History from Africa to the United States* (New York, 1995), 3–13. George E. Lewis, "Singing Omar's Song: A (Re)construction of Great Black Music," *Lenox Avenue* 4 (1998): 69–92. Robert M. Crunden, *Body and Soul: The Making of American Modernism* (New York, 2000), 153–154.

69. Floyd, *Power of Black Music*, 37, 8–10. Lewis, "Singing Omar's Song," 71, 87. For contrast, see Jason Berry, "African Cultural Memory in New Orleans Music," *Black Music Research Journal* 8 (1988): 3–12.

70. Cable, *Grandissimes*, 252. Blesh, *Shining Trumpets*, 159. Bechet, *Treat It Gentle*, 45. In *Bedouin Hornbook*, we again find Mackey echoing this discourse, including its patriarchal bent, describing the "generation by generation" that is the "default" recourse on the "underside of recognition." It is like a "stutter," he says, that results not from a situation where the tongue is "obstructed" but rather from its inflation in "pursuit of options" that make "emphasis" indiscernible from "obsession." One example of this stuttering is the sentence, "I don't know your father but I know your father's father," parlayed into the next line, "I don't know you but I know your father's father but I know your father's grandfather," which continues without end ("And so on."). This "receding, self-correcting withdrawal into a cave of ancestors" is an example of the movement that Mackey elsewhere terms the "'broken' claim to connection." Here, as elsewhere, I would note again that Mackey is best heard repeating what we have already been hearing from Sidney Bechet, and before him, from Bras-Coupé. Mackey, *Bedouin Hornbook*, 28–31, 42.

3. Uncle Remus and the Atlanta Police Department

1. Lee J. Vance, "Folk-Lore Study in America," *Popular Science Monthly* 43 (1893): 586–588, 596, 598. William Wells Newell, "On the Field and Work of a Journal of American Folklore," *Journal of American Folklore* 1 (1888): 3–7. Joel Chandler Harris, *Uncle Remus, His Songs and His Sayings: The Folk-Lore of the Old Plantation* (New York, 1880). *New York Times*, 1 December 1880. "Dialect Writers," in *The Cambridge History of English and American Literature*, 18 vols., ed. A. W. Ward, A. R. Waller, W. P. Trent, J. Erskine, S. P. Sherman, and C. Van Doren (New York, 1907–1921), 2:347–366. Stella Brewer Brookes, *Joel Chandler Harris—Folklorist* (Athens, Ga., 1950). Kathleen Light, "Uncle Remus and the Folklorists," *Southern Literary Journal* 7 (Spring 1975): 88–104. Eric J. Sundquist, *To Wake the Nations: Race in the Making of American Literature* (Cambridge, Mass., 1993), 323–359.

2. Melville Jean Herskovits, *The Myth of the Negro Past* (New York, 1941), 263, 272–273. Robert Hamill Nassau, *Fetichism in West Africa: Forty Years' Observation of Native Customs and Superstitions* (London, 1904), 276. It was not uncommon for researchers working the other side of this argument to scoff at the proposition that the stories told by Uncle Remus could have been "an independent conception among the aborigines of Africa" as there was in their minds no such thing as African culture. A. Gerber, "Uncle Remus Traced to the Old World," *Journal of American Folklore* 6 (1893): 264.

3. Harris, *Uncle Remus, His Songs and His Sayings*, 4–10. Joel Chandler Harris, *Nights with Uncle Remus: Myths and Legends of the Old Plantation* (Boston, 1883), xi–xlii. Charles Frede Hartt, *Amazonian Tortoise Myths* (Rio de Janeiro, 1875). Joel Chandler Harris, "Negro Folk Lore," *Atlanta Constitution*, 9 April 1880. Vance, "Folk-Lore Study," 597. Early commentaries on the controversy include the following: A. F. Chamberlain, "African and American: The Contact of Negro and Indian," *Science* 17 (1891): 85–90. Frank Gouldsmith Speck, "The Negroes and the Creek Nation," *Southern Workman* 27 (1908): 106–110. J. H. Johnson, "Documentary Evidence of the Relations of Negroes and Indians," *Journal of Negro History* 14 (1929): 21–43. A standard account of the controversy and its implications is Alan Dundes, "African Tales among the North American Indians," *Southern Folklore Quarterly* 29 (1965): 207–219. A recent, excellent discussion is Brad Evans, *Before Cultures: The Ethnographic Imagination in American Literature, 1865–1920* (Chicago, 2005), 51–81. Harris eventually expressed his disdain for the professional folklorists in a parody, "The Late Mr. Watkins of Georgia: His Relation to Oriental Folk-Lore," in *Tales of the Home Folks in Peace and War* (Boston, 1898), 97–113.

4. Harris, "Negro Folk Lore," 9 April 1880. On the history informing the Chinese professor, see Kenneth Pomeranz, *The Great Divergence: China, Europe, and the Making of the Modern World Economy* (Princeton, N.J., 2001).

5. T. F. Crane, "The Diffusion of Popular Tales," *Journal of American Folklore* 1 (1888): 8–15. William Wells Newell, "Additional Collection Essential to Correct Theory in Folklore and Mythology," *Journal of American Folklore* 3 (1890): 23–32. Franz Boas, "The Occurrence of Similar Inventions in Areas Widely Apart," *Science* (1887): 485–486. James George Frazer, *The Golden Bough: A Study in Magic and Religion* (London, 1890). Johann Gottfried von Herder, *Outlines of a Philosophy of the History of Man*, trans. T. O. Churchill (London, 1800). Jacob Grimm and Wilhelm Grimm, *Household Tales*, trans. Margaret Hunt (London, 1884; first published 1857). For the long-term impact on the culture concept, see Alfred L. Kroeber and Clyde Kluckhohn, *Culture: A Critical Review of Concepts and Definitions* (New York, 1952). See also George W. Stocking Jr., *Race, Culture, and Evolution: Essays in the History of Anthropology* (Chicago, 1982; first published 1968).

6. Evans, *Before Cultures*, 51–81. On Remus's centrality to this debate, it is useful to consult the annual reports on current research in the new folklore journals. In 1889, *Folklore* describes the evidence for the diffusion thesis only to concede that the case "cannot be deemed to be wholly solved" until "thorough and scholarly" attention is paid to the "problem" of the "origin" of the Uncle Remus tales. E. Sidney Hartland, "Report on Folk-Tale Research in 1889," *Folklore* 1 (1890): 113. Three years later the journal would again frame the "burning question of folk-tale diffusion" around Remus. Noting that "the place of origin

of any folk-tale" is often "regarded as insoluble," the journal argues that such "disbelief" is "premature" given the promising research that was already being done into Uncle Remus's Tar Baby story. E. Sidney Hartland, "Report on Folk-Tale Research," *Folklore* 4 (1892): 82, 85, 90. Other research on Remus and diffusion includes the following: T. F. Crane, "Plantation Folk-Lore," *Popular Science Monthly* 18 (April 1881): 824–833. James Mooney, "Myths of the Chero-kees," *Journal of American Folklore* 1 (1888): 97–108. Gerber, "Uncle Remus Traced to the Old World." W. A. Clouston, "'Uncle Remus' and Some European Popular Tales," *Notes and Queries* (1890): 301–302. Joseph Jacobs, *Indian Fairy Tales* (London, 1892), 251–253. E. M. Warren, "Uncle Remus and 'the Ro-man de Renard,'" *Modern Language Notes* 5 (May 1890): 257–270. Lee J. Vance, "Plantation Folk-Lore," *Open Court* 2 (1888): 1029–1032, 1074–1076, 1092–1095. William Taylor Thom, "Some Parallelisms between Shakespeare's English and the Negro-English of the United States," *Shakespeariana* 1 (1884): 129–135. Louis Pendleton, "Notes on Negro Folklore and Witchcraft in the South," *Journal of American Folklore* 3 (1890): 201–207. C. W. Previte Orton, "Uncle Remus in Tuscany," *Notes and Queries* 10 (1904): 183–184. John M. McBryde, "Brer Rabbit in the Folk Tales of Other Races," *Sewanee Review* 19 (April 1919): 185–206. On the global history of the principal case, see Aurelio Espinosa, "Notes on the Origin and History of the Tar-Baby Story," *Journal of American Folklore* 43 (1930): 129–209.

7. David Wells, "Evolution in Folklore: A New Story in an Old Form," *Popular Science Monthly* 41 (1892): 45–54. On the philosophy of folklore collection at Hampton and "the chain that connects the American with the African Ne-gro," see Alice M. Bacon, "The Study of Folk-Lore," in *Africa and the American Negro*, ed. John Wesley Edward Bowen (Atlanta, 1896), 191. On the Hampton Folklore Society, see Donald J. Waters, *Strange Ways and Sweet Dreams: Afro-American Folklore from the Hampton Institute* (Boston, 1983). Uncle Remus is invoked to anchor the African diaspora in the following cases: William Owens, "Folk-Lore of the Southern Negroes," *Lippincott's* 20 (1877): 748–755. Chatelain Heli, *Folktales of Angola* (New York, 1894), 22. W. S. Scar-borough, "Negro Folk-Lore and Dialect," *Arena* 17 (1896–1897): 186–192. An-nie Weston Whitney, "Negro American Dialects," *Independent* 53 (1901): 1079–1081, 2039–2042. A. B. Ellis, "Evolution in Folklore: Some West African Prototypes of the 'Uncle Remus' Stories," *Popular Science Monthly* 48 (1895): 93–104. Henry C. Davis, "Negro Folk-Lore in South Carolina," *Journal of American Folklore* 27 (1914): 241–254. If some collectors sought to prove that the "Uncle Remus stories" were told "wherever the African race is distrib-uted," others suggested they had merely stumbled upon native informants who looked like Remus and told the same stories, and still others crafted fictional conceits, more or less explicitly modeled on Harris, to frame their work.

Robert Hill, *Cuba and Porto Rico with the Other Islands of the West Indies* (New York, 1899), 233. W. L. Weber, "Mississippi as a Field for the Student of Literature," *Publications of the Mississippi Historical Society* 1 (1898): 16–24. Arthur Fraser Sim, *Life and Letters of Arthur Fraser Sim* (Westminster, U.K., 1896). Ellen C. Parsons, *A Life for Africa* (New York, 1898). Poultney Bigelow, *White Man's Africa* (New York, 1898). James Bryce, *Impressions of South Africa*, 3rd ed. (New York, 1900). Charles Jones Jr., *Negro Myths from the Georgia Coast Told in the Vernacular* (Boston, 1888). Mary Pamela Milne-Home, *Mamma's Black Nurse Stories: West Indian Folklore* (London, 1890). A. M. H. Christensen, *Afro-American Folk Lore Told Round Cabin Fires on the Sea Island of South Carolina* (Boston, 1892). Charles L. Edwards, *Bahama Songs and Stories* (Boston, 1895). Patricia C. Smith, *Annancy Stories* (New York, 1899). Florence Cronise and Henry W. Ward. *Cunnie Rabbit, Mr. Spider, and the Other Beef: West-African Folk-Tales* (London, 1903). Anne V. Culbertson, *At the Big House, Where Nancy and Aunt 'Phrony Held Forth on the Animal Tales* (Indianapolis, 1904). Walter Jekyll, *Jamaican Story and Song: Annancy Stories, Digging Sings, Ring Tunes, and Dancing Tunes* (London, 1907). Mary Tremearne and Newman Tremearne, *Fables and Fairy Tales for Little Folk, or Uncle Remus in Hausaland* (Cambridge, U.K., 1910). Andrews Wilkinson, *Plantation Stories of Old Louisiana* (Boston, 1914). Ambrose Gonzales, *With Aesop along the Black Border* (Columbia, S.C., 1920). Elsie Clews Parsons, *Folklore of the Southern Sea Islands* (Cambridge, Mass., 1923). Frank Worthington, *Little Wise One* (London, 1924). At present, the excellent standard work on the African origins of the tales is Florence E. Baer, *Sources and Analogues of the Uncle Remus Tales* (Helsinki, Finland, 1981).

8. Benjamin Brawley, *The Negro in Literature and Art*, rev. ed. (New York, 1921; first published 1918), 165–179. Arthur H. Fauset, "American Negro Folk Literature," in *The New Negro: An Interpretation*, ed. Alain Locke (New York, 1925), 238–244. *Song of the South* (Walt Disney Film-Studio Productions, 1946). Sterling Brown, *The Negro in American Fiction* (Washington, D.C., 1937). Sterling Brown, "Negro Folk Expression," *Phylon* 11 (1950): 318–327. Alice Walker, "The Dummy in the Window: Joel Chandler Harris and the Invention of Uncle Remus," in *Living by the Word: Selected Writings, 1973–1987* (San Diego, 1988). Peggy A. Russo, "Uncle Walt's Uncle Remus: Disney's Distortion of Harris's Hero," *Southern Literary Journal* 25 (1992): 19–32. See also the popular collection based upon the Disney adaptation of Harris's writing, Marion Palmer, *Walt Disney's Uncle Remus Stories* (New York, 1946). A brilliant and scrupulous reassessment of the Uncle Remus legacy, one of the high points of this critical movement, is Darwin T. Turner, "Daddy Joel Harris and His Old-Time Darkies," *Southern Literary Journal* 1 (1968): 20–24. Also useful and representative is the take on Uncle Remus in Robert A. Bone, *Down Home: A History of Afro-*

American Short Fiction from Its Beginnings to the End of the Harlem Renaissance (New York, 1975), 19–41.

9. C. Alphonso Smith, "Joel Chandler Harris," in *Southern Literary Studies*, ed. Howard Odum (Chapel Hill, N.C., 1927), 128–129. Harris, "Negro Folk Lore," 9 April 1880. Paul H. Buck, *The Road to Reunion* (Boston, 1937). Rayford W. Logan, *The Betrayal of the Negro, from Rutherford B. Hayes to Woodrow Wilson* (New York, 1965). Sundquist, *To Wake the Nations*. David W. Blight, *Race and Reunion: The Civil War and American Memory* (Cambridge, Mass., 2001).

10. Joel Chandler Harris, "Uncle Remus as a Rebel," *Atlanta Constitution*, 14 October 1877. Joel Chandler Harris, "A Story of the War," in *Uncle Remus, His Songs and His Sayings*, 175–185. Nina Silber, *The Romance of Reunion: Northerners and the South, 1865–1900* (Chapel Hill, N.C., 1993). Karen A. Keely, "Marriage Plots and National Reunion: The Trope of Romantic Reconciliation in Postbellum Literature," *Mississippi Quarterly* 51 (1998): 621–648. On the marriage plot and politics, see Doris Sommer, *Foundational Fictions: The National Romances of Latin America* (Berkeley, Calif., 1993).

11. Harris, "A Story of the War," 183. Harris, "Uncle Remus as a Rebel." Elsewhere in his writings, Harris plays on the theme of the ex-slave's return to the master. Joel Chandler Harris, "Blue Dave," in *Mingo and Other Sketches in Black and White* (Boston, 1884), 171–234. Joel Chandler Harris, "Daddy Jake the Runaway," in *Daddy Jake the Runaway: And Short Stories Told after Dark* (New York, 1896; first published 1889), 1–82.

12. Harris, *Uncle Remus, His Songs and His Sayings*, 7, 3–4, 11. Smith, "Joel Chandler Harris," 128–129. On folklore as the antidote to blackface, see also Joel Chandler Harris, "Plantation Music," *The Critic* 3 (1883): 505–506.

13. W. E. B. Du Bois, *The Souls of Black Folk* (Chicago, 1903). On the development of Atlanta, see Franklin M. Garrett, *Atlanta and Environs: A Chronicle of Its People and Events* (New York, 1954). James Russell, *Atlanta, 1847–1890: City Building in the Old South and the New* (Baton Rouge, La., 1988). For a contemporary account of the changes in the cityscape, see Ernest Ingersoll, "The City of Atlanta," *Harper's New Monthly Magazine* (December 1879): 30–43.

14. Henry Grady, "The New South," *Atlanta Daily Herald*, 14 March 1874. Joel Chandler Harris, *The Life of Henry W. Grady, Including His Writings and Speeches* (New York, 1890). Paul Gaston, *The New South Creed: A Study in Southern Mythmaking* (New York, 1970).

15. Wallace P. Reed, ed., *History of Atlanta, Georgia* (Syracuse, N.Y., 1889), 244–286. Regarding the racial politics of Atlanta's modernization, see Alexa Wynelle Benson, "Race Relations in Atlanta, As Seen in a Critical Analysis of the City Council Proceedings and Other Related Works, 1865–1877," MA thesis, Atlanta University, 1966. Regarding the uneven distribution of the new public amenities made available by the city government, see Tera W. Hunter, *To 'Joy My*

Freedom: Southern Black Women's Lives and Labors after the Civil War (Cambridge, Mass., 1997), 44–73.

16. Atlanta Policeman's Relief Association, *The History of the Atlanta Police Department* (Atlanta, 1898), 9. There is one advertisement from 1874 that even goes so far as to represent the new organization of "uniformed police" as one of the "seven wonders of Atlanta." *Atlanta Constitution*, 1 March 1874.

17. James Henry Hammond, "Hammond's Letters on Slavery," in William Harper, James Henry Hammond, William Gilmore Simms, and Thomas Roderick Dew, *The Pro-Slavery Argument, As Maintained by the Most Distinguished Writers of the Southern States* (Charleston, S.C., 1852), 129–131. Henry Grady, "The New South," in Harris, *Life of Grady*, 90.

18. The first annual report from the Chief of Police gives an excellent account of the methods used by the reorganized department; *Atlanta Constitution*, 7 January 1875. William Mathias and Stuart Anderson, *Horse to Helicopter: The First Century of the Atlanta Police Department* (Decatur, Ga., 1973). Eugene J. Watts, "The Police in Atlanta, 1890–1905," *Journal of Southern History* 39 (1973): 165–182. Howard Rabinowitz, "The Conflict between Blacks and the Police in the Urban South, 1865–1900," *Historian* 39 (1976): 62–76. Hunter, *To 'Joy My Freedom*, 120–129. Statistics, including information on police funding and ratio of police per capita, are from Reed, *History of Atlanta*, 244–286. See also William Cleveland Duke, *The Policeman: His Trials and His Dangers* (Atlanta, 1911).

19. Reed, *History of Atlanta*, 287–298. Watts, "Police in Atlanta," 172. *Atlanta Constitution*, 19 May 1877. *Atlanta Constitution*, 25 May 1877. On the concurrent renovation of the city jail, see *Atlanta Constitution*, 26 April 1872. On the distinctive role of the minor judiciary in the modernization of southern justice, see Christopher Waldrep, *Roots of Disorder: Race and Criminal Justice in the American South, 1817–1880* (Urbana, Ill., 1988).

20. Alex Lichtenstein, *Twice the Work of Free Labor: The Political Economy of Convict Labor in the New South* (London, 1996), 37–125. Joseph P. Reidy, *From Slavery to Agrarian Capitalism in the Cotton Plantation South: Central Georgia, 1800–1880* (Chapel Hill, N.C., 1992), 215–241. Edward L. Ayers, *Vengeance and Justice: Crime and Punishment in the Nineteenth Century American South* (New York, 1984), 185–265. On a related case, see David M. Oshinsky, *"Worse than Slavery": Parchman Farm and the Ordeal of Jim Crow Justice* (New York, 1996). See also W. E. B. Du Bois, "The Spawn of Slavery: The Convict-Lease System in the South," *Missionary Review of the World* 24 (1901): 737–745. For a valuable first-person account of the system, see A Georgia Negro Peon, "The New Slavery in the South—An Autobiography," *The Independent* 56 (25 February 1904): 409–414.

21. Lichtenstein, *Twice the Work*, 1–16, 73–104.

22. Philip Abrams, "Notes on the Difficulty of Studying the State," *Journal of Historical Sociology* 1 (1988): 58–89.

23. Harris, *Life of Grady*, 9–80. For Grady's reflections on the *Daily Herald*'s mission, see *Atlanta Constitution*, 18 April 1880.

24. Richard Terdiman, *Discourse/Counter-Discourse: The Theory and Practice of Symbolic Resistance in Nineteenth-Century France* (Ithaca, N.Y., 1985). For contrast on the symbolic operation of the newspapers, see Benedict Anderson, *Imagined Communities: Reflections on the Origin and Spread of Nationalism* (London, 1983).

25. These excerpts are taken from the following installments of "Police Points" in the *Atlanta Constitution*: 4 December 1878, 12 September 1878, 14 November 1877, 14 February 1879, 4 December 1878, 28 January 1879, 4 August 1876, 14 January 1878, 22 November 1877, 1 November 1877, 4 August 1876, 1 November 1877, 14 November 1877, 11 January 1878, 27 October 1877, 4 August 1876, 31 October 1877, 9 January 1879, 27 October 1877.

26. The celebrated police court reporter at the *Daily Herald* from 1872 to 1876 was Bill Moore. *Atlanta Daily Herald*, 30 August 1873. The police court columns in the *Constitution* were expanded after Grady arrived, but it was not until the 1890s that they would again be elaborated to the extent that they had been at the *Daily Herald*. For the history of police court reporting in the penny press in New York, including a profile of George Wisner, see Alexander Saxton, "Problems of Class and Race in the Origins of the Mass Circulation Press," *American Quarterly* 36 (1984): 211–234.

27. On inbound black migration and the changing demographics and growth in Atlanta's population, see Allison Dorsey, *To Build Our Lives Together: Community Formation in Black Atlanta, 1875–1906* (Athens, Ga., 2004). The novel anti-vagrancy strategies employed by the police department are detailed in Watts, "Police in Atlanta."

28. These excerpts are from anti-vagrancy editorials and articles in the *Atlanta Constitution* on the following dates: 29 July 1885, 29 August 1877, 12 April 1879, 30 July 1879, 16 February 1878, 24 January 1879, 26 November 1879.

29. *Atlanta Constitution*, 3 June 1877, 30 July 1879, 29 August 1879. The DeFoors were murdered on 25 July 1879. On the DeFoor case, also consult *Atlanta Constitution*, 27 July 1879, 29 July 1879, 31 July 1879, 2 August 1879, 12 August 1879, 15 August 1879, 17 August 1879, 21 August 1879, 14 January 1881, 22 August 1884. For a prescient and early account of the critical theory of deviance amplification, see Stuart Hall, "Deviancy, Politics, and the Media," Stenciled Occasional Paper, Centre for Contemporary Cultural Studies (Birmingham, U.K., 1971).

30. For the explicit equation between anti-vagrancy and economic development, see *Atlanta Constitution*, 15 September 1878, 30 July 1879, 24 January 1879, 1 December 1878, 24 January 1902, 26 June 1901, 25 January 1879.

31. David F. Gottschalk, *Veiled Visions: The 1906 Atlanta Race Riot and the Re-shaping of American Race Relations* (Chapel Hill, N.C., 2005), esp. 35–56. Kevin K. Gaines, *Uplifting the Race: Black Leadership, Politics, and Culture in the Twentieth Century* (Chapel Hill, N.C., 1996), 47–66. On violence and social reform, see Charles Crowe, "Racial Violence and the Social Reform Origins of the Atlanta Riot of 1906," *Journal of Negro History* 53 (July 1968): 234–256. There is also a novel about the riot: Thornwell Jacobs, *The Law of the White Circle* (Nashville, 1908).

32. For the police complaints about public apathy in Atlanta, see Mathias and Anderson, *Horse to Helicopter*, 20–22. For the anti-lynching editorial, see *Atlanta Constitution*, 9 June 1877. On the perceived difficulty of drawing the line when it came to lynching, see *Atlanta Constitution*, 19 May 1893. On the broadest contours of this debate, see Dan T. Carter, *When the War Was Over: The Failure of Self-Reconstruction in the South, 1865–1867* (Baton Rouge, La., 1985).

33. Gaines, *Uplifting the Race*, 47–99. Booker T. Washington, *The Negro in Business* (Chicago, 1907), 270.

34. Gaines, *Uplifting the Race*, 152–178, 47–66, 179–208. Dorsey, *To Build Our Lives Together*, 54–121.

35. Watts, "Police in Atlanta." Rabinowitz, "Conflict between Blacks and the Police." See also Terry John Thornbery, "The Development of Black Atlanta, 1865–1883," PhD diss., University of Maryland, 1977.

36. Henry Grady, "In Plain Black and White: A Reply to Mr. Cable," *Century Magazine* 29 (1885): 909–917. Hunter, *To 'Joy My Freedom*, 44–144. Dorsey, *To Build Our Lives Together*, 122–166. Rabinowitz, "Conflict between Blacks and the Police." *Atlanta Constitution*, 8 December 1870, 27 September 1881, 17 August 1883. An earlier complaint about this recalcitrance was posted by Henry Grady in the *Atlanta Daily Herald*, 5 May 1875.

37. Hunter, *To 'Joy My Freedom*, 44–144. *Savannah Tribune*, 18 September 1897. For examples of critical journalism coincident with the initial cycles of the *Constitution*'s advocacy for the Atlanta police, see *Savannah Tribune*, 8 January 1876, 15 January 1876, 22 January 1876, 26 February 1876, 11 March 1876, 18 March 1876. "Georgia Justice" is a miscellany that appeared in the *Tribune* in the 1870s, and "Horrors of the Chain Gang" and "Chain Gang Outrages" are regular columns that ran in the *Tribune* in the 1890s. John W. Blassingame, "Before the Ghetto: The Making of the Black Community in Savannah, Georgia, 1865–1880," *Journal of Social History* 6 (1973): 463–488.

38. *Savannah Tribune*, 4 March 1876, 15 July 1876, 26 February 1876, 15 January 1876, 14 November 1896, 7 April 1894, 14 April 1894, 18 May 1895, 23 May 1896, 1 October 1892, 22 January 1876, 26 November 1892. "Only last week," the *Tribune* explains in one editorial, "a policeman went into the home of a citizen and shot him dead. Does this show that policemen will protect citizens?" "The

officer," the paper decides, "should be brought to justice. The law should brand him as a murderer as he is branded by the laws of God." *Savannah Tribune*, 2 January 1897.

39. *Savannah Tribune*, 12 June 1897, 26 August 1893, 21 May 1892.

40. *Savannah Tribune*, 13 June 1896. *Atlanta Weekly Defiance*, 28 October 1881.

41. Here I am framing the arguments in the *Defiance* and *Tribune* through the discussion of contract and warfare in Michel Foucault, "*Society Must Be Defended*": *Lectures at the College de France, 1975–1976* (New York, 2003).

42. *Savannah Tribune*, 19 December 1889.

43. "Roundabout in Georgia," quoted in Bernard Wolfe, "Uncle Remus and the Malevolent Rabbit," *Commentary* 8 (1949): 40–41. On Harris's early career, see Walter M. Brasch, *Brer Rabbit, Uncle Remus, and the "Cornfield Journalist"* (Macon, Ga., 2000), 1–58. See also Paul M. Cousins, *Joel Chandler Harris: A Biography* (Baton Rouge, La., 1968). Eric Montenyohl, "From Old Si to Plantation Storyteller: The Evolution of Uncle Remus," MA thesis, University of North Carolina, 1975. Bruce Bickley, *Joel Chandler Harris: A Biography and Critical Study* (Boston, 1978), 15–62. Sundquist, *To Wake the Nations*, 323–347. In 1880, Sidney Lanier remarked that the common thread joining the urban sketches to the plantation sketches is the ability to demystify archaic systems of belief that could potentially get in the way of New South progress. He identifies Uncle Remus as a "famous colored philosopher of Atlanta, who is a fiction so founded on fact . . . as to have passed into true citizenship and authority." Lanier quotes at length an urban sketch in which Remus hears about a "cullud lady" who has been communicating with "sperrits" and has learned that "jedgment day aint fur off." Remus has no truck with these forms of belief: "w'en it comes ter deze yer sines in de a'r an deze yer sperrits in de woods, den I'm out. . . . I hear talk er [negroes] seein' ghos'es all times er night an all times er day, but I aint never seed none yit." Remus finally explains that when he has "an' nuff grease fer ter make gravy" then he "ain't keerin' much wedder folks sees ghos'es or no." For Lanier, Remus's no-nonsense attitude embodies the pragmatic spirit of the New South Creed: "There may be signs of danger to the republic; there may be ghosts of dreadful portent stalking around the hustings and through the Capitol corridors . . . but meantime it is clear that we will have nothing to eat unless we go into the field and hoe the corn and feed the hogs." Ghosts are a danger to the republic, in this reading, because they distract black workers from their responsibilities, making them potentially into "beggars and criminals." For Lanier, the value of the Remus tales is their ability to cut through this tissue of black vernacular belief. Sidney Lanier, "The New South," *Scribner's Monthly* 20 (October 1880): 840–851.

44. "Uncle Remus and a Democratic Christmas," *Atlanta Constitution*, 9 December 1876. "Uncle Remus's Politics," *Atlanta Constitution*, 28 November 1876.

"Uncle Remus as a Weather Prophet," *Atlanta Constitution*, 18 August 1878. "Uncle Remus on Color," *Atlanta Constitution*, 4 May 1879. "Uncle Remus's Vote," *Atlanta Constitution*, 8 December 1878. "Uncle Remus and the Savannah Darkey," *Atlanta Constitution*, 14 November 1876. On the leased convict labor that made possible the Air-Line Train, see Lichtenstein, *Twice the Work*, 37–72.

45. "Uncle Remus and the Emigrants," *Atlanta Constitution*, 4 August 1878. "Uncle Remus as an Emigrant," *Atlanta Constitution*, 18 March 1878. Joel Chandler Harris, "Views on the African Exodus," in *Uncle Remus and His Friends* (Boston, 1892), 315–323. On the emigration movements scorned by Remus, see Stephen Angell, *Bishop Henry McNeal Turner and African-American Religion in the South* (Knoxville, Tenn., 1992).

46. Joel Chandler Harris, "Turnip Salad as a Text," in *Uncle Remus, His Songs and His Sayings*, 196–197. "Uncle Remus Makes a Confession," *Atlanta Constitution*, 17 August 1879. On street vending, see Dorsey, *To Build Our Lives Together*, 41–42. For legal context and contrast, see Regina Austin, "'An Honest Living': Street Vendors, Municipal Regulation, and the Black Public Sphere," *Yale Law Journal* 103 (1994): 2119–2131. On vending and vernacular property, see Dylan C. Penningroth, *The Claims of Kinfolk: African American Property and Community in the Nineteenth-Century South* (Chapel Hill, N.C., 2003).

47. "Uncle Remus and a Democratic Christmas," *Atlanta Constitution*, 9 December 1876. "Uncle Remus on Color," *Atlanta Constitution*, 4 May 1879. "Uncle Remus as a Murderer," *Atlanta Constitution*, 11 August 1878. "Uncle Remus in the Role of a Tartar," *Atlanta Constitution*, 7 July 1878. "Uncle Remus and the Fourth," *Atlanta Constitution*, 6 July 1879. On the all-around valor of Tige Anderson, see "Police Points," *Atlanta Constitution*, 27 September 1881, 28 January 1879, 25 January 1879. For Remus in the police court, see Joel Chandler Harris, "Uncle Remus in Limbo," in *Uncle Remus and His Friends*, 248–253. Remus speaks to the police court reporter in "A Story of a Blind Horse," in *Uncle Remus and His Friends*, 243–247.

48. This surrogacy is apparent, for instance, in "Uncle Remus as a Murderer," "Uncle Remus in the Role of a Tartar," "Uncle Remus as an Emigrant," "Uncle Remus and the Savannah Darkey," "Uncle Remus and the Emigrants," and "Jeems Rober'son's Last Illness." For Remus's proposed gunslinging, see "Uncle Remus's Church Experience," *Atlanta Constitution*, 21 January 1877. For talk with a vagrant called Pegleg Charley, see "Uncle Remus Preaches to a Convert," *Atlanta Constitution*, 21 July 1878. Officer Jarrel's well-phrased question is from "Uncle Remus as a Murderer."

49. Joel Chandler Harris, "Negro Folk Lore," *Atlanta Constitution*, 20 July 1879. Harris, "Negro Folk Lore," 9 April 1880. "Uncle Remus's Folk-Lore: The Story of the Deluge and How It Came About," *Atlanta Constitution*, 14 December

1879. The parody in the *Constitution* adjacent to "The Story of the Deluge" concerning black participation in electoral politics is titled "The Mule as a Reformer."

50. "Uncle Remus's Folk-Lore: Brer Rabbit, Brer Fox, and the Tar-Baby," *Atlanta Constitution*, 16 November 1879. Espinosa, "Notes on the Origin and History." On the conflict of manners in this story as a "significant Africanism," see Herskovits, *Myth of the Negro Past*, 272. Without denying the African lineage, it is necessary to take account of the immediate historical coordinates that are written into the tale as it is presented in the *Atlanta Constitution*. These coordinates draw "The Wonderful Tar Baby Story" into line not only with urban sketches, like "As to Education," that appear in the final section in *Uncle Remus, His Songs and His Sayings*, but also with soon-to-be-archetypal scenes from films like *Birth of a Nation* and *Gone with the Wind* that portray, in Margaret Mitchell's phrasing, "niggers pushin' white folks off the sidewalks" as a by-product of emancipation. Joel Chandler Harris, "As to Education," in *Uncle Remus, His Songs and His Sayings*, 222–223. *The Birth of a Nation* (1915, dir. D. W. Griffith). *Gone with the Wind* (1939, dir. Victor Fleming). Margaret Mitchell, *Gone with the Wind* (New York, 1936), 520. Regarding the social form of these scenes, see Bertram William Doyle, *The Etiquette of Race Relations in the South: A Study in Social Control* (Chicago, 1937).

51. "Uncle Remus's Folk-Lore: Brer Rabbit Again Grossly Deceives Brer Fox," *Atlanta Constitution*, 21 December 1879. "Negro Folk Lore: The Story of Mr. Rabbit and Mr. Fox, as Told by Uncle Remus," *Atlanta Constitution*, 20 July 1879. "The Fox Goes a Hunting but the Rabbit Bags the Game," *Atlanta Constitution*, 15 February 1880. "How Brer Rabbit Saved His Meat," *Atlanta Constitution*, 21 March 1880. "A Plantation Legend: The Sad Fate of Mr. Fox," *Atlanta Constitution*, 18 July 1880. See also "Uncle Remus's Folk-Lore: Ole Brer Rabbit, He's a Good Fisherman," *Atlanta Constitution*, 22 February 1880. The foods listed in the text are featured in tales collected in Harris, *Uncle Remus, His Songs and His Sayings*.

52. "The Story of Mr. Rabbit and Mr. Fox, as Told by Uncle Remus." "Uncle Remus's Folk-Lore: Why Brer Possum Is a Peaceful Citizen," *Atlanta Constitution*, 23 November 1879. "Uncle Remus's Folk-Lore: Ole Brer Rabbit, He's a Good Fisherman." For Remus's pan-toting song, see "Christmas Play-Song, As Sung by Uncle Remus (Myrick Place, Putnam County, 1858)," *Atlanta Constitution*, 12 October 1879. For Brer Rabbit in the police court, see "Brer Rabbit in the Collard Patch," *Atlanta Constitution*, 10 January 1902. Examples of related pan-toting songs appear in the following folklore collections: Will H. Thomas, *Some Current Folk-Songs of the Negro* (Austin, Tex., 1936; first published 1912), 8. E. C. Perrow, "Songs and Rhymes from the South," *Journal of American Folklore* 25 (1915): 135. Dorothy Scarborough, *On the Trail of Negro Folk-Songs*

(Cambridge, Mass., 1925), 135–136. On pan-toting in Atlanta, see Hunter, *To 'Joy My Freedom*, 60–66, 131–136. An example of how pan-toting was treated in the police court reports is "Old Lazy Cyril," who is said to have received "His grub by hook or crook: / He ceased to beg and ceased to fret / And 'stood in' with a cook," *Atlanta Constitution*, 9 June 1901. For a positive argument representing pan-toting as legitimate source of customary income, see *Savannah Tribune*, 29 July 1911.

53. June Jordan, "A Truly Bad Rabbit," *New York Times*, 17 May 1987.

54. Reidy, *From Slavery to Agrarian Capitalism*, 8, 40, 69–70, 151–152, 224–227. Penningroth, *Claims of Kinfolk*, 47–50, 64–67. Barbara Fields, *Slavery and Freedom on the Middle Ground: Maryland during the Nineteenth Century* (New Haven, Conn., 1985), 182–193. Steven Hahn, "Hunting, Fishing, and Foraging: Common Rights and Class Relations in the Postbellum South," *Radical History Review* 26 (Fall 1982): 37–64. Alex Lichtenstein, "That Disposition to Theft, With Which They Have Been Branded: Moral Economy, Slave Management, and the Law," *Journal of Social History* 22 (1988): 413–340. James C. Scott, *Domination and the Arts of Resistance: Hidden Transcripts* (New Haven, Conn., 1990), 19, 163–166. Robin D. G. Kelley, " 'We Are Not What We Seem': Rethinking Black Working-Class Opposition in the Jim Crow South," *Journal of American History* 80 (1993): 75–112. For comparison, Peter Linebaugh, *The London Hanged: Crime and Civil Society in the Eighteenth Century* (London, 1991).

55. Harris, *Uncle Remus, His Songs and His Sayings*, 32. Regarding the formal necessity involved in frame narration, see Peter Brooks, *Reading for the Plot: Design and Intention in Narrative* (Cambridge, Mass., 1984). For a description of the evolution of the frame narrative between the first two Uncle Remus books, see Sundquist, *To Wake the Nations*, 324–327.

56. Obviously the landmark here is Thomas Hobbes, *Leviathan* (London, 1651). On uncertainty, self-possession, and anthropomorphism in the state of nature as it is shown in Hobbes, see Sheldon S. Wolin, *Politics and Vision: Continuity and Innovation in Western Political Thought*, rev. ed. (Princeton, N.J., 2004; first published 1960), 214–256.

57. Harris, "Negro Folk Lore," 9 April 1880. *New York Times*, 10 October 1895. Page is quoted in Burton J. Hendrick, *The Training of an American: The Earlier Life and Letters of Walter H. Page, 1855–1913* (Boston, 1928), 332.

58. Although many trickster stories collected in these years were flush with contemporary references to policing and labor disputes after emancipation, it became a truism that Brer Rabbit was a stand-in for the slave, and the trickster tradition was a cultural survival from slavery. For contrast, consult the following collections, which emphasize the oral tradition's evolving present tense: Arthur H. Fauset, "Tales and Riddles Collected in Philadelphia," *Journal of American Folklore* 41 (1928): 529–557. Zora Neale Hurston, "High John de Conquer,"

American Mercury 57 (1943): 450–458. Harry Oster, "Negro Humor: John and Old Marster," *Journal of the Folklore Institute* 5 (1968): 42–57. This critical emphasis on the present's continuity with the past is also evident in early literary adaptations of the trickster tradition by African American writers. Charles W. Chesnutt, *The Conjure Woman* (Boston, 1899). William Wells Brown, *My Southern Home: or, The South and Its People* (Boston, 1880).

59. Theodore Bacon, *What the Lawyer Owes to Society, An Address Delivered Before the Graduating Classes at the Seventy-Second Anniversary of Yale Law School* (New Haven, Conn., 1896), n.p.

60. Many details from "Uncle Remus and the Fourth," including its characterization of police, are changed when the tale is republished as "The Fourth of July" in *Uncle Remus, His Songs and His Sayings*, 228–231. Remus has a comparable conflict with an excursionist on July Fourth in a sketch published the previous year, "Uncle Remus in the Role of a Tartar."

61. *Savannah Tribune*, 7 April 1894.

62. On Tige Anderson, see *Atlanta Constitution*, 27 September 1881, 29 July 1879. Unlike in the other urban sketches collected in *Uncle Remus, His Songs and His Sayings*, where interlocutors are designated as "policeman" or "police officer" rather than by name as they are in the newspaper, Anderson disappears altogether from "The Fourth of July" sketch after it is revised for book publication. *Uncle Remus, His Songs and His Sayings*, 205, 210, 222, 228–231. Additional facts on Anderson are contained in Jerry Cook, "A Brief History of George T. Anderson, C. S. A." (unpublished manuscript).

63. *New York Times*, 13 July 1874. On July Fourth celebrations, see Mitch Katchun, *Festivals of Freedom: Memory and Meaning in African American Emancipation Celebrations 1808–1915* (Amherst, Mass., 2006).

64. On the "bad nigger" character type, John W. Roberts, *From Trickster to Badman: The Black Folk Hero in Slavery and Freedom* (Philadelphia, 1989).

65. Frederick Douglass, "The Meaning of the Fourth of July to the Negro, 1852," in *The Life and Writings of Frederick Douglass*, 2 vols., ed. Philip S. Foner (New York, 1950), 2:192. For contrast on violence and the timeframe of revolution, see Walter Benjamin, "Critique of Violence," trans. Edmund Jephcott, in *Reflections* (New York, 1978), 277–300. This question as well as its answer—the shut eye of Tige Anderson—are deleted from *Uncle Remus, His Songs and His Sayings*.

66. It is worth recalling that Uncle Remus is represented as a folk artist even before he leaves Atlanta to become a plantation storyteller. In the closing lines of "Uncle Remus's Politics" from November 1876, Remus walks away singing a spiritual. Two months later, the *Atlanta Constitution* dispensed with the narrative preparation when it published another spiritual, "Uncle Remus's Revival Hymn." "Uncle Remus's Plantation Play Song" and "Christmas Play Song: As

Sung by Uncle Remus" were both reels. Appearing in October 1878 and 1879, they were prefaced only by their place and time of performance ("Putnam County—1858"). The newspaper also printed "Plantation Proverbs" and "Home-Made Axioms" from Remus. These newspaper selections were supplemented in the songs section of *Uncle Remus, His Songs and His Sayings* by work songs and serenades, and they were annotated as "transcriptions" with language that was "in the highest degree characteristic." *Atlanta Constitution,* 18 January 1877, 12 October 1879, 18 December 1879, 9 December 1879, 25 December 1879. Harris, *Uncle Remus, His Songs and His Sayings,* 149–171.

67. On the "obscure ideals" expressed in these tales, see Octave Thanet, "Folk-Lore in Arkansas," *Journal of American Folklore* 5 (1892): 122. Richard Wallashek, *Primitive Music: An Inquiry into the Origin and Development of Music, Songs, Instruments, Dances and Pantomimes of Savage Races* (London, 1893). Henry E. Krehbiel, *Afro-American Folksongs* (New York, 1914). James Weldon Johnson, *The Book of American Negro Spirituals* (New York, 1925). Du Bois, *Souls of Black Folk,* 254–255.

68. David Levering Lewis, W. E. B. Du Bois, vol. 1: *Biography of a Race 1868–1919* (New York, 1993), 79–149.

69. Booker T. Washington and W. E. Burghardt Du Bois, *The Negro in the South: His Economic Progress in Relation to His Moral and Religious Development* (Philadelphia, 1907), 64. Anna Julia Cooper, *A Voice from the South, By a Black Woman of the South* (Xenia, Ohio, 1892), 224–225. James Weldon Johnson, "Preface to the Original Edition," in *The Book of American Negro Poetry,* rev. ed. (1931; first published 1922), 9–10.

70. Brawley, *Negro in Literature and Art,* 198, 189. Fauset, "American Negro Folk Literature." Twain quoted in Julia Collier Harris, *The Life and Letters of Joel Chandler Harris* (Boston, 1918), 169–170. Alain Locke, "The Negro's Contribution to American Art and Literature," *Annals of the American Academy of Political and Social Science* 140 (1928): 235–236. William Stanley Braithwaite, "The Negro in American Literature," in *The New Negro,* 32. W. E. B. Du Bois, *The Gift of Black Folk: The Negroes in the Making of America* (Boston, 1924), 296.

71. Sterling Brown, "Negro Folk Expression," 318–327. For background, see Henry Louis Gates Jr., "The Trope of a New Negro and the Reconstruction of the Image of the Black," *Representations* 24 (1988): 129–155. Like Du Bois, Brown would pause to reflect on the irony of this inheritance, contemplating his own connection to Harris by writing about the experience of having been turned away from the Wren's Nest, the Harris family home, which was turned into a segregated tourist attraction after it was sold to the Uncle Remus Memorial Association in 1913. See Sterling Brown, "Georgia Sketches," *Phylon* 6 (1945): 225–231.

72. W. E. B. Du Bois, *A Pageant in Seven Decades, 1868–1938* (Atlanta, 1938). W. E. B. Du Bois, *Dusk of Dawn: An Essay toward an Autobiography of a Race*

Concept (New York, 1940), 67. W. E. B. Du Bois, "My Evolving Program for Negro Freedom," in *What the Negro Wants*, ed. Rayford Logan (Chapel Hill, N.C., 1944), 31–70. Ralph McGill, "W. E. B. Du Bois," *Atlantic Monthly* 216 (November 1965): 78–81. W. E. B. Du Bois, *The Autobiography of W. E. B. Du Bois: A Soliloquy on Viewing My Life from the Last Decade of Its First Century* (New York, 1968), 222. William T. Ingersoll, *The Reminiscences of William Edward Burghardt Du Bois* (Sanford, N.C., 1972). For Du Bois's early criminology, see W. E. B. Du Bois, "The Negro and Crime," *The Independent* (May 18, 1899): 1355–1356. W. E. B. Du Bois, *The Philadelphia Negro: A Social Study* (New York, 1899). W. E. B. Du Bois, "The Negro as He Really Is," *World's Work* 2 (1901): 848–866. W. E. B. Du Bois, ed., *Some Notes on Negro Crime, Particularly in Georgia* (Atlanta, 1904). On Sam Hose and the shift from science to politics in Du Bois's thinking, see Lewis, *W. E. B. Du Bois*, 226, 228, 333–337, 363–364, and 408. On this general intellectual trajectory in his career, see Cornel West, *The American Evasion of Philosophy: A Genealogy of Pragmatism* (Madison, Wis., 1989), 138–150. On the lynching of "Sam Hose," whose true name is Samuel Wilkes, see the following: National Association for the Advancement of Colored People, *Thirty Years of Lynching in the United States: 1889–1918* (New York, 1969; first published 1919), 56–58. Mary Louise Ellis, "Rain Down Fire: The Lynching of Sam Hose," PhD diss., Florida State University, 1992. Philip Dray, *At the Hands of Persons Unknown: The Lynching of Black America* (New York, 2002), 1–16. For background and comparative cases in the contemporary cultural ferment of spectacle lynching, see Jacqueline Goldsby, *A Spectacular Secret: Lynching in American Life and Literature* (Chicago, 2006).

73. On Harris's political moderation around this time, see his late series of articles on the race question, published as the anti-black rhetoric of Georgia politicians was near its peak. Joel Chandler Harris, "The Negro as the South Sees Him," *Saturday Evening Post*, 2 January 1904. Joel Chandler Harris, "The Negro of To-Day," *Saturday Evening Post*, 30 January 1904. Joel Chandler Harris, "The Negro Problem," *Saturday Evening Post*, 27 February 1904. An early, also oblique, example of Harris's moderation on the vagrancy question is Joel Chandler Harris, "Free Joe and the Rest of the World," *Century* 29 (1884): 117–124.

74. *Atlanta Constitution*, 8 May 1897. For reporting on Sam Hose, see *Atlanta Constitution*, 13 April 1899, 14 April 1899, 15 April 1899, 16 April 1899, 19 April 1899, 21 April 1899, 23 April 1899, 29 April 1899. For the Georgia governor's race and Atlanta Riot of 1906, see Gottschalk, *Veiled Visions*, 35–56.

75. *Newnan Herald and Advertiser* quoted in Dray, *At the Hands of Persons Unknown*, 1–16. Ida B. Wells, *Lynch Law in Georgia* (Chicago, 1899). For elaboration on Wells and additional fact-finding on the Sam Hose case, see Mary Church Terrell, "Lynching from a Negro's Point of View," *North American Review* 178 (June 1904): 853–868.

76. McGill, "W. E. B. Du Bois," 78. *Atlanta Constitution*, 13 April 1899. On Du Bois and criminality, consult the following: Gaines, *Uplifting the Race*, 152–178. Fred Moten, "Uplift and Criminality," in *Next to the Color Line: Gender, Sexuality, and W. E. B. Du Bois*, ed. Susan Gillman and Alys Eve Weinbaum (Minneapolis, 2007), 317–349. Nicole A. Waligora-Davis, "W. E. B. Du Bois and the Fourth Dimension," *New Centennial Review* 6 (2007): 57–90.

77. Du Bois, *Dusk of Dawn*, 117.

78. Du Bois, *Souls of Black Folk*, 121, 117, 124, 128, 121, 151.

4. The Black Tradition from George W. Johnson to Ozella Jones

1. Victor Emerson, "The Making of a Disc Record," *Columbia Salesman* (September 1907). *New York Age*, 5 February 1914. F. W. Gaisberg, *The Music Goes Round* (New York, 1942), 8, 41–42. Jim Walsh, "Favorite Pioneer Recording Artists: George Washington Johnson," *Hobbies* (September 1944): 27. Jim Walsh, "Favorite Pioneer Recording Artists: In Justice to George Washington Johnson" [Part 1], *Hobbies* (January 1971): 37–39, 50, 91. Jim Walsh, "Favorite Pioneer Recording Artists: In Justice to George W. Johnson" [Part 2], *Hobbies* (February 1971): 37, 39–40, 50, 92. Allen Koenigsberg, *Edison Cylinder Records, 1889–1912* (New York, 1987). These sources and my summary of Johnson's legend and career are drawn from Tim Brooks's remarkable research. Tim Brooks, *Lost Sounds: Blacks and the Birth of the Recording Industry, 1890–1919* (Urbana, Ill., 2004), 13–71. There is a great *Lost Sounds* companion, which is available from Archeophone Records, ARCH-1005, 2005. Many of George W. Johnson's recordings and many related works are accessible online from the Cylinder Preservation and Digitization Project, housed at the Donald C. Davidson Library at the University of California at Santa Barbara, http://cylinders.library.ucsb.edu.

2. Ernest Hogan, "All Coons Look Alike to Me," Berliner 1610, 1896. Arthur Collins with Vess Ossman, "All Coons Look Alike to Me," Edison Record 7317, 1899. *Phonogram* (January 1891), 23, quoted in Brooks, *Lost Sounds*, 30. Edward A. Berlin, *Ragtime: A Musical and Cultural History* (Berkeley, Calif., 1980). Sam Denison, *Scandalize My Name: Black Imagery in American Popular Culture* (New York, 1982). James H. Dormon, "Shaping the Popular Image of Post-Reconstruction American Blacks: The 'Coon Song' Phenomenon of the Gilded Age," *American Quarterly* 40 (1988): 450–471. Lynn Abbott and Doug Seroff, *Ragged But Right Black Traveling Shows, "Coon Songs," and the Dark Pathway to Blues and Jazz* (Jackson, Miss., 2007). For further comment on the supposed differences between the "vocal apparatus of the negro" and "that of the white man," see "Negro Music," *Musical Visitor* 24 (1895): 179.

3. Gaisberg, *Music Goes Round*, 8. For the review that established the terms for Dunbar's initial reception, see William Dean Howells, "Life and Letters,"

Harper's Weekly 40 (1896): 630. We have no data on the make-up of Johnson's listening audience, but we know that his songs, like Dunbar's poems, were esteemed on both sides of the color line.

4. *New York Times*, 13 October 1899. *New York Tribune*, 13 October 1899. *New York Sun*, 29 November 1890, reprinted in *New York Age*, quoted in Lynn Abbott and Doug Seroff, *Out of Sight: The Rise of American Popular Music, 1889–1895* (Jackson, Miss., 2002), 103–104. *New York Herald*, 13 December 1899. *New York Herald*, 21 December 1899. *New York Sun*, 22 December 1899. *New York Times*, 22 December 1899. Gaisberg claims that Johnson was found guilty and hanged; Walsh repeats the claim in 1944 and then corrects it in 1971. Brooks, *Lost Sounds*, 49–58.

5. Brooks, *Lost Sounds*, 15–58. Emerson, "Making of a Disc Record." See also *New York Age*, 5 February 1914. The story about Edison and Johnson is widely reported. David Nasaw, *Going Out: The Rise and Fall of Public Amusements* (New York, 1993), 122. "George W. Johnson," Wikipedia, 20 December 2007, http://en.wikipedia.org/wiki/George_W._Johnson (accessed 12 January 2008).

6. J. B. McClure, ed., *Edison and His Inventions Including the Many Incidents, Anecdotes, and Interesting Particulars Connected with the Early and Later Life of the Great Inventor* (Chicago, 1889). For an overview of the development of the Edison cult and its mythologies, see Matthew Josephson, *Edison: A Biography* (New York, 1959).

7. On the tendency among collectors in the nineteenth century to claim that the black voice resisted transcription and musical notation, see Ronald Radano, *Lying Up a Nation: Race and Black Music* (Chicago, 2003), 164–229. Concerning the cultural precedents that influenced early thinking about sound reproduction, see Johnathan Sterne, *The Audible Past: Cultural Origins of Sound Reproduction* (Durham, N.C., 2003). Lisa Gitelman, *Scripts, Grooves, and Writing Machines: Representing Technology in the Edison Era* (Stanford, Calif., 1999). Friedrich A. Kittler, *Gramophone, Film, Typewriter* (Stanford, Calif., 1999). On the implications within the law, see Jane M. Gaines, *Contested Culture* (Chapel Hill, N.C., 1991).

8. Edison is quoted in Jacques Attali, *Noise: The Political Economy of Music*, trans. Brian Massumi (Minneapolis, 1985), 91–92. Jesse Walter Fewkes, "A Contribution to Passamaquoddy Folklore," *Journal of American Folklore* 3 (1890): 257–280. George A. Miller, "Canning Negro Melodies," *Literary Digest* 52 (27 May 1916): 1556–1558. "The phonograph," Miller writes, generalizing the Edison's line from individuals to peoples, "with its power of bringing back dumb and forgotten voices . . . performs an invaluable service for us in keeping alive and in our memories the songs of past generations" (Miller, "Canning," 1556). On Edison's contribution to ethnography, see especially Erika Brady, *A Spiral Way: How the Phonograph Changed Ethnography* (Jackson, Miss., 1999). The

idea that Edison saw the phonograph as technology for preservation rather than mass replication is also advanced in Attali, *Noise*, 87–132.

9. Here I am reversing the terms of the story that is often told about this historical transition. Rather than alienating the voice from the body, the phonograph appears to have grounded the black voice in the body, if not the black soul. For contrast, see Walter Benjamin, "The Work of Art in the Age of Mechanical Reproduction," in *Illuminations*, ed. Hannah Arendt, trans. Harry Zohn (New York, 1969), 217–251. For an additonal point of contrast, see also Alexander G. Weheliye, *Phonographies: Grooves in Sonic Afro-Modernity* (Durham, N.C., 2005). My thinking here is ancipated, at least in part, by Béla Bartók's provovative if truncated suggestion that Edison needs to be understood as the "father of modern folk-song studies." Bartók, *Hungarian Folk Songs*, Folkways FE4000, 1950. For contrasting background, representing the black folk artist's presumed aversion to technology, see Joel Chandler Harris, "The Phonograph," in *Uncle Remus, His Songs and His Sayings: The Folk-Lore of the Old Plantation* (New York, 1880), 201–202.

10. For an example of the critical tendency that contrasts "authentic floating folk lyrics" to "vaudeville-based novelty songs," see William Barlow, *"Looking Up at Down": The Emergence of Blues Culture* (Philadelphia, 1989), 142.

11. George W. Johnson, "The Laughing Song," Ko-L'ar Music, 1894. Sam Devere, "The Whistling Coon," *Daly Brothers K. H. K. South Carolina Cloe Songster* 13 (1878): 13. For the production history of "The Laughing Song," see Brooks, *Lost Sounds*, 31–32. Edward James, *The Amateur Negro Minstrel's Guide* (New York, 1880), 8. Regarding the enlarged open mouth and penetration, see Michael Rogin, *Blackface, White Noise* (Berkeley, Calif., 1996), 111, 176–177.

12. "Epithet, n.," *Oxford English Dictionary*, 2nd ed. (New York, 1989). On exemplification as a mode of reference that refers back to the category that denotes it, see Nelson Goodman, *Languages of Art: An Approach to a Theory of Symbols*, 2nd ed. (Indianapolis, 1976). On the double sense in which this type of existence is supernumerary, see Alain Badiou, *Being and Event*, trans. Oliver Feltham (New York, 2005), 201–231, 327–343.

13. Jean-Paul Sartre, *Being and Nothingness*, trans. Hazel E. Barnes (London, 1986; first published 1943), 67. Frantz Fanon, *Black Skin, White Masks*, trans. Charles Lam Markmann (New York, 1967). These statistics are calculated in W. Fitzhugh Brundage, *Lynching in the New South: Georgia and Virginia, 1880–1930* (Urbana, Ill., 1993). On the phenomenology of this threat, see especially Richard Wright, "The Ethics of Living Jim Crow: An Autobiographical Sketch," in *American Stuff: An Anthology of Prose & Verse by Members of the Federal Writers' Project, with Sixteen Prints by the Federal Art Project* (New York, 1937), 39–52.

14. Charles Penrose, "The Laughing Policeman" (Columbia Records FB1184).

15. George Kelling and James Q. Wilson, "The Police and Neighborhood Safety: Broken Windows," *Atlantic Monthly* 127 (1982): 29–38. On the mythology of a golden age of policing, see Ian Loader, "Policing the Social: Questions of Symbolic Power," *British Journal of Sociology* 48 (1997): 1–18.

16. Kelling and Wilson, "Broken Windows," 30.

17. Kelling and Wilson, "Broken Windows," 35. *Papachristou v. City of Jacksonville*, 405 U.S. 156 (1972). Jeffrey S. Adler, "A Historical Analysis of the Law of Vagrancy," *Criminology* (1989): 209–229. Marcus Dirk Dubber, *The Police Power: Patriarchy and the Foundations of American Government* (New York, 2005), 120–138.

18. Penrose, "The Laughing Policeman." The phrase "Hey, you there!" is borrowed from Louis Althusser, "Ideology and Ideological State Apparatuses: Notes towards an Investigation," trans. Ben Brewster, in *Lenin and Philosophy* (London, 1971; first published 1970), 127–186.

19. Penrose, "The Laughing Policeman." Kelling and Wilson, "Broken Windows," 30. At several points in this analysis, I am drawing from from Eric L. Santner, *On the Psychotheology of Everyday Life: Reflections on Freud and Rosenzweig* (Chicago, 2001).

20. I am attempting to describe here a process that has been termed by Eric Santner, among others, as "interpellation without identification." Santner, *On the Psychotheology of Everyday Life*, 25–85. On the police power as sovereignty that disposes, rather than convinces or commands, see Dubber, *The Police Power*, 71–77. On the police power to dispose and its representation in early slave codes, see Dubber, *The Police Power*, 61–62.

21. On the mechanical coin banks to which the song alludes at its ending, see Bill Brown, "Reification, Reanimation, and the American Uncanny," *Critical Inquiry* 32 (Winter 2005): 175–207.

22. Daniel François Auber, *Manon Lescaut* (Paris, 1856). The best seller among the many laughing records from the succeeding decades is the phenomenally popular "Okeh Laughing Record," Okeh-4678, 1922. Uncle Dave Macon's laughing in time is also specially relevant. Uncle Dave Macon, "Run, Nigger, Run" (Vocacion 5060). On mechanics, I am drawing from Robert R. Provine, *Laughter: A Scientific Investigation* (New York, 2000).

23. William Francis Allen, Charles Pickard Ware, and Lucy McKim Garrison, *Slave Songs of the United States* (New York, 1867), vi. Dorothy Scarborough, *On the Trail of Negro Folk-Songs* (Cambridge, Mass., 1925), 245. Charles Peabody, "Notes on Negro Music," *Journal of American Folklore* 16 (1903): 151–152. Frances Kemble, *Journal of a Residence on a Georgia Plantation, 1838–1839* (New York, 1863), 218. C. Vann Woodward, ed., *Mary Chesnut's Civil War* (New Haven, Conn., 1993), 214. James Weldon Johnson and J. Rosamond Johnson, *Books of American Negro Spirituals* (New York, 1969; first published

1925–1926), 30. On the transcription of slave music and the trope of the sublime, see Gary Tomlinson, *Music in Renaissance Magic: Toward a Historiography of Others* (Chicago, 1994). Jon Cruz, *Culture on the Margins: The Black Spiritual and the Rise of American Cultural Interpretation* (Princeton, N.J., 1999). Radano, *Lying Up a Nation*.

24. "Contributor's Club," *Atlantic* 67 (1891): 143–144. Louise Pound, *Poetic Origins of the Ballad* (New York, 1921), 158. See also Frederick Louis Ritter, *Music in America* (New York, 1883), 392–400. At this juncture, I am seeking to describe the interface between these familiar laments about the resistance of black music and the claims made by Edison about the phonograph as a functioning solution to problem cases where transcription is either impossible or inadequate. See Thomas Edison, "The Phonograph and Its Future," *North American Review* 126 (1878): 530–536.

25. Ralph Ellison, *Invisible Man* (New York, 1995; first published 1952), 581.

26. John A. Lomax and Alan Lomax, *American Ballads and Folk Songs* (New York, 1934), xxxiv. John A. Lomax, *Negro Folk Songs as Sung by Lead Belly*, "King of the Twelve-String Guitar Players of the World," *Long-Time Convict in the Penitentiaries of Texas and Louisiana* (New York, 1936). John A. Lomax and Alan Lomax, *Our Singing Country, a Second Volume of American Ballads and Folk Songs* (New York, 1941). John A. Lomax and Alan Lomax, *Folk Song: U.S.A.* (New York, 1947). The recordings created by John and Alan Lomax in 1933–1935 are available along with their subsequent work at the Archive of Folk Culture, American Folklife Center, Library of Congress. The commercial albums featuring black music recorded in the field by the Lomaxes and their colleagues between 1933 and 1946, first released by the Library of Congress, are currently reissued by Rounder Records in the series *Deep River of Song* (Rounder 1821–1832). Also available are the recordings created by Alan Lomax with Magnacord paper tapes at Parchman Farm in 1947–1948. *Prison Songs: Murderous Home* (Rounder 1714). *Prison Songs: Don'tcha Hear Poor Mother Calling* (Rounder 1715). John Lomax, *Adventures of a Ballad Hunter* (New York, 1947). Alan Lomax, *The Land Where the Blues Began* (New York, 1993). Carl Engel, *Archive of American Folk Song: A History 1928–1939* (Library of Congress Project, Works Project Administration, 1940).

27. John Lomax quoted in *Report of the Librarian of Congress for the Fiscal Year Ending June 30, 1933*, reprinted in Engel, *Archive*, 24. H. Bruce Franklin, *Prison Literature in America*, 2nd ed. (New York, 1989). Jerrold Hirsch, "Modernity, Nostalgia, and Southern Folklore Studies: The Case of John Lomax," *Journal of American Folklore* 105 (Spring 1992): 183–207. Nolan Porterfield, *Last Cavalier: The Life and Times of John Lomax 1867–1948* (Urbana, Ill., 1996). Benjamin Filene, *Romancing the Folk: Public Memory and American Roots Music* (Chapel Hill, N.C., 2000), 47–75. Marybeth Hamilton, *In Search of the Blues: Black*

Voices, White Visions (London, 2007), 71–124. Patrick B. Mullen, *The Man Who Adores the Negro: Race and American Folklore* (Urbana, Ill., 2008).

28. Howard W. Odum and Guy B. Johnson, *Negro Workaday Songs* (Chapel Hill, N.C., 1926), 71. John Lomax's research proposal to the Library of Congress, quoted in *Report of the Librarian of Congress for the Fiscal Year Ending June 30, 1933*, reprinted in Engel, *Archive*, 22–24. John Lomax, "Report of the Honorary Consultant and Curator," quoted in *Report of the Librarian of Congress for the Fiscal Year Ending June 20, 1935*, reprinted in Engel, *Archive*, 32–34. John Lomax, "Field Experiences with Recording Machines," *Southern Folklore Quarterly* 1 (1937): 58–59.

29. John Lomax, "'Sinful Songs' of the Southern Negro," *Musical Quarterly* 20 (1934): 182. John Lomax, *Adventures of a Ballad Hunter*, 128–129. Lomax and Lomax, *American Ballads and Folk Songs*, xxvii. Lomax and Lomax, *Our Singing Country*, 379.

30. John Lomax, "Report," reprinted in Engel, *Archive*, 33.

31. John Lomax, "'Sinful Songs,'" 181.

32. John Lomax, "'Sinful Songs,'" 177, 184.

33. John Lomax, "'Sinful Songs,'" 179. Charles K. Wolfe and Kip Lornell, *The Life and Legend of Leadbelly* (New York, 1992). Leadbelly's Library of Congress Recordings have all been reissued by Rounder Records in a series produced by Alan Lomax (Rounder 1044–1046, 1097–1099).

34. John Lomax, *Negro Folk Songs as Sung by Lead Belly*, xiii, 45. *New York Herald Tribune*, 3 January 1935. Richard Wright famously summarized the consensus about Leadbelly seeded by Lomax. "It seems," Wright held, "that the entire folk culture of the American Negro has found its embodiment in him." Richard Wright, "Huddie Ledbetter, Famous Negro Folk Artist Sings the Songs of Scottsboro and His People," *Daily Worker*, 12 August 1937.

35. John Lomax, *Negro Folk Songs as Sung by Lead Belly*, 39. John A. Lomax, "Self-Pity in Negro Folk-Songs," *Nation* 105 (1917): 140–141. "After Lead Belly, Iron-head," *Time* 27 (6 April 1936), 17. Of course, it is also this same natural-born singer who greets Handy at the train station, and it is this same character who appears in many histories of the black tradition, including landmarks like Sterling Stuckey's "Through the Prism of Folklore: The Black Ethos in Slavery" (1968). In this essay, Stuckey proposes that the songs and stories collected by folklorists during and after slavery are evidence that disproves the proposition about black dependency advanced in Stanley Elkins's *Slavery* (1959). Folklore demonstrated the creativity and independence that scholars like Elkins were keen to deny. This was an argument that helped to set the agenda for an entire generation of scholarship that shifted scholarly attention away from the study of victimization to the demonstration of agency. By his own admission, Stuckey builds his case from "John and Alan Lomax's theory that the songs of the folk

singer are deeply rooted 'in his life and have functioned there as enzymes to assist in the digestion of hardship.'" He cites, as an extension, Alan Lomax's claim that black music "'expresses the same feelings and speaks the same basic language everywhere'" as another "working principle" in the essay. Folk-songs are enzymes. Folk singers are people who sing about themselves. Folk expression makes the continuity and collective consciousness in the black tradition. These are claims that follow directly from the primary declension of the race concept—from law to culture—that we have been tracking in this book. Pointing out the fact of this borrowing is not an attempt to fabricate guilt by association; rather, it is to inquire into what have become the structural conditions for our historical understanding of black culture. Sterling Stuckey, "Through the Prism of Folklore: The Black Ethos in Slavery," *Massachusetts Review* 9 (1968): 419–420. Stanley Elkins, *Slavery: A Problem in American Institutional and Intellectual Life* (Chicago, 1959). For an enlargement of the argument in the 1968 essay, see Sterling Stuckey, *Slave Culture: Nationalist Theory and the Foundations of Black America* (New York, 1987).

36. Gates Thomas, "South Texas Negro Work Songs," in *Rainbow in the Morning*, ed. J. F. Dobie (Hatboro, Penn., 1965; first published 1926), 166. For another early example, see Howard W. Odum, "Folk-Song and Folk-Poetry as Found in the Secular Songs of the Southern Negroes," *Journal of American Folklore* 24 (1911): 354–355. For perhaps the best-known version of the verse, Jimmie Rodgers, "Blue Yodel No. 9" (Victor 23580), reissued as Rounder 1060.

37. Reese Crenshaw, "Trouble," recorded by John Lomax at State Prison Farm, Milledgeville, Georgia, 15 December 1934. Reissued on *Red River Runs: Library of Congress Field Recordings from the South-Eastern United States* (Flyright-Matchbox 259). Jesse Wadley, "Alabama Prison Blues," recorded by John Lomax at Bellwood Prison, Atlanta, Georgia, 11 December 1934. Reissued on *Field Recordings*, vol. 2: *North Carolina and South Carolina, Georgia, Tennessee, Arkansas 1926–1943* (Document Records 5576). Bruce Bastin, *Red River Blues: The Blues Tradition in the Southeast* (Urbana, Ill., 1986), 52–71. On confession and secularization, see Peter Brooks, *Troubling Confessions: Speaking Guilt in Law and Literature* (Chicago, 2000).

38. Ozella Jones, "Prisoner Blues," recorded by John Lomax at State Farm, Raiford, Florida, 4 May 1936. Reissued on *Field Recordings*, vol. 7: *Florida, 1935–1936* (Document Records 5587).

39. Lomax and Lomax, *Our Singing Country*, 364–366.

40. Ed Bell [Barefoot Bill], "Bad Boy" (Columbia 14526-D). Reissued on Ed Bell, *The Complete Recorded Works 1927–1930* (Document Records 5090). Many pop songs were transcribed in the field as folk music, among them "The Laughing Song," which is for example transcribed and retitled as "The Happy Coon" in

Frank C. Brown, *The Frank C. Brown Collection of North Carolina Folklore*, vol. 3 (Durham, N.C., 1952), 510.

41. Lomax and Lomax, *Our Singing Country*, 364–366. The idea that the blues combines the vocal style of the field holler with accompaniment patterns from blues ballad tradition is an argument that was first made systematically in the remarkable writing of Paul Oliver. For example, Paul Oliver, *The Story of the Blues* (London, 1969), 22–25.

42. This is very close to what Nathaniel Mackey has called, in several instances, the performance of meta-voice or the pursuit of an alternative voice. For example, see Nathaniel Mackey, "Cante Moro," in *Disembodied Poetics: Annals of the Jack Kerouac School*, ed. Anne Waldman and A. Schelling (Albuquerque, 1994), 71–94. In this connection, see "Black Mo'nin' and the Sound of the Phonograph," in Fred Moten, *In the Break: The Aesthetics of the Black Radical Tradition* (Minneapolis, 2003), 192–211. For overvocalizing, see Lawrence Kramer, *Music and Poetry: The Nineteenth Century and After* (Berkeley, Calif., 1984), 132. For a similar point, put differently to the general case of lyric, see Robert Kaufman, "Lyric's Constellation, Poetry's Radical Privilege," *Modernist Cultures* 1 (Winter 2005): 209–234.

43. Alan Lomax, liner notes to *Roots of the Blues* (New World Records 80252-2): 6–7. "More such irrefutable documents will emerge as field coverage improves," Lomax concludes. For an example of how this composite track has been cited and put to use by cultural historians, see Ted Gioia, *Delta Blues: The Life and Times of the Mississippi Masters who Revolutionized American Music* (New York, 2008), 23.

44. Nathaniel Mackey, *Bedouin Hornbook* (Los Angeles, 1997; first published 1986), 7. Archie Shepp, *Four for Trane* (Impulse A71).

ACKNOWLEDGMENTS

The first word is for Deborah McDowell, my mentor and most important teacher. It was her guidance and intellectual example that kept the writing on track at the start. Special thanks as well to those who took the time, at various stages, to read the full manuscript: Ed Ayers, Stephen Best, Saidiya Hartman, Abdul JanMohamed, Eric Lott, Colleen Lye, Teju Olaniyan, Sam Otter, Marlon Ross, and Scott Saul.

For their engagement with the ideas in this book, I thank Elizabeth Abel, Aaron Bady, Dorri Beam, Alex Benson, Kelvin Black, Adam Boardman, Mitch Breitwieser, Natalia Brizuela, Reginald Butler, Anthony Cascardi, Brandi Catanese, Karlyn Crowley, Brent Edwards, Richmond Eustis, Cathy Gallagher, Marcial Gonzalez, Grace Hale, Mark Healey, Richard Hutson, Chuck Jackson, Greg Jackson, James Kim, Michael Laine, Ben Lee, Heather Love, Annie McClanahan, Fred Moten, Donald Pease, Kent Puckett, Megan Pugh, Mark Rifkin, Joseph Roach, Mike Rubenstein, Sue Schweik, Andrew Strickler, Corey Walker, Cheryl Wall, Robyn Wiegman, Kara Wittman, and Edlie Wong.

For help tracking down sources, I thank Kathie Bordelon, Brad Evans, Nicole Waligora-Davis, Irene Wainwright, and Mary Helen Washington.

Research for the book was ably assisted by Audrey Wu Clark and Shawn Salvant, and by librarians and archivists at the Bancroft Library at the University of California, Berkeley; the City Archives at the New Orleans Public Library; the Kenan Research Center at the Atlanta History Center; the American Folklife Center at the Library of Congress; and the Cylinder Preservation Project at the University of California, Santa Barbara.

Fellowship support for the book was provided by the University of California President's Research Fellowship for the Humanities, the University of California Humanities Research Fellowship, the Carter G. Woodson Institute for African and African American Studies at the University of Virginia, and the Doreen B. Townsend Center for the Humanities at the

University of California at Berkeley. Additional support was generously given by the University of California Hellman Family Faculty Fund and the University of California Junior Faculty Research Grants.

I thank Alexandra Quinn for help processing texts, Jill Tarlau for advice about book design, Phoebe Kosman for sharp editorial suggestions, John Donohue for careful copyediting, and Lindsay Waters for his patience and continuing interest in the project.

I am grateful to my parents and sister for their love and support, and to my extended family, now scattered from New Orleans to San Francisco to Washington, D.C., for the wonder and happiness they bring to my life.

Kim Magowan has been this book's closest reader, its fiercest interlocutor, and a rock-solid companion over the years that it has taken to get the writing finished. I simply could not have done it without her. To Nora Magowan Wagner and Camille Magowan Wagner, what is there to say? You have changed my life in ways I did not think possible. Nothing could mean more to me than the prospect of our keeping company in the time to come.

INDEX

(grandfather of Sidney Bechet), 109;
Atlanta, Georgia and, 128–134; Uncle Remus
stories and, 158–159, 169–175; legitimacy
of, 202

Police officers, 136, 158, 171

Police power: slave codes and, 4–6; public
safety and, 6–7, 12–15; limitations on, 8–12;
natural law and, 15–18; vigilante violence
and, 18–20; the black tradition and, 20–24;
vagrancy and, 38–42, 139–141; Robert Charles
and, 47–51; Robert Charles Song and, 51–52,
53–54; discretionary authority and, 71–73;
legal status of slaves and, 74–75; *The
Grandissimes* (Cable) and, 80–81, 83; Bras-
Coupé and, 85; equality and, 87; Atlanta,
Georgia and, 134, 141–153; Uncle Remus
stories and, 168, 170–171, 173–175; lynchings
and, 180–184; "The Laughing Song" and,
199–200; "The Laughing Policeman"
(Penrose) and, 200–202, 204–208;
"Broken Windows" (Kelling and Wilson),
202–204

Policing the Southern City (Rousey), 61

Political activism, 46, 145–146, 175

Political functions of folklore, 123–125, 126, 155,
159–160, 176

Political speech, Bras-Coupé and, 76–77

Pollock, Frederick, 71

Popular music, 195–196, 215–216, 222, 230

Pound, Louise, 211

Powell, John Wesley, 118

Power of Black Music, The (Floyd), 113–114

Prentice, William Packer, 13, 15

Price, Richard, 23

Prieur, Denis, 64, 66, 68, 70, 71, 72–73

Prigg v. Pennsylvania (1842), 38, 75

Primitive Culture (Taylor), 81

Prisons, 215–222, 227–228, 230

Proctor, Henry Hugh, 143

Professional controversies, folklore origins and,
118–122

Progress, historical, 64–65, 102, 168

Property ownership, 143–144

Property rights, 12, 13, 14, 73–74, 164–165,
166–167

Publications, of black folk songs, 30–31

Public safety, 4–5, 6–7, 12–15

Pufendorf, Samuel, 17–18

Punishment, deterrence and, 17–18

Race relations, 122–124

Race riots, 46–47

Racial epithets. *See* Epithets

Racial equality, 87, 90, 102

Racial profiling, 48

Racial slavery, blackness and, 1

Racial Uplift Movement, 143–144

Racism, appeals to self-preservation and, 18–20

"Ragged songster," character of: blues music
and, 25–28, 56–57; folklorists and, 33, 34;
song collectors and, 36–38, 40–41; W. C.
Handy and, 45; George W. Johnson and,
194–195. *See also* Vagrancy

Ramsey, Frederick, Jr., 56, 97

Really the Blues (Mezzrow), 103

Reason-of-state tradition, 13–14

Reconstruction Era, 123–125, 126, 127–128, 134–141

Recorder's Court, 131–132, 137–138, 140–141, 147,
158

Recording industry, 31–33, 185–186, 188, 189–194

Reform efforts, police forces and, 62–68, 72,
130, 131–134

Reid, John, 103

Reliques of Ancient English Poetry (Percy), 35

Rice, T. D., 29, 189

Ritson, Joseph, 35

Robert Charles Song, 45, 47, 51–55

Roots of the Blues (Lomax), 235

Rousey, Dennis C., 61

Rural setting, Uncle Remus and, 159–169

"Sad Fate of Mr. Fox, The," 162–163

Sales, phonograph records and, 185–186

Savannah Tribune, 145, 146–151, 174–175

Scarborough, Dorothy, 30, 210

Science of Rights, The (Fichte), 16–17, 74

Second Treatise of Civil Government (Locke), 16

Select Collection of English Songs (Percy), 35

Self-consciousness, blues music and, 28

Self-defense, 75, 150–151, 166–167

Self-expression: blues music and, 26–27, 28,
42–43, 56, 57; character of the "ragged
songster" and, 33–34, 35; John Lomax and,
227–228; criminality and, 228–234